The Daily

BOOK OF
MOTORING
ANSWERS

The Daily Telegraph

BOOK OF
MOTORING
ANSWERS

Honest John

ROBINSON
London

Robinson Publishing Ltd
7 Kensington Church Court
London W8 4SP

First published by Robinson Publishing Ltd 1997
This edition published 1999

A copy of the British Library Cataloguing in Publication Data is
available from the British Library

ISBN 1–84119–098–5

Designed and typeset by Editburo, Lewes, East Sussex

Printed and bound in the EC

10 9 8 7 6 5 4 3 2 1

CONTENTS

INTRODUCTION

What you need to know about this book before you start reading and using it

This *Daily Telegraph* book gives you the answers to the most-asked questions about cars and motoring. How do I know this? Over the last five years I have replied to more than 22,000 letters. Most people sought information. But many also provided it, particularly about older cars. So, whether you're worrying about your next MOT, or you want to know a bit more about a car owned by your grandad in the 1920s, the chances are you'll find it in these pages.

Condition of Sale

You don't have to be in the motor trade to enjoy this book. You don't need to be an enthusiast. You don't even have to be remotely interested in cars. All you need to be is a car owner or driver, or simply someone looking for an answer to a car-related question – past or present. While you're looking, I hope you'll also find plenty to amuse, stimulate and maybe even annoy you enough to write to 'Honest John' at *The Daily Telegraph*.

But, a word of warning: since all this went to press long before you laid out your money, and since I could not know for certain exactly what was going to happen in the future, I can't guarantee that everything in this book can be 100 per cent up to date. So, just like unwarranted cars at auction, you buy this at your own risk. Neither I, nor *The Daily Telegraph*, nor Robinson Publishing, nor anyone else mentioned or involved will accept any liability whatsoever for any inaccuracies or the dating of any information in this book. Of course, unlike cars at auction, you can sneak a look inside and give it a 'read-test' in the bookshop, so you know exactly what you're getting before you make a bid to the cashier.

About the chapter headings

In editing more than 20,000 questions and answers down to 1,000 or so, I had to categorise them. So what happened was that the chapter headings more or less decided themselves. This year there are new chapters, such as 'Alternative Transport'. Others, including 'Catalytic Converters', have been incorporated into more general sections.

About me

I don't have time to do much buying and selling any more. But I still get down to the auctions around once a week. And I have my own comprehensive computer databank of auction prices from the beginning of 1992 – so I always know exactly which way the market is going compared to the past month, the past year, and up to six years ago.

My first contact with the motor trade was in 1959 when I started cleaning cars for Ron at Sports Motors on Orpington High Street. Ron's stock included a 1926 AC Roadster at £225; a 1930 Austin Nippy at £90; a 1932 Lagonda 2 litre two-seat special at £225; a 1938 Jaguar SS 100 at £275 (multiply by somewhere between 100 and 250 to find out just what an investment some of this older stuff has been). Ron also had comparatively modern cars, such as a pair of 1949 Riley three-seat Roadsters, MGAs, TR2s, a Buckler, a Berkeley and a gigantic Buick. Sports Motors folded in 1960, but Pete the Painter's murals remain to this day, hidden behind the dry-lined walls of the carpet shop that replaced it.

I bought my first car in 1964 and did my first deal the year after when I sold it. The car was a 1959 BMW Isetta 300, spotted rocking gently on the roof of a fabric-bodied Alvis 12/50 saloon in Shire Ted's scrapyard. 'I can drive that when I'm 16,' I thought. The car duly arrived on the end of a rope behind a 1938 Oldsmobile and, being the canny man he was, Ted gave me £2 back from my £20. Reconstruction began, and test runs were undertaken round a neighbour's garden. On my 16th birthday the bubble burst forth onto the road. A year later I sold it for £60.

Further gains (and losses) were made on a 1959 Riley 1.5 bought for

£250; a 1942 Ford Jeep, bought for £20; a Thames Camper bought for £175; a modified Minivan bought for £125; a 1949 Rover P3 bought for £40; a Wolseley Hornet and plenty of other tackle, including a rear-engined Renault and a two-stroke Saab. Then, by writing the ads for a Rolls Royce dealer, I got into advertising.

Four years of this was spent conveniently close to London's Warren Street, where I shared bank, pubs and caffs with the street's car traders and did a few deals on Simcas, Minis, VW Beetles, 2CVs, Fiats and Alfas. Apart from acquiring a pair of 'D&AD' pencils, I have to admit I never really made it in adland. The recession didn't help. Then, deep in the midst of the Gulf War, I had a brainwave: I would launch a completely new type of car magazine about nothing but used cars. The aim was simply to set it going, and then flog it for £10,000 and carry on in the ad game, but instead I became indentured into the penury of freelancing features for car magazines. Since this involved reporting on car auctions, watching wasn't enough. Before long, I was back to buying cars and turning them round – retail, trade or on commission – to supplement the mag money into enough to live on.

For four months I commuted between London, Amsterdam and Nice, working on pan-European launches for the Mazda Xedos 6 and RX7. Then it was back to buying and selling, a column in *Car Week*, and an auction column in *The Daily Telegraph*'s 'Motoring' section. Life was moving along quite nicely. Then, at a contributor's Christmas party in a room above a pub in Soho, my editor, Eric Bailey had an idea.

I'd arrived at the party fresh from an auction where I'd spent £17,250 on three Vauxhalls in the space of 20 minutes, then moved them on to earn a mere £250 each. Eric thought, '£250 a car. He's far too honest for that game', and 'Honest John' was born.

In the ancient tradition of all agony columns, the first questions were made up, and they ran on the back cover of *Telegraph* 'Motoring' in the issue of 21 January 1995. The response was phenomenal: within months I was answering up to 150 genuine letters a week. By year three, the weekly mailbag sometimes hit 500. By year four, I'd even got myself onto television.

What you'll find in this book is a distillation of the best and most interesting questions and answers, mostly from the last year, but some going back to January 1995.

AIR CONDITIONING

Airconomic size

" A friend and I both have similar Volvo 960s with climate control as standard. He has his permanently turned off as he has been told that air conditioning increases petrol consumption. I can understand that installing aircon, with its heavy components and drive belts, will increase fuel consumption compared with an unencumbered engine, but I cannot understand how, once aircon is installed, switching it on or off can affect mpg. "

When you switch the aircon on, an electric clutch then gives positive drive to the compressor pump which requires a few bhp of engine power to turn. It then clutches out when the desired temperature is reached. On a 960 with between 170 and 204 bhp, the effect on both performance and fuel consumption will be negligible except if the aircon is used to provide maximum refrigeration on a very hot day. Aircon should be run at least once a week and serviced at least every two years. If it isn't, the bill for repairing it will be many times greater than the savings on petrol from not using it.

Power drain

" *I have a new Daihatsu Charade 1.3 automatic fitted with power steering and air conditioning. I have heard that the PAS and aircon will affect the power the engine is able to transmit to the front wheels. As I live in a mountainous area, is it better to turn off the aircon when climbing mountain roads? Is it also better not to use the air conditioning at all in winter months when the car heater is being used constantly?* "

Power-steering and air-conditioning pumps do absorb some power. The PAS pump takes roughly 3–5 bhp, and an aircon pump between 5 and 10 bhp. The effect of this is more likely to be felt in small-engined cars and large, underpowered cars, particularly automatics, than in cars with an adequate power and torque output. So, yes, use of the aircon will reduce available power and will increase the fuel consumption of your Charade to a perceptible degree. But whether you need to switch the air conditioning off when ascending a hill will depend on how sluggish the car feels. In winter you need to use the aircon at least once a week or the seals in the system, which are lubricated by the gas, will dry out and eventually start to leak. But this is no hardship because aircon is an excellent de-humidifier.

Aircon aggro

" *The air conditioning in my 'H'-registered Ford Scorpio became ineffective and I took it to a local specialist garage for re-gassing (this had been done once before, elsewhere). They tested it, then filled it with refrigerant which promptly leaked away. This cost me £70.50 and I was advised that a new condenser was required, at a cost of £333.53 plus five hours of labour at £150 – all-up cost £638.65 including VAT. Is this reasonable? Is there no other more economical way of dealing with a leaky condenser?* "

No. And I'm afraid this is a normal, reasonable charge for the work involved. Air conditioning is an excellent extra but, for it to last, it must be used regularly and properly serviced every couple of years. Eight years is a pretty good life for a condenser anyway.

More hot air

" *In June 1997 my 'H'-registered Honda Accord was broken into and the air-conditioning system was damaged. It was repaired by an aircon specialist at a cost of £825, paid by the insurance company. Since this happened in the winter, I did not have cause to use the air conditioning until summer 1998 when I discovered it was not working. I took the car back to the Honda agent which had subcontracted the original repair to the specialist, and was asked to pay £56.99 for diagnosis of the fault as a gas leakage and a further £899.87 to have it repaired. I strongly feel that it should be repaired entirely free of charge as the original repair was obviously not satisfactory. I enclose copies of the relevant correspondence.* "

The Honda agent gave you specific instructions to use the air conditioning for 20 minutes a month in order to keep the system properly lubricated. This you failed to do, so the problem which developed is entirely your own fault.

Aircon specialsts

" *I am retiring soon and am considering purchasing my company car, which is a three-year-old Vauxhall Omega 2.5TD Estate with 53,000 miles on the clock. Can you please advise if it is possible to retro-fit air conditioning?* "

Air-conditioning retrofit specialists and maintenance specialists include: Motor Climate (0121 766 5006); Alpinair, 174 Honey Pot Lane, Stanmore, Middlesex (0181 204 9633); Coolair UK Ltd, Kingsley Road, Lincolnfields, Lincoln LN6 2TA (01522 682288).

ALTERNATIVE TRANSPORT

Knackered

" *Forty years ago I bought my house in the centre of the village within ten minutes walk of schools, cricket club, the station, several pubs, the workman's club, two supermarkets and an off-licence. Now, my knees are knackered, and I have to drive to most of the aforementioned facilities. We already had to suffer the absurdity of catalytic converters, which increase CO_2 emissions by at least 10 per cent plus hydrogen sulphide, and now you tell me that I must drive at least 7–10 miles to avoid condensation damage to my engine and exhaust system. So to keep my car healthy, it seems that I must either move sevenmiles away, or clog up the roads by driving the extra miles for my medicinal pint. Can you suggest a car, ancient or modern, that will tolerate journeys of less than a mile?* "

Anything electric. But, of course, for these sort of trips you don't need to haul all the baggage of a full-sized car. The smart thing to do is to invest in an electric bicycle or an electric buggy.

Mobility mugging

It turns out that there's a bit of a racket going on over mobility scooters. Elderly people are phoning 0800 numbers, being visited by high-pressure salesmen and 'persuaded' to pay up to twice what they could be paying. Price variations included: £1,100–£2,045 for a Sunrunner CH2 (RRP £1,495); £1,320–£2,545 for a Sovereign CH5 (RRP £1,850); and £2,475–£3,445 for a Sprinter CH7CD (RRP £2,750). All prices are pre-VAT and the lowest prices quoted still allow a profit margin of 25–30 per cent. The Electric Vehicle Association recommends anyone considering an electric mobility scooter to contact the British Healthcare Trades Association first on 01732 458868 before phoning any 0800 numbers.

Short-run solutions

As mentioned many times, the quickest way to destroy a car and to pollute the neighbourhood is to use it for short runs of less than three miles. More solutions have been flooding in.

A reader from Oxford tells us that the famous Velosolex is now being imported to the UK by Hamlet Motor Ltd of Boars Hill, Oxford (tel: 01865 327170). It is built to the original specification on the original French tooling in Hungary, runs on unleaded, will take off from a standstill without pedalling, can reach 23 mph and travels 200 miles on a gallon. The price is £698 including VAT, plus £25 registration tax, £15 VED, £62 annual insurance, a few pounds for a numberplate and the cost of a crash helmet.

The Raleigh Select Electric, price £1,000, requires no licence, numberplate or helmet (though a cycle helmet is advised). The motor proportionally assists – rather than completely replaces – pedalpower, effectively doubling the effort expended by the rider. The machine is also reasonably light at just 57 lbs (26 kg), has six-speed Shimano derailleur gears and a range of 25–30 miles on one charge. You can obtain a brochure from any Raleigh cycle stockist or visit the Raleigh website at http://www.raleigh-bikes.com. Raleigh Industries Ltd, Nottingham NG7 2DD, tel: 0115 942 0102.

The exciting new American EMB (Electric Motor Bike) Lectra 24 is being imported by Charlie Tomkins at Motorcycle City (01252 400000). Top speed is 45 mph, maximum acceleration 0–30 mph in 5 seconds and range up to 30 miles on one charge. Unfortunately, after shipping, import duty, VAT and profit, the price is a bit steep at £3,999 on the road.

A reader from Woodbridge recommends the 24 volt TGA Electrobike 212, which uses three-speed Sturmey-Archer hub gears to get you up hills without having to pedal. Another from Porthmadog sent details of the range of TGA electric bicycles and tricycles. Prices start at £545 for the rather clumsy looking, front-wheel-drive Electrokit Bike. The nicer, rear-drive Electrobike 212 starts at £765. The Tri-Pacer Electra tricycle is £1,050. And the Tri-Shopper Electric tricycle (with the advantage of a large 'boot') is £1,475. Optional extras such as lights can increase these prices fairly substantially, but no helmets, licences, registration plates or insurance are presently required to use any of them (apart from the Velosolex) on the road. TGA Electric Leisure is situated at Factory Lane West, Halstead, Essex CO9 1EX, tel: 01787 478430.

A reader from Reigate has an £800 TGA Electrobike 212 but does not think much of the build quality. He does, however, recommend Yamaha's new £900 electric bike and the £1,200 Honda Sky mobility scooter which requires no pedalling.

The Heinzmann Brilliant Fold-it is a front-wheel-drive folding bicycle with adequate power to take off from a standstill. It costs £1,150– £1,250; tel: 0181 608 1829.

As for the £130 Sinclair Zeta II electric bicycle motor (tel: 0171 837 6150), an owner in Pershore thinks his is 'absolute rubbish'. He tells us: 'The clutch is a piece of cord to lift the tiny motor off the wheel, the traction onto the front wheel is by an eighth of an inch rubber band and the throttle is a simple on/off switch.' But his main gripe is that he needs two fully-charged batteries to cover a ten-mile journey over ground that, apart from two short hills, is absolutely flat. He also points out that it would be no good for my first correspondent (see "Knackered", above) because his knees would not let him pedal the bicycle which is the only way to get the thing going or to get it up the slightest incline.

Another suggestion for those prepared to 'get on their bikes' but who don't want to pedal is the Italian-built electric Scoiattolo that comes in men's, women's or unisex styles, with two gears for flat or hilly areas. It costs £875 plus VAT and £20.00 delivery from the Marsden Weighing Machine Group (tel: 0118 935 1655).

A reader from Cambridge manages to 'recycle' his own electric bikes from old mopeds, using either battery mower motors or car starter motors. These cost him around £80 in parts, though the price would obviously be more if he built one for you (tel: 01223 860892).

For more advice on electric vehicles, contact The Electric Vehicle Society (tel: 01933 276618; website: www.evn.co.uk) and the Battery Vehicle Society (tel: 01258 455470).

Yet more short-run solutions

" Do you have any practical advice to help what must be thousands of motorists with petrol-driven cars who only need to make short journeys? You have mentioned Velosolexes before, and electric motorcycles, but, frankly, for a couple of pensioners travelling mostly to the local shopping complex, this does not appear to be a very attractive alternative. "

A warm engine starts more easily, does itself less damage in starting and quickly gets 'off choke' so pollutes less and is more economical. Kenlowe makes a device known as the 'Hotstart' which is a combined immersion heater and pump, run from mains electricity, which gets the engine block up to temperature before you start it (tel: 01628 823303 for information and suitability, because it won't fit all engines). To keep the battery fully charged, an Airflow

Automatic Battery Management System, again run from the house mains, is a good idea (tel: 01635 569569). The other answer for those who only need a vehicle for short runs is a micro car. The smaller the engine you start up, the less condensation and less pollution you generate.

Micro machines

" *I have seen some tiny cars in France and Spain, which must surely represent the answer to reducing urban pollution for those who only need or want to travel short distances. Can you tell us more?* "

Reliant is now importing Ligier micro cars from France. They are right-hand-drive, UK and Euro Type-Approved, have a 505 cc two-cylinder Lombardini diesel engine and open belt Variomatic transmission. In de-restricted UK specification, they should have a top speed of 55–65 mph and give 85 mpg. They should qualify for an extremely low CO_2-based rate of VED as from next October. And, after changes in licence regulations in 1996, they can also be driven on the same motorcycle licence as a Reliant three-wheeler. Price, around £6,500. More details from Reliant Cars Ltd, Cannock Road, Chase Terrace, Burntwood, Staffs WS7 8GB, tel: 01543 459222, fax: 01543 459444. Reliant is also importing Piaggio Ape micro pick-up trucks and vans and will probably take on the cheaper Ligier Due Microcar in the near future. A second microcar contender is Aixam UK Ltd, of 4200 Waterside Centre, Solihull Parkway, Birmingham Business Park, Birmingham B37 7YN, tel: 0121 224 5720. Aixam has been building microcars since 1975 and offers a range of convertibles, and two- and four-seater hatchbacks with diesel engines from

276 cc to 479 cc. The UK range is all RHD and is all powered by the 479 cc Kubota diesel engine which gives up to 55 mph and up to 90 mpg. Prices start at £6,530 on the road with a year's VED for the two-seater Utility, or £6,630 OTR for the four-seater Economy, rising to £8,050 for the four-seater Super. Ex-Reliant boss Jonathan Heynes is importing a range of right-hand-drive fibreglass monocoque models actually called Microcars. Eventually these will be available with two or four seats, 505 cc petrol or diesel Lombardini engines and will cost from £6,592 on the road, including a three-year warranty; Microcar UK, Park House, The Grange, Wolverton, Stratford CV37 0HD, tel: 01789 730094. Others micro car makers include JRD and Erad, who will be watching the UK market to see how sales go. And we shouldn't forget the LHD 599 cc six-speed 87mph SMART car, from the KSB Motorgroup at prices from £5,995, tel: 0181 995 3837, website: http://www.ksb.co.uk, and Wheelbase, tel: 01932 252515.

Boot-size electric scooter

" On a visit to Italy I came across an ingenious scooter. It folds for ease of transport and has a small battery which fits snugly under the footrest platform. Unfortunately, it bore no marks by which I could identify the manufacturer or details of where I could make enquiries about buying one. Can you help? "

Nick Hopkins of Guernsey imports similar rear-drive MZ 'Charly' electric scooters, built in former East Germany. The top speed is 20 kph and maximum range 25 km, so they are really only suitable for local shopping or transport from the car park to the office (tel: 01481 46662). Another possible supplier is 'Board Silly' on

0181 964 3000. It is also thought that, unlike an electric bicycle, you would need a number plate, lights, helmet, driving licence and insurance to run one in the UK, but these needlessly oppressive restrictions may soon be relaxed for a means of transport with such 'green' credentials.

Getting warmer

" *Could you please explain how you would keep warm in an all-electric car in the winter? A useful by-product of the internal combustion engine is heat. Surely an electric heater would be a tremendous drain on the batteries, drastically reducing the vehicle's range in cold weather?* "

The Citroën Berlingo Electrique has a petrol heater fed by a 5 litre tank to keep you warm while you benefit from its 60 mph top speed or 60 mile range (you don't get both at the same time). The batteries are stored beneath the load area (same size as the Berlingo diesel van) and also provide a low centre of gravity for secure roadholding. It's very impressive and at £9,120 plus VAT, plus a lease deal of £2.50 a day for the batteries, provides the first viable electric van I have seen in the UK. Perfect for zero pollution stop/start city-centre deliveries (though, of course, if the electricity is generated by the burning of fossil fuels, pollution is merely transferred from one area to another). Citroën also has another clever idea up its sleeve: the Saxo Dynavolt. This is an electric Saxo with a small two-cylinder direct-injected petrol auxiliary motor tucked under the back seat where the petrol tank would normally be. Its combined starter motor and alternator helps to re-charge the batteries on the move when out of urban conurbations, giving the car a range of up to 200 miles and a top speed of up to 70 mph. Arriving early next year, the Toyota Prius is the best hybrid car yet. This combines a 1,496 cc 58 bhp VVT-i engine with a bank of nickel metal hydride batteries and a 40 bhp electric motor. Excess power output charges the batteries, which are also charged by regenerative braking when descending hills. The petrol engine switches itself off at rest and the car moves off on its electric motor, only starting its petrol engine when needed. It works remarkably well and the car even has a lively feel to it.

Electric car conversions

" Have any of the car manufacturers cracked the electric car nut yet? Our two cars cover around 5,000 miles a year each, almost exclusively on three miles of country lanes to and from work. As you keep telling us, a vehicle with an internal combustion engine is entirely unsuitable for this sort of use. "

Alternative Vehicles Technology (AVT) has written to say that it offers 'affordable electric cars'. Unfortunately 'affordable' is only relative, because its 'lowest cost complete conversion' works out at £5,500 including batteries and charger but excluding the cost of the car to be converted – either a Mini or an old-model sump-gearbox Metro, now at least nine years old. However, kits are available for home conversions from £2,995, excluding charger and batteries. The company also offers a conversion of the later and better Rover Metro or Rover 100 and of micro-vans, including the Bedford Rascal, Daihatsu Hijet and Suzuki Supercarry. AVT is in the process of developing its own AVT 100E electric car, but quotes prices from £16,995 to £19,995, *plus* batteries which cost from £1,481 to £2,070 including VAT. AVT claims top speeds from 56 mph for its £16,995 (plus battery) PM2 model, to 'over 120 mph' for its £17,996 (plus battery) S192 model. The theory of electric cars is spot-on for people who use their cars for short journeys only, a job for which internal combustion engines are particularly unsuited. Unfortunately, as yet, AVT's complete vehicle prices are still too high to attract the levels of interest they deserve. AVT can be contacted at Blue Lias House, Station Road, Hatch Beauchamp, Somerset TA3 6SQ, tel: 01823 480196. The Electric Car Association also operates from the same offices. A reader from Manchester reports unfavourably on Varta semi-traction batteries and warns readers to source their batteries from a British supplier instead.

On yer bike

" *Any motorist who wishes to become an 'eco warrior' and cycle to work instead of driving should visit http://www.living-room.org/ bikepeople/ slackers.htm. Or, if they send me 50p plus a stamped, addressed envelope, I will send them a copy of my article, 'Cycling for Slackers' which describes how cycling to work can be achieved with a minimum expenditure of energy and emission of CO_2. By the way, I am the bearded Devon cyclist reviled by Jeremy Clarkson at every opportunity for having the temerity to question the juvenile antics of 'Top Gear' presenters. But I should add I am also a keen motorcyclist and quite like driving my wife's MX5, sometimes.* "

Well, that's all right then. For those who can't key in the website address (of which I may be one), Tony Collins's postal address is 18 Edwin Road, St Thomas, Exeter EX2 8JF.

ANIMALS IN CARS

Doggy wagons

Four years ago I was asked to list the most suitable estate cars for transporting dogs. The reader specified that candidates must have tie hooks for harnesses or dog cages, a reasonably low rear sill and, preferably, no exposed seat pins which could damage a large dog's skull or ribcage. What follows is an updated list:

- Audi A4 Avant: tie hooks, no pins, 3 × 3 point belts.
- BMW E36 3-Series Touring: tie hooks, protected pins, 2 ×3 point belts.
- Citroën Xsara: tie hooks, no pins, 2 × 3 point belts.
- Citroën Xantia: tie hooks, no pins, 3 × 3 point belts, suspension lowers to help older and smaller dogs jump in.
- Citroën Berlingo Multispace: tie hooks, small pins, 2 × 3 point belts.
- Daihatsu Move: no pins, 2 × 3 point belts.
- Daihatsu Grand Move: no pins, 2 × 3 point belts.
- Fiat Marea Weekend: tie hooks, no pins, 2 × 3 point belts.
- Ford Mondeo: tie hooks, exposed pins, 3 × 3 point belts.
- Honda CRV: tie hooks, 2 × 3 point belts.
- Land Rover Freelander 5 door: tie hooks, 3 × 3 point belts.
- Mazda 626: tie hooks, no exposed pins, 2 × 3 point belts.
- Mazda Premacy: no exposed pins, 2 × 3 point belts, separately removable rear seats – like Scenic.
- Mercedes A Class: tie hooks, no exposed pins, 2 × 2 point belts, completely removable rear seats.
- Mercedes C Class: tie hooks, no exposed pins, 3 × 3 point belts.
- Mercedes E Class: tie hooks, no exposed pins, 3 × 3 point belts.

- Mitsubishi Space Star: tie hooks, no exposed pins, 3 × 3 point belts, rear sill protector, slide-forward as well as fully folding and reclining rear seats.
- Nissan new Primera SLX: tie hooks, no exposed pins, 3 × 3 point belts.
- Peugeot 306: tie hooks, semi-exposed latches, 2 × 3 point belts.
- Peugeot 406: tie hooks, no pins, 3 × 3 point belts (option of rear facing 6th and 7th child seats).
- Renault Megane Scenic: tie hooks, no pins, 3 × 3 point belts, slide forward as well as reclining and completely removable rear seats.
- Renault Kangoo Combi: strong tie hooks, no pins, 2 × 3 point belts, 5 doors (very practical for dogs – and cheap at £9,750).
- Renault Laguna: tie hooks, no pins, 3 × 3 point belts (option of rear facing 6th and 7th child seats).
- Seat Cordoba Vario: no exposed pins, 2 × 3 point belts, very high sill.
- Skoda Felicia: tie hooks, exposed pins, 2 × 3 point belts.
- Skoda Octavia: tie hooks, no pins, 2 × 3 point belts, high sill without optional false floor.
- Suzuki Wagon R: tie hooks, no pins, 2 × 3 point belts.
- Suzuki Baleno: tie hooks, no pins, 2 × 3 point belts.
- Toyota Corolla: tie hooks, no pins, 3 × 3 point belts.
- Toyota Avensis: tie hooks, no pins, 3 × 3 point belts.
- Toyota RAV4 5-door : tie hooks, no pins, 2 × 3 point rear belts, also a low rear loading sill and a completely flat floor when the rear seats are folded
- Vauxhall new Astra: tie hooks, no pins, 3 × 3 point belts.
- Vauxhall Vectra: tie hooks, no pins, 3 × 3 point belts.
- Vauxhall Zafira: tie hooks, no pins, 2 × 3 point belts, 7 seats.
- Volkswagen Golf Mk III: no hooks, exposed pins, 2 × 3 point belts.
- Volkswagen Golf Mk IV: four strong tie hooks, no exposed pins, 2×3 point belts (3×3 point belts optional), built-in dog guard.
- Volkswagen Passat: tie hooks, exposed pins, 2 × 3 point belts (3 × 3 point belts optional, covers for exposed pins available).
- Volvo V40: tie hooks, no pins, 3 × 3 point belts.
- Volvo V70: tie hooks, no pins, 3 × 3 point belts.

BODYWORK AND APPEARANCE

Chips and scratchings

" *In the past you have mentioned firms that specialise in removing minor dents, painting in stone chips, and repairing damaged windscreens. Any chance of a quick reprise?* "

For minor dents of the supermarket carpark variety, call Dentmaster (0800 433687), Paint Technik PDR (0800 298 5455) or Dent Devils (0402 936728) who will put you on to their nearest operator. For stone chips and upholstery repairs try Chips Away on 01562 755678. (Paint Technik also 'invisibly' repairs minor paint damage.) For repairs to cracked or scratched plastic bumpers, call Plastic Technik on 01296 682105. For plastic trim and upholstery repairs call Magic Mend on 0800 901 902 or Trimline Systems on 01202 480 881. For repairs and renovation of leather upholstery call Patrick Russell Leather on 0181 878 3976. And for chipped or scratched windscreens, call Glas Weld Systems on 0800 243 274 (or 01372 362362 in Surrey). On modern cars with bonded windscreens this is better than having the entire screen replaced because removing the old one can damage the car body, leading to leaks and rust. (Autoglass and Auto Windscreens and many others offer a similar service.)

Seeing red

" The roof and bonnet of my red VW Golf Mk III, which is just over three years old, have faded badly and the car is now out of its three-year paint-work warranty. Fortunately my local VW agent has taken the responsibility to re-paint the offending areas. I would like all VW owners to be apprised of the situation so that they can report the signs of this happening to VW within the prescribed period. "

Oxidation of the pigment was always a problem with VW, Audi and Seat 'Tornado Red' and is also a problem with red paint generally, due to a reduction in the lead content to a safer level. I have found that solid, non-metallic finishes can usually be cut back with a mildly abrasive polish, such as Mer, but this, of course, reduces the thickness of the paint. For modern metallic finishes, I prefer dust-free Autoglym Super Resin Polish, followed by Autoglym's Extra Gloss Protection sealant. A tip about polishing is to use cheesecloth, work top to bottom with a circular motion, and always throw the cloth away after use to prevent bits of grit caught in the cloth from damaging your paint. Some valeting companies also offer to professionally seal the paint. VW/Audi has now re-named its non-metallic bright red 'Flash Red' and covers it with a clear lacquer to prevent oxidation. Seat has kept the name 'Tornado Red' and also covers it with a clear lacquer. Because of this, 'Tornado Red' is one of the many extra cost options when ordering a VAG car in Europe.

Killer car washes?

" *Do automatic car washes damage a vehicle's paintwork? I shall soon be in possession of a new Mercedes Benz. As I am not in the first flush of youth I have tended to use an automatic wash at a local filling station but am worried about the effect of the rotating nylon strings on my pristine new paintwork.* "

Nylon brush type car washes can inflict a network of fine scratches on the paint or, in the case of metallics, on the clear lacquer top coat. One answer is a 'brushless' carwash of the type developed by Karcher which does the job by high pressure water jets. The other is a hand-held 'Jetwash'. Both offer the additional advantage that you don't need to retract or remove radio aerials, luggage racks and other appendages that can be damaged by car wash brushes.

Galvanised into action

" *Can you supply me with the names of any motor manufacturers which galvanise their car bodies? I am interested because I find that mechanical components these days seem to far outlast the bodyshells which surround them.* "

I'll have a stab, but this list won't be complete. I should also add that there are two types of galvanising used on car body components: 'hot dip' galvanising (true galvanising) for some unseen underbody parts and the much smoother 'electro galvanising' for external body panels. Galvanisers include Audi, BMW, Fiat (Punto, Bravo, Brava, Marea); Ford (Focus); Mercedes Benz (all models); Mitsubishi (Galant, new Space Wagon); Porsche; Renault (Espace floorpan); Seat (Arosa, new Toledo); Saab (all models); Subaru (Impreza, Legacy); Renault

(Megane and Scenic); Vauxhall (new Astra);
VW (Lupo, Golf Mk IV, Bora, Passat); Volvo
(S70, V70, S80).

Aggravating alloys

" *The alloy wheels of my 1993 Toyota Camry V6 GX are beginning to
show their age. I cannot justify the cost of replacing them, so ask where in
the North East or the Midlands I can have them restored?* "

One of my directories shows up A1 Wheel ren-
ovations of 345 Bilston Road, Wolverhampton,
tel: 01902 871422. Readers in the South might
like to try Spit & Polish of Tonbridge, Kent
(01732 367771) or Wheelbrite of London (0171
431 9015). The cost is likely to be £30–£50
per wheel.

Perforated Passat

" *I have a 1994 'M'-reg. VW Passat saloon which seems to have sprung a
leak. Noticing that the front nearside carpet seemed wet, I lifted it and
found the underlay to be soaked. I had to remove the underlay to let it dry
out. I then found the rest of the carpet and underlay to be the same. There
is no visible sign of any water coming into the car, so what could it be?
It has been suggested that at some time the door panels have been
removed and not re-sealed properly. Short of buying a wet-suit, can you
suggest a cure?* "

Get a Haynes manual and prepare yourself for
a long and tedious job. What has probably
happened is that the plastic membranes
between the door panels and the door frames
have perforated and are allowing water to seep
into the car. You need to remove the door panels
(which is why you need the Haynes manual to
help you locate all the re-usable plastic pins),
and you need to replace the membranes. You

can either cut your own from builders' DPC plastic membrane, or buy the VAG self-adhesive items which cost around £10 a door. Most cars will also suffer some ingress of water if the drain holes in the ventilation plenum chamber in front of the windscreen become blocked, the sunroof drain pipes become blocked, the windscreen seal goes, or any breaches occur in the door seals. And if you are unfortunate enough to be the driver of an early Vectra, you may find that grommets in the wheelarches have been pushed in, allowing water to enter from there.

BRAKES

Unstoppable

" Recently a friend and I both suffered a motorist's nightmare. The brakes failed on our 300 Series Volvos – fortunately while driving slowly. Both cars are eight years old, two of the many such cars still on the road, often driven by elderly people. Would you therefore please advise all owners to have the servo rubber connecting hose checked? This is about two inches long, half an inch in diameter and situated close to the throttle mechanism on the carburettor. In both cases, the rubber hose had perished from within with no visible external signs. "

Thank you for this warning. The pipe is a cheap part, easily replaced, so no hardship is involved. Without the servo assistance this pipe helps to provide, the brakes will feel hard and perhaps too hard for many elderly people. But they will still work if you are able to push the pedal forcefully enough.

Braking the bank

" My six-year-old Honda Concerto has developed a fault in its ABS pump. Honda has quoted £1,400-plus for a replacement! Where on earth can I find a reconditioned or second-hand pump? Alternatively, since I am advised that my normal braking will not be affected, must the ABS be functioning to pass the MOT? "

This is a familiar lament of owners of ABS-equipped cars, especially those who live in coastal regions. The best advice to you and all other owners of ABS cars kept in areas subject to severe salty condensation is to change the brake fluid every year. What has happened is that the brake fluid has absorbed this condensation and this in turn has corroded the internal surfaces of the ABS pump. I don't recommend a 'reconditioned' or second-hand ABS pump. And, since the ABS pump is an integral part of the braking system, the car won't pass an MOT unless the ABS is functioning correctly, or the entire braking system has been dismantled and replaced with a non-ABS system.

Brake fluid warning

" *I recently purchased a ten-year-old Proton and, though I'm happy with the car as a 'buy', while touring the Lake District I noticed the brakes were a bit 'squidgy' when descending the passes. Leaving them to cool for a while restored a firm pedal, but needless to say I changed the fluid at the first opportunity. The liquid that came out looked as old as the car. Now that it's the holiday season, surely it would be an opportune moment to repeat your warning to readers to change their brake fluid regularly, or risk running out of brakes!* "

Said and done. The 'squidginess' is caused by condensation absorbed by the hygroscopic brake fluid. Discs become extremely hot when descending long hills, the heat is transferred to the calipers, and inside the calipers the water in the brake fluid boils. While water is not compressible, steam is, and this is why brakes feel spongy.

'Hygroscopic Horror'

" *Brake fluid. Aaargh! Your reply to the letter about failing ABS pumps (see 'Braking the Bank', above) inspires me to call again for the abolition of that hygroscopic horror, that rust-breeding, paint-stripping bastard child of radiator anti-freeze 1923-style, known as brake fluid – still used almost universally, though not, I believe, by Rolls Royce and Citroën who sensibly prefer mineral oil. Of course, 75 years ago, when seals and hoses were of natural rubber, mineral oil could not be used. Surely all these components are synthetic now? But with the force of habit and the vast investment in making the horrible stuff I don't expect any change. What do you think?* **"**

You're right. Rolls Royce adopted the Citroën system which uses non-water-absorbing 'Liquide Hydraulique Minerale' (or LHM for short). This allows some components of the Citroën hydraulic system, such as the brake doser valve (equivalent of the master cylinder) to be built to such fine tolerances that they are self-lubricating and function without any seals at all. But LHM is still susceptible to grit and dirt and lack of use and needs to be changed every four to five years. This leads into another benefit of the Citroën system in cars such as the Xantia. To change the LHM, all you have to do is set the suspension to its lowest setting. The LHM then returns to the reservoir, which can be removed, the old LHM disposed of, the reservoir replaced and refilled without any need for bleeding. The alternative that could and should be adopted for conventional braking systems is DOT 5 Silicone brake fluid, one supplier of which is Automec (01280 822818). Because this never needs replacing, brake manufacturers scandalously refuse to recommend it in their braking systems, insisting instead on their own Glycol-based hygroscopic DOT 2 or DOT 3 fluids which do need replacing frequently. Cars with pre-DOT-rated seals in their braking systems cannot use silicone brake fluid. But all cars with DOT-rated seals can, provided, and only provided, the entire braking system is pressure-bled first and at least a litre of DOT 5 silicone fluid is flushed through to get rid of the residue before the bleeding nipples are closed. If any old brake fluid remains in the system it could cause problems. However, always remember if you do change to 'non-recommended' brake fluid, you could put yourself in a dodgy legal liability position in the event of any brake failure.

Handbrake failures

" *I'd like to bring your readers' attention to the ineffectiveness of hand-brakes on some modern vehicles, in particular the Chrysler Voyager manual [Editor's note: automatics have a transmission lock]. My daughter purchased a 'nearly new' 2.0 litre version about six months ago and found that the handbrake was so weak that on two occasions the vehicle 'ran away' – fortunately without injury.* "

The handbrake travel on a Voyager is very long, but the design is such that it requires very little strength to pull it on fully. I found that, on my own steep driveway, I needed to release the brake a full four clicks before the vehicle began to roll away. The answer, to preventing any possibility of a vehicle rolling away if the handbrake fails, is always to leave the car in first or reverse gear when you park and, if parking on a hill, to point the front wheels towards the kerb. Saab sensibly forces you to put the gear lever into reverse before you can remove the ignition key.

Rusted discs

" *On 17 October 1997 we purchased a second-hand Citroën Relay 2.5 turbodiesel van from a Citroën agents under the impression that it had belonged to the chairman of the garage company. The van was first registered on 24 August 1995 and the mileage on the date of purchase was*

10,505. We have just taken it for its first MOT and been told that the front brake discs are badly pitted with rust. We were quoted £300-plus for new discs and pads. In fact we had the discs and pads fitted and a new MOT test at Charley Brown's Auto Centre for £249 all-in. They are giving us a written report on the state of the discs. Can we recover any of this expenditure? "

10,505 miles in 26 months is an extremely low mileage for a van. 100,000 miles would be normal. So I suspect that it has been sitting around for most of its life and where it was sitting will have affected the rate of corrosion of the discs. If the van was standing on grass, then the discs will have corroded quite quickly. A company by the name of Vehvac offers a good cure for this which is an in-situ disc re-grinder to take off surface corrosion and restore the discs to 'as new' (01732 868080). You might try getting the Citroën agent which sold you the car to agree to allow a Small Claims Court to arbitrate over this matter, but the agent may well argue that having to replace discs at three years old is fairly normal these days.

Warped mind

" *I bought a three-year-old 76,000 mile Honda Prelude VTEC in 1996 at a discount because of front-wheel wobble while braking. I knew the reason was warped discs, had both them and the pads replaced at a cost of £145, and the problem was solved. 10,000 miles later, brake judder was so severe I had the discs skimmed. I had them replaced again after a further 4,000 miles, skimmed after another 6,000 miles, skimmed again at another 4,000 miles, then the problem returned after yet another 2,500 miles. Honda UK was unable to suggest a better solution, such as cross-drilled discs and competition pads, so what is the reason for the warping? I don't consider myself to be a heavy braker.* "

Heavy braking in itself does not necessarily warp discs. But holding the car on the brakes after heavy braking can. Say, for example, you are approaching a roundabout on a dual carriageway. Assuming you have been sticking to the speed limit, you could be braking from 70mph to a standstill. If you then hold the car on the footbrake because of traffic on the roundabout, you prevent the heat you created in stopping from dispersing in the area of the disc clamped by the pads. The heat differential between this part of the disc and the rest of it can cause the disc to warp. The other reason this can happen is wear in the brake calipers which prevents the pads from retracting properly after braking and again causes localised overheating.

BUYING AND SELLING

£10,000 bath in two years

" *I purchased a new Citroën Xantia SX 2.0i automatic with air conditioning from my local Citroën agent in June 1996. With the allowance on my existing car, it cost me £17,600. Two years later, in June 1998, I made enquires about replacing it with a new Xsara 1.8iSX automatic. I was quoted £15,700 including ABS and, after the part-exchange of my 10,870 mile Xantia, was quoted a balance of £8,100. This means that in two years and 11,000 miles, my Xantia has lost £10,000. In 44 years I have owned or driven 23 cars and have never experienced a loss of anything like this amount. Please can you explain?* "

For five years, list prices of mass-market cars in the UK have been ludicrously high. But private buyers (who make up about 30 per cent of the UK new car market) supported these prices by paying them and by paying excessively high prices for used cars less than two years old. Now reality has dawned. In Spring 1998, used car values began to tumble. By Spring 1999 100,000 unsold 'T'-reg. cars were being offered at discounts of up to 40 per cent. But in your case, the message is, keep the Xantia. Forking out £10,000 over two years just to get behind the wheel of a new and smaller car makes no sense at all.

Old bikes

" *Could you please tell me the best way to dispose of my late husband's motor cycle which is more than 60 years old and in need of restoration? Also, how much should I ask for it? The motorcycle is a BSA 498 cc, first registered on 24 August 1934. I have the original Kent County Council log book.* "

Advertise it in *Old Bike* magazine, but first speak to the editor, Ken Hallworth, to get a good idea of how to price it. *Old Bike*, Clayside Barn, Alstonfield, nr Ashbourne, Derbyshire DE6 2FS, tel: 01335 310407. Sell it quickly to someone with a recognised collection or someone prepared to MOT and SORN the bike, in case new EU 'end of life' regulations come into effect demanding that the bike be destroyed.

Collectors' price

" *Eighteen months ago I purchased from a Mercedes agent a 1985 left-hand-drive Mercedes W123 240TD manual estate car with a genuine mileage of 3,500. This vehicle had been imported from Germany and stored by an enthusiast who had to sell it to finance a divorce. With much trumpeting, the Mercedes agent displayed the car in its showrooms and I purchased it for £9,995. Now, 18 months later, I find that my needs have changed and I wish to dispose of the vehicle. It has completed a total of 17,000 trouble-free miles, has been serviced by the agent and remains in immaculate condition. But the agent has refused to re-purchase it for reason of 'excess stock'. Enquiries elsewhere suggest a trade price of between £2,500 and £3,000, and my advertising campaign has produced no serious leads despite bringing the price down from £8,995 to £6,995. This means that I am likely to lose more than £7,000 on the vehicle. What sensible yet effective means do I have at my disposal to challenge the selling price set by the agent, to persuade the agent that gross overcharging is not a sensible business policy, and to encourage the agent to take the car back at a price commensurate with that which we paid?* "

None whatsoever. Old cars with spectacularly low mileages often sell at ridiculously high prices. In February 1998, British Car Auctions sold a 1975 Jaguar E-Type Series III Roadster with just 650 miles from new for £70,500, plus commission. I was there and watched two bidders fight it out in £250 bids all the way from £50,000. But the fact is, once that car has been driven another 10,000 miles, most of this value will disappear. An extra 10,000 miles is likely to cost the owner the thick end of £40,000. As a private sale, your car might be worth around £5,000. Only a mug would pay more, but that doesn't mean to say you won't find one.

'Time warp' Audi

" I will be 82 years old very soon and feel that the time has come to give up driving. I started in 1932, so it will be a very sad day for me. I shall have to sell my Audi 80, bought in 1974, not quite a 'classic' but not far off. The condition is excellent and the mileage a mere 38,965. I have all the relevant papers. Could you advise me as to the price I should ask? "

You're right. It isn't a classic. But, since the Audi 80 was only launched in the UK the previous year, it does have 'time warp' value, either to Audi UK (tel: 01908 679121) or to a film hire company such as Carriages Vehicle Agency (tel: 01737 353926). I'd ask a straight £1,000 and see how you get on. If you get no joy, try Club Audi (tel: 01525 750502). And, finally, try a photo ad in *Classic Car Weekly* (tel: 01733 465430) which costs £20 a week, or £40 for three weeks, stressing the 'time warp' factor. But be very careful over people responding to advertisements. When they call, ask for their phone number and call them back (land lines, not cellphones), so you at least have a handle on them. Keep the car locked up and hidden away. Never open the door to anyone after dark, whatever their protestations about 'getting lost' (they won't be able to see the car properly anyway). And only arrange appointments to view when a younger, stronger relative or friend is available to oversee matters. The best way to take payment for the car in exchange for its keys and documents is in cash actually inside your bank where you can bank the money straight away.

255,000-mile M5

" *I wish to sell my 1986 BMW M5 which has given me wonderful service for the last ten years. It is totally original, has full BMW agent service history and has covered 255,000 miles with barely a murmur. The agent is not interested in a part-exchange and suggests selling privately. Can you please tell me what price would be reasonable and where I should advertise?* "

Try it at £2,500 (not £2,499 in this case) and be prepared to settle for £2,000. Your best media bet is probably a photo ad in *Classic Car Weekly* (tel: 01733 465430). It's a 'classic', so you won't be expected to put the mileage in the ad, but if any caller asks tell them straight away and don't fudge the issue. Another possibility is a classic car auction which takes 'neo-classics'. Apparently only 180 RHD Mk 1 M5s were built.

Who sells SLs?

" *Where can I buy a good, second-hand Mercedes Benz 280 or 300SL sports car with some degree of confidence about the mechanical state of the car and its mileage? I live in the Chichester area, but would be prepared to travel up to 100 miles.* "

Silver Arrows of Putney specialise in 1963–71 'Pagoda Top' Mercedes SLs, the best of which are the later 280s. They advertise regularly in the *Telegraph's* 'Forecourt' section and their number is 0181 789 8525. I don't recommend the later 'Ribside' roadsters for a number of reasons: they look like fairground bumper cars; they can never attain the 'classic' status of a 'Pagoda Top', much less that of a proper 1957–63 300SL roadster; they rot and body repairs can set you back a lot more than the repaired car is worth; an engine rebuild on a 280 or 300 'Ribside' is megabucks and again can cost more than the repaired car is worth.

Beautiful Beetle

" *I am seeking advice on the most advantageous way to dispose of my sister's VW Beetle which originally belonged to her late husband. The car is 1,498 cc, first registered 7/7/70, recorded mileage is 39,000 and the colour is Diamond Blue. It is in excellent condition. Some indication of a price would be appreciated.* "

If it really is 'excellent', I wouldn't be embarrassed to ask £2,750. You may have to settle for a bit less than this because, from your photograph, it looks as though the nearside front wing has been re-sprayed a slightly different blue. But honest, 'genuine' VED-free 1500 cc Beetles like this are becoming hard to find, and if it's 100 per cent rust-free you might find yourself holding a doorstep auction once the VW enthusiasts get wind of it. Try a photo ad in *Classic Car Weekly* (tel: 01733 465430) or one of the numerous magazines catering specifically for Type 1 Beetles. New rear-engined Beetles are still available from Mexico, subject to SVA quota, at £7,495 OTR from Beetles UK (tel 01454 228999), who also do new 'Bay Window' Type 2 VW vans from £9,995 plus VAT.

How to lose £1,200 a month

" *I purchased a used 10,000-mile 1997-registered Mercedes Benz C180 Esprit Estate from a Mercedes agent in September 1997 and paid £23,000. My requirements then changed and five months later I decided to trade it in for a Mitsubishi Shogun at the same dealership. The best it would offer me was £17,000, a drop of £6,000. I understand that there is a glut of 'C Class' Mercedes on the market, evident from the large numbers on the agent's forecourt. But is this typical? Have other readers had the same experience?* "

Yes, it is typical, both generally, and now of 'C Class' Mercedes when they are offered for trade-in so soon after purchase. Long-term residuals in percentage terms, however, remain better for Mercedes than for other makes, and for this reason they should be seen as long-term rather than short-term purchases. Another factor affecting 'nearly new' Mercedes prices when you were trading-in was a glut of cancelled RHD Far East export cars which were diverted to the UK at huge savings.

Karmann Ghia Type 3

" *Please could you give me an approximate value for our VW Karmann Ghia Type 3 which we bought new on 1 July 1969 and which we believe to have been the last one imported (it was to special order)? The car has now covered 61,227 miles (with MOTs to confirm this), is used regularly, and the bodywork is in first-class condition.* "

Practical Classics magazine said £4,600 in 'Condition 1' or £2,700 in 'Condition 2' (body parts are hard to get). If yours is in perfect condition, because of its historical significance, it could be worth £5,000–£6,000. VW suggests that its museum in Wolfsburg might be interested. There are several VW-specific magazines on the bookstalls which would be a good place to advertise. And there are so many VW Clubs that, rather than attempt to list them, I'll give you the address of The Association of British VW Clubs: c/o J. Daniel, 66 Pinewood Green, Iver Heath, Bucks, tel: 01753 651538.

Played for a sucker

" *I have read with interest your replies and the recent article on importing cars from Europe. I was particularly impressed with the Alfa Romeo 156, so I test-drove one at my local Alfa agents. The car came up to expectations and I decided to purchase one. From then on my story goes downhill. After a fleeting glance at my 'L'-reg. Audi 2.0 16v Coupe the salesman offered me trade price for it against full list price for the Alfa – for which I was asked to wait seven months. In a follow-up call, the salesman stated that his franchise was not prepared to offer a discount. For a car which is available £5,000 cheaper in Holland to be sold in the UK without even a modest discount is scandalous. I sincerely hope that your articles and replies on the subject and the campaigns being waged on TV by Anne Robinson on 'Watchdog' and Quentin Willson on 'Top Gear', and in the Daily Mirror will have the effect of bringing us a true Common Market.* "

Fiat managed to limit official imports of the 156 to the UK at first so that the company could demand and get full list price on every private sale. But, by Spring 1999, specialists such as Motorpoint of Derby were advertising new 156 1.8 Twin-Sparks for £14,699 (a £3,000 saving) from stock and I know one trader who bought a 156 2.0 Twin-Spark with Sport Pack 3 in Germany for Dm35,300 (£11,800) plus VAT. Fiat has even issued official RHD price lists for Belgium and Holland which detail exactly what you get for your money. (I know because I have them.)

Toyota discounts

" I am thinking about buying a new Toyota Corolla and have seen advertisements by companies which import these cars to the UK via Ireland and other countries at special lower prices. I went to my local Toyota agent to check the savings available, but he did not know the models described in the advertisement as 'Terra' and 'Luna'. Can you tell me if these have the same spec as models on sale in the UK? If I were to send a completed order form, the company involved requires a power of attorney over the sale. Is this a safe and normal practice, and does it have any disadvantages for me? "

Since Corollas are roughly twice the price in the UK that they are in Japan, you should be able to walk into any Toyota agent in the UK and ask for a discount of at least 10 per cent off the UK 'on the road' list price. This will include the UK importer's three-year warranty. An imported Corolla won't have the three-year warranty, will not be to UK spec, will not have the second-hand value of a UK-spec car, and may even have been illegally imported into the UK which could render it subject to confiscation. So, no, giving the import agent power of attorney is certainly not advisable. Personally importing a car with full European Certificate of Conformity is a different matter, but the car needs to be at least £2,500 cheaper, all taxes paid, to work out less than one bought with a proper warranty at a 10 per cent discount from a UK agent.

Neo-classic Volvo

" I have a 1972 Volvo 144 GL fuel injection automatic, in gold, with black leather seats and a sunshine roof. I have owned it since new, have always had it serviced by Volvo agents, and it is the most comfortable car I have ever driven. But now my age and rheumatism demand a car with power steering. There is rust in only two places: the bottom front of the offside

front wing and in the spare wheel well. How do you suggest I sell this car, and how much can I expect for it? "

A couple of years ago, this model was worth no more than buttons. But now it's inside the 'Historic Vehicle' qualification for VED exemption, things have changed. Auctioneers H&H at Buxton recently realised £1,106 for a 71K 144 and £2,415 for a 1972 144DL. Whether your car will appeal in the same way is a bit of a gamble because it depends on the right private buyer being there on the day. But the auction route is worth a try (see list of classic car auction houses at the end of this chapter). Another possibility is to put the car in a photo ad in a magazine such as *Practical Classics* or *Classic Car Weekly* (tel: 01733 465430). State one owner from new, give the mileage, mention VED exemption, ask £1,750 and see what offers you get.

On a Roller

" *I am a 70-year-old pensioner and my lifetime dream has been to own a Roller. I can't afford a new one, so what am I likely to get for around £10,000?* "

Anything up to a 1980 Shadow II. Shadow IIs are much improved over Shadow Is in terms of handling and steering. But, with their chrome bumpers, there's no doubt that Shadow 1s look better. Rough Shadow 1s start at around £3,000; Shadow IIs at around £5,000. It's very important not to get a rough one disguised as a good one. If you can find a Shadow with original paint, even if it's almost worn through with polishing, that's a good sign. If the car is one-owner or one-family-owned, that's even better. And if it comes with a full service history plus a file of specialist bills, that's better still. The first place to look for body rot and filler is where the 'A' pillars meet the scuttle. Auctions aren't a bad source as long as you only bid for cars entered directly by their long-term owners or by executors. The Hanwell Car Centre (tel: 0171 436 2070) specialises in these models and also hires them out, so you could spend a weekend driving one to make sure it's what you really want before committing to a purchase. From October 2000, annual VED for Rolls Royces which do not qualify as 'Historic Vehicles' could be prohibitively high.

Buying a jam sandwich

" *As one who searches for style and performance on a shoestring I've lusted after a 3.0 24v Senator ever since Vauxhall stopped making them and 'Top Gear' gave them a rave review. After that, prices rose overnight and it was like looking for a cuckoo at Christmas. But I've just found and bought an ex-police Senator. It's strictly a no-frills muscle machine with bags of space and all the oomph I could wish for. The odometer says it's only done 70,000 miles and, although the rear suspension's a wee bit noisy, its looks and performance seem to bear this out. It's also clearly never worn an illuminated roof rack. So how was it used? Could the mileage be true? Did police Senators have modified suspension and engines? And is it worth feeding back some of the frills such as electric windows with a view to getting a better price on resale?* "

The best place to buy a Senator was one of the twice-monthly ex-police sales held on Tuesday or Thursday evenings by West Oxfordshire Motor Auctions on the old A40 at Witney (tel: 01993 774413). Throughput of ex-police vehicles is now running at 120 to 150 a week. Thames Valley Senators usually came off the fleet at about 110,000 miles, and the service docket often itemised new clutch and catalytic converters at the 80,000–90,000 mark. These cars were prepped for auction with all police markings removed and all holes filled in. But there won't be many more because, although Senators were kept in storage for several years for the police, the last were registered on 'N' plates. The new bargain ex-police car is a Volvo T5 estate, many of which are automatics because this increases front tyre life. I think your car may have been a driver training car, which explains the groaning rear suspension. Yes, suspension was stiffened at the rear to help carry all the police clobber in the boot, but, though Surrey Police helped get gremlins out of the Senator's emissions control system, the engines weren't uprated. The Achilles heel of manual Senators is their Getrag 5-speed gearbox which tends to become troublesome at around 120,000 miles. Rebuilds are very expensive because special tools are required, but second-hand replacement boxes can be obtained from the Vauxhall Spares Centre of Romford on 01708 384720. A specialist in reselling these cars, tidied up and fully sorted, is Portaploy on 01256 322240.

Older than it seemed

" On 23 May 1998 I signed an order for a used Honda Civic 1.5i VTEC-E, first registered on 25 July 1997, and paid a deposit of £350. I was surprised to see that the price included 12 months extended warranty, because a new Honda comes with a two-year warranty. On querying this I discovered that the reason was that the car had first been registered in Jersey in 'late 1996'. In fact, the Honda agent admitted in writing that 'many of our Hondas arrive this way'. The agent still holds my £350 deposit and states, 'I really want you to have a car supplied by us and I would very much welcome the opportunity to sit down with you and discuss a way to sort this out.' What's the story about registering all the vehicles in Jersey? "

It's one of the oldest tricks in the book and it stinks. After sitting around unsold on an airfield for between 6 and 18 months, cars are exported to Jersey to serve time on the island's rental fleets. Once they've been there for long enough they can be re-imported to the UK VAT-free and re-registered in the UK according to the date they were registered in Jersey. Old Austin Metro 1.3s, production of which ended in 1989, were coming back in 1991/92, being registered on 'J' plates, and plenty of people were conned into believing they were new. To establish when your Honda was built, pull out the ashtray and check the date stamp underneath. With 'Just in Time' production, it won't have been more than a couple of weeks before the car was assembled. Since ashtrays can easily be swapped, you then need to confirm this with date stamps on other plastic components. If this confirms that you're buying a 1996 car and not a 1997 car, you should pay the 1996 price, not the 1997 price. According to 'Glass's Guide', the dealer wasn't overcharging, but, since prices have slid rapidly since you started doing the deal, I'd ask him to reduce the bottom line by at least £500. If he refuses, go to Trading Standards and report him for misleading you into believing the car was younger than it is.

How to net a car

" *You mentioned that there were not many Citroën SM 2.1TD SX estate cars around. I ran a search on the 'Car Hunter', part of the regional press 'AdHunter' internet website, and found four XM estates in the trade advertisement section. The email address of 'Car Hunter' is: http://www. autohunter.co.uk/car.* "

Thank you. I checked this out myself and found

no less than 906 privately advertised Citroens in total. However, searches can be confined to regions and specific models, so you don't have to wade through an endless list. It is definitely a useful service. Another website for new and used car buying is http://www.autobytel.co.uk; and every car advertised in the regional *Autotraders* goes on their website: http://www.autotrader.co.uk.

Part-exchanging for a 'nearly new'

" *This is a tale of caution to those who believe they are getting a bargain from the 'nearly new' car supersites. In early May, I accompanied my son to Trade Sales in Slough and the Great Trade Centre at White City to look at Mondeos and Escorts. At Slough he was told that his car, a 'G'-reg. Sierra 1.8LX with low mileage and in good condition, owned almost from new, was worth probably £1,650 subject to survey. We returned to Slough two weeks later to discover that the part-exchange value of the Sierra against a nearly new Escort had slumped from £1,650 to £1,000. At White City we were offered £500. Both admitted that the car was in good condition. I then advised my son to go to a franchised Ford agent. This he did, and purchased a 1.8 litre 16-valve Escort, less than one year old, with £1,500 worth of extras. Although the price of this Escort was dearer, after being given £2,000 for his trade-in he was £200 better off and also gained the security of a warranty. The moral of this story is that, although places like Slough and White City offer cheaper cars, their trade-in policy can leave you worse off than a Ford agent. They basically want cash sales. If you have cash, however, do what I have done in the past: Go to the auctions. If you are buying a six-month-old car, you will get it for the price they pay (they buy at auctions) and you will get the remainder of the warranty.* "

The situation isn't anything like as cut and dried as this. First of all, what had seemed a bullet-proof trade in cars under £2,000 died virtually overnight. Trade Sales and The Great Trade Centre picked this up as it happened, but a franchised agent would take much longer and would not discover that the £2,000 Sierra was worth £500 until he tried to trade it out. Second, 'nearly new' prices have been collapsing since Spring 1998, and by Spring 1999 the rate of collapse had accelerated. Trade Sales and The Great Trade Centre only buy some of their 'nearly news' at auction. They buy the bulk of them direct and know full well that they have to compete with auction prices to stay in business. As for them preferring cash sales, not so. Trade Sales of Slough prefers to sell cars on finance. To move metal, it will even undercut auction prices and take its profit on the finance. The Great Trade Centre has done more over the years to pull used car prices down to a sensible level than any other dealer in the country.

Ted's wisdom

" As a pensioner whose wheels are his legs, trying to survive on £74 a week necessitates a different type of motoring from that of most Telegraph readers. I had a 'D'-reg. Metro City, bought six months earlier for £300, and I put on 7,000 miles before the MOT ran out. I asked the MOT garage to give it an MOT pre-check, which they did, prescribing two new tyres and realigning the front wheels at a cost of £132. I agreed and the work was done, but then the car failed its MOT on a list of other counts for which I was quoted a total of £447 to put right. So I said, "Put my old tyres back and I'll scrap the car." The garage refused, telling me that if I wanted my car back I would have to pay £132 plus £25 for the MOT. So I gave them the log book and let them keep the car under their mechanic's right of lien. I then went out and bought a 61,000 mile 'B'-reg. Metro Vanden Plas with ten months MOT for £280 – a lot less than the £447 I'd have had to pay to get my old car back on the road. Cheap second-hand cars are now at rock bottom prices, so when the Vanden Plas fails its MOT, I'll scrap it and buy another old car with a long MOT. Seems far more sensible to me than spending more than the car is worth on repairs. I'll even be doing my bit for the environment and jobs in the motor industry by helping to get old cars off the road. "

Good thinking from our regular correspondent Ted Stupple. But you have to make sure you either buy cars like this from private owners who have had trouble selling them, or you buy them at a part-exchange auction. In April 1999, a friend picked up a one-owner 111,000-mile Vauxhall Carlton with a long MOT at one of these sales for £65 all in. When we went to drive it out of the compound we found that the tank still contained at least a tenner's worth of petrol. He sold it that afternoon for £350.

Test drives

" Car manufacturers already know how to overcome the difficulty experienced by private buyers in the UK of obtaining a test drive in the exact model of car they want to buy. When I moved to work in Brussels in 1990 I was offered cars to drive by the manufacturers' own test centres on the outskirts of the city. This gave informative extended experience at the wheel by allowing the use of the car without limitation for an entire weekend. "

This is coming to the UK and will be here before 'block exemption' ends in 2002. 'Block exemption' is the system by which manufacturers award and control the franchises which sell their cars, allowing only one within each 'sales area'. Because block exemption is clearly a restrictive trade practice, it will be banned throughout Europe by 2002 and effectively any large trade organisation will then be able to buy cars direct from the factory at the ex-works price. So what the manufacturers have done is to get rid of smaller franchises and combine others into larger units in which they have at least a 51 per cent shareholding. Or they allocate franchises to large trading groups with which they have special arrangements. By 2002, private buyers will be able to do just as you did in Brussels: visit and buy at a large Daewoo-like regional showroom where they can test-drive a much wider range of models than those available at a conventional franchised dealer; then have their car serviced or repaired at local 'satellite' service and repair centres (which is why Ford bought 'Kwik Fit'). Cars should also be a lot cheaper, because whenever manufacturers try to hype prices via the outlets they still control, big operators will be able to move in and undercut them – forcing manufacturer-controlled prices back into line.

Time for a 'nearly new' car

" *After seven years I have decided to sell my 41,000-mile 1990 'G'-reg. Citroën BX16 TGS Meteor which has been serviced since I bought it by the same specialist Citroën garage. In its place I can get a Ford Mondeo, Vauxhall Vectra or Toyota Avensis from the car-hire firm where my daughter works. The car would be about three months old. Assuming I can sit equally easily in the Mondeo, Vectra and Avensis (I am 6ft 2in tall), which of these would you recommend? I understand that the prices are heavily discounted compared to the normal market.* "

With 6,000–9,000 miles and at 3–6 months old, direct from the rental company, these cars should be between £8,000 and £9,000 – no more. If you like sporty handling and plenty of 'feel-good factor' go for the Mondeo. If you prefer the balance of a three-year warranty and fuel consumption the right side of 40 mpg on a run, go for the Avensis. This has an unaggressive, nice, smiley 'face', so another benefit is that it is less likely to provoke road rage in others.

Dumping an old friend

" *I have just retired and am starting to wonder whether to change my 'H'-registered, pre-cat Vauxhall Cavalier 1.6L hatchback. It was first registered in February 1991 to a vehicle hirer, and I bought it in June 1992 with 20,500 miles on the clock. It has been serviced regularly, has never caused me a moment's trouble, had new tyres last year, now has a registered 65,000 miles and seems to be running better than ever, getting 40–42 mpg on long runs and around 35 mpg in everyday use. There are no signs of rust. My first question is, should I change it? Have I had the best out of it and is it now running into an age when it's going to start costing me money? The second question is, what should I buy instead? A newish replacement hatchback of a similar size, say for £10,000 or so, including part-exchange, would seem appropriate, but I don't like the idea of airbags and really don't want a 'cat'. Alternatively, with the same budget and specifications, what springs to your mind from the 'pre-cat, pre-bag' era? Something a little more upmarket, perhaps. I can fit 14ft of it into my garage, and width is no problem.* "

You have the perfect car. A rust-free 91H pre-cat Cavalier with designed-in low maintenance costs (even changing the clutch is a cheap half-hour job), that runs on Premium Unleaded petrol. So the only possible reason you could have for swapping cars is sheer boredom. If you get rid of your Cavalier and replace it with something more exciting that promptly breaks down every other week, drinks petrol and costs you a lottery win in maintenance, you will forever rue the day. So the only sensible advice I can give you is to keep the car, happy in the knowledge that it has virtually stopped depreciating and that the only problem you might eventually have is with the carburettor.

Citroën price appeal

" *I was fascinated to read how your reader from Northampton stood to lose £10,000 if he part-exchanged his two-year-old Xantia for a Xsara (see '£10,000 bath in two years', above). But the trick seems to be to buy your Xantia 'right' in the first place. In April 1997 I was looking to change my five-year-old ZX for a new one, at that time listed at £11,500. But when I visited my Citroën agent I found he had just purchased ten 'N'-registered Xantias from Citroën UK. By the time I decided to buy one (overnight, as it happens) there were only two left: a 1.9TD SX at £10,300 and a 1.9D LX at £8,995. I bought the 1.9D LX, received £3,500 in part exchange for my ZX (which had cost me £8,800 new five years before), and ended up with an 'as new' Xantia with only 400 miles on the clock, complete with a two-year Hallmark warranty, 12 months VED and a full tank of diesel for a total outlay of £6,000 cash. Needless to say I am delighted with the car, which never does less than 40 mpg. If there are any drawbacks to this kind of purchase, I can't think of them.* "

You got yourself a bargain because, whenever Citroën finds itself stuck with excess stock, it doesn't try to manipulate the market by holding cars back. It lets them go for sensible money. The other aspect of this is that you're very happy with your purchase and with Citroën generally. Ford did much the same thing with Fiestas and Mondeos in Spring 1999. Makes sense to me.

Hello, Dolly

" *I own a red and white Citroën Dolly 2CV6 Special, 'D'-reg., in first-class condition. It has only done 20 miles in the last year bringing the total milage to 24,000. I have no more need to use it, so should I sell it? Or should I keep it off the road as a future collectors item?* "

The Tin Snail's 50th anniversary was covered in detail in *Telegraph* 'Motoring' on 18 May 1998. Yours is desirable in one sense because it was built during the last years of production at Levallois, Paris. 2CVs built in Portugal, from 1988 to 1990, were not as well put together. But Dollies built in 1985/86 have a reputation for a rust-prone rear panel and floorpan. The 2CV soldiered on in the UK until October 1990, and a bit longer in the rest of Europe. A few people have zero-mileage examples of the last cars 'tucked away' in the hope of making a bit of money, but are strongly advised to MOT and re-SORN them every year (see the section on 'Storing a Car'). But nearly 7,000,000 2CVs and their derivatives were produced and aficionados are already picky about which are the ones to have, so I don't think you'll make a killing by hanging on to yours. See if you can interest a member of the Citroën Car Club, tel: 07000 248258. Graham Draper at Garage Levallois restores 2CVs to better than new, tel: 01243 555556, and is always interested in buying good cars to start from. Likewise the Tin Snail Company, tel: 01903 823880.

Low p/x offer

" *I am now driving my second Mercedes Benz and expect to trade it in for a new 'A' Class in September. I did not trade in the first because I was offered an extremely low price by the agent and so ended up selling it myself for the full retail price given in* What Car? *magazine. However, this time round, I am high on the agent's list for 'A' Class deliveries so am more or less tied to him. He has offered me £1,600 less than the trade price listed in* What Car? *for a 1994 C180 Elegance. Is there an ombudsman I can appeal to over this matter?* "

You must be joking. Trade prices offered by agents are determined by supply and demand and on a car such as the C Class are always likely to leave a margin of £1,500–£2,000 to cover the agent's stocking and preparation costs, warranty and profit. A few years ago, demand for the C Class exceeded supply, but the reverse is now true and many Mercedes agents are being extremely cautious in their valuations of trade-ins, particularly of manual C180s. At auction at the time you wrote I saw Mercedes C180 Classics bid to less than £9,000 against a guide value of £10,625, and this explains why the agent offered you £1,600 less than guide price.

Fancy a Yank

" Call me daft if you will, but I have always fancied a 'Big Yank' from the period 1955–60. Apart from telling me to forget it, any advice would be appreciated. I have up to £7,500 to spend and would consider one for less to rebuild. "

Ask your newsagent to get you a copy of *Classic American* magazine and have a root through that. Apart from cars for sale, it gives lots of useful advice and will direct you to the appropriate club.

Ex-lease versus private

" I'm puzzled by a reply in which you appear to state that ex-fleet cars disposed of at 50,000–80,000 miles and 2–4 years are not too good. I am sure I have read previously that you recommended just such cars as these because repairs and servicing are included in the lease costs and would have been done properly. "

You're right to bring this up. The more mileage a car clocks up every year, the less chance the engine has to cool down. Since most engine wear occurs on start-up and the highest level of engine wear is in cars driven short distances, it usually makes more sense to buy low in years

and high in miles rather than the other way round, if the price is more or less the same. Detailed computer print-outs of the maintenance the car has undergone are more reliable than stamps in service books as proof of the maintenance which has occurred and of the mileage showing on the odometer. But, fleet managers are notoriously penny-pinching – it's their job to be. So if a car is coming up for a big service close to the end of its lease, they'd rather offload it before the big service than after. For the same reason, they replace expensive tyres with cheap tyres and sometimes damaged panels with second-hand ones. More worrying than this, though, is the influence fleet managers have on 'manufacturer' service intervals. These now seem to be moving towards a service regime which suits a car which will run for two to three years and cover 50,000–80,000 miles, with absolutely no regard for the problems faced by any subsequent owner due to inadequate servicing during the car's fleet life. I think this is carrying cost-cutting too far. But if private owners also comply with fleet-based servicing regimes, there remains no benefit in buying an ex-privately owned car rather than an ex-fleet car.

Ageism in the showroom

" *I am now 45 years old and have found that the drive towards youthfulness in car showrooms has led to the belief that potential customers will not buy cars from salespeople of 40 years old or more. That makes car sales a dead-end career, because if you do not make sales manager or dealer principal by your mid-30s, you don't just get 'passed over', you find yourself out of a job. How do your readers feel about this? Would they prefer to buy from a 20-year-old, or from a 50-year-old?* "

B&Q, the DIY chain, have a sympathetic policy towards the employment of older sales people and find that older customers like it. Dixons are the same. The proportion of private car purchasers over the age of 40 must be well over 50 per cent. So I have a lot of sympathy for your point of view. The problem comes from the fact that, behind the scenes, selling cars is a highly aggressive occupation and that success is measured in terms of units sold and profit per unit, which also includes profit on finance deals, warranties, insurance and other peripherals. I asked *Telegraph* readers the age range they preferred to be sold to by. Only 6 per cent were happy to deal with car sales staff under 25. Eleven per cent didn't mind dealing with 25–30-year-old salespeople. Twenty-eight per cent had no objections to 30–35-year-olds. Forty-five per cent were fine with 35–40-year-olds. Seventy-seven per cent liked sales staff aged 40–45. Eighty-two per cent felt at ease with 45–50-year-olds. And 76 per cent liked to deal with sales staff over the age of 50. The average age of male respondents was 60.7 years and of female respondents 61.4 (the split was 252 to 136). But only 48 per cent were both over 40 and stated a definite preference for sales staff over 40. Nevertheless, the conclusion has to be that, if garages want to sell cars to *Telegraph* readers, they will do better with sales staff aged at least 35.

Ex-Ministry

" As a consequence of living a stone's throw from the sea and working in Southampton Docks, any vehicle I own is subject to virulent salt water corrosion. I am therefore considering purchasing an ex-MoD Land Rover Defender 90 diesel (preferably ex-RAF, as I believe they are the best) to act as our second car-cum-utility. Could you advise me where the MoD sells its surplus vehicles at auction? "

British Car Auctions runs regular 'drive through' auctions at its Blackbushe Airport Centre on the A30 between Hartley Wintney and Blackwater (tel: 01252 878555). The MoD and Lex Defence sales are on Fridays. But the problem with ex-MOD vehicles is that they are not registered or MOT-tested, so, unless you have trade plates and trade insurance, you cannot legally drive them back to base. If you'd rather buy from a dealer who has pre-registered and MOT-tested the vehicle, the best place to look is in *Exchange & Mart*.

RAC sportscar inspections

" Back in March 1998 I paid £3,200 for a 1983 Porsche 924 on the strength of an RAC Used Car Inspection, which itself cost me £239. As soon

as I bought the car I found that neither the windscreen washers nor the heated rear window worked, and that the driver's electric window was very sluggish, none of which was mentioned in the report. Two thousand miles later, during the last week in May, I found that the rear-mounted gearbox was hanging loose. After another 1,000 miles and a further six weeks I heard grinding noises and took the car into Halfords, where I was told the car needed new rear brake drums and new front discs and pads. I complained to the RAC, which denied all responsibility. The garages that made the repairs were horrified to learn that the car has passed an RAC inspection. Halfords said that if the RAC doesn't thoroughly check something as fundamental as the brakes, then what exactly does it do during its four-hour inspection? ""

As we have discovered before, a purely visual used car inspection which involves no dismantling and no engine compression testing is of limited value when purchasing a 15-year-old Porsche. But, in your case, the RAC inspector did state 'fit bolt to gearbox bellhousing torque tube (missing)', so that was definitely covered. The discs and pads are ticked as inspected and you admit in your letter to the RAC that the discs themselves were relatively new. It is possible that the pads could have worn so severely in 3,000 miles of use that the backplates damaged the discs. Rear drums are not removed as part of an RAC test, so any internal wear would not have been spotted. My view is that anyone thinking of buying a used Porsche should first pay for an HPI check, pay for a new MOT test of the car, and, if the results of the first two are favourable, have a Porsche specialist go over it, perform a compression test on all cylinders, and provide a repair estimate.

Hot little number

Thanks to a notice helpfully displayed by British Car Auctions, I can let readers in on the hotline for checking if your MOT certificate is genuine. The number is 0891 615977, calls cost 50p a minute, and the service provides a check on the serial number of your certificate. This hotline can tell you if the MOT certificate that came with a car you purchased is false or stolen, and is definitely worth ringing if you have just bought a grey-imported Japanese car. But it can't tell you if anything has been 'missed' in a genuine MOT inspection.

Little-flown Spitfire

" *I would like to sell my late wife's Triumph Spitfire 1500. The car was first registered on 2 February 1981, has done under 7,500 miles, was Ziebarted when new, has always been garage-stored, and is in excellent rust-free condition. I would greatly appreciate any suggestions you may have as to the best way for me to endeavour to sell the car.* "

Ultra-low-mileage sports cars for which unleaded conversions are readily available have been achieving very high prices at classic car auctions. Last year, a 15,000 mile 79V Spitfire 1.5 made £5,294 including commission at BCA Blackbushe. Assuming your car is freshly MOT-tested and either taxed or SORN'd, and can be driven through the hall, I think it stands a chance of making £5,000–£7,000 at auction. There is a list of classic car auction houses at the end of this section.

Under-age smokers

" *I am thinking of changing my car, and the prospect of a youngish, high-mileage, well maintained ex-fleet car appeals. I would be more interested in a 2-litre turbodiesel than any other, in the price range £5,000–£7,000. Do you have any phone numbers or addresses where such cars can be obtained, preferably in the north of England or the Midlands?*

And what things should I be careful to look out for in a car that has done a high mileage in a short time? "

The best place in the country for these sort of cars is The Great Trade Centre, Hythe Lane (off Scrubbs Lane), White City, London NW10, tel: 0181 969 5511. It's also worth checking out Arriva Used Vehicle Sales, London Street, Smethwick, Birmingham B66 2SH, tel: 0121 558 5141, and Motor Nation, Mackadown Lane, Garretts Green, Birmingham, tel: 0121 786 1111; and look for other similar operations in north-west editions of the *Autotrader* and *Exchange & Mart*.

Unprepared for sale

" *Do all second-hand car dealers not bother to prepare their cars for sale and simply leave it to their customers to ask for faults to be rectified prior to purchase? The last time I bought a used car I indicated that I would do so providing the dealer carried out a 12,000-mile service, replaced the timing belt, fitted two new tyres, replaced the front discs and pads, replaced two wiper blades, fitted a new radio aerial mast, replaced a fog-light, and supplied me with its internal invoice for the work, which came to £652.63.* "

Unless the car is sold under a manufacturer's 'Approved Used' scheme which requires that work of this type is carried out before the car is offered for sale, the answer is 'yes'. The used car trade is in such a parlous state that many dealers simply cannot afford to prepare cars for sale unless they have customers for them. Had they gone to town on the car, then found no punter for it, they would not only suffer a loss when trading the car on, they would face the additional loss of the cost of the preparation work and the VAT on it which they aren't allowed to reclaim.

Not quite Jeep enough

" *I have a 1948 Willys Jeep. It is basically the same as the wartime one. Indeed, it has not done many miles, as it came from the Swiss airforce and was only used as a battery carrier for starting aircraft. I have it in wartime colours and, by purchasing an Aberdeen-registered car, was able to transfer 'USA 521S' to it. What could it be worth? I don't use it much. Please advise how to go about selling it with a suggested venue.* "

Willys built 361,349, Ford built 277,896 and American Bantam built 3,000 MB Jeeps for the war effort between 1940 and 1945. But from 1945, Willys also produced a civilian 'Universal' Jeep Model CJ2A with side-mounted spare, drop-down tailgate and column gearshift. CJ2As, CJ3A M38 Jeeps and Jeeps licence-built by Hotchkiss and Delahaye after the war are not worth as much as a genuine wartime MB – I'd say about £3,000 for yours at auction (list at end of section).

190SL

" *Can you direct my search for a Mercedes 190SL of the 1964 era in reasonable condition and at a reasonable price?* "

The Garage on The Green has just sold one, but is in the process of negotiating for another (0171 384 1100). The fortnightly Collectors Car Auction List (0181 534 3883) showed an RHD 1961 model coming up at Coys 'True Greats' Auction on 26 November (0171 584 7444), estimated at £20,000–£25,000. Over the past four years these cars have achieved between £8,500 (for a restoration project) and £66,500 (for a rare factory 'Renn-version'), but a price range of £15,000– £25,000 for a good, usable example is about right. The model years were 1954 to 1963. Most are left-hand-drive.

Little and large

" *I recently read an article about old bubble cars in BBC* Top Gear *magazine regarding a man in Oxfordshire who rescues and sells them for restoration. I would dearly love to contact him, but try as I might to get someone at the magazine to answer my messages, they do not reply. British Telecom seems to list no one trading under the name 'Alan's Unusual Automobiles'. Also, can you tell me if there is a club for Messerschmitts in the UK?* "

The story, by Mark Holmes, ran in issue 61 (October 1998) of *Top Gear* magazine, featuring the large Alan Hitchcock and his stock of little cars. Alan advertises every week in *Classic Car Weekly*. His telephone number is 01367 240125. And he's a super bloke, take it from me. But Alan's Unusual Automobiles is a part-time operation, as he needs to support the business with another job several days a week. The clubs are: Messerschmitt Owners Club, c/o Eileen Hallam, The Birches, Ashmores Lane, Rusper, West Sussex RH12 4PS; and the Register of Unusual Microcars, c/o Jean Hammond, School House Farm, Hawenbury, North Staplehurst, Kent TN12 0EB, tel: 01580 891377. In 1998, the address of the separate Messerschmitt Enthusiasts Club changed to: Colin Archer, Kitterick, Shaftesbury Avenue, Woking, Surrey GU22 7DU, tel: 01483 769270.

'Big bumper' to go

" *Regrettably, the time has come to replace my almost immaculate 1991 VW Golf GTi 16v 'big bumper' 3-door model with lower-than-average mileage. The car has been very well cared for by Colin Marshall of Wheelbase Garage in Hersham, Surrey (01932 252515), where, incidentally, customer service on a scale rising from 1 to 10 comes in at around 15. Although my local VW agent has offered a very good part-exchange price, I suspect I could obtain a better deal privately. Where should I advertise a vehicle like mine so as to attract only genuine interest? I am keen to avoid a stream of would-be boy racers knocking on my door and demanding a test drive.* **"**

Try *Rabbit*, the magazine of Club GTi. For trade ads, phone Ashley Buck on 0411 023021. *Rabbit* went bi-monthly from January 1999, so waiting for your ad to appear is now much less of a problem (membership enquiries to Club GTi, PO Box 2747, Brighton BN2 4HT). Another route, free of charge to Golf owners, is a photo ad in *The Golf* magazine, but they don't run every ad readers send them and if you don't price the car right you'll get no interest.

Beating import prices

" *Last November I purchased an 'S'-registered Renault Megane Scenic 2.0RXE with metallic paint and eight miles on the clock from Motorpoint of Derby (01332 347357). I had intended to import, but at their price of £13,599, going through all the hoops of importing one personally simply wasn't worth it. The only annoying feature is that the French dealer offered to include side airbags which were not available on the car I bought. My car is also missing an important feature of our Toyota Corolla: a light to tell you that one of the doors is open.* **"**

By the end of September 1998, every 'nearly new' specialist in the country had a good selection of pre-registered Renaults. The same thing happened in March 1999. Excluding the extra cost of metallic paint, this reader saved £3,146 on the UK list price of his Scenic. And this for a proper UK-supplied car with no question-marks about warranty.

How not to buy a classic

" *Most English people would regard retiring to a villa in Spain, with a swimming pool and a cheap turbodiesel in the driveway, as bliss. But, with all the lovely roads in our area and low traffic density, I couldn't help hankering after a sports car. I did my research, and eventually settled on a Porsche 912. My reasoning was: wonderful looks, good build quality, cheap to insure and a cheap-to-maintain, VW-derived, flat-four engine. So then I began to look for one, faxing several specialists who brought them in to the UK from the USA. Only one got back to me with a car and suggested we overcame the problem of viewing by having the car independently inspected at a cost of £200. The inspection report duly arrived, stating it to be 'a good sound vehicle, very good in the mechanical department…with an excellent gearbox with no faults'. It went on to itemise £1,000 of minor work, which I committed to. In September, I travelled to the UK to pick up the car. It looked excellent with its new coat of paint, but the drive back to London was simply hell. I couldn't get the five-speed box into first gear unless I came to a complete halt, then double declutched. Idling was so uneven that I stalled at several roundabouts during London's rush-hour. The gear knob came off and fell on to the floor. Next morning revealed more faults. The spare tyre was bald (despite a fresh MOT). Trim was missing from above the drivers knees. The warm-air hose to the carbs was crushed and had a 4-inch split. The air filters were full of carbonised insulation. The motor pinked under partial load. Then, when the rain started, it became obvious that the car leaked like a sieve. So, less than 24 hours after I collected the car, I phoned the dealer to ask him to take it back. The dealer himself had gone on holiday, but his second-in-command agreed. The next morning, I handed the car back, but the chap had a shock in store. He told me he couldn't refund my money. Only his boss could do that. But he did give me a receipt for the car. Then when I arrived back in Spain a fax arrived from the owner of the business stating that there was nothing wrong with the car and no refund was due, but he would try to sell the car for me on commission. Needless to say, legal action has now begun, but it's all very half-hearted and I'm out of pocket for just under £10,000. So all I can do on the basis of my experience is urge your readers to always check a second-hand car yourself before handing over any money.* "

You said it. I don't have full sales figures, but can tell you that the 1,582 cc Porsche 912 was introduced in Germany in September 1965 at chassis no. 350800. The Targa was launched in September 1967 at chassis no. 128.7.0001 (they changed the numbering system). And, according to an old 'Glass's Guide', the model lasted until September 1969, chassis no. 129.00.0412. So your car was a 1960s pre-galvanised Porsche with a leak-prone targa top. On 2 December 1998 someone tried to sell a truly horrible, deeply suspect, but shiny red 912 at a car auction I happened to be attending. Top bid was £2,950, which the auctioneer pronounced to be 'less than two-thirds what they want'. To me, £2,950 was at least £2,000 too much, but genuine, really good 912s have been known to make as much as £7,000.

1926 Fiat for sale

" *I have a 1926 Fiat 503B open tourer with dickey seat which I wish to sell. It is in quite good condition with new brake linings, new head gasket and re-wound magneto. It has not been on the road since 1993 but would, I am sure, pass its MOT. I have tried the Fiat Owners Club and Auto Italia magazine, without success. What do you suggest?* "

I'd have thought that the best medium for advertising a car like this would be *The Automobile* magazine, which is exclusively pre-1960 and has a readership passionately interested in very old cars. Use a photograph and take any advice the magazine's staff give you when placing your advertisement (tel: Roger Banks or Margaret Clark on 01932 864212). Your other option, of course, is a classic car auction (see the list of auction house phone numbers at the end of this section).

Executor's sale

" *As executor to a will, I have to dispose of a Saab 96 produced on February 8 1972 with a mileage of 33,500 and a current MOT. I also have the service booklet showing that it has been maintained on a regular basis. I know it is in excellent condition, but is not quite pristine. Would you please advise what you would consider the value to be and the best method of selling the vehicle? Is there a Saab Owners' Club you could put me in touch with?* "

Ask £2,500–£3,000. A classic car auction is the best means of disposal because it's cut and dried and avoids any arguments with beneficiaries over the price you get (list at end of section). The two clubs are: Saab Enthusiasts Club, c/o William Glander, 4 Rochdale Avenue, Calne, Wilts SN11 9AX, tel: 01249 815972, and Saab Owners Club of Great Britain Ltd, c/o John

Wood, PO Box 900, Durham DH1 2GF, tel: 070
7 171 9000; email: membership@saabclub.co.uk
Website: http://www.saabclub.co.uk.

Getting a better deal

" *I was about to part-exchange my 'J'-reg. Seat Ibiza GLX for an 'N'-reg.
VW Polo 1.4CL when I noticed a letter in your column about Ford Direct.
So I called in to Bristol Street Motors, Cheltenham to see what sort of deal
they could offer. Whereas the VW agent wanted £6,000 after allowing
£1,500 for my Seat, Bristol Street offered me a 1998R Ford Escort 1.6iLX
with less than 10,000 miles for £6,300, after allowing £1,700 for my Seat.
What's more, the Ford came with a two-year Ford Direct warranty and a
nice bunch of flowers for my wife.* "

Well done. New VWs hold their value well
because they aren't 'over-supplied', discounts are
minimal, quality is perceived to be 'a cut above'
the rest, and they carry a certain snob appeal.
But VWs are not – and never were – the second-
hand 'bargains' that year-old Fords can be.

The value of low mileage

" *How much difference does low mileage make to the value of a car? My
1991J Range Rover Vogue V8 SE automatic with leather seats, 32,000
miles and main agent servicing every 6,000 miles was stolen in October
last year and I'm still trying to agree a value with the loss adjuster.* "

As long as the public is daft enough to place an
excessive value on low mileage, 'low mileage' will
continue to be valued excessively. At the time
you wrote, 'Glass's Guide' valued a 92J Range
Rover Vogue SE with 40,000 miles at a reasonable £925 more than one with the average 65,000
miles. A fair settlement for your car would be
about £9,000, but the service history worries me.
A service every 6,000 miles works out at once

every 16–17 months, which is nothing like often enough for a car kept and used in London.

Millennium glut?

" *I have an 'M'-registered Vauxhall Corsa 1.5TD, which is in excellent condition, regularly serviced and has done 70,000 miles. While it will probably run for another five years without too many problems, once the odometer passes 100,000 miles it will not be an attractive sales proposition. Having read that second-hand car prices are falling, particularly with the possibility of a glut of such cars on the market next year, would you advise that I attempt to sell the car before the end of 1999?* "

I don't think the used car market will be over-supplied during year 2000 for one very good reason: the end of leaded petrol. The British Car Auctions 1998 Used Car Report showed that, in the UK in 1997, more than 9,000,000 cars were over ten years old. Separate figures from the Petrol Retailers Association estimate that by the end of the year there will still be around 2,300,000 cars on the roads with soft valve seats. Many of these, driven relatively slowly on short runs, will survive for a few more years on un-leaded petrol dosed with additives. But there will still be a significant fall-out of cars that aren't worth the cost of an unleaded cylinder head conversion, that become uneconomic to run using an additive, and that are likely to be scrapped over the winter of 1999/2000. While the owners may not have the money to replace them with new cars, they will want relatively cheap cars that can run on unleaded or diesel and this demand should increase values of cars five to eight years old. At the same time, 'Millennium fever' seems likely to persuade a lot of people to want Year 2000 'V'-reg. cars and Year 2000 'W'-reg. cars – there will only be two months of the '2000 V'. Their part-exchanges will partly meet the extra demand generated by the end of unleaded, but I still think demand will pull the values of five- to eight-year-old cars up over 1999 levels. With this in mind, I would only swap your Corsa now if you can get an amazing deal on the car you replace it with.

Clockwatch register

" *I thought your readers might like to know that the majority of British Vehicle Rental and Leasing Association members now lodge mileages on disposal on the BVRLA database. This now contains more than 2,000,000 mileages and is managed on our behalf by Vehicle Mileage Check, one of the agencies used by dealers for this purpose. We are about to enter into contracts for HPI/National Mileage Register and CNN/Experian for them to access these mileages too. This greatly reduces the potential for comparatively young but high-mileage ex-fleet cars to be 'clocked back' by unscrupulous traders before sale to members of the public.* "

This has always had my full support and can be accessed by HPI (01722 422422), AA/Experian (0800 234999), or ABS (0800 3895169), as part of their checking service. I even played a small part in introducing BMW Finance to the BVRLA mileage register. There is no excuse for any fleet vendor not registering a mileage on disposal, either with the BVRLA or with the DVLA or with both, because every V5 Registration Document has a place to register the mileage, while V5s issued after 1 January 1998 even have a slip to register mileages when cars are sold into the trade.

Falling sales

" *I can give you one good reason why Rover's sales halved over 1998: the so-called 'streamlining' of its dealer network. In Cornwall alone this has disenfranchised many smaller, family-owned and well loved local dealerships which were pillars of the community and which derived their success from being so. When their franchises were yanked away and consolidated into larger dealerships, gaping holes were left in these communities that were rapidly filled by the awarding of Nissan, Proton and a number of other franchises to the former smaller Rover agents. The management of Rover has only itself to blame for the results of its 'streamlining' exercise.* **"**

There is a great deal of truth in what you say. When Rover franchises were taken from well liked and respected garages in market towns, the locals were hardly going to hike 30 miles to the nearest city with a Rover franchise just to buy a Rover. But that's not to say that every smaller Rover agent with a local monopoly was well liked and respected. There were one or two bad apples in the barrel.

Barking up the wrong tree

" *In December 1998 I bought at public auction a 1995 BMW 740i, previously owned by BMW themselves, with a full BMW service history, and showing five green service lights. The car needed four new tyres, a full set of brake discs, a full set of brake pads and new rear shock absorber mounting bushes to make it roadworthy and legal to use. I complained directly, several times, to Bernt Pischetsrieder, but all the response I ever got from BMW was words to the effect of 'caveat emptor' since I bought the car at auction. Is this the way BMW cares about its image and its customers?* **"**

Thank you for sending me a detailed file on your case. The car was previously owned by BMW Financial Services Ltd which leased it to Hillsdown Holdings PLC. It was sold by BMW Financial Services at auction in the South of England. You then bought it at auction in the North of England. Neither BMW, nor BMW Financial Services Ltd, can be held responsible for the description of the car or its condition when you bought it at this auction. The most likely scenario is that a trader bought the car at a BMW Finance auction in the South, then re-sold it at auction in the North. Between auctions, a number of things could have happened. If the service indicator wasn't showing five green lights, the trader could have reset it with a simple £15 tool. He might also have had the mileage on the odometer reset so the reading was no more than a few miles after the last stamped service. Fortunately, BMW Financial Services Ltd logs mileages on disposal onto the British Vehicle Rental and Leasing Association databank which is held by Vehicle Mileage Check (tel: 01663 766047), so you can check the exact mileage. As a general rule, leasing companies almost always dispose of their cars before a big service involving major replacements and anyone who buys cars on a regular basis at auction knows this. Your one and only right of redress is against the trader who sold the car at auction if the mileage was mis-described. Under most auction house terms and conditions you only have until the end of the day's trading to obtain a refund if the car is otherwise misdescribed.

In the 'Family' way

" *I recently had to part with a Peugeot 505 diesel 'Family' estate car. It drove very well and gave all passengers excellent seats – seating eight at most. The model that I had was fitted with two sunroofs. I see plenty being driven around, but not so many for sale. Do you know where I can get one in good condition. Age is not important. Condition is everything.* "

A specialist such as Shadoxhurst Garage, near Ashford in Kent (tel: 01233 732811) will offer the best choice of Peugeot 505 'Family', Citroën CX Safari and Renault Savanna seven-seaters. For economy, go for a diesel. Obviously, you could do better searching the used car sites, the auctions and the private ads, but because these vehicles are comparatively rare, the cost of finding a bargain will very probably outweigh any saving. You should also try a Mitsubishi agent for an old-shape Space Wagon. If he hasn't got one, Mitsubishi has a nation-wide stock locator system to help find the right vehicle.

Net discounts

" *I currently own a Vauxhall Cavalier 2.0GSI which I bought from the company where I was previously employed and with which I have had very few problems in 100,000 miles. I would now like to replace it before running costs escalate and I am considering a new Astra. Is there any quick way of finding dealers who give the best deal to a cash buyer? I have a substantial number of points on a GM credit card to help offset UK prices so I do not want to buy abroad.* "

With its galvanised body, the Astra is a good long-term bet – particularly the 2.0 litre DI. Two well established brokers who can be recommended are: Steve Tokatlian at Quote to Quote on 0171 603 9999 (6 lines); and Pat Lawless at Carfile on 01335 360763/360022 (9.15–5.45) or 0410 081984 (evenings and weekends). Neither broker asks for a deposit. Alternatively, if you have access to the Internet, try New Cars Direct at http://www.newcarsdirect.co.uk.

Por que?

A number of readers have written to ask what was the point of my article, '*Por favor, senor*, do you have any bargains?' This used a story from a Spanish magazine to show what cars the Spanish were able to buy for 'on the road prices' of Ptas2,000,000 (around £8,750). Readers are questioning the fact that many of the featured models were Spanish market specials, available only in left hand drive. The point of the story is encapsulated in Janet Daley's words in *The Daily Telegraph* of 16 February 1999. In her leader page article, she wrote, 'For many years, British consumers have been uncomplaining sitting ducks for a lazy, profiteering retail sector that has complacently carved up the market for almost everything from groceries to electrical goods.' My story was timed to precede yet another official EU price comparison showing that the British still pay far more for their new cars than our continental cousins, and to give further ammunition to those pressurising the UK government into doing something about it.

Letting it rip (off)

" *Thank you for your timely article on Spanish versus UK 'on the road' car prices. I have just made a choice between a Renault Megane RN 1.9DTi, a Honda Civic 2.0iTD and a Skoda Octavia GLX 2.0TDI. In the end, I went for the Honda and with no p/x got one discounted to Ptas2,500,000 with metallic paint, aircon and a four-year warranty included. At Ptas240 to £1, this translates to £10,416. A sunroof, ABS and remote keyless entry are not standard in Spain (though with only three days rain in the last five months I don't feel much need for ABS).* "

Thank you for keeping us all reminded. A Honda Civic 2.0TDI with aircon currently lists at £15,200 on the road in the UK with a three-year, 90,000-mile warranty. The Monopolies and Mergers Commission is not scheduled to make its report on UK car pricing until December 1999, which has given the industry an extra nine months to squeeze what it could out of blinkered UK car buyers who know no better.

Why can't I sell this car?

" *For the past three years I have been the proud owner of a 1968 MGC/GT, which is in stunning condition with a full, documented history. I have promised my wife that I will sell the car to finance another project, but can't sell it. I've advertised in classic magazines, Owners Club magazines, newspapers, etc., but still no takers and, frankly, very little serious interest. I can't imagine that at £7,250 I'm asking too much money, given the huge quantity of spare parts which go with the car. Any suggestions? I'm desperate.* "

Your price is way over the top. Fine for an MGC Roadster with an unleaded conversion. But you're asking two grand more than I've ever seen an MGC/GT sell for. In the circumstances, the best suggestion I can make is to try a classic car auction which, by the auction process, will set an accurate value on the car.

Size matters

" *Can you offer any advice on how to sell my left-hand-drive Mercedes S600 coupe. It was UK-registered in 1996, but was previously used on the continent and has been allocated an 'M' registration It has covered approximately 60,000 kilometres, is charcoal metallic in colour with black leather upholstery, has recently been serviced when all brake discs and pads were replaced, has a current MOT certificate and is running on Mobil 1 synthetic oil. Mercedes Benz franchise holders show no interest.* "

Last year, another reader wanted to know where he could get an S600 Coupe as cheaply as possible and I recommended someone outside the MB franchise chain. This led to howls of protest from the franchisees, so first I have to suggest that you go to MB UK on 01908 245000 and ask if they can put you onto a franchisee who has a market for LHD S600 Coupes. If you have no success there, then you have no alternative but to look elsewhere. Have a word with Tom Hartley or Tom Hartley Junior on 01283 762762. And consider entering the car for a British Car Auctions 'Top Car' sale at either their Blackbushe or Measham auction centres (01252 878555 or 01530 270322). On the vexed question of value, these awesome £100,000 cars have been written down heavily of late and even an RHD 'M'-reg. S600 Coupe would not fetch more than £30,000 in the trade. Subtract the disadvantage of LHD and you're probably looking at between £20,000 and £25,000. To help offset this car's considerable thirst, a smart move by the new owner would be an LPG conversion. Call the LPG Gas Association on 01425 461612 or visit their website at http://www.lpga.co.uk.

£6,375 in 8 months?

" On 1 August 1998 I purchased a new 'S'-registered, British-built Honda Civic 1.6iLS automatic in 'Sicilian Red Pearl' paint with air conditioning. I paid £15,875 in cash. It was my third successive brand new Honda Civic, the previous two having been Japanese-built 4-door models. I then noticed in the press that Rover had brought down its prices and, with the Rover 400 Series having the same basic body as the Honda Civic 5-door, I wish to go back to a 4-door saloon. The Rover agent offered me a 4-door Rover 416 automatic for £15,800 but all he would give me for my 'S'-reg. Civic was £9,500. Surely it hasn't depreciated that much in eight months? "

It hasn't depreciated £6,375 in eight months. The part-exchange offer merely reflects what the car is worth at eight months old and blows the whistle on the fact it was never worth anything like the £15,875 you paid for it in the first place. In Spain, a British-built Honda Civic 1.6iLS 5-door automatic with air conditioning is £11,800 on the road. That's what it should be here.

E-Type yearning

" *In 1966 I drove a TR3 and was contemplating buying an E-Type. Then I met my wife and events took a different course. But now that I am approaching retirement I hanker after fulfilling my life-long ambition. I can afford £15,000–£20,000, which I think will limit me to an SII 2+2 FHC. What should I look for when buying? Where can I get parts? And what can I run one on when Four Star is withdrawn?* "

There are obvious disadvantages of buying an E-Type at a classic car auction. As Quentin Willson has warned, these can be thieves' kitchens where the worst kind traders offload glittering rubbish to over-excited billies with no possibility of any comeback. On the other hand, they can be the best way of getting a good car for the least money. So, now that you have time on your hands, pay a visit to a few classic car auctions and start learning from experience. You'll soon spot the cars being hawked from sale to sale and you'll begin to develop an eye for what's genuine and what's not. The best way to find out which cars are coming up at which auctions is to subscribe to *The Collectors Car Auction List*, which also carries an up-to-date results list (tel: 0181 534 3883). I'm going to have to be brief, but, when looking at an E-Type, first check the solidity of the 'tub' and use a Teslec Ferristor (01257 271105) or similar tool to detect any filler. A small Maglite torch will also be handy for looking underneath (be prepared to get dirty – best clothes mark you out as a target at a classic car sale). If the engine is cold, take the cap off the expansion tank and look for rusty coolant (you may have to budget for flushing out the cooling system, which involves removing engine core plugs). One school of thought says that all Jaguar engines already have exhaust valve seat inserts hard enough to run gently on Superunleaded. But I don't subscribe to this, because if you aren't going to rev the engine there's no point in having an E-Type. I reckon you will need to have the exhaust valve seats and the valves themselves replaced with parts of high chrome content, if that has not already been done. Martin Robey is the main source of E-Type parts these days (tel: 01203 386903). If you want to buy through a specialist dealer, it's worth talking to Robert Hughes on 01932 858381 and David Marks on 01159 405370.

Classic Car Auction Houses

- AMA, Aylesbury, tel: 01296 339150.
- Barons, Sandown Park, tel: 01703 840081.
- BCA Blackbushe (A30 Surrey/Hants), tel: 01252 878555/877317.
- Brooks, various locations, tel: 0171 228 8000.
- Cheffins, Linton, Cambridgeshire, tel: 01223 358731.
- Christies, London, tel: 0171 389 2851.
- Coys, various locations, tel: 0171 584 7444.
- Greens, Millbrook Test Centre, tel: 01684 575902.
- H&H, Pavilion Gardens, Buxton, tel: 01925 730630.
- Husseys, Marsh Barton, Exeter, tel: 01392 425481.
- Lambert & Foster, Maidstone, tel: 01892 832325.
- Philips, Exeter, tel: 01392 439025.

- Purely Classics, Southend, tel: 01702 461600.
- RBR Sales, Doune, Scotland, tel: 0131 449 2465.
- RTS, Godmanchester and Norwich, tel: 01603 418200.
- Sothebys, various locations, tel: 0171 493 8080.
- Stags Classic Commercials, Devon, tel: 01882 255533.

CAMPERS AND CARAVANS
(SEE ALSO 'TOWING')

Big bang theory

" With the growing popularity of LPG as a fuel for motor vehicles, it surely makes sense to require such vehicles to display a HAZCHEM plate to warn firefighters of the potential danger. Since the secondary fuel is almost invariably petrol, and since both fuels are stored in or around the rear of the car, any fire started by a rear-end collision is likely to result in an explosion as the gas cylinder overheats in the flames. Unless a warning plate is displayed, firemen who don't see the LPG/CNG filler will be unaware of the extra danger they face. "

Anyone who has witnessed a motor-caravan or camper fire when the CNG gas bottles go off will know exactly what you mean. But all tanks for current-generation LPG conversions incorporate pressure relief valves to take the pressure off the gas gradually. In cases where the petrol tank has exploded in a car that is fitted with both a petrol tank and an LPG tank, in spite of the heat created by this the LPG tank has not exploded. To be 100 per cent safe, responsible installers do in fact apply a HAZCHEM sticker.

The answer to 'VLUS' problems

" *A little while ago I read your comments on how VLUS (Very Little Use Syndrome) can affect van-based campers and motorhomes. You referred to problems with gearboxes and other components designed to cope with 100,000 miles in two years in a van, but not 20,000 miles in ten years in a motorhome. I think I may have found the solution. For the past ten years we have owned a Bimobil demountable camper which, when travelling, sits on the bed of a Peugeot 504 pick-up. (In fact, it's now sitting on the bed of its second 504 pick-up.) Its short length gives it a great advantage over a towed caravan or articulated outfit. It can be demounted on site and the vehicle used separately. And outside the holiday season which, let's face it, is most of the year, the camper can form a useful 'granny flat' in the garden while the 504 with its pick-up back replaced carries on working for its living.* "

A great idea; very sensible. But it has to be said that, though your Bimobil is more sophisticated, demountable camper backs for pick-ups have been going strong in the USA for at least 30 years.

Piggyback campers

" *Further to the letter about demountable camper backs and your reply that they have been popular in the USA for years, your readers might be interested to hear that we offer a range of them. They are designed to fit standard world-market pick-ups such as the Toyota Hi-Luxe, etc., so that a working or leisure vehicle can be transformed into a comfortable camper in just 20 minutes. And, because the camper backs are demountable, the pick-up and the camper can be separated for individual use once the destination is reached.* "

I think this idea is far better than having the running gear of a camper, coachbuilt motorhome or caravan mouldering in the drive-way for most of the year, accumulating all the problems and dangers associated with 'Very Little Use Syndrome'. More information from Niche Marketing, Park House, Park Lane, Manby, Lincolnshire LN11 8UF, tel: 01507 327172.

CAR DESIGN AND EQUIPMENT

To the point

" *I had a puncture in my RAV 4. When I tried to jack it up by the sill, I found the jack was too short. I then read the driver's manual which tells you to jack it up by the suspension arm mounting. This lifted it high enough to replace the punctured tyre with the standard-size spare.* "

Sound advice. Before jacking any car you should always RTFM ('Read The Flippin' Manual'). But if you have fitted oversize tyres to your 4x4 you may find you need either a substantial block of wood to put under the jack, or a longer jack. A good tip is, once you have got the punctured wheel off, shove it under the jacked-up axle. Then, if by mischance, the car falls off the jack before you get the spare wheel bolted, the axle has something to land on.

Fixed wheels

" *On Easter Bank Holiday Saturday, my Fiat Cinquecento Sporting suffered a puncture. My passenger took out the virgin jack, jacked the car up, removed the wheel nuts, but was then unable to remove the wheel. A policeman came and couldn't remove it either, even with a crowbar. So I had to have the car 'recovered' to our village garage which did not open until the Tuesday. Several days and £60 later, I was told that where aluminium wheels are bolted to steel hubs, and especially to cast iron brake drums, the two metals can corrode themselves together. The wheels should be removed every six months and any corrosion wire-brushed off.* "

A timely tip. The same is also common on the current generation of Range Rovers. Lavender Hill Garage has developed a special device for removing them. A very small amount of copper-based grease should help prevent this sort of corrosion, but be careful on disc-braked wheels because any excess grease flung onto the disc will badly affect the braking.

Unprotected

" *The present-day cost of cars to private motorists in the UK usually makes them our second-most valuable possessions. Vehicle density on our roads has never been higher. Yet manufacturers offer less protection from minor bumps to the vehicle than ever before. My son recently purchased a £46,000 Audi A8, had a minor scrape at the front in a public garage, and was landed with a repair cost of £200, which he paid himself to protect his no claims discount. There must be thousands of cases of minor damage that could have been avoided if cars were better protected against the consequences of minor bumps.* "

Cars are designed primarily to protect pedestrians and occupants from injury and only secondarily to protect themselves. That said, 'damageability' and 'repairability' account for a significant proportion of insurance premiums. By making their cars less likely to suffer minor damage and easier to repair if they do, manufacturers can earn insurance premiums two to four groups lower than would otherwise have been the case. MGFs for example, have clever impact-absorbing and replaceable 'crush boxes' behind their flexible fronts which protect both the occupants and the structure of the car. Ford's improvements to the Fiesta from October 1995 earned it two places lower in the groupings.

Alloy wheels and steel spares

A number of Ford and Nissan owners have written to say that only on suffering their first puncture did they discover that the nuts or bolts for their alloy wheels were not compatible with their steel 'spare' wheels. If your car has alloy wheels and a steel spare, check the owner's manual to make sure you know where the nuts or bolts for the steel spare are stored. If the car is second-hand or fitted with aftermarket alloy wheels, you may have to go out and buy a set of nuts or bolts to suit the temporary steel 'spare'.

Who needs five seats?

" *Having had an incurable interest in cars for many years I called to see a Renault Megane Scenic. This is a most interesting vehicle and, I understand, is very popular. Behind the driver is a row of three individual fully-upholstered seats, each with a proper lap/diagonal safety belt. I wondered how much they were likely to be used in the hands of a private owner, so I conducted my own survey by counting the number of passengers in cars I pass in my local travels. After a few months I had recorded that less than ten per cent of these cars contained more than two occupants. Many carried only one. As the rear seat of my Volvo spends its life in the garden shed I wondered why I am expected to pay for expensive seating I never use. This led me to consider other equipment which comes as standard which I have paid for but never (or rarely) use. I never use the radio or cassette player or the airbags. I find central locking a menace. I don't need a boot spoiler (I am not Tazio Nuvolari). And I do not really care for lots and lots of little valves working themselves to death under the bonnet. Power steering? Yes please, and a sun roof if you insist. Many years ago on a visit to the Motor Show I was attracted by the cloth seats on tubular frames of the original Renault 4.*

These were comfortable, inexpensive and would be perfectly adequate for the little-used rear compartment of most cars, so why not fit them? Manufacturers continue to add features which add to the cost of the vehicle. Surely there must be a market for basic transportation? "

Most private motorists either have families or are sociable and need at least five proper seats often enough to justify carting them about in the car all the time. Add a touch of 'Hyacinth Buckett' syndrome and it's not hard to see why stripped-out, basic cars or combi-type window vans don't sell in their millions in the UK. Citroën had to launch its ultra-practical Berlingo Multispace here with a huge canvas sunroof and in bright metallic colours to get it off the ground. It wasn't until a year later that the company dared to introduce more practical basic versions without the sunroof with starting prices £1,000 less. But if you want an even cheaper simple, basic vehicle with power steering and no back seat, get a van. The Citroën Berlingo van, Renault Kangoo van or VW Polo Caddy van will suit you down to the ground.

On reflection...

" *In October last year I bought my wife a car which, while meeting our needs in almost every way, is dangerous to drive in sunny weather. The car is an Audi A3 SE and the reason it is dangerous is that the light-coloured dashboard top reflects so brightly in the windscreen that it seriously impairs the driver's ability to see the road ahead. Through the Audi agent, Audi replied that no one else had complained of this. What's the answer?* "

This problem has come up a few times in the past. It afflicts almost any car, from a Fiesta to a Passat, which has a light coloured dash-top or parcel shelf during the periods of the year when the sun is low in the sky. Back in 1996, a reader from Ottery St Mary supplied an answer in the form of black self-adhesive Fablon 'Velour' from a DIY shop (order code 65217 – 450 mm wide) cut to shape and stuck to the reflecting areas. Though it shrinks over time, it totally eliminates reflections, and can easily be removed with white spirit prior to sale of the vehicle. Your alternative is to try and ignore the reflection. The more you become upset about it, the more you will see it and the more likely it is to cause problems.

Why only one rear foglamp?

" *Last year I bought a new Renault Clio. The rear light clusters are mirror images of each other. But, despite being wired, the nearside cluster has no rear foglamp bulb and a plastic moulding actually prevents a light-bulb being inserted. Why should this be?* "

Because two rear foglamps can be confused with brake lamps, especially on motorways. False signals from the idiots who drive too close and continually have to brake are already a serious problem on motorways because they create a knock-on effect causing panic-braking accidents futher back, so any fitting that can be confused with brake lights should be avoided. Readers occasionally ask if one rear fog light on the 'wrong' side when driving in Continental Europe in fog might lead other drivers to think your car is a motorbike and smack into your rear end. But, unless they are driving at a lunatic speed for the conditions, they would see your rear pair of driving lights and realise you are driving a car in plenty of time to slow down.

Highlights and lowlights

" Our 'K'-registered Land Rover Discovery had rear light clusters on the side pillars in which all the lights were fitted and all worked. Our current 'R'-registered Discovery has the rear lights and indicators in the rear bumper, and only the stoplights, reversing lights and rear foglights in the side clusters. This makes the rear lights and indicators much more vulnerable and less visible, especially when towing a small trailer the lights of which are also close to the ground. I was told by someone in the motor trade that the change was required by an EU Directive because the high lights were deemed to cause dazzle but, if that is the case, why are these lights still set high in the rear pillars of cars like Volvo V70's, Renault Laguna estates, Fiat Puntos and Ford Focuses? "

My understanding of Directive 76/756 EEC is that the rear driving lights and indicators must be visible from behind when the back door of the vehicle is open. Since 1 January 1998, EU Whole Vehicle Type Approval Directive 70/156 EEC has required that all passenger cars sold within the EEC comply with Directive 76/756 EEC. V70s, Laguna estates, Puntos and Focuses all have upward opening 'hatchbacks'. The Discovery has a side-opening rear door with a spare wheel attached which obscures the rear pillar lights on one side when it is open.

A load of lip

" I kept a copy of the review of a Skoda Octavia Estate written by Mark Hales. In it he wrote of 'handy features like a level floor with no loading lip'. Imagine my disappointment after waiting for the UK launch in September to find that the demo model I was shown had a loading lip several inches deep. Did they change the design, or was Mark Hales mistaken? "

There are two different floor heights for this and the VW Golf Mk IV estate (both cars share the

same floorpan). The lower floor height gives an increased load volume and ensures the load is carried closer to the car's centre of gravity. But an oddments tray is available to fit between the spare wheel well and the load area floor to raise the floor to sill height.

Narrowing it down

" *When will British manufacturers specify electric folding door mirrors as the norm? The standard British garage does not allow easy parking for a reasonable sized car such as a Mondeo. Maybe it's the garage door manufacturers' fault, but whichever way, you would have thought the two could have worked together for each other's benefit.* "

There aren't any British volume car manufacturers. Though some design is still done in the UK, most is Japanese, European or American.

(The Chrysler Neon is the only medium-sized car I know of with expensive electric folding mirrors.) The real problem is mean-minded, cost-cutting developers who cram as many houses as they can into as little space as they can get away with. And if that means tiny rooms you can't swing a cat in and narrow garages you can't get a car into, it's our fault for not measuring up properly before we make the biggest purchase most of us ever sign up to.

Verona vilified

" *I have a Ford Mondeo Verona and have complained to Ford about its 'space-saver' spare wheel which can only be used for speeds of less than 50 mph. I recently had a puncture on a Saturday afternoon which could not be repaired until Monday. I had to used the space saver for 30 miles at the suggested speeds, after which the tyre went flat and I had to pump it up to get the car to the tyre fitters. In my letter to Ford I stated that I did not think their car would be regarded as a reliable form of transport and that using the spare was dangerous and probably technically illegal. I also asked them to suggest how I could carry a proper 205/55 × 15 alloy spare which is too big for the spare compartment. Their reply merely stated that the space-saver was legal and safe and that other makers fitted an identical type of 'emergency wheel'. They obviously think I am unreasonable in expecting a full-size spare wheel. Do you? And can you suggest a solution?* "

The spare wheel compartment of a Mondeo easily takes a 185/65 R14 spare wheel because that's exactly what is nestling in the spare wheel compartment of my 98R Mondeo. The Verona is a cut-price special which, with its alloy wheels, metallic paint and air conditioning, appears to offer more than a standard Mondeo 1.8iLX. But you can't have everything for the reduced price. Most Fiats have space-saver emergency wheels, Citroens have standard-size emergency wheels which may not match the size of the road wheels exactly. And most makers from Ford to Mercedes offer a steel space-saver emergency wheel on models fitted with alloy wheels. These wheels are not 'technically illegal'. Honourable exceptions to the practice are VW/Audi, who now supply full-size alloy spare wheels with their official UK imports.

Man and machine in disharmony

" *I was amazed to read that you have bought a Ford Mondeo. Can I give you and your readers some facts regarding this car? In August 1997 I sold my 11-year-old Sierra 1.8GLX automatic and bought a Mondeo 2.0 Ghia auto. The Sierra never failed to start and gave me over 115,000 trouble-free miles. I was told the Mondeo was an improvement over the Sierra. In reality it is much worse. It developed a water leak, flooding the rear compartment with six inches of water. The driver's door seal had come adrift. Then it flooded again and has gone back for further investigation. Are there cars built by robots that don't leak? Other unwelcome improvements over the Sierra include: (1) The electric mirror switch is in the middle of the dashboard instead of in the driver's door; (2) The passenger seat adjuster sticks out so far that anyone with short legs can't put their feet on the floor; (3) The car cannot be driven in fog because the elements of the Quickclear windscreen make it like driving behind a net curtain; (4) Unlike the Sierra, the heating in the front is almost useless and it is impossible to get hot air in the front footwell; (5) The tape or CD box lid contains cup-holders for rear seat passengers, but does not fold out flat enough for it to be of any use; (6) The rear shelf is no longer hinged in the middle, so any oddments stored on it fall off when the hatch is opened; (7) The car has no bumpers; (8) The coloured side protectors are useless; (9) The Mondeo has far less internal storage space than the Sierra; (10) The Mondeo has a greater turning circle than the Sierra; (11) The Mondeo's back seats do not fold down flat like the Sierra's. I could go on. If Ford had spoken to its Sierra designers it might have got more of the small things right, and solved the big problems like building a leak-proof car.* "

Why be amazed? My Mondeo was less than ten months old and I got if for £8,039, at which it represented excellent value. A second 10,000-mile service, a fresh pollen filter, fresh batteries for the remote key and putting right four known faults has set me back another £163.29. Repainting the damaged roof was £190, including new sealing strips. So for £8,392.29, I have an air-conditioned 2.0 litre Mondeo with no faults and what seems to me to be a better specification than your £18,000 Ghia.

With knobs on

" *Am I alone in thinking that modern press-button-controlled car radios are a driving hazard? One button feels much like another and you have to look down to see what you are pressing. It is now difficult to get a radio with an analogue volume control. In my opinion, the old-style radios with two large knobs were much safer and quicker to use. The best combination would be to have analogue controls with a digital frequency display. A cassette-recording facility would also be useful to catch all those ends of programmes. What think you?* "

You are not alone. Volvos have knobs for volume, station and function/waveband; the kit in the Mitsubishi Space Star I recently drove had knobs; so does Ford's 6000 RDS EON. Fiat's ergonomic dashtop radio/cassette player in the Bravo/Brava is a reasonable compromise. The very first Philips 'in-dash' radio/cassette players back in the 1970s had recording facilities that could be used as dictating machines. My biggest gripe is the siting of radios. Fiat has it right in the Bravo/Brava, as does Mitsubishi in the Space Star. VW used to have it right in the Golf/Jetta Mk II. But far too many radios are sited so low that, unless they have remote steering wheel or column controls, they are positively dangerous to use on the move.

CAR HIRE

Hiring something special

" *Next year is my father's 60th birthday. To make it special we wish to send him and my mother away for a night in a hotel and we would like them to be able to drive there in a classic car. Something like an Austin Healey or an MGA would be appropriate. So far my attempts to locate a classic car hire company have been in vain. Can you help? I also read somewhere of a 'classic car timeshare' club. Do you have any details.* "

The Classic Car Club (tel: 0171 713 7313, fax: 0171 713 7316) is a sort of 'classic car timeshare' which costs £500 to join and £1,750 a year membership subscription. This gives access to around 40 days of use of fifty classic cars, from Fiats to Ferraris, according to the points-per-day required for each car. A good classic car rental company is Bespokes on 0181 421 8686, fax: 0181 421 8588. Its fleet includes E-Types, older 911s, Aston Martins and Ferraris, with prices from £350 a day, and it also does long-term contract hire. Modena, on 01676 535596, offers Lotus, Ferrari and Porsche. Miles & Miles Prestige Car Rental offers new BMWs, Jaguars and Mercedes (tel: 0171 591 0555). Carriages Vehicle Agency (01737 353926) offers a wide variety of classic vehicles from a 1920s Dennis bus, through 1930s Rolls Royces, to a 1970s VW

Beetle cabriolet. Ray Tomkinson (01204 533447) offers a range of 'classic taxis' from 1930s Austin Landaulettes to late 1970s Checker Cabs. Hanwells of London has a late-model Rolls Royce and Bentley rental fleet (0171 436 2070). Budget Rent-a-Car (now owned by Team Rental) aims to offer anything from a Harley Davidson motorcycle to a Jaguar XK8 convertible (look in the Yellow Pages). Euro Style in London (tel: 0171 624 1313) offers TVRs, Boxters, SLKs, Range Rover 4.6HSEs and even a Bentley Azure.

Holiday hire car insurance

" *When I go to visit my daughter in California I plan to hire a small car for local travel – otherwise I will be marooned in a small area. I am in my mid-70s, I have fully comprehensive insurance, an international driving licence translation and a clean driving record. What additional insurance would you recommend to cover for possible problems?* "

Your UK policy does not provide comprehensive cover for a hire car in the USA and you do need to be very thoroughly covered in that litigious country. As well as the basic hire car insurance, you need Collision Damage Waiver (called Loss Damage Waiver in the USA) to cover you against any damage you may do to the hire car (and usually subject to an 'excess'). You need Theft Protection Option to cover you if the car is stolen. You need Supplementary Liability Insurance to cover you for claims of up to a million dollars against you (set-up whiplash claims are common against foreigners in hire cars). Your travel insurance should cover you against personal injury to yourself. I should warn you that the cost of the insurance will probably amount to more than the cost of hiring the car and that you may run into age restrictions. It might be better to use your UK travel agent to arrange the hire of the car with an international company such as Hertz, Budget, Avis or Alamo and also the insurances before you go. If you do this, make sure the agent states your age on the proposal forms. A reader from Chichester reports that Avis offers LDW, supplementary liability insurance up to $1,000,000 and accident/medical insurance in the USA with no upper age limit.

True price of 'low rent' cars

" I was fascinated to read your reply concerning the insurance add-ons when hiring a car in the USA (see 'Holiday hire car insurance', above). I recently went to Miami on business and had to hire a car at short notice. Freefoning around from the terminal indicated Alamo to have the cheapest mid-range base rate at $42 a day. After insurances, loss damage waiver, supplementary liability insurance, state tax, battery and tyre wear charge, etc., the total cost for ten days' hire of a Pontiac Somethingorother was $810. Car hire in the USA is not cheap. It's actually cheaper, car-for-car, in Italy, where I go a lot, and I always thought Italy was expensive. Please remember also to check the time the car is taken out. Alamo, for example, charge extra hire time at $15 an hour, plus, plus, plus. "

A reader from Cardiff adds that if you arrange the hire of the car in the UK at a special rate, it is vital to take all the documentation with you. If you don't you may find yourself downgraded to a basic car that corresponds with the rental rate you paid.

Overseas liability insurance

Insurance Brokers Marcus Hearn & Co. Ltd now offer annual Extended Liability Insurance for multiple hirings for £75 a year. Apparently, this

£75 can be less than the cost of similar cover offered by American car hire companies for just two weeks. The only problem I can see is opposition at the other end from the car hire company, many of which make hardly any of their income from hirings and virtually all of it on the 'add ons'. As a result, you might find yourself pressured into paying for the hirer's liability cover as well as the annual cover you bring with you. But I still recommend Marcus Hearn's Annual Travel Policies. Our family has one. For information, contact Jeffrey Klipp at Marcus Hearn & Co. Ltd, tel: 0171 739 3444.

Car hire for older drivers

" *Which car rental companies are prepared to hire cars out to drivers over the age of 70?* "

Avis, Budget and National Car Rental.

CHASSIS AND SUSPENSION

No bearing on the matter

" *Two weeks ago, I put my wife's 1989 Mini into a garage for its MOT. It failed and needed a new nearside shock absorber and offside track rod end. Four days later, the offside front wheel bearing seized up. I took the car back to the garage and was told it was a coincidence. There was no reason why they should have picked up the problem during the MOT. A week later, the same bearing seized up again. The garage apologised and replaced it FOC. But I'm still wondering if there is any way they could have damaged the bearing while replacing the o/s track rod end. I asked two or three fitters from other places and they all thought it was unlikely. Now I'm worried that the new bearing won't last more than another week.* "

Depends on how they removed the old track rod end and on the tracking they then set up. If they had to whack it with a club hammer to get it off the steering arm, then this may have cracked the bearing carrier. It's more likely that too much toe out, set after the new track rod end was fitted, prematurely wore out the old wheel bearing and its replacement. If you notice any scuffing on the inside of the o/s front tyre tread, then there is too much toe-out and the tracking needs adjusting. But the most likely explanation is that too much 'thrust' was put on the first replacement bearing.

Soggy steering

" *I drive a 1992 VW Jetta 1.8GX which has now covered 121,000 miles. Just lately, the steering has become more and more vague, lighter and floating. There is a tendency to lose control when driving over anything more than a matchstick, and surface water is scary. I put new tyres on, but they made no difference. You can wiggle the steering wheel around while driving on the straight and not much will happen. Nevertheless, it remains quite driveable apart from in the wet. Do you think it is the steering rack, or something more esoteric? Have you had this problem with any of your Jettas?* "

Before you go to the frightening expense of new struts, strut-top bearings and a new steering rack, get the suspension bushes and the front wheel alignment checked. If at some time you have hit a pothole or whacked a kerb, you may be suffering from excessive toe-in and this will certainly lead to the symptoms you describe – especially in a power-steered car such as yours. The new tyres will take about 200 miles to scrub in.

A car called 'Wanda'

" *I recently purchased a 1994N BMW 518iSE with 41,000 miles showing. I am concerned by the steering on motorways at higher speeds, where it requires constant attention to keep the car travelling straight. Passing lorries and riding over undulations in the surface cause it to veer away. I took it back to the BMW agent who sold it to me and, after they checked the steering over, I was told it was perfectly normal as the model is fitted with recirculating ball steering which is not as positive as a rack and pinion system. I find it difficult to accept that wandering steering can be a characteristic of a car developed in a country like Germany with its Autobahn system.* "

A reader from Woodstock came up with the definitive reasons why old-shape BMW 5-Series may start to 'wander'. It's partly to do with tyre choice, partly suspension alignment, partly uneven wear on the tyres from parking manoeuvres and partly worn rear subframe bushes which create a self-steering effect that requires constant steering input to correct. His check list reads: (1) stick to the original Uniroyal tyres and don't switch to wider rims with low-profile tyres; (2) always change the front tyres as soon as the outer shoulders wear down; (3) check the rear subframe and replace any worn bushes (a £200 job); (4) check the front steering components and replace any worn items; (5) check and replace any worn suspension units and bushes; (6) only then, have the four wheel alignments re-set.

Primera points

" *I recently bought an 'Approved Used' 1995 Nissan Primera 2.0SLX four-door automatic saloon with two previous owners and a recorded 35,300 miles from a Nissan agent. The car came with up-to-date service history, Vehicle Mileage Check certificate, HPI Report, 'Nissan Assured Ownership Benefit', a preparation check and is immaculate in every sense of the word. The only query I have is from ex-Primera owners who ask me if I have had any trouble with the car's multi-link suspension, front and rear, warning that repairing defects can cost around £300. What are the early signs of defects, so I can spot them before the 12-month warranty expires?* "

The bushes of the multi-link suspension eventually dry out. This is rarely serious at the back and easily solved by spraying the links with WD40 (be careful not to get any on the brake discs). At the front, it can be more of a problem, necessitating replacement pre-bushed suspension arms. The first signs are clonkings and a weird feeling through the steering on full lock (though, of course, full lock should only be used in emergencies because of the strain it imposes on the driveshafts). That said, this is the only major problem area of an automatic 2.0 litre Primera (on manuals, the gear change can become sloppy). All cars deteriorate in some way over time, but the 2.0 litre Primera is the most bulletproof three- to eight-year-old mass-market family car I know of, and it's British built.

Bum steer

" *I have a 1993 Honda Prelude 2.3 automatic with 67,000 miles on the clock and four-wheel steer. The car had been trouble-free until a few days ago when a warning light came on indicating problems with the four-wheel steer. The agent tells me it needs a new control unit at a cost of £1,450 plus fitting, that he has never seen this problem occur before, and that, because the system is fail-safe, it is all right to continue to drive the car in two-wheel steer mode only.* "

Check with an MOT station that the car will pass in the 'fail safe' mode and check with your insurer that cover will not be affected. If you get a positive response in both cases, then you can afford to ask yourself if you need four-wheel steer so much that it's worth paying £1,450 for it.

'Flailing arm' suspension

" *I was interested to read of the apparent evolution in suspension that came with the 1996 version of the Escort. I purchased an estate version of one of these for my wife and, while she has never criticised the suspension or handling, we are very unimpressed with its rate of front tyre consumption. Two new front tyres were needed at 12,000 miles and, shocked by this wear rate, I had the suspension alignment properly checked by laser equipment. All was found to be in order and I was told that the premature tyre wear had 'probably arisen due to the driver's abuse of the power steering system'. If the new Focus shares the Escort's suspension set-up, will it be an equal contributor to the profitability of tyre manu-facturers?* "

The Focus does not share the Escort's suspension set-up. To put it bluntly, its suspension is light years ahead of that of the Escort, which is one reason why the Focus was voted 'European Car of The Year'. The fundamental flaw with the Escort was always the rear trailing arms. In cornering, under any kind of load, these flexed uncontrollably. For 1992, with the launch of the Zetec 1.8 16v engine, the arms were strengthened by beefy anti-roll bars bolted to each arm at two points down their lengths. Under hard cornering, the arms still flexed. For 1996 the suspension was improved again, but the basics were the same. For the Focus, this compromised rear suspension has been completely ditched and a proper, fully-independent 'control blade' system applied. I go along with the words of the alignment specialist. Heavy front tyre wear is often attributable to drivers using power steering to turn the wheels while the car is stationary. Stand and watch while this is being done and you will actually see rubber being worn away on the road surface.

CHERISHED REGISTRATIONS

'JSO 11' for sale

" *My father died just after Christmas and left a 20-year-old Austin Allegro with the registration number 'JSO 11'. The car is taxed and has a current MOT. We wish to sell the car, but expect to gain considerably more for the registration than for the car itself. A registration company has already offered to give us £1,500 on sale of the registration, but does not want the car. Would it be better to sell the registration privately and sell the car to an Allegro enthusiast?* "

Since the car is taxed and MOT-tested, there is no problem in transferring the registration to another car, but it may be worth transferring it to a retention certificate (£80 + £25) before the VED and MOT run out. (You need form V778/1 – which comes with instructions – from your local Vehicle Registration Office.) To simply transfer a registration from one vehicle to another, in which case the donor vehicle will be allocated a new age-related registration, costs £80 and requires form V317 which also comes with full instructions. The extra workload on a reduced number of Vehicle Registration Offices means that transferring registrations is no longer as quick or simple as it used to be, so allow at least four weeks. Elite Registrations (01380 818181) offers to value registrations by post (but not by telephone). To shift the Allegro, try *QUARTIC*, the magazine of the Allegro Club International, 20 Stoneleigh Crescent, Stoneleigh, Epsom, Surrey KT19 0RP.

Goodbye, Dolly

" *I have decided to part with my car, a 1979 Triumph Dolomite 1500 Highline in yellow with 47,000 miles which I have owned since new. The body is rusting, but otherwise there is nothing wrong with it. It was suggested that maybe we could sell the number plate: 'RKB 97T'. How much do you think we could get for the car or the number plate, separately or together? And how do I go about selling it? The car has not been taxed or insured since last year because it was not being used.* "

You can't sell the registration separately unless the car is MOT-tested and taxed, and to be taxed it has to be insured. From your description it doesn't seem like Classic Car Auction fodder, and is probably worth no more than £200 without MOT or tax. I don't think you'd get enough for the registration separately to justify the cost of putting the car through the MOT, insuring it and taxing it. You could try selling it through the club, which is Triumph Dolomite Club, 39 Mill Lane, Arncott, Bicester, Oxon OX6 0PB, tel: 01869 242847; email: triumph.dolomite.club@london.almac.co.uk.

Registration valuation service

" *Your readers might like to know that, for a fee of £25, they can have their cherished registration valued. They will receive a signed valuation certificate within 28 days. Alternatively, should they be thinking of buying a cherished registration, for a slightly higher fee we can provide a valuation within 24 or 48 hours. The Cherished Number Dealers Association can be contacted on 01788 538303 or via our website, which is hhtp://www.cnda.co.uk. Our postal address is 9 North Street, Rugby CV21 2AB.* **"**

Finding a reg.

In the same week, two readers asked how they could go about finding specific registrations they wished to buy and transfer to their own cars. The answer is to call the DVLA Hotline on 0181 200 6565. This will tell you if a specific number is available for transfer. If you just want to find out if a registration has been assigned to a vehicle, write to Customer Enquiries (Vehicles), DVLA, Long View Road, Swansea SA6 7JL, or fax them on 01792 783657. If it has been asigned, because of the Data Protection Act the DVLA cannot supply the keepership details unless you show 'reasonable cause', such as wishing to check the mileage of a car you want to buy or to take civil action against a driver who damaged your property. To obtain a list of previous owners under these circumstances, write to: Fee Paying Section, DVLA, Swansea SA99 1AL, enclosing a cheque for £5 made out to 'Department of Transport'.

Bequeathing a reg.

" *I am the 'owner' of a personalised registration mark of some value, but it is currently held on a retention certificate. In the event of my death before this mark is transferred to another vehicle, would those who inherit my estate become 'owners' of the mark or would 'ownership' revert to the DVLA automatically? If the latter is normally the case, is there anything I can do to ensure that my family does not lose the mark and therefore its financial value?* **"**

The rules on the notes which come with form V778/1 are clear on this point. They allow the recorded keeper of a vehicle with a cherished registration to transfer the mark to a retention certificate for 12 months – and for extensions of the period on the retention certificate to be purchased at the rate of £25 a year – otherwise the keeper's right to the mark lapses. The right to keep the mark on a retention certificate is not transferrable. Your best bet therefore is to use the form 778 Retention Document to assign the mark to a vehicle other than a moped or motorcycle owned by a member of your family. The £80 you paid to transfer the mark to the retention certificate also pays for this.

Keeping a cherished reg.

" *I have a personalised registration plate, bought from the DVLA, which is on my present car. When I am ready to part-exchange the car I will want to transfer the plate to my new car. Can you tell me how the dealer who buys my car will re-register it, and what registration number he will get bearing in mind that the car will probably be five years old?* "

Now that the number of Vehicle Registration Offices has been reduced there can be a delay of a month in transferring a registration from one car to another. To stay on the road with both cars, it may be better to transfer your personal registration to a retention certificate at the time of part exchange, using form V778/1, which comes with full instructions. The transfer costs £80 and the retention certificate £25. Your old car will then be allocated a registration with a prefix appropriate to its date of first registration. The new car will have to be registered to a standard date plate first, then, after you take delivery, you can use the appropriate form to re-assign the registration on the retention certificate to the new car at no further charge. There is a bit of hassle involved as you will also have to change the registration on the car's insurance certificate.

Age-related

" *In 1980, I laid up my 1960 Morris Minor, reg. 'WDP 383'. A couple of years ago I telephoned one of the cherished number agents advertising in* The Daily Telegraph *and was told that the number could not be transferred unless the car was MOT-tested and bore a current, free, VED disc. It now does, but if I sell the plate what will I get instead? And will the car still be VED exempt?* "

You will get another 'age related plate'. But the replacement plate cannot ever be sold for transfer. Your car will continue to be VED exempt. However, should you decide to take it off the road for any reason, you are now obliged to make a Statutory Off Road Notification (SORN) to the DVLA.

Selecting a 'select mark'

" *Under its 'Select Marks' scheme, the DVLA is currently offering registrations with the prefix A, B, H, J, K, L, M, N, P, R and now S. Why no C, D, E, F or G prefixes? Are there any plans to utilise these prefixes in the future?* "

The DVLA began selling 'Select Marks' in 1990 when the prefix was H. But a forward-thinking person in the authority had made sure that when prefixes A to G had been allocated, the numbers 1–20 were held back. As Bs and Cs with these numbers have now been released for sale and will be followed by D to G when the DVLA judges the time is right. To make an enquiry about Select Registrations,

write to Select Marks Marketing, DVLA,
Swansea SA6 7JL.

Lapsed registrations

" *I have a 1934 Armstrong Siddeley 17 hp 2.4 litre saloon and a 1957
Matchless G11 600 cc motor cycle, both with lapsed registrations due to
my lack of knowledge of the change in the regulations. I still have the
original documents. Please can you advise me how to reclaim the old
registrations?* "

You need booklet V848, 'How to Register Your
Old Vehicle', and forms V765 and V55/5 which
you can obtain from your nearest Vehicle
Registration Office – confusingly listed under
'Transport, Department of' in the telephone
directory. Since you have the original log
books and can thereby prove the entitlement
of the car and the bike to their registration
marks, you should be able to revive them if
they have not already been reallocated. (Other
acceptable forms of proof include pre-1983 tax
discs or pre-1983 MOT certificates). The evidence must be accompanied by recent photographs of the vehicles. You then need to send
your completed application to a relevant
owners club (listed on V765/1) for authentica-
tion. (The club may charge for its services and
may wish to inspect the vehicles.) Once the
application is authenticated, you can send the
application in for processing. If you are
successful, the registrations will not be
transferrable, so cannot be sold for transfer to
another vehicle. As the DVLA very reasonably
states, 'This arrangement helps to safeguard
entitlement by removing the incentive there
would otherwise be for spurious claims to
attractive old registration marks.' The relevant

DVLA Customer Enquiry Line is 01792 772134. However, under proposed new EU regulations, you may find you are obliged to MOT and SORN the cars every year or they could be compulsorily removed from your property and destroyed.

Petty offences

" *I notice an increasing trend for non-standard lettering to appear on number plates. Have the regulations been relaxed, or are the police just turning a blind eye?* "

No, the regulations have not been relaxed. Instead they have been strengthened. This is not the petty offence it may seem, either, as police speed cameras can't always read some of these registrations correctly. The latest initiative is to punish people who alter the spacing or the typeface by withdrawing their entitlement to a cherished number plate. If they have many thousands of pounds tied up in their cherished registrations, this could hit the N1GELs of this world very hard. But it won't do much to get rid of the real problem of standard registrations in script faces. As I've written before, drivers who try this open themselves to being stopped for a Construction & Use offence, which will be followed by a document check, possibly a breath test and maybe an inspection of the car for any other irregularities.

CLASSICS AND NOSTALGIA

Horsepower tax

" *When you describe an old car as a '10/26', what do the '10' and the '26' mean? I know that the RAC may have rated what was loosely known as a 10 HP car at perhaps 9.8 HP for road tax purposes, but how was this rating actually arrived at?* "

Useful question, to which there is no straight answer until you come to the 1920s. Prior to then, '10/26' could have referred to estimated 'horse-power'/'brake-horsepower', or it could have meant estimated 'brake-horsepower' at two different engine speeds. By the 1920s it was more or less standardised to mean estimated nominal 'horse-power'/'brake-horsepower' as measured on an engine brake. The explanation of the RAC rating is on page 17 of Culshaw & Horrobin's *Complete Catalogue of British Cars 1895–1975* (ISBN 1-874105-93-6). RAC HP is the square of the cylinder bore in millimetres multiplied by the number of cylinders, the result then divided by 1613. So a 4-cylinder car, nominally a 10 HP, with a cylinder bore of 63 mm would have an RAC rating of 9.84 HP. The undesirable result of this taxation formula was a profusion of narrow-bore, slow-revving, long-stroke engines, and it was not until after taxation according to RAC formula ended in 1948 that high-revving 'oversquare' engines began to appear in large numbers in the UK. Confusingly, some marques, notably Wolseley, continued with designations such as '16/60' up to 1971, yet also designated their cars by the number of cylinders, such as '4/44' and '6/90'.

A.B.C.

As easy as A.B.C.

" *I have a photograph, taken in the mid-1920s, showing my mother in a car which I believe was an A.B.C. I understand that Tommy Sopwith was responsible for the manufacturer of A.B.C.s and, following aircraft principles, installed an air-cooled engine. Filling with petrol caused some confusion, as what appeared to be a radiator cap was really the cap to the fuel tank. I would be interested in more information about this car.* "

A.B.C. Motorcycles were built using spare post-WW1 capacity by the Sopwith Aircraft company at Kingston-upon-Thames from 1919 until 1923, after which production was transferred to France. The bikes and their 398 cc flat-twin engines were designed by the same Granville Bradshaw who was responsible for the flat-twin A.B.C. car. The All British Engine Company was originally based at Brooklands (there is an A.B.C. motorcycle, reg. 'XF 502', on display at the Brooklands museum). But, by 1919, Harper Bean had taken a controlling interest in the company and moved it to a 20-acre site in Hersham, Surrey. The cars were built between 1920 and 1929 and the first had a flat-twin air-cooled engine of 1,203 cc which put out an impressive 35 bhp. A problem was that the engine was designed down to a cost and, in G N Georgano's words, 'was noisy, hard to start, inefficiently lubricated and liable to breakages, especially of the very long exposed push-rods'. But the A.B.C. was fast for its size, capable of 60 mph. By 1924, a much-improved 1,326 cc 'Super Sports' version had been introduced with twin carburettors and 40 bhp. A total of 8,000 A.B.C.s were built, but electric starters and front brakes were always deemed to be 'optional extras'. All commentators testified to the danger of having the fuel tank topped up with water by over-eager filling station attendants. A correspondent from Hereford swears blind that a fellow college student at Kingston in the mid-1950s had a two-seater aluminium-bodied sports run-about, badged 'A.B.C. No. 3' which he described as 'a Sopwith A.B.C.' and which had not one but two 600 cc horizontally opposed A.B.C. motorcycle engines and a rear-mounted fuel tank rather than the confusing 'fuel radiator'. Given the Granville Bradshaw connection, it's possible that this was either a prototype or a 'special' produced at the Kingston Sopwith factory rather than at the Hersham A.B.C. works.

AC

Buckland Tourer

" *Back in 1948 I crewed as navigator in some club rallies. The owner-driver was my sister's boss, and I was recruited as a recently demobbed RAF navigator. The car was an AC Buckland Sports drop head, finished in cream with red leather upholstery – a lovely car with good performance, particularly for those early days after the war when any new car was hard to get. I lost touch with the owner when he died and I wonder what happened to the car. Although I have been a keen follower of cars and motor sport, I have not seen any reference to this AC model since those days. I know the company went on to produce the Ace and the Aceca, but what happened to the Buckland? And what was its specification?* **"**

I also remember the Buckland, because a friend of my father's owned one from the fifties to the seventies and it was the first car in which I was driven at 90 mph on the clock. My most abiding memory was the wind roar tearing through its complex folding top and sounding like a hurricane. The owner was Dr Philip Edmonson, who lived at Redcar. The car itself had AC's venerable 1,991 cc ohc six, which dated back to the mid-1920s and sported three SU carburettors to develop 76 bhp. The Buckland tourer had cutaway doors with flaps in the side-screens for hand signals that accounted for some of that wind noise. The model range was built from 1947 to 1956. In the mid-1970s there was a warehouse/showroom on Buckingham Palace Road, and I helped arrange for the car to be sold on consignment there.

A reader from Biggleswade later wrote to tell us he purchased a dark green AC Buckland tourer, reg. 'HGG 459', in Devizes in 1996, and that at least one other remains in the same area. He tells us that the engine needed quite a lot of work, but has now settled down and that, though the top speed is listed at 89 mph, the car cruises happily at 60 mph.

AC aficionado

" *I, too, became involved with AC Buckland tourers between 1967 and 1970, and owned one tourer and two 2-Litre saloons. They weren't all they were cracked up to be. The engine dated back to 1919 and had cast-iron* *bores in an alloy block which caused continuous cylinder head gasket problems. Piston rings also broke regularly, heads had a tendency to fracture, and the ash frame of the alloy body was prone to rot. However, the better of the saloons took a family of six on several continental tours and the Buckland managed a memorable trip exploring the vineyards of the Rhine and Moselle. I kept a detailed log of services, repairs etc. on all three cars, together with registrations and chassis numbers, which I would be glad to pass on to anyone who is seriously interested. Looking back at the notes now, I can't imagine how I ever found the patience and time to do all the work.* "

This was of great interest to Mike Smith of the AC Owners Club Buckland Register, 1 Melbourne Street, Bratton, Westbury, Wilts BA13 4RN, tel: 01380 830351. He sent me a list of the forty-five surviving cars, which confirmed that this reader's Buckland, NKR 179, is still a 'runner', incredibly in Mike Smith's own hands.

Allard

Emigrated Allard

" *I recently purchased a 1948 Allard model 'L' touring car. The previous owner was a Mr Frank Savage who bought it in 1962 when he lived in England and worked for Amoco there. According to 'Allard, the inside story', my car is one of 191 'Model L' four-seater tourers built in 1946, 1947 and 1948. The ID number is 7195654-MOD 71L. The chassis number is 520, the reg. is 'DVD 567' and it was delivered on 31/3/48 to Gloucester. Mr Savage bought it from Paradise Garage and thinks it was previously owned by a woman who found it uncomfortable and tricky to drive. There is a dash plaque: 'Performance Cars Ltd – The Sports Car People'. On the badge bar are AA, Gloucestershire county, Allard Owners Club and Wiltshire county badges. Can you give me the address of the Allard Owners Club and any other tips for discovering the history of this car?* "

Allard Owners Club, c/o Michelle Watson, 10

Brooklyn Court, Woking, Surrey GU22 7TQ, tel: 01483 773428. 'VD' is a Lanarkshire registration, 1930–1948 records of which are held by The Kithead Trust, De Salis Drive, Hampton Lovett, Droitwich Spa, Worcs WR9 0QE, tel: 01905 776681. (It may be that one of the owners bought the registration because it matched his initials or his name was 'David'.)

All British Ford

'All British' and proud of it

" *I wonder if you have ever come across a car by the name of the 'All British Ford'. Many years ago a friend of mine took me to a garage in the Banbury area where I was shown a couple of these cars. I believe that the total production numbered three. They were designed and built by a man at Moreton-in-Marsh in the twenties or early thirties, I would guess, and each was quite different. As far as I remember they were quite professionally made and I believe that the intention was to market them rather than merely construct them as specials. I saw two cars at the garage of Charlie Metcalf who had obtained them from Mr Ford, by then consigned to an old folks' home. One of the cars was a flat-twin and the other a more sporting V4.* "

The cars were built by inventor Bertie Ford in Kenilworth, in the period 1918–1920. Models included a flat-twin water cooled model and a V4 sports car which had, in Nick Baldwin's words, 'an ingenious two-stroke engine with stepped pistons and atmospheric valves. Most parts were cast and machined in house.' Sadly the 1920s recession and competition from better-funded manufacturers killed off the project, but two prototypes apparently still survive. The V4 is registered 'UF 51' and there is a picture of it on Page 13 of *A–Z of Cars of the 1920s* (ISBN 1-870979-53-2).

David Culshaw finished this story by sending a definitive history of Bertie Ford's 'All British Ford' V4 car. It was fitted with a 'racing' body from a 10/30 Alvis known as 'Yodol Dodol Doh' which C M Harvey had driven in the 1921 JCC 200-mile race at Brooklands. Only one prototype V4 car was made and Bertie Ford built all of it except the body himself. He later sold it to Ivor Lindsell and Charles Arnold, who were partners. It languished with them in a partially dismantled state until 1957 when they sold it to Tom Porter who put it back into running order. Porter also acquired the other flat-twin water-cooled prototype when Bertie Ford's garage was scheduled for demolition to make way for road widening. Porter subsequently sold the ABF V4 to Peter Russell, who got it back onto the road briefly before the gearbox broke up. He repaired this, then used the car as everyday transport in Scotland and attended the Brooklands reunion with it in 1980. A few years later Russell sold it at auction to US collector Charles Schalebaum, who exported it to the United States, then later sold the car to Stanley Wanlass. Wanless kept the car in a shed for many years until DeWayne Ashmead of Fruit Heights, Utah bought it from him. Thinking it was a re-engined 10/30 Alvis, Ashmead had wanted to restore it back to the car as driven by C. M. Harvey in the 1921 JCC 200, but Culshaw persuaded him that only the body was originally 'Alvis'. The chassis, suspension, axles and running gear were all hand-made by Bertie Ford and the car would have far more historical significance left as it was.

Many thanks to a reader from Leominster who supplied two mid-1950s photos of the ABF in its complete form with headlights, mudguards and screen. These may prove invaluable for DeWayne Ashmead's restoration of the car.

Alldays and Enfield Allday

Allday to Aston

" *My recollection is that my father had an Enfield Allday of about 10 HP. He cherished it as a really well-engineered car which, I suspect, proved too expensive to produce at a profit in those days. It was utterly reliable and reached a top speed of 59 mph on the speedo. I well remember yearning that it would reach the magic mile-a-minute.* "

Alldays & Onions Pneumatic Engineering Co. of Birmingham acquired the Enfield Autocar Company in 1908. The two ranges of cars were then rationalised and most were sold under both brand names until 1916. The main models from 1913 were a 990 cc V-twin Midget cyclecar with air cooling and, from 1914, a four-cylinder 1100 cc version with a bullnose radiator, which must have been the model you had. Production wound down during the First World War, and the last year was 1916, which could explain why only six were built in that year. After the war, the company was re-named 'Enfield Allday' and continued building cars, including the astonishingly advanced, backbone-framed, five-cylinder radial-engined 'Bullet' of 1919. The Enfield Allday 10/20, 10/30 and 12/30 were beautifully engineered but, with chassis from £380 and a sports saloon listed at £795, they were extremely expensive. In his *A–Z of Cars of the 1920s*, Nick Baldwin tells us that only 100 were produced between 1920 and 1926. 10/20s had 1,488 cc side-valve engines and three-speed gearboxes; 12/30s had 1,757 cc side-valvers and four-speed gearboxes. Highly developed versions of the 10/20 with twin over-head inlet valves and front-wheel brakes were raced by the works manager, A. C. Bertelli, in 1921–1922, but then he left to help form the company that became Aston Martin.

Alvis

Fast lady

" *For many years, my 1932 Alvis Speed 20, originally registered MV 6348, was like a giant Meccano set. Now I've got it back to a restored 'rolling chassis', I'd like to find out about its past. The Alvis Owners Club tells me that its first owner was Miss B. J. M. Streather of Golders Green, London, who drove the car in the 1933 RAC Rally when it was described as a 'two door saloon'. However, body builders Vanden Plas record it as a coupe while a gentleman who rode in it fifty years ago remembers it being open-topped. Legend has it that it competed at Brooklands and also in sand racing, which might account for its utterly clapped out condition when I bought it in 1968. It lost its Vanden Plas body in about 1947 when it was converted to a shooting brake and was later cut down to a two-seater. Although I want to fit a drophead body, I would dearly like to see some photos of the car in its original form and learn more about Miss Streather and the events in which she competed.* "

A reader from the Isle of Man, wrote to tell us that he has found the rallying history of MV 6348 in an old book, *British Rally Drivers 1925–39* by Donald Lowbourne. It seems that the car, driven by B. J. M. Streather, was entered in the RAC Rallies of 1933–1936, described as an 'open two seater' with the registration NV 6349 (misprint?) taken from a photo in a contemporary *Motor* magazine (the picture could, of course, have been of a different car). Roger Ramage of the Brooklands Museum tells us that

Miss B. J. M. Streather also drove an SS in the JCC Rally at Brooklands on 25 March 1939, so perhaps by that time she had sold the Speed 20. The Alvis Owners Club celebrated the marque's 75th anniversary at Brooklands Museum on 14 June 1998.

Mayfair Madam's origins unfold

" *I have owned my 1933 Alvis SA 16.95 HP, reg. 'KY 4232' for ten years, yet know nothing of the first 46 years of its life. According to the Alvis factory record, it was despatched to Messrs Waterhouse in Bradford on 14 April 1933, but a plaque on the dashboard states 'This car was supplied by Gaffikin Wilkinson & Co. Ltd., 17a Hanover Square, W.1., tel Mayfair 3425.' I bought the car in London and was told it had come from 'a large house in the New Forest' in 1978 and had possibly been owned by someone called Bibby. My investigations and the Alvis Owners Club have drawn a complete blank. The car is still very original and unworn, suggesting it either led an easy life or lay unused for a long period. In 1978 it was red and black, but the last owner changed it to ivory and black. Does anyone remember this car? I would really appreciate any information about its early life.* "

The factory record describes the car as a sports saloon with body by Charlesworth, coachworks number 12692 (most of Charlesworth's fine work at the time was for Alvis). The seats are brown leather. The car was originally fitted with four lamps. Engine number: 10751: chassis number: 10301; car number 15307; originally fitted with one Zenith carburettor, but later converted to three SU's. The body and wire wheels were originally painted black, but at some time in the car's history the flanks became red or maroon. An SA 16.95 had a 2,148 cc six-cylinder engine with a bore of 67.5 mm and a stroke of 100 mm. Using the

RAC formula, this worked out at 16.95 HP. A reader from Salisbury met the owner, Geoffrey Bibby, in 1961 and was employed by him in a garage business in Salisbury. Bibby had built up a collection of pre-war cars, one of which was the Alvis, and my correspondent remembers it being take to Southampton for an overhaul of the coachwork, which was when the red and black finish was applied. He left Bibby's employ in 1966. Another reader, this time from Honiton, wrote to tell us that Bibby purchased the car from a scrapyard in Honiton in the late 1950s. Yet more details come from Romsey, where a reader tells us that Bibby lived at 'Forest Edge', Wood Green, Fordingbridge, which still has an enormous 90-foot garage ideal for a car collector. It seems that Bibby exchanged the house in 1985 for a flat in Spain, and died in 1991 or 1992.

More Alvis ancestry

" *I have been trying to fill in some gaps in the past life of my 1966 Alvis TF21 (GVC 473D). I have contacted the DVLA, but their records only go back to computerisation in 1973/74. I have also gleaned as much as I can from the Alvis Owners Club. But can you tell me if any organisation keeps records of pre-computer 'VC' registrations?* "

Yes. The Museum of British Road Transport, Hales Street, Coventry CV1 1PN has 'VC' registration records from 1949–1975. Tel: 01203 832418; fax: 01203 832421. A very useful book, *How to trace the History of Your Car* by Philip Riden, ISBN 1-898937-25-7, price £5.95, lists all registration records which have been preserved and where they are kept.

Amilcar

One-wheel-drive

" *At the beginning of the Second World War I owned a CGSS Surbaisse Amilcar with aluminium racing chassis and body. As I was only a very junior army person, I was very cost-conscious and overcame the severe tyre wear caused by the solid back axle by removing the drive key for one of the half shafts. It actually worked surprisingly well. The car was of 1929 vintage, registered 'YX 15', and I often wonder what happened to it.* "

The Amilcar & Salmson Register (10 Monument Green, Weybridge, Surrey KT13 8QS) wrote: 'In response to your reader's query regarding Amilcar 'YX 15', chassis no 19727, this car was rescued from a junkyard outside Chelmsford by my brother and myself in around 1960. It was there because it had broken its transmission, presumably as a result of your correspondent's misguided efforts to reduce his tyre wear. As the hubs are retained by a key and taper, I find it hard to understand how he did not lose a rear wheel, unless he welded the retaining nut to the shaft. My brother replaced the engine and gearbox with units from a Riley 9 and the car still exists in that form, having recently been sold through the trade to a man in Holland. The body when rescued was the standard Amilcar steel 2-seater with pointed tail, undoubtedly the original one. No Amilcar chassis was ever made of aluminium.

Ansaldo

Ansaldo, anyone?

" *I am interested in anything made by Diatto or Ansaldo. The earliest rather vague information I have about this 1925 Ansaldo 4C 1850 is that it was rescued from a breakers yard in, I believe, Barking in the 1950s, the number-plates and all paperwork having been lost. At some time prior to this, perhaps pre-war, it had been fitted with the body of a 1925 Fiat 501 tourer in place of the original. It is a very long shot, but somebody might remember it from between 1925 and the early 1950s before it was sold for breaking, as it was a fairly unusual make in this country.* "

Can anyone remember this car? Does anyone know when it lost its original Weymann body and acquired the Fiat tourer body? Any Ansaldo anecdotes to Frank Lugg, 460 Baddow Road, Chelmsford, Essex CM2 9RD.

Another two Ansaldos

" *My late father bought an Ansaldo for my sister. The car's design impressed me immensely as a young man, although I do not know what happened to it following the outbreak of war. I believe the Ansaldo tourer 4C had an 1800 cc engine, although they later produced a sporting version, and I wonder if my sister's car was one of these.* "

A specification list shows that four-cylinder Ansaldos had two engine sizes back to 1923. The standard engine was 70 mm x 120 mm, giving a swept volume of 1,847 cc, and this became the 4C '12/40' in 1926. Increasing the bore to 72.5 mm brought the swept volume up to 1,981 cc, and this became the 4CS '14/50'. The fact that your sister's car had wire wheels would tend to indicate it was a 4CS according to the spec sheet. The battery looks a bit vulnerable, sitting uncovered at the rear of the nearside running board. Meanwhile, a reader from Manchester sent a photo of another wire-wheeled 1926 Ansaldo 4CS, this one a full drop-head coupe with dicky seat, rear-mounted spare and no battery on the running board. His uncle purchased it in around 1933 for £12 (then the equivalent of two weeks' pay), stripped it right down to the chassis and fitted high-compression pistons.

Argyll

Magnificence restored

" *Though you have covered the Argyll factory at Alexandria near Glasgow before, I thought you might be interested to hear of its restoration. As you know, prior to restoration, the building was last used as a torpedo factory during WW2. I used to weep whenever I passed the decaying and vandalised ruin. The planners and restorers are to be congratulated in giving this building a fresh new lease of life as a shopping arcade, and for incorporating a small museum dedicated to the cars the factory was built to produce.* **"**

The museum address is Motoring Memories Heritage Centre, Loch Lomond Outlets, The Argyll Building, Main Street, Alexandria, tel: 01389 607862. (Director: Tim Amyes. Alexandria is on the A82 North of Glasgow.)

Armstrong Siddeley and Siddeley Deasy

Not Armstrong, but certainly Siddeley

" *I remember a Siddeley car with a pointed front and the radiator behind the engine. Can you tell me more about it?* **"**

It's a Siddeley-Deasy, probably an 18/24 as the bonnet in the photo you sent doesn't look long enough for a six-cylinder 24/30. These were built from 1911 to 1919 in Coventry, after J. D. Siddeley left Wolseley to join the Deasy company, but before Armstrong-Whitworth merged with Siddeley-Deasy. There's a 1912 Siddeley-Deasy Althorpe Cabriolet at the Museum of British Road Transport, Coventry.

Stretch Armstrong

" *I have had a number of arguments over Armstrong Siddeleys. General opinion seems to be that all Armstrong Siddeleys had a pointed nose. Yet the one my father owned in the early 1930s had a flat front. I still remember riding in this 'tank' of a car with nine others from Weymouth to Lulworth Cove. My father was very proud of its gate-change gearbox and the huge amount of space inside, which happily accommodated all the* *people in the photograph. Any information on this particular model would be greatly appreciated.* "

In 1923 Armstrong Siddeley introduced its first four-cylinder car, the 1,852 cc ohv 4/14, which was distinguished from its more luxurious brethren by a flat rather than a pointed radiator. The 4/14 continued in Mk II form to 1929, but in the meantime, in 1927 a 1,900 cc side-valve six-cylinder 'Fifteen' model had also been introduced, sharing the 14's flat radiator until 1931, and I think this is the model which was owned by your father. The three-speed gate-change gearbox was standard and a four-speed pre-selector an option. It had sophisticated features such as foot-pumped, one-shot, chassis lubrication. The engine was smooth and, while by no means powerful, it was flexible, which is why it was able to pull that heavy body and all those passengers from Weymouth to Lulworth Cove. David Potter of The Armstrong Siddeley Owners Club has directed readers with questions and information about old Armstrong Siddeleys to Peter Sheppard, ASOC, 57 Berberry Close, Birmingham B30 1TB. Having purchased the bulk of the original company spares from Rolls Royce in 1972, and having embarked on its own re-manufacturing programme, the club is well placed to help with spare parts, so if you have an Armstrong Siddeley it would be well worth joining.

Hurricane hits Oldham

" *My late husband, Clifford Woolley, owned an Armstrong Siddeley Hurricane, reg. FBU 222, when we lived at of 33 Whetstone Hill Road, Derker, Oldham, Lancashire. The car was sold in Oldham to our old friend Ken Healey, who had a shop in Waterloo Street, Oldham, shortly prior to July 1961 when we left the town. It would be interesting to know what happened to the car.* "

Post-war Oldham 'BU' registration records don't seem to have been preserved. But you may strike lucky by contacting the Armstrong Siddeley Owners Club, c/o Peter Sheppard, 57 Berberry Close, Birmingham B30 1TB, tel: 0121 459 0742. Alternatively, a reader may write to tell us that he or she now owns the car. I remember getting a lift to school in one of these in the 1950s, and, as with the AC Buckland, the noise of the wind blowing through the Elastoplast-mended hood certainly did sound like a hurricane.

Arrol Johnston

Arrol Aster

" In 1929, my parents replaced their Arrol Johnston with an Arrol Aster car. Could you please let me know where I can obtain a picture of either of these cars, particularly the Arrol Aster? "

Pages 25–26 of Nick Baldwin's A–Z of Cars of the 1920s (ISBN 1-870979-53-2), or pages 52–53 of The Complete Catalogue of British Cars 1895–1975 by Culshaw & Horrobin (ISBN 1-874105-93-6). Arrol Johnston merged with Aster in 1927, but the resulting company, which built its cars at Heathall, Dumfries, only lasted a few years. Its products included a Cozette super-charged 17/50, a straight-eight sleeve-valve 23/70, and the company was noted for reconstructing Sir Malcolm Campbell's 1928 Bluebird car.

Beach racer

" Did Arrol Johnston ever go in for racing?. I have a photograph of what I believe to be an Arrol Johnston, taken prior to the 1914–18 war, which I *believe was raced on the sands at Southport. I expect it is very doubtful that this car is still in existence, but might it, perhaps, be in a museum?* "

The Museum of Transport, housed at Kelvin Hall, 1 Bunhouse Road, Glasgow (tel: 0141 287 2720) has two Arrol Johnstons of the period: a 1906 TT replica 18 HP (currently out on loan to the Grampian Transport Museum, Alford, Aberdeen) and a 1912 15.9 HP. The 18 HP TT car was designed by J. S. Napier and won the Tourist Trophy in 1905; it had a conventional radiator and bonnet. The sand racer appears to be a modified 15.9 HP, built from 1910 to 1925, with two different strokes of 120 mm and 140 mm giving 2,409 cc and 2,815 cc respectively. Sand racing, involving hair-raising sideways drifts, was popular at Southport right up to the outbreak of the Second World War.

Aston Martin

Phantom Disco Volante?

" *In the late 1950s, at the corner of Heaton Moor Road, Redish Lane and the Stockport-to-Manchester A6, there was a colony of shops. Overnight, the last shop on the Stockport side became a very cramped car showroom holding three cars at the most. These included a Paramount, like those sold in 1998 from the Duncan Rabagliati collection. But the gems were parked in a cobbled alleyway beside the showroom. One was the ex-works HWM Jaguar, XPE 2. The other was an Aston Martin, registered RZ 1500, with a bizarre 'flying saucer' body. A plaque in the engine compartment stated, 'Bodywork by South Wraxall Garages, Bradford-on-Avon, Wiltshire'. The engine and instrumentation were conventional Aston Martin, probably a DB2 or DB2/4. I have always wondered whether the chassis was fitted with this body from the outset and why a small Wiltshire garage was entrusted with the job of building it. After a couple of months in business, the Stockport showroom vanished as quickly as it appeared.* "

The Aston Martin Owners Club confirmed the chassis number of this DB2/4 as LML/810, its engine number as VB6J/279 and that it had been built for Lord O'Neill. Chassis number LML/802 was bodied by Vignale and a number of other carrozzeria including Bertone built 'spider' bodies on DB2/4 chassis. But LML/810 was originally sold in October 1954 as a standard 2/4-seater saloon car with rear luggage 'hatch' by agents John Patterson Ltd. If the car ever went back to the Feltham works, or to the later Newport Pagnell factory, AM archivist Roger Stowers may have a record of it (tel: 01908 610620). Build sheets and other records for the Feltham-built cars are held by Aston Service of Dorset on 01202 574727. South Wraxall Garages of Bradford-on-Avon is not listed as a body-builder in the *A–Z of British Coachbuilders*, so I'd be as fascinated as you if any readers can tell us more about this Disco Volante body.

Atalanta

Lost city motor

" *My neighbour is in his eighties. When he left college in the 1930s, he tells me he started his own firm making motor cars. It's hard to conceive of such a thing today. The name of his car was the 'Atalanta'. Do any such cars exist today, and is there anywhere one might be seen?* "

The company was started by Albert (or Alfred) Gough as HGS Motors in 1935. Gough already had 24 years of motor industry experience, having spent the last three as chief engineer at Frazer Nash, so your neighbour must have been one of his friends who joined him in the venture at Staines. These were A. E. (Peter) Crosby, R. E.

Scott, Walter Hamill and two young graduates, N. G. Watson and P. N. Whitehead. Car production lasted from 1937 to 1939, and the cars themselves were extremely good looking. The very advanced specification included independent suspension front and rear, 16-inch hydraulic brakes, and Gough-designed four-cylinder ohc engines of 1,496 cc and 1,996 cc, with twin carburettors or a Shorrock supercharger situated in line with the crankshaft. Sadly, Gough's brilliant but unfettered enthusiasm soon used up the funds supplied by partner Whitehead. At this point, Dennis Poore, Joan Brotchie and Midge Wilby then came to the rescue, Wilby taking over Watson's shares. Later versions built in 1938/39 had 112 bhp 4.3 litre Lincoln Zephyr V-12 engines and three-speed gearboxes in the original chassis. Douglas Blain tells the story over five pages in the November 1997 issue of *The Automobile* magazine, to the magazine's usual very high standard, and back copies are available from Enthusiast Publishing Ltd, tel: 01932 864212. I'll bet your neighbour would be thrilled to receive a copy of it. The car in Blain's article was re-built by TT Workshops of Westbury (01373 823603) for Craig Davis of Pebble Beach, California. I'm afraid I can't find any Atalantas listed in UK museums.

Austin

Pedal car to peddle

" *The nursery school, which is part of our parish church, has asked me to value a pedal car which they wish to sell. It is in the style of an Austin Devon/Dorset produced in the late 1940s. I cannot find a maker's name, but the number stamped in the boot is 30060. The car is very scruffy but complete, with the exception of the headlamps. An offer of £200 has been made and my inclination is to advise acceptance unless you suggest otherwise. "*

If the bonnet and boot open, there's a dummy engine and the tyres are pneumatic, it's an Austin J40. As it is, it could fetch £400 at auction, and fully restored with hubcaps and working electric headlights it could make £750. An example of its sister car, the more desirable Austin 7 Pathfinder 'racer', sold for £2,250 at BCA Blackbushe in October 1995. A specialist in these is C.A.R.S. of Brighton, tel: 01273 601960, and they have produced a book on the subject.

Seven's hidden past

" I have a 1935 two-seater Austin 7 tourer with an APD military body (no. 2884), finished as an APE 'Opal'. She was first registered BNF 551 in Manchester on 12 July 1935, chassis number 226776. I have her history from 20 May 1977, but would like to know what happened to her in between. "

Would readers with any information please contact Dr Bernard Juby on 01926 450241. 'NF' Manchester registration records from 1968 to 1974 still survive at The Archives Department, Central Library, St Peter's Square, Manchester M2 5PD, tel: 0161 839 1980, fax: 0161 839 3808 (there may be a search fee). Earlier records seem to have been destroyed, but if there was a change of ownership within this period, they may have it.

Whatever happened to Pobble?

" Pobble was a 1907 Austin racing car belonging to Oscar Thompson, one of the founder members of Brooklands Automobile Racing Club. In

1907, Oscar's sister Muriel won the first Ladies' Race held there driiving Pobble. When war broke out in 1914, Oscar had Pobble converted to an ambulance and drove it with the French 7th Army in the Vosges, carrying between 300 and 400 wounded men to relative safety. For this, Pobble was awarded the VC in the British racing press. The French would not accept women drivers, so Muriel joined the all-women F.A.N.Y. Convoys driving a different vehicle, possibly a Fiat, and during four years of service on the Western Front she was awarded the Military Medal, the Croix de Guerre and the Ordre de Leopold II for bravery under fire. I am currently preparing an entry on Muriel Thompson for the New National Dictionary of Biography, in the course of which I have been in touch with John Grainger at The Brooklands Museum and the Austin Vintage Register. We know Pobble survived the first three years of the war, but not whether it ever came home. We should all like to know. Can any of your readers help? "

I think that Pobble was based on either a 5,843 cc Austin 40 HP or, possibly, an 8,764 cc 60 HP model which was itself the basis for Austin's 1908 Grand Prix '100 HP' cars, one of which survives at The Heritage Motor Centre at Gaydon. All had four-cylinder engines at a time when S. F. Edge was proving the superiority of six cylinders in his Napiers. Would readers with any information about Pobble contanct Lynette Beardwood on 0171 730 2058?

Sporting Seven

" *In 1932 I purchased for £80 an Austin 7 which rejoiced in the description 'Sportsman's Coupe'. It was different from most Austin 7s as it had no side windows apart from those in the doors. As far as I can remember, the registration began with 'VE'. At the time I was a Frigidaire service engineer and the car had a hard life carrying gas cylinders, electric motors and my tools. Flat-out it did a genuine 45 mph and I became very fond of it. I replaced it after two happy years with a Morris 8, which I in turn replaced with a Vauxhall 14 which had torsion bar suspension and went off bang periodically. I am now 91 and have had all the TRs. The TR2 was my favourite. Quite lethal. I also had a Renown, which was a much under-rated car, and a very disappointing Riley. I am now hooked on reliable Renaults, but can you tell me anything about my first Austin 7?* "

A reader from Totnes has the only known survivor of a Swallow two-seater with its original coupe hard top. But his is a non-standard 1928 model, fitted in 1934 with twin gearboxes for the Lands End Trial and restored in this format. The Austin Seven Owners Club, c/o T. Simkins, 5 Brook Cottages, Riding Lane, Hildenborough, Kent TN11 9LJ, will be able to tell you more. May I also refer you to two books: the 544-page *Austin Seven Source Book* (Purves), price £29.99, and the 221-page *Austin Seven* (Harvey), price £19.99, both from Mill House Books, tel: 01205 270377.

The Wey to success

" *I am renovating a 1930 Austin 16/6 coupe with special Magnet body-work built at Addlestone under the Weymann patent and commissioned by Pass and Joyce, the West End Austin agents. I am familiar with the history of the Weymann system and that it was licensed out to other coach-builders. But what I can't understand is why the body of my car, actually built by Weymann itself at its own works, carries a licence number. It has been suggested that this may be because all Weymann bodies built in the UK were effectively licensed by the original French company. Can any of your readers confirm this?* "

May I refer you to Nick Walker's excellent *A to Z of British Coachbuilders 1919–1960* (ISBN 1-870979-93-1). At the risk of repeating much of what you already know, he tells us: 'Charles Terres Weymann was a Frenchman with a background in aviation. This experience led him to believe that a [car] body should be as light as possible, and at the same time flexible.' He devised a system of an extremely light wood frame over which fabric was tightly stretched. Important components such as seats were mounted directly to the chassis, so the body did not have to bear their weight. And to prevent creaks from the frame as it flexed, the separate sections of it were held together by steel fish-plates at a distance of around 4 mm apart. The Weymann system was announced in France in 1922 and in Britain in 1923. Weymann's initial approach was to appoint licensees rather than set up his own factory as he had done in France. And, to award these licences, he set up a subsidiary named Weymann Motor Body Co. The first sub-licences were awarded to Rover, Chalmer and Hoyer and Elkington, later followed by Cadogan, Gurney Nutting and Windover. In 1925 the company decided to set up its own UK factory, formed as Weymann's Motor Bodies (1925) Ltd, and bought the Cunard company, together with its coachworks in London's Putney High Street. Despite competing with its sub-licensees, the Weymann system was so successful that many more coachbuilders adopted it. Weymann's own output also grew rapidly, necessitating the purchase of the old Bleriot Whippet/Eric Longden factory in Addlestone, coincidentally close to the River Wey and Weybridge.

Autovia

Twin engines

" *Peter Dron has listed production cars with two engines. He did not mention the Riley Autovia – or did this have a doubled-up (four- to eight-cylinder) motor rather than two separate engines?* "

The Autovia had a 2,849 cc overhead valve V8 – effectively two four-cylinder Riley 1.5 litre blocks at 90 degrees, with three camshafts, one operating the inlet valves and the other two the exhaust valves. The ultimate '4 to 8' car was the 1935– 1939 Alfa Romeo 8c-2900 which comprised two four-cylinder blocks in line with twin magnesium-bodied superchargers driven from the centre. A wonderful attempt was made to recreate this car in the form of the Appenine Three Nine, using two Alfa 105 Series 1,991 cc blocks, which appeared at the 1996 Birmingham Motor Show. Sadly, there were insufficient takers and the beautiful prototype was sold by Coys on 15 May 1997 for just £68,813, including buyer's premium. Gordon Thomas, secretary of the Autovia Car Club, later added that I was right to say that the Autovia V8 was based on the concept of two Riley 12/4 engines cast as a single block in V formation. But, sadly, very few parts are interchangeable. Only between 36 and 44 were made in 1937 and 1938, of which possibly twelve survive and seven are roadworthy. The car was the brainchild of Victor Riley who, after failing to convince his board, set up a separate company and employed Charles van Eugen from Lea Francis to develop the car. Gordon Thomas would be grateful for any information or pictures readers can supply – The Autovia Car Club, tel: 01787 237676.

Bean

Has Beans

" *Are there any Hadfield Beans left anywhere? My father took the family on holiday to Somerset in his Hadfield Bean sports tourer in, I believe, 1930. I think that the car had a 3-litre 4-cylinder engine, that the bonnet and wings were finished in British Racing Green and that the body was made of plywood with a black fabric covering. Father used to call it 'the poor man's Bentley'. The cars were made at West Bromwich and I think the registration was XY 7777. The car had a tram-lever handbrake and a crash gearbox gate-change alongside the driver's seat. Father used a strong cord loop to hitch his artificial leg out of the way (he lost his right leg on the Somme) and drove with great spirit using the hand throttle on the steering wheel. How he managed to use the clutch and the foot brake at the same time I don't know, but I do remember him paying half a crown to drive the Bean for four laps around Brooklands. When he died in 1937, the car was sold to a Cranleigh scrap dealer for £5.* "

The Hadfield Bean 14/70 Sports had a 2,297 cc side-valve four-cylinder engine with Ricardo turbulent head that could push it to 70 mph. Gearbox was a four-speeder, brakes were Dewandre servo-assisted, reducing the pedal pressure necessary for a safe stop, so this may have been one of the reasons why your father chose the car. There is a Bean lorry and a 1925 14 HP twin-spark tourer at the Black Country Living Museum, Tipton Road, Dudley DY1 4SQ (information from Dr E. R. Clark, tel: 01902 755262.) The National Motor Museum at Beaulieu has a 1928 Bean 'Short 14'. And there is a Bean Car Club, c/o Gerry Langham on 01628 25387. No examples of the Hadfield Bean 14/70 Sports are known by the club to have survived.

Belsize

The family Belsize

" *Our family's first car was a Belsize. It was a light grey colour and, after two or three years, my father bought a wonderful new accessory for it – a simple, hand-operated windscreen wiper. I have happy memories of being driven along in the dickey seat at the back. Is there anything you can tell us about Belsize cars? Ours was bought in Canterbury and registered 'FN', but I don't remember the number.* "

Belsize grew out of Marshall and Co which was based in Manchester and began making cars in 1900. By 1914 the company employed 1,200 men and was building 50 vehicles a week. Models included a 9 hp, a 15/20 (your family car) and a 14/30 straight eight of which only a few were built. American-style removable wheel rims were a useful feature. Sadly, Belsize collapsed in 1924 with debts of £500,000. An expert on Belsizes is Rodney Fowler, Tithe House, Chelford Road, Knutsford, Cheshire WA16 8LY, tel: 01565 651051, fax: 01565 754204. Colin Chambers of The Belsize Garage of Tunstall

Street, Openshaw, Manchester M11 1FB, tel: 0161 223 0120, is looking for a Belsize to restore.

Father's first car

" *My father had a Belsize Bradshaw 9 HP in the 1920s. Can you tell me anything about it?* "

The Bradshaw was designed by Granfield Bradshaw, had an oil-cooled V-twin engine of between 1,094 and 1,370 cc, and was built from 1921 to 1924. Nick Baldwin tells us it was advertised as 'the no trouble light car', but unfortunately it was anything but and hastened the demise of the old Manchester company, which went into receivership in the mid-1920s. However, your father might have been lucky and got a 10/20 which had the same body but a more reliable four cylinder 1,131cc overhead valve engine.

Bentley

Derby Bentley's history sought

" *I bought a 1931 3.5 litre Bentley, reg. BGF 69, in 1960 in Hove and sold it there two years later. The original colour was grey. It had cable brakes and a straight-through (by then blanked off) exhaust. I believe the body was by Park Ward. Can you throw any light on its history, both before and after my ownership?* "

It could not be a '31. That was the year, sadly, that Bentley went into receivership. Negotiations followed to absorb the company into D. Napier and Son, but these fell through and by 20 November 1931 a syndicate calling itself 'The

British Central Equitable Trust' had acquired the assets of the company. A week later, it was announced that Rolls Royce had purchased Bentley from the Trust, but it was not until April 1932 that W. O. Bentley joined Rolls Royce and plans for a new sporting car were announced. The first of these 'Derby Bentleys', based on the Rolls Royce 20/25, with Vanden Plas open touring bodywork, was not delivered until October 1933, so your car would have to be 1933 or later. Simon Toll (who took over from Bill Port) at the Bentley Driver's Club (01844 208233) had a look in the club's records and confirmed that 10ft 6in chassis B63BL and engine Y6BC were assembled in 1934, fitted with a Park Ward Saloon body, and despatched to H. M. Bentley & Sons of Hanover Court on 26 June 1934 at an invoiced price of £1,100. The car was then sold to its first owner, Kenneth Walker of Knill Court, Kington, Herts at a price of £1,232 14s 9d. 'GF' is a London registration, first issued in March 1930, but it may well have been transferred to your car from an earlier vehicle. The BDC knows no more, apart from that the car was sold in 1971.

Mystery Movie Star

" I bought a 1928 3-litre Mulliner-bodied Bentley saloon on Good Friday, 1964, and still have it. The registration is PN 148 and the chassis number ML 1522. The car was found sharing an orchard with a number of other vehicles which I understood had been rescued from a film company a year or two previously to escape being scrapped. The front wings were painted white, the car was facing a late 1930s Ford Anglia tourer with a registration ending 665, and behind is was a large box van, possibly in the livery of The Salvation Army. Other vehicles rescued from the film company included several Rolls Royce Silver Ghosts, an upright hearse body, the chassis of a B-Type bus and a straight-eight Packard *which had been converted to a breakdown truck bearing the name 'Standish Garage', which I believe was in the Notting Hill area. The Packard had to be moved to extricate the Bentley. I remember some of the spark plugs being removed in order to pour neat petrol into the combustion chambers, then a large 24 volt battery being applied to the 6 volt starter. My Bentley was supplied new by Gaffikin and Wilkinson of Hanover Square and in my ownership has twice been over the Grossglockner Pass (8,212 ft).* **"**

First, a heartfelt thanks to this reader for preserving a six-window Bentley saloon. Far too many lost their bodies (and a piece of history), to be turned into replica Vanden Plas tourers. Does anyone have any idea which film this Bentley could have starred in?

Bitter

Bitter virtues

" *While on holiday during the first week of October in Buxton, Derbyshire, I stayed at a hotel where there was a convention of keen motorists, all driving exotic-looking motor cars badged 'Bitter'. There were about a dozen, in superb condition with luxurious white leather interiors, and one of them displayed a short history inside its screen from which I gathered they are German and that Bitter went out of business some years ago. I have never seen or heard of this make before. Have you?* **"**

Yes. They are based on the Opel Monza, built from 1981 to around 1986, and later models had 6-cylinder engines bored-out to 3,848 cc by Manzel, developing 210 bhp. New, they were extremely expensive for the time at £39,000, which was a lot more than a Jaguar XJS or Mercedes SEC. Only 19 1984/86 RHD 3.9 litre models were officially imported to the UK and

I've only ever seen three at auction. A 58,000-mile 1984 model bid to £11,600 at BCA Measham on 2 August 1994; a 35,000-mile 85C sold for £6,988 including commission at BCA Blackbushe on 12 February 1996; and a 74,000-mile 1986 model bid to £6,000 at BCA Blackbushe on 16 December 1998. The club is: Bitter Owners Club, c/o P. Griffith, Medina Garden Centre, Staplers Road, Wootton, Isle of Wight PO33 4RW, tel: 01983 883430, website: http://www.uk-classic-cars.com/bitter.htm.

Black Prince

Cyclecar conundrum

" *Here is a Mystery Motor photo that stumped Bill Boddy, the readers of* Motor Sport *and even the National Motor Museum at Beaulieu. I'd be really pleased if you could help. It shows my Grandfather and Grandmother with their baby (my mother) in Grandad's first car. My mother was born in 1920 and looks about a year old in the photo. The photo will have been taken near the village of Yalding in Kent.* "

I'm almost 100 per cent certain (and have Nick Baldwin's *A–Z of Cars of the 1920s* to thank) that this is a 'Black Prince' built in small numbers by H. G. Wright & Co of Barnard Castle, County Durham between 1919 and 1924. The wheel size, body shape, squalk-hooter on the running board, fuel cap on the scuttle and starting lever on the side of the bonnet are all an exact match. Engines were single or twin-cylinder Precision or Union 2.75 HP which drove through a two-speed belt or an Albion gear transmission. 'Suspension' was provided by the resilience of the seasoned ash frame.

Bleriot Whippet

Mr Whippet?

" *Looking for interesting old family photos for my daughter's collection I came across a snapshot of my late father in a 1920s cyclecar. When my father and uncles reminisced about this car, I seem to remember them referring to a 'Bleriot Whippet'. Could this be that machine? I would welcome any information you have. Is there any connection with Louis Bleriot who made the first Channel crossing by air in 1908? I believe his 54-year-old grandson is hoping to celebrate the anniversary of this by repeating the feat on 25 July. The progress in aviation seems incredible since those days. But when I compare the performance of my very handsome Citroën Xantia turbodiesel estate with that of my own first cars in the 1950s, I realise there has been progress on the ground too.* "

Yes, the car is a Bleriot Whippet, and you are right about the connection with Louis Bleriot. The French company established a factory at Brooklands and built Bleriot aircraft there until 1916. The company then moved to a new factory in Addlestone, less then two miles away, was renamed the Air Navigation & Engineering Co. Ltd, and began to make AVRO aircraft. Three years later, in 1919, the French Bleriot factory started making a cyclecar designed by English designers Jones and Marchant and initially named after them. But when production commenced in Addlestone in 1920, the cars became 'Bleriot Whippets'. Until 1921 they had pulley and belt 'infinitely variable' transmissions and centrally mounted air-cooled 997 cc Blackburne V-twin engines developing 14 bhp at 2,000 rpm. To keep up with light cars such as the Austin 7, in 1922 they gained chain drive with a reverse gear and, in 1923, shaft drive with a conventional 3-speed gearbox. Altogether, several hundred were made. There's an interesting picture of one, taken from above, on page 44 of Nick Baldwin's *A–Z of Cars of the 1920s*. Nick writes that Eric Longden cars were made in the same factory. When the company went into liquidation in 1928, the factory became the English home of the Weymann coachworks.

Botwood

'Body by Botwoods'

" *I am searching for examples of cars that were either bodied or supplied by Botwoods Ltd of Ipswich (also known as Botwood & Egerton) prior to 1918. Botwoods was started as a coachbuilding firm in 1875, which changed to supply the growing market for car bodies. By 1906 the company letterhead shows that Botwood & Egerton held the sole area wholesale and retail rights for Argyll, De Dion, Gladiator, Darracq, Siddeley, Wolseley and Humber. Botwoods became a subsidiary of Mann Egerton & Co. Ltd in 1918, but continued to trade as Botwoods Ltd until 1983.* "

There is a slightly different account of Botwoods, but much of interest, in Nick Walker's *A-Z of British Coachbuilders 1919–1960* (ISBN 1-870979-93-1). He tells us that the forerunner of Botwood of Ipswich, established on his own account by William Botwood in 1875, was Bennett & Botwood, which is known to have existed before 1861. When William died, his two sons took over and re-named the business W. T. and S. E. Botwood. They took an agency for Gobron Brillie cars and started building cars on imported chassis. Reggie Egerton joined the business in 1902, his brother Hubert having already established Mann Egerton in Norwich. The company started a separate coachbuilding operation known as Botwood & Egerton and it flourished, at one time building batches of bodies for Napier. But in 1910, Reggie fell out with the Botwoods and set up under his own name as Egerton's (Ipswich) Ltd. The Botwoods also formed a company known as Botwoods Ltd. Then, after more problems in 1914, William Botwood left the company. And in 1918, your great grand-father, Samuel, sadly died at the early age of 44. A year later, the company was taken over by Hubert Egerton's firm Mann Egerton, but Botwoods Ltd continued operating under its own name as coachbuilders until the mid-1920s, bodying Sunbeams and Minervas. If any-one can help this piece of personal research, please contact my correspondent Tim Hopes on 01488 658355.

BSA cars

First front-drive BSA?

" I had a front-wheel-drive BSA three-wheeler. It was new in 1929 and I bought it in 1939 in Torquay for £10. It would do 68 mph with the wind behind it on the Bovey straights, and I believe petrol was 2/- a gallon at the time. We went all over the place, mostly Dartmoor, and rode 'four-up' frequently. It had levers on the steering wheel with which I could drive it instead of using the accelerator pedal. I passed my test in Fulham in 1937 after seven lessons at 2/6d a go. I sold the BSA for £16 a couple of years later – I seem to remember it was because petrol rationing came in. Anyway, I came to London and it wasn't a London car. Those were the days: nothing much on the road and police turned a 'blind eye' to us young nurses. "

Yours must have been one of the first, because the BSA three-wheeler was not officially announced until November 1929. It caused a big stir due to advanced features including front-wheel-drive, independent front suspension, and unheard-of three-wheeler luxuries including reverse gear, electric start, full weather protection and an easily removed rear wheel. The original engine was a 1,021 cc Hotchkiss-designed air-cooled overhead-valve V-twin. 68 mph must have been quite exciting. The BSA Front Wheel Drive Club is chaired by Peter Cook, of Two Chimneys, Pinks Hill, Wood Street, Guildford, Surrey GU3 3BW, tel: 01483 570433; Membership Secretary is Barry Baker, 164 Cottimore Lane, Walton-on-Thames, Surrey KT12 2BL, tel: 01932 225270, website: http://members.aol.com/bsafwdc/home.htm.

Brough Superior

A very superior Brough

" *Along with her Christmas card, an old friend advised that the* Banbury Guardian *has reported the discovery of a rare 500 cc Brough Superior motorcycle, found under a tarpaulin following the owner's unexpected death. It was to be auctioned by Sotheby's on 7 December 1998 and was expected to make £6,500. The 1964 book by Ron Clark,* Brough Superior – the Rolls Royce of Motorcycles, *tells me that only nine machines were manufactured at 100 guineas apiece (a huge sum for a 500 cc bike), and of these nine, only three survived. I wonder. The price realised at Sothebys would be of interest. The book also includes a photograph of T. E. Lawrence leaving Brough's Haydn Road works on UL 656, a Brough Superior SS100 in 1929. He later wrote, 'The 100 goes like stink still. All its pristine manners came back to it and it seems to me the best thing I have ever ridden.'* "

As far as I can gather, the Sotheby's Brough failed to sell, but a 1937 990 cc Brough SS100 sold for £38,900 including premium at a Brooks Motorcycle Auction at the Classic Bike Show in

May 1999. Two interesting articles about T. E. Lawrence appeared in a national newspaper and in *The National Geographic* during January 1999. It seems that he owned or borrowed seven Brough Superiors in all, the first in 1922, and covered a total of 299,000 miles on them. UL 656 was not his last SS100. 'Boanerges', the SS100 he was riding on the day of his death, was registered GW 2275. Though 'Boanerges' was capable of 108 mph, the accident was not caused by high speed. On 13 May 1935, Lawrence crested a hill in Dorset at about 40 mph to be confronted by two boys on bicycles. In swerving to miss them, he crashed at an estimated 20 mph, fractured his skull, and died six days later. The motorcycle was then returned to the Brough works and re-sold. Its whereabouts were discovered some 30 years ago and it is currently owned by John Weekly, who would like to sell it to a UK museum (but wants £1,000,000 for it!). Even Lawrence's death was not in vain. Hugh Cairns, the neurosurgeon who tried to save him, was so shocked by the brain damage caused by such a low speed impact that he began a campaign which led to crash helmets becoming compulsory in the UK. This, of course, has saved many thousands of lives.

Four-wheel Broughs

" Can you possibly give some information about the Brough Superior, which was a sporty convertible of the 1930s? I remember being impressed by the built-in hydraulic jacking system. A control in the floor just ahead of the driving seat enabled selection of the wheel to be jacked, and by inserting and pumping a short handle the desired wheel could be raised off the ground. "

Motorcycle manufacturer George Brough's cars were in limited production in Nottingham from 1935 to 1939. Like contemporary Railtons, the first had 4,168 cc side-valve Hudson straight-eight engines delivering an impressive 125 bhp. Later models, such as the Alpine Light Sport, used a supercharged Hudson straight-six. A total of around 75 of both types were built. The company's swansong was the XII with under-slung chassis, handsome Charlsworth body and a 4,387 cc Lincoln V-12 under the bonnet. Charlesworth also build the 'Wentworth' saloon bodywork for the stunning, but ill-fated, Invicta Black Prince.

Bugatti

£75 Bugatti

" *In the summer of 1945 my pal and I (both Army despatch riders in the Royal Corps of Signals) were mooching around Mestre, near Venice, when we came across a Bugatti in a garage yard. The owner wanted to sell it to us for £75, as civilians at the time were desperate for money and food. Our problem was how to scrape together £75 on our Army pay of 24/6d a week, and how to get the car back to the UK. Sadly, we declined, and gave him some cigarettes for his kindness in showing us this beautiful machine. Could you identify the type?* "

Hugh Conway of The Bugatti Trust has identified the Bugatti as a Type 37A 1.5 litre racing model which was similar in most respects to the 2.3 litre 35B. A Type 43 Grand Sport has different bodywork. However, famous Bugatti owner and racer Hamish Moffatt thinks it is a Type 35B or 35C, as the brake drums are correct and this model was sometimes fitted with wire rather than cast alloy wheels. He thinks that the reason for no outside gear lever is that the gearbox and engine had been removed and replaced with more mundane units when the owner found himself unable to repair the originals. The Bugatti Museum at Prescott Hill, Gotherington near Cheltenham, is open to visitors and can be contacted on 01242 677201.

Buick

Amateur photographers

" *In the early 1930s my grandparents took a picture of an accident where the adverse camber of the road had the effect of rolling their car into a field. I believe the car was a 'Marquette'.* "

A photo of the same car, back on all four wheels and now parked outside 'Johnsons 8-hour Snapshot Service', shows signs of the damage sustained. It also shows my correspondent's grandparents, none the worse for their unexpected excursion. The 'Marquette' was a small side-valve 6-cylinder Buick which, according to G. N. Georgano, had more in common with the 1929 Pontiac than with the rest of the Buick range. 13,850 were built in its first year, but during 1930 it was decided to withdraw the model and it ceased to be listed at all early in 1931. This incident shows the benefit of an all-steel body though. Accidents like these were commonplace in Yorkshire and Lincolnshire in the 1930s. My grandad told me that whenever he ended upside down in a field, he simply rolled the car back onto its wheels and drove out through the gate.

Chamberlain

Time for a tractor

" *While on holiday in Western Australia recently, I visited a tractor museum at Whiteman Park, just north of Perth. I was the only visitor and I thought you might be interested in one of the exhibits. It is a Chamberlain, of Australian manufacture and, in order to advertise the marque, a special model was built with longer gearing and a bench seat so that it could be used for three consecutive circumnavigations of the country. I was told that 20 of these tractors are to set out in 2000 to drive straight across Australia from east to west. A contact for the museum is Phil Wyndham, The Tractor Museum of Western Australia, tel: 00619 94573376.* "

This is the kind of thing that gets Nick Baldwin even more excited than the prospect of Lincolnshire pork sausages for breakfast. In fact, he's written a book, *Classic Tractors of the World*, ISBN 0-89658-394-5 (superb photography of unusual vehicles), which includes the Chamberlain story. The tractor in question was a Chamberlain Champion, christened 'Tail End Charlie' for its part in the endurance event. To survive the 10,413 mile distance, the drivers must have been pretty tough, too. They weren't all that slow about it either as the 10,413 miles were covered in just 19 days – a non-stop average of 22.8 mph – and Nick tells us that, with the right gearing, Chamberlains were capable of 65mph.

Cord

Lost Cord

" *I am trying to trace missing parts of the history of my 1937 Cord 812 RHD 4-seater phaeton, reg: FYF 924, chassis no. 1270; engine no. FB 2205;*

body no. C91 645. Also, can anyone tell me anything about RSM (Automobiles) Ltd of 26 Bruton Street, Berkeley Square, London W1 and 6 North Audley Street, Grosvenor Square, who were agents for Auburn cars before WW2? I am particularly interested in import figures for Cords from 1936 to 1937, and any sales records too if they exist. My car was owned until 1949 by a Dr James Sim who lived in Harby Road, Leicester. It was then creamy yellow, but was resprayed black in 1949 at Modern Motors, Wigston Road, Oadby. It was also used as a prop for a photo-shoot of the Beatles in the late 1960s. I would be very grateful for any help anyone can give me. **"**

Would readers with any information please write directly to Barrie Sly, 'Wearhurst', 15 Biddick Lane, Fatfield, Washington, Tyne and Wear NE38 8AB.

Pull the other one

" *In the late 1920s my uncle chauffeurred a long American car which he says had front-wheel drive. What could it have been?* **"**

It was a front-wheel-drive Cord L-29, which preceded the 'coffin bonnet' Cord 810/812 and was Erret L. Cord's first successful front-wheel-drive model. Despite having a solid front axle, an early type of universal joints and a lack of traction on slippery hills, it sold 4,400 between 1929 and 1932 when the Depression killed it off. It had a 125 bhp, 4,934 cc Lycoming straight-eight under that long bonnet. Some were bodied in England by Freestone & Webb, which held a Weymann licence and helped start a fashion for coupes without running boards. There should be a spare wheel between the driver and the front wing. E. L. Cord had bought Auburn in 1924 and Duesenberg in 1926, but the radical L-29 was the first car to bear his own name.

Coventry Premier

Sent to Burma

" *In Burma*, circa *1924, my dad had a car with a two-cylinder engine which he said was a Coventry Premier. We called it 'Chuff Chuff'. I sat on my mother's lap in front and the Punjabi batman was in the dickey together with tins of petrol, oil and water. It boiled regularly climbing the Burma hills. I remember that, when all the reserve water was used up, the batman had to collect water from a stream at the side of the road. The car looked a bit like a Rover 8, though the Rover was air-cooled. Do you have any information on the Coventry Premier?* "

The Coventry Premier was originally a three-wheeled cyclecar. But first it grew a fourth wheel. Then, following a merger with Singer, in place of its water cooled 1,056 cc V-twin (rated at 8 HP), it acquired the Singer 10's 1,097 cc 'four'. Gradually, more and more Singer 10 components were used and it became a cheaper version of the Singer. Oddly enough, there's a picture of an 8 HP, identical to your father's car, stripped down for a 1921 Brooklands 200-mile race on page 381 of Culshaw & Horrobin's *Complete Catalogue of British Cars 1895–1975.*

Crosley (American)

The one-'s' Crosley

" *In 1946–47 I saw a couple of American mini cars called Crosley. With all the enthusiasm of a twelve-year-old, I then collected what little information was available. The Crosley was about the size of a Renault 750 and was a two-door four-seater saloon with a sloping tail, tiny wheels and a four-cylinder 600 cc ohc aluminium engine, with beam axle suspension front and rear. A year or two later I saw a new version, now pathetically complying with automotive convention by adopting a three-box shape.*

Are there any photographs, brochures or road tests? Can one still be found anywhere? **"**

Not to be confused with the English Crossley, the Crosley car was launched in 1939 by Powel Crosley and built in Cincinnati, Ohio. Pre-war versions had a 582 cc aircooled twin. But things started getting really interesting after the war when Crosley started using 722 cc four-cylinder water-cooled COBRA engines, originally developed for the US Navy. It was fabricated of oven-brazed copper and sheet steel and, according to a period advertisement, developed 'up to 26.5 bhp'. The ad gave a length of 145 in, a width of 49 in, a wheelbase of 80 in, a weight (with full petrol tank) of 1,155 lbs and a cruising speed of 50 mph. At least six body styles were offered: 'woody' station wagon, four-seat roll-top convertible, four-seat fastback sedan, pick-up, panel delivery van and sport utility. For reasons of reliability Crosley replaced the fabricated engine with the cast iron CIBA engine in 1949 and launched the famous 'Hotshot' roadster which out-performed MGTCs and even boasted Goodyear disc brakes. Production continued until 1952. Because Crosley bodies were small and light, many were used for 'Altereds' (a type of dragster) in the 1950s and 60s. A good mailorder bookshop such as Mill House Books (tel: 01205 270377, email: MHBooks2@aol.co) should be able to offer you a copy of *Crosley and Crosley Specials*, which is a Brooklands Books compilation of old magazine articles and costs £9.95. Many years later Lloyd Taylor and Ted Tyce revived the concept of the fabricated engine with a twin-cam version, designed primarily for powerboats, and standard performance of the 2,212 cc version was 175 bhp at 6,500 rpm. You'll find a full technical article about this in *Hot Rod* magazine, December 1961. Your best bet for old magazines such as *Hot Rod* is Autobooks of Ditchling, tel: 01273 84500.

Crossley (English)

Crossley recalled

" *I have nostalgic memories of my father's first car – a Crossley 25/30, the body of which was built for a Glasgow Motor Show of 1920/21 by a firm Halstead of Kings Heath, Birmingham. It was a huge beastie, registration OE 5025, coloured dark blue, nominally a five-seater with a four-speed gate-change gear lever on the right of the driver and the accelerator pedal between the enormous rubber-covered clutch and brake pedals (rear-wheel brakes only). It had an 18 gallon tank situated under the rear tonneau and a rack which could carry one or two custom-built luggage trunks when required. My father's car was enhanced by a horrible looking serpent bulb horn whose open fanged mouth was supported on the right front wing. In place of the normal wire-spoked wheels it was fitted with coned discs which, to my mind, spoiled its appearance. It had a canvas hood of inordinate ugliness when raised and it took two of us to do the job. It had a four-cylinder engine with massive cast iron pistons and sported, I believe, a C.A.V. electric lighting system of two headlights and two minute sidelights also situated on the front wings. Its radiator was, of course, distinctive, but my most abiding memory was of a horrendous return journey from Liverpool to Birmingham, beset by a series of punctures. These necessitated slow progress from Talke (near Stoke-on-Trent) and we finally arrived at Lichfield long after midnight with one inner tube completely destroyed and the outer tyre cover stuffed with grass (believe it or not), to spend the remainder of the night at a local hotel when we should have been home long since. Those tyres seemed to have been the largest ever fitted to a touring car. I was then ten or eleven years old. Unfortunately I have no photographs of this monster, but thought you might be interested in telling us a little more about this Manchester-built job.* "

The 25/30 was descended from the 20/25 of First World War staff car and Royal Flying Corps tender fame. It had a 4,530 cc – and later 4,950 cc – four-cylinder sidevalve engine, cone clutch, spiral bevel rear axle and threequarter elliptic rear springs which gave a comfortable ride and led to it being favoured by royalty. The wheels were probably wires covered with discs and those discs certainly would not have helped with the puncture repairs. You're right about the tyre size. I've seen the name Halstead, but it does not feature in Nick Walker's *A-Z of Coachbuilders*, so I'm wondering where I did see it. There is a Crossley Register, c/o Malcolm Jenner, Willow Cottage, Lexham Road, Great Dunham, Kings Lynn, Norfolk PE32 2LS, tel: 01328 701240.

Crouch

Why walk when you can Crouch?

" *75 years after the event I am wondering why my parents used to refer to their first car as 'The Crouch'. Was this a nickname due to its small size? I remember there was a seat at the back beyond the hood in what they called 'The Dicky'. This is where I had to sit. My grandsons are interested and would like to know if you can help.* "

Yes, it is a Crouch 8/18 of the period 1919 to 1923. The Crouch family of Cook Street, Coventry, built around 400 three- and four-wheeled, mid-engined Crouch Carettes before the First World War. After the war, the four-wheeler was revived, first as the 8 HP with the same mid-mounted V-twin motor of 1,115 cc, later growing to the front-mounted longer-stroke 1,248 cc 8/18. As far as I can gather, post-war 8s and 8/18s had the slope-front radiator of your parent's car, while earlier Carettes and later Crouch models had a square profile, beaded-edge radiator. They were comparatively quiet, refined and well built cars for the period. Front-engined four-cylinder models followed the 8/18, and Stirling Moss's father, Alfred, had some success at Brooklands in a 90 mph Anzani-engined Crouch 12. After a business failure in Australia, the company folded in 1927, having built a total of between 2,000 and 3,000 cars.

Daimler-Benz

Manchester's first motor

" *I feel sure you will be interested in the first motor vehicle in Manchester, delivered by my late partner's grandfather and his father, Mr Arthur J. Cotton, who described the journey as follows: 'It was in 1897. I was only 14 at the time and had just started work with my father who was manager of a Manchester firm of carriers. The firm decided to buy a motor car, and my father and I went to Coventry to fetch it. We had never seen one before and the chief engineer of the firm of makers gave us a few lessons in driving. From the moment we set off on our journey to Manchester to the moment of our arrival we were beset with hostile crowds and some people went so far as to throw stones at us. They didn't seem to like the contraption at all and thought it was fraught with the gravest dangers to them. It took us three days and three nights to cover the 100 miles.' Unfortunately we do not know the make of the vehicle, but it may possibly be a Daimler.* "

You're right. Nick Georgano describes the vehicle in some detail in his *Complete Encyclopaedia of Commercial Vehicles*: 'Though the Daimler parcels van driven by J. S. Crichley in the Emancipation run of November 1896 was an imported vehicle, the Coventry-Daimler concern had such a model available early in 1897. It had a 4 HP vertical-twin engine, tube ignition, three-speed gearbox with horizontal dial-type selector, and side chain drive.' Sutton & Co. and the brave Cotton father and son are to be congratulated on their foresight in the face of such hostility from the mob and the idiot populist politicians of the day.

Darracq

Back from the saw bench

" *As early as 1900, Alexandre Darracq laid down a production run of 1,200 cars – a staggering figure for those days. He had recognised that motoring was only going to be really popular if cars were comparatively cheap. The early 6.5 HP model was improved in mid-1901. From the known engine numbers, probably less than 1,000 6.5 HP cars were built and around a dozen survive today. It may cheer some of your readers to see our restoration of a 1901 'improved'-model Darracq (dated by the Veteran Car Club). It had been in a French farmyard and, after being used as a tractor, the final indignity was being jacked up to drive a saw bench by means of a strap round the back wheel.* "

The more letters that come in, the more I learn, and I have been struck by the immense importance of Darracq in the development of the European motor car. Just as in the USA Ransom E. Olds predated Henry Ford in series-producing motor cars, Darracq pre-dated Renault, Austin, Morris, Rover and the rest in Europe. 'Genevieve' wasn't just an eccentric one-off; she represented the leading edge in popular car design in the early 1900s.

Day-Leeds

In the family Day

" *My name is Day and I believe that my great grandfather, Job Day, built a car by the name of the Day-Leeds. The only information I have is from page 119 of Culshaw & Horrobin's Complete Catalogue of British Cars. This tells me that four models were built between 1912 and 1924: an 8.9 HP and three 10 HP types. Do you have any more information about these cars and, even better, do you know if there are any still in existence?* "

Nick Georgano confirms that automatic tea packing machinery manufacturers Job Day & Sons of Leeds began to make motor cycles in 1912, and the two-cylinder 8.9 HP cyclecar the following year. But this was soon replaced by the four-cylinder 10 HP, first with Turner engines and later with four-cylinder side-valve engines of Day's own design. Capacities were 1,286 cc, 1,131 cc and 1,266 cc, all with a stroke of 100 mm. The cars were reliable and usually carried either open two-seater or coupe bodies built by Lockwood & Clarkson of Leeds. Prices rose from £195 in 1915 to £500 in 1920, but would have had to fall again soon after, along with the rest of the market. As far as I know there are none in any UK museums, but readers might come forward with the whereabouts of any survivors.

De Dion

Third car in Worcester

" *A family photograph shows Mr and Mrs Edward Worth (my great-uncle and aunt) and family of Rodborough, Stroud, in the third car to be registered in Worcestershire. AB 1 was owned by Lord Dudley, and AB 2 by Mr Roland Worth (another great-uncle). From the ages of the children, the year seems likely to be 1904. We should be interested if you would identify the type of car and see if it corresponds with our date. Does anybody know what happened to the car?* "

Almost inevitably the car is a De Dion Bouton, the most numerous of all veteran cars mainly because the French had the good sense to mass-produce horseless carriages while the British were still throwing stones at them. The Veteran Car Club of great Britain should be able to tell you what happened to AB 3. Speak to Margaret Golding, Jessamine Court, 15 High Street, Ashwell, Hertfordshire SG7 5NL, tel: 01462 742818.

Deemster

Anyone got a Deemster engine?

" *Crazily, at 64 years of age, I am starting the most difficult resurrection of a vintage car that I have ever tackled. The car is a Deemster 10 HP, made in 1919. I was wondering if any of your readers can supply any information about, or the source of, an original Deemster 62 mm bore x 90 mm stroke engine or parts. Any help, no matter where in the world, would be welcome, and I will arrange to collect all the parts. I hope your readers will be able to assist in this worthwhile project.* "

The Deemster 10 hp was launched by the Ogden Motor Co. Ltd of Acton, West London, in 1914 and, of course, timing was not on its side. It was re-launched after the First World War in 1919. Deemster made its own 4-cylinder 1,086 cc engines which apparently had good low-speed pulling power and, since the car was light, its three-speed gearbox did not handicap it unduly. Like the contemporary Morris Cowley, it had a 'bullnose' radiator but five-stud rather than three-stud artillery wheels. One of these cars, fenderless and fitted with wire wheels, was entered for a Brooklands 200-mile race in 1921. There had been plans to transfer production to the USA, but they fell through. If anyone has any Deemster parts or knows where any might be, please telephone my correspondent G. K. Hadfield on 01827 373466.

Delage

£125 Delage

" In 1949 a group of school friends purchased a 1931 Delage D6 saloon, registration GT 4819, for £125 from Deep Mill Filling Station, Great Missenden, Bucks. After a very happy association, we parted company from 'Janine' (as we had named her) in the early 1950s to University Motors of Stratton Street, London W1. The group of friends re-established contact four years ago, and now meets annually for a 'reminiscence lunch'. We know nothing of the car's history prior to our ownership or since. Is there anyone out there who can fill us in? "

The Delage Club, a subsection of the VSCC, will be able to tell you if the car is in a member's hands and, even if not, may have some information. The secretary is Peter Jacobs of 'Cloud's Reach', The Scop, Almondsbury, S. Gloucs BS12 4DU. Or perhaps some of our readers may know.

DFP

Bentley connection

" I am compiling details of all the cars we have had in our family and need some help. Prior to a Humber coupe, which I remember in 1926, my *father owned a DFP. I think it was French, but I would appreciate any information and, if possible, where I might find a photo or drawing.* "

The intitials stand for Doriot, Flandrin and Parant, and there is a photograph of a 1924 12 HP DFP tourer in Georgano's *Complete Encyclopaedia of Motorcars*, if you can find a copy. Doriot and Flandrin had worked for both Clement-Bayard and Peugeot, and built voiturettes until Parant arrived on the scene. They then progressed to larger 2.4 litre and 2.8 litre fours, a 25/30 HP six and a very successful 1.6 litre 10/12 four. W. O. and H. M. Bentley had the UK concession for these cars and ran the later 10/15 in competition with some success. A sporting 2.0 litre 12/40 arrived in 1914 and Bentley persuaded the company to fit aluminium pistons which pulled the top speed up to 65 mph. W. O. Bentley finished 6th in the 1914 TT in one of these. Then, of course, the First World War intervened and, after W. O. Bentley set up as a manufacturer in his own right in 1919, DFP lost its biggest export market. Also, by then, the price of the 12/15 had risen from £290 in 1914 to £675. The company lasted until 1926, when it was taken over by Lafitte.

Ford

Follow the van

" *Our company, which supplies frying oil and batter flours to fish and chip shops, celebrated its centenary in 1999. After having a Model T van and a Model A van, the company purchased a Model BB van, registered XJ 4061, in 1932. This remained the backbone of our fleet until 1952 and stories relating to the old BB are something of a company legend. It was a black morning when XJ 4061 was finally consigned to the scrapman. However, true to form, it escaped and was seen that same afternoon disappearing down Queens Road with four fairground trailers in tow and our striking 'VAW' logo still on display. We have a 'flatnose' Morris Cowley 14/28 van. But we would dearly like to find and restore XJ 4061 if, indeed, there is anything left to restore. Do any of your readers know if the old Ford BB van survived?* **"**

Carter's Steam Fair still operates a Ford AA van, but not a BB. Ray Mullard of Guildford is also trying to find an old Ford van, this one a car-based Model A, with Berkshire reg. RX 7011, in which he travelled through most of Berkshire, Oxfordshire, Hanmpshire and Wiltshire erecting combine harvesters and grain dryers and repairing farm machinery. Anyone with any news on these vans please call Tony Rogers on 01706 364211 or Ray Mullard on 01483 235678.

Is the Pilot extinct?

" *The Ford Pilot was a majestic looking car and it always held a fascination for me. The father of a friend had one in the early fifties and I occasionally went for a ride in it, but was never allowed to drive. In later years, I have watched the specialist press, but have never seen one advertised. Nor have I seen one mentioned in your columns. Is the model extinct? If not, where can I buy one?* **"**

It's rare, but not extinct. They occasionally crop up at auction. Brooks sold one in May 1998 for £6,882 and Parkes sold one on which £10,000 had been lavished in June for £5,294. The car was basically the pre-war 'European' 20 HP V-8, in production from 1947 to 1951, with a 'retro' front and a proper 30 HP 3,622 cc sidevalve V-8 under its bonnet. 22,155 were built, but, sadly, they proved to be ideal 'stock cars' and many MOT failures ended their days on the oval cinder track. More recently, Pilots in poor condition have been cannibalised to build 'retro' hot rods. You should take a look at *Multicylinder*, the magazine of the Pre-'50 American Auto Club which incorporates the Ford V-8 register. To get the magazine, you'll have to join the club, c/o Mike Sandy, 38 Knightwood Road, Hythe, Southampton SO45 6JL, tel: 01703 849685. Ginger Dann of D & M Autos, Wokingham (0118 973 0711) is a Pilot enthusiast with a 1950 saloon and a very rare 1951 Pilot panel van. He has also built a Pilot 'stretch' limousine, knows the cars inside out, and offers to help anyone interested in V8 Pilots. The Early Ford V8 Club of America is represented in the UK by Chris Sanders, 12 Fairholme Gardens, Cranham, Upminster, Essex RM14 1HJ.

Frazer Nash

Jenks's Frazer-Nash

" *I took a photograph of a 'chain gang' Frazer-Nash for the late, great Dennis Jenkinson in 1945 and, as far as I know, it was the first four-wheeler he ever owned. Even in those days he was a great archivist and insisted on having a photograph of every motorcycle or car he owned. I just happened to be the nearest photographer and had helped to finance it by buying his very nice Norton. Alas, Jenks was always short of money and soon reverted back to two wheels, but I wonder what became of the car.* "

Dennis Jenkinson's Frazer-Nash Archives live on at Coxon House, Newton Road, Henley-on-Thames, Oxon RG9 1HG, tel: 01491 411491. This is actually a Toyota franchise, but the records are kept there and messages are soon passed on – as I discovered when none other than John Aldington returned my call. YG 2122 is four-cylinder and Meadows-engined, and was built for Alan Marshall, of Wilkinsons Liquorice

Allsorts and Pontefract Cake fame, who was an active trials campaigner. Dennis Jenkinson owned it from 1945 to 1946 and sold it to Charles Bulmer, who kept it until 1951. It's still around, still in the capable hands of a Frazer-Nash Owners Club member and still being used for the purpose for which it was built. Any snippets of information about GN, Frazer-Nash and HRG will be welcomed by the Archives.

Goliath

Early German Alfasud

" *I was very interested in Kevin Ash's article in the* Telegraph *on the Bimota bike, and in particular its twin-cylinder direct-injected two-stroke engine. However, this was not the first two-stroke to employ direct injection, as Borgward in the early 1950s developed a similar system for their vertical twin Goliath 700E and 900E saloon cars. The Bosch mechanical fuel injection system injects direct into the cylinders at a pressure of some 40 ATH (560 lbs/sq in). The oiling system uses a separate Bosch pump mounted on the injection pump and drip feeding oil into the air intake as well as lubricating the injection pump. As I own the only RHD Goliath 900E known to survive, I can confirm the need for accurate setting-up of this type of injection system. The petrol is injected at BDC and the ignition timing is critical.* "

Borgward later developed a flat-four 1,093 cc four-stroke engine for a model variously known as the Goliath or the Hansa. Lloyd cars were also build by Borgward in Bremen during the same period, and later Lloyds had a smaller 897 cc version of the four-stroke flat-four (Revell now do a 1:18 scale die cast model of the 25 bhp Lloyd Alexander TS, price £22.99). A reader from Hazel Grove then sent further information derived from a 1950s World Car Catalogue, which tells us that saloon versions of these flat-four front-drive cars developed 40 bhp at 4,250 rpm and had a usefully flat torque curve. 'Full use of the synchronised four-speed gear-box makes it possible to obtain astonishingly high average speeds even with a full load of passengers, and on mountain roads the car reveals its best feature, inasmuch as it can be accelerated painlessly from the lower gears.' The tester also found it to have 'excellent road-holding qualities' with 'remarkably light steering'. Top speed was 80 mph, 0–50 mph in 15.5 seconds; 0–100 kph (62 mph) in 24.8 seconds; and 0–75mph in 39.8 seconds. Average fuel consumption was 36.2 mpg. The coupe version developed an extra 15 bhp and did 84 mph, bringing it even closer to the concept of the 1,186 cc, 73 bhp, 90 mph Alfasud of 1972.

Hillman

Aero Minx

" *Can you tell me anything of the history of the little Hillman Aerominx two-seater coupe which I bought for £155 in Birmingham in about 1935? I never saw more than one other. How many were made, for example? And what was the cost new?* "

The National Motor Museum at Beaulieu charged £4.10 for the information that 649 Aero Minxes in total were built at a price of £245 each. Nick Walker's *A–Z of British Coachbuilders 1919–1960* (Bay View Books) showed that this reader's car was a 1933 Aero Minx coupe designed by Freddy March, heir to the Duke of Richmond and Gordon, and was built either by Carbodies or by Compton's Ditton in 1933 only. A reader from of Leominster, an expert in all things Humber and Hillman, came up with information from a register which he ran in the 1970s. Aero Minx chassis numbers were: (1933) AM100 onwards; (1934) AM 18150 onwards, but not in regular sequence; and (1935) AM 19001 onwards, again not in regular sequence. He thinks that total production of Aero Minx Saloons, coupes and roadsters was less than 500. The cars competed successfully in road trials such as the MCC London–Exeter, London– Edinburgh and London–Land's End, and also appeared in relay races at Brooklands where, apparently, they 'had the legs of the smaller MGs'. By the late 1970s the Aero Minx register (now moriibund) listed five March coupes, 18 Sports Tourers, four drophead coupes, three Cresta saloons and three open two-seaters.

Honda

Zzzzzzzs

" *Your recent review of modern microcars reminds me of a Honda 'Z' which I owned in the early 1970s. It had a lively 600 cc engine which I think was air-cooled, and the only colour available was bright orange. Do other readers remember this model, which I think was Honda's first move into cars in the UK?* "

Honda's first car exported to the UK was the S800 coupe and roadster from 1965–1970, which is fondly remembered for its 70 bhp at a then-incredible 8,000 rpm. The N360/N600, a Mini-sized four-seater, followed from 1966–1974. The 45 bhp N600 was good for 80 mph – as a friend of mine, who had one in the 1960s, delighted in proving. The 'Z', with the same 598 cc air-cooled twin as the 600, followed, and lasted from 1970 to 1975. They suffer badly from tinworm, but there are still a few about in the hands of enthusiasts. Honda's microcars were killed off with the advent of the Civic in 1972, which set new standards of refinement for its class.

Horstman

Not as German as it sounds

" Although I am now 87 years old I still have a keen interest in cars, particularly the Classics. I remember, as a boy, being driven in a two-seater open car which I think was a Horstman. It had a kick-start in the cabin. Was there such a car? "

Sidney Horstmann came from a clock-making family which had resided in Britain for many generations. He began building cars in James Street West, Bath, just before the First World War broke out, and quickly changed his name to 'Horstman'. Historians note the cars as having been 'interesting' and 'including all manner of eccentricities'. That explains the kick-start, which was a pedal acting on an Archimedes screw. There was no chassis forward of the fly-wheel and the front suspension was slung from an aluminium casting which formed the engine sump. The gearbox was incorporated into the rear axle. Several versions were built, the most powerful available with a supercharger, but by that time the kick-start was a thing of the past.

Hotchkiss

Seven stay hot in Hotchkiss

" On his return from Burma in 1930, my father imported a seven-seater Hotchkiss convertible from France. We spent six magical months in

Barton-on-Sea, exploring the New Forest and visiting Southampton to see the magnificent ocean liners. We used to dare father to dash through the Ford at Brockenhurst with the top up and the sidescreens on. And we used to egg him on to overtake long queues of cars making their way back to London after a Sunday at the seaside. The car had a QQ number because, to avoid paying duty, Daddy never registered the car in Britain. Sadly, for the same reason, he had to take it back to France within 12 months. Those were heavenly days. Safe for children, young girls and old people, and we had no need for locks on the car or even the house. We danced for Amy Johnson when she visited Bournemouth after her triumphal flight. "

These Hotchkiss AM80s with their six-cylinder ohv 3,015cc engines were reckoned to be well-nigh indestructible, so there is a chance that, if it survived being requisitioned by the Germans during the Second World War, this car may still be around. Unfortunately, the temporary QQ registration won't help to find it.

'Hot-kisser'

" Could your readers help me trace PO 9877? This was a 1929 Hotchkiss I purchased from a family in the Hampton Court/Shepperton area which gave me great service during my youth in the mid-1950s. It had a four-seater open tourer body and four-cylinder engine of about two litres. Though I joined the VSCC, I never found out much more about it. What I can say is that it held its own very gamely against the Healey 100/4s and TR2s owned by my more affluent friends. The main problem was stopping it, because its drum brakes were rod operated in compression and, understandably, the rods used to bend. Eventually the magneto packed up, I couldn't obtain a replacement, and the car had to go. "

Your car was a 2.5 litre Type AM2, generally regarded as an excellent fast tourer of the day. Pity it wasn't the 3.0 litre six-cylinder AM80 which joined the Hotchkiss line-up in 1928, as this car had an exceptionally smooth seven bearing ohv engine with vibration damper, and both suspension and brakes were rated as very good. The AM80 grew into the AM80S, then the 620, then the 686, and had an excellent rally career winning the Monte Carlo in 1932, 1933, 1934 and 1939. You might be able to trace PO 9877 through the British Hotchkiss Society, Hon. Sec. Michael Edwards, 'Wooton Tops', Sandy Lane, Boars Hill, Oxford OX1 5HN.

Hudson

Supercharged Antipodean

" *Can you help identify a car seen in Australia at a classic car rally in Melbourne? The triangular badge is not an Alvis triangle and the machinery between the dumb irons is nothing like a Bentley blower. The whole thing was quite enormous, but very professional, and clearly not some backyard job. I thought I was quite auto literate, but it is a mystery to me. Someone must know.* "

The car you describe is a Hudson Super Six, dating from from between 1916 and 1926, and the engine was a 4.5 litre high-compression side-valver, successful in long-distance trials and even coming 9th in the 1919 Indianapolis 500. Hudson sixes continued from 1927–29, after which manufacture was confined to 'Essex' models and all Hudsons had eight cylinders. The supercharger is a Rootes-type Amhurst Villiers device similar to that fitted to 'blower' Bentleys, but with downdraught carburettors instead of SUs. It's a beautiful installation and the finned alloy casting provided a degree of 'charge cooling'. This Hudson is a famous car. There is a tradition of Australians radically modifying vintage motors. In 1928, John

'Jumbo' Goddard bought a standard 3-litre Bentley. By 1973 it sported a twin turbocharged 500 bhp 8 litre Bentley engine, and was timed at Ghent in 1973 at 158.2 mph.

Terror-plane

" As a life-long car enthusiast I am intrigued to know more about a car I recently saw parked in Sutton-on-Sea, Lincolnshire. It was badged, 'Terraplane', and in design smacks of 1940s America with a bulbous radiator grille, encased spare wheel on each front wing, and a flat, one-piece rear end. The car was registered ADF 463. Could you enlighten me about this hitherto unknown manufacturer? "

The Terraplane gradually replaced the Essex as Hudson's low-cost line between 1932 and 1934, running through to 1937. It began with a conventional 2.6 litre side-valve straight-six and three-speed gearbox, would do 70 mph, and sold for £295 in the UK. A 4 litre straight-eight side-valver with 94 bhp followed in 1933, was good for 85 mph, and formed the basis of Railton cars built at Cobham in Surrey. 1934 Terraplanes had a choice of 3.5 litre or 2.6 litre Hudson straight sixes. Hydraulic brakes arrived in 1936. But the model name was dropped in 1937, becoming simply the Hudson 112. Several body-shapes were available, mostly characterised by a very heavy rear overhang.

Humber

Very old Humbers

" I have a photograph of a car, which I think was a Humber, taken in 1920 or 1921 at either Meols or Hoylake on the Wirral. Could you tell me *anything about the make of car and whether it is likely to have survived? The registration was FM 856.* "

I thought at first the car was a Humber 15.9, built from 1919 to 1925, though the frameless windscreen and the shape of the sidelamps suggest it might have been an earlier '14' built between 1914 and 1919 – quite an advanced car in its day despite the First World War interrupting development. Stewart Thorpe of The Humber Register has kindly offered to help readers trace what happened to any pre-1933 Humber they may once have owned. No less than 750 of these cars and motorcycles still exist in enthusiast ownership throughout the world. Stewrat's telephone number is 01270 522422, but please remember, this is only for pre-1933 Humber cars and motorcycles, not for later Humber models. The Pre-1933 Humber Register itself is run by A. Demaus, The Hop House, Stagbatch Farm, Leominster, Herefordshire HR6 9DA.

Jaguar SS

SS cars were re-named Jaguar after the Second World War, for obvious reasons. Letters to do with the marque are listed under *SS*.

Jensen

Jensen-Ford

" *The news that the Jensen marque is to be revived reminds me that my first car purchased in 1958 for £40 was a 1937 Jensen 4.25 litre saloon with aluminium body and wire wheels. But it had been fitted with a Ford V8 engine which had no radiator fan, so every few miles it boiled over. It gave 19 mpg, but at more than four bob a gallon this proved an expensive luxury for a student, so I sold it six months later.* **"**

The July 1998 issue of *Practical Classics* magazine includes a fascinating six-page history of the marque and its other projects, such as the Austin A40 Sports, the Volvo P1800 and the Sunbeam Tiger. Your car may have been an 'H'-type 4.25 litre, the bonnet of which usually covered a 16-plug 4,200 cc 120 bhp Nash straight-eight (Lincoln Zephyr flathead V-12s were also fitted to this model). But it's more likely to have been an 'S'-type, which ran a standard 3,622 cc Ford V-8 with special heads and twin SU carburettors which also put out 120 bhp. It should have had Dewandre servo-assisted brakes and a Columbia two-speed back axle, giving six forward speeds.

541

" *A friend recently sent me a print of a Jensen I once owned, taken at a picnic site in Norfolk around 1960. I can't remember much about it except that it was built in the 1950s, had a lorry engine with three carburettors, and that the door locks used to freeze up in winter. Can you tell me what model it was? I have heard that later Jensens were fitted with Chrysler engines.* **"**

Bob Stoddart of Hexham, Northumberland, had one of these for sale, so I phoned him to check the details. The 541 was launched at the Motor Show in 1953, (1954 model year, Series 1) with a very attractive fibreglass GT body, Austin 'A135' 3,993 cc triple-carb ohv engine (derived from the engine in the Austin K Series truck), overdrive gearbox, aerodynamic front radiator flap and 115 mph top speed. Jensen built 226 of these, followed by 193 541Rs – now up to 150 bhp with a 123 mph capability, disc brakes and still with the radiator flap. The last six-cylinder Jensen was the begrilled 541S of 1960–63, of which 127 were built, and these were followed by the Chrysler V-8-powered CV8 Mks I, II and III, of which 68, 250 and 181 were built. Jensen then went over to the steel-bodied Interceptors. Anyone interested in Bob's red 1955 541, chassis number 541 585633, should call him on 01434 604221. It's a regular runner and, when we spoke, he had just returned from a trip to Edinburgh in it. Spares for fibreglass-bodied C-V8s, 541s and earlier Jensens are available from Copredey Bridge Garage, near Banbury, tel: 01295 758444. Spares for steel-bodied 1960s and 1970s Interceptors and Jensen Healeys are supplied by Martin Robey, tel: 01203 641951. The two clubs are: Jensen Owners Club, c/o Keith Andrews on 01625 525699; and The Jensen Club, c/o Caroline Clarke on 01296 614072.

Kelvin

Any Kelvins out there?

" I have a photocopy of the only leaflet, in Spanish, known to be in existence for the Kelvin car. Fourteen or fifteen were built between May 1904 and the end of 1906 and, apparently, none were sent abroad. The car's engine was later developed into a marine engine – a job it was particularly well suited to, running on both petrol and paraffin – and they were installed in thousands of fishing boats. Did any Kelvin cars survive? "

Nick Georgano printed the same picture, courtesy of the Museum of Transport, Glasgow, in his 1968 *Encyclopaedia of Motorcars*. He tells us they were built by the Walter Bergius Car &

Engine Company of Glasgow, which was still in business manufacturing Kelvin marine engines in the late 1980s. Though Georgano tells us that 'an unusual feature was the use of solid tyres', your leaflet lists these as two of four tyre options which determined the retail price of the car. With solid 810 x 65 tyres front and 810 x 80 rear, it was £370; with 810 x 90 pneumatic tyres, it was £380; with 'Sirdar' solid tyres 870 x 65 front and 870 x 80 rear, it was £382; and with 'Ducasble' cushioned tyres 810 x 90, it was £385. The four-cylinder engine had a bore and stroke of 90 x 121 mm and developed 16 HP at 950 rpm. Alastair Smith, curator of the Glasgow Museum of Transport (coincidentally situated in Kelvin Hall) knew of none in existence, but was very interested to receive a photocopy of the Spanish leaflet.

King Dick

King Dick?

" *A friend of mine during my youth in the 1950s told me that his father had owned a 'King Dick' car in the 1920s. Could this have been true, or was he pulling my leg?* "

Automobile historian David Culshaw wrote to tell us that the reader was 'almost certainly referring to the Abingdon car. This Birmingham company produced various tools after the cessation of car manufacture, and the "Abingdon King Dick" range of spanners is well known'. Apparently an Abingdon King Dick is a pedigree breed of bulldog, which features in the company's advertising. The Abingdon is mentioned briefly on page 462 of Culshaw & Horrobin's *Complete Catalogue of British Cars* (ISBN 1-874105-93-6), where we are told it was a 1,496 cc 11.9 HP Dorman-engined light car, built during 1922/23. The Abingdon also appears with an illustration on page 14 of Nick Baldwin's *A–Z of Cars of the 1920s* (ISBN 1-870979-53-2). Subsequently Griff Roberts wrote to tell us that he is the managing director of Abingdon King Dick, which still produces a wide range of ratchet spanners, socket tools, torque wrenches and screwdrivers at its factory at Unit 11, Roman Way, Coleshill Industrial Estate, Birmingham B46 1HG, tel: 01675 467776; email: info@kingdicktools.co.uk.

La Buire

Museum piece

" *I recently discovered a photograph taken shortly after the First World War either in Cardiff or Caerphilly. It shows my late father at the wheel of a car he chauffeured for a titled person in Glamorgan. What we would like to know is the make and model of the car and any of its history. I think I can recall my father telling me it was a Darracq.* **"**

I used a magnifying glass to scrutinise the radiator badge in the photo that accompanied this letter, and I was able to decipher something I thought looked like 'BUTRA' or 'GUIRE', plus the words 'AUTOS' and 'LYON'. Then, because I was filming at The National Motor Museum, Beaulieu, I took the photo along to see if the archivists could identify the car. It didn't take them long. It's a LA BUIRE, built in Lyons probably between 1912 and 1913, and certainly not after the First World War, by which time the radiator shape had changed to a 'V'. The museum charges a research fee of £15 an hour, £10 for simple mail/fax enquiries, and £7.50 a day for personal callers to use its facilities. Please always include a stamped addressed envelope with anything you send to: Reference Library, The National Motor Museum, Beaulieu, Hants SO42 7ZN, tel: 01590 612345, fax: 01590 612655.

Lagonda

Lovely Lagonda

" *More than 35 years ago, I bought a 1930 Lagonda 2.0 litre Speed model from a man in Derby. It was completely dismantled, crankshaft out, not a nut on a bolt. I was told that this 'kit' had passed through a number of hands in that state. The log-book (reg: GJ 5890) was duly returned to London where it was promptly lost. I therefore never had a list of previous owners. However, I do remember that one owner's address was (Something) Hall, Loughborough. Does anyone remember this car?* **"**

'GJ' is a London registration, current between May and July 1930, but records have been destroyed. Can anyone help? I'll pass the information on to my correspondent, who deserves it after all that work.

Lagonda diesel

" *I have a 1936 Lagonda LG45 saloon, reg. NRL 633, which I am planning to restore. The car has not been used for the past 30 years and I enclose a letter, dated 7 March 1967, from a Mr H. Oswell of Acomb House, Hexham, Northumberland, who originally installed the car's Gardner 4LK diesel engine. I have not been able to trace Mr Oswell and would be very grateful if anyone who knew him or the car could get in touch with me by telephoning 01344 622972.* "

This is more than usually interesting to me because I lived in Hexham, Northumberland, during the 1960s, but don't remember the car. There was a superb scrapyard in Acomb (pronounced 'Yeckum') near Hexham, owed by the excellent Edward Heslop (known as 'Shire Ted'), which contained a lot of kit like this in the 1950s and 1960s. H. Oswell's fascinating letter (slightly edited) reads:

'I originally constructed this car in 1949/50, and the Gardner engine was first put in a 1934 Lagonda M45. In 1957 the M45 chassis was giving trouble and so I fitted it into a 1936 LG45. I sold it about two years later and must have done the best part of 200,000 miles in it. You are quite right in guessing that the rev counter figures indicate top gear road speed. As far as I can recall, the overall ratio worked out at 25 mph per 1,000 rpm. The reason why the speedo is not connected is that I replaced the original gearbox with one from an Alvis Speed 25. The original box was a right-hand gate Meadows and rather unsatisfactory. The Alvis one was a great improvement, of much better design, and with synchromesh on all four speeds as far as I can remember. Of course, the Alvis ratios are quite different, so the speedo drive would not be correct, but it would be possible to fit a small intermediate gearbox in the speedo drive to rectify this. I hope this has been of some help and wish you luck and good – if rather smelly – motoring. I never did discover how to keep the smell of diesel oil out of the interior.'

Since this car has spent most of its life as a diesel, I think it would be a great mistake to try to restore it to its original petrol power. Another Lagonda diesel, this time a 1934 M45 fitted with a Gardner 4LK by Walker Brothers of Wigan in the late 1930s, came to light in the Preston area and was reported by Nick Baldwin in *Diesel Car* magazine in September 1997. There is a full story of Walker's 4LK conversions available from Tom Meadows, 8 St Mary's Gate, Wistaston, Crewe CW2 8HH (price £7 in 1997, but it might cost more now).

Land Rover

LHD Landy sought

" *We are trying to find a left-hand-drive 80-inch Land Rover Series 1. It was built in April 1951, originally for export to Cuba, but factory-registered LNX 406 in July 1951. It was dark coloured, possibly Bronze Green, and bore an RAC badge. This vehicle was sold to Macrae & Dick of Inverness in February 1952, but in-between was evaluated by the Belgian authorities, and led to Land Rover supplying Minerva with knocked-down kits from which the steel-bodied Minerva TT Land Rovers were built. These were unique in having sloping rather than upright front wings. Early this year a*

Minerva TT Register was set up to record as much as is possible about these vehicles for posterity, so if any of your readers know anything of Minerva TTs, or of LNX 406, I'd be grateful if they would get in touch. "

Of course, it's entirely possible that the helm and pedals of LNX 406 were swapped over to the right, but if any reader knows what happened to it, please contact Mike Hardiman, 8 Balmoral Close, Stoke Gifford, Bristol BS34 8NL, tel: 0117 969 0552. There are a couple of Minerva TTs mouldering into some undergrowth in the central island of one of the rides at the 'Autotron' (signposted from the A2 near Rosmalen, east of S'Hertogenbosch in Holland).

Leon Bollee

Great Horseless Carriages

" *My main reason for writing is the suicide-seat three-wheeler, which you identified as a 1905/06 Riley. Back in 1896 or 1897, my late uncle, Wilfred Le P. Webb was a draughtsman with The Great Horseless Carriage Company of Coventry. He drove my father in one of its products, a similar, but lever-steered vehicle of French design, from Coventry to Cheltenham where the tricycle was photographed.* "

Barely visible to the naked eye is the script 'Leon Bollee' on the crank-case of the tricycle. Leon was the son of Amedee Bollee, who was famed for developing steam road vehicles. His three-horsepower three-wheeler of 1895 had a single air-cooled cylinder of 650 cc, three forward speeds and belt final drive. According to Nick Georgano, it was faster than any other petrol driven vehicle of the time. In 1895, Harry Lawson's 'British Motor Syndicate' bought the British patent rights to the Leon Bollee, and his

'Great Horseless Carriage Company' assembled and later marketed it as the 'Coventry Motette'. Eleven were entered by Lawson's company in the 1896 Emancipation Run (the first London to Brighton) to celebrate the repeal of the 'Red Flag Act'. All eleven Leon Bollees reached Brighton and the company was subsequently re-named MMC (Motor Manufacturing Company).

Leyland

When Leyland made the best car in the world

" *A relative of mine was an apprentice with Leyland Motors in the 1920s and in sorting out his effects I found a photograph of a Leyland Straight Eight. Parry Thomas was Chief Engineer and designer for Leyland at the time and I understand that the Leyland Eight was his concept, assisted, of course, by Reid Railton. The car was ahead of its time, with novel features such as vacuum servo brakes, and I understand it appeared in many different guises. Have any survived? As many will remember, Parry Thomas was killed on Pendine Sands driving 'Babs', his Thomas Special, on a World Land Speed Record attempt.* "

The Heritage Motor Centre at Gaydon has the sole surviving Leyland Eight, a rakish 1927 Leyland Eight Thomas Special built from spare parts held by Thomson & Taylor at Brooklands after production of fourteen to eighteen Leyland Eights ceased. Advanced features of John Godfrey Parry Thomas's car included coil ignition, hemispherical combustion chambers, overhead cam, automatic chassis lubrication and, as you say, vacuum servo brakes. With twin carbs, the output of the bored-out 7,266 cc engine was 145 bhp, top speed was well over 90 mph, and many believe it to have been the best car in the world of its day. The Liberty aero-engined Highham Parry Thomas Special, christened 'Babs' and driven by Parry Thomas broke the World Land Speed Record at 169.3 mph on Pendine Sands, Carmarthenshire, in 1926, then broke its own record at 171.02 mph the same year. Malcolm Campbell replied with 174.88 mph in the Napier-Campbell in 1927, and Parry Thomas was killed on Pendine Sands trying to beat this when a rear wheel collapsed and a drive chain broke. 'Babs' was then buried in Pendine Sands, but was recently unearthed and restored. Thomson & Taylor are now back in the used sports car business at Cobham in Surrey.

Le Zebre

Earned its stripes

" *Some 30 years ago I lived in Grimsby. Next door to us lived a lady who had recently celebrated her 100th birthday. Sadly, she didn't make 101, which meant that her house was cleared and into my possession came the following items: a Le Zebre Type 'D' road test reprinted from* The Auto *of 16 June 1922; an article from* The Daily News *about the 1921 Motor Show; a newspaper advertisement for Le Zebre priced at £325; a page from* The Light Car and Cyclecar *of 23 July 1921 on the 10 HP Le Zebre; and* The Book of Le Zebre, *which amounts to an owner's manual. The importers even offered free insurance on every car sold and a deferred payment plan ('Live now, pay later'). I don't know if these items have any value, but they are not doing any good in my filing cabinet. Incidentally, I am an old-car buff. An Austin Ruby occupies my garage and consigns my new cars to rust away on the drive.* "

The best thing to do with these items is to offer them to Brian Heath, editor of *The Automobile* magazine. He may be able to make a feature out of them or, at the very least, direct you to a Le Zebre enthusiast who wants them badly. *The*

Automobile, Enthusiast Publishing Ltd, 'Holme-rise', Seven Hills Road, Cobham, Surrey KT11 1ES. Le Zebre lasted from 1909 to 1931, beginning with a single-cylinder 600 cc cyclecar and graduating via the 950 cc, later 783 cc, 8/10 to a two litre model.

Loughborough College Motor Club

Lagonda's life located

Following my correspondent's request for information about the past of his 1930 2.0 litre Lagonda Speed model, reg. GJ 5890 (see 'Lovely Lagonda' above), several readers responded. One, from Petworth, tells us there is a chance that the Loughborough owner was a student at Loughborough College living in one of the halls of residence (Hazelrigg or Rutland) on Ashby Road. There is a flourishing motor club, patron Bob Gerard, which is still going strong and which may have the car on its records. Club members in 1948–1951 owned a 4.5 litre sleeve-valve Minerva (once owned by G. L. Baker, who held a Brooklands 100 mph lap certificate); an Aston Martin International; an early Bertelli Aston Martin; a three litre Sunbeam; an Austin Seven Ulster; an Aero Morgan; a Healey Silverstone and numerous motorcycles. The next mail brought a letter from a Loughborough reader who has traced the chairmanship of the motor club in 1939 to H. A. Wharry. Wharry himself then wrote to tell us that the Lagonda registered GJ 5890 was owned by Malcolm Sayers and had to be handicapped in club events because it was so much more powerful than other members' cars. A reader from

Bishopsteignton positively identified the 1950–1954 owner of the car as his great friend S. R. Philcox, then resident at Hazelrigg Hall, Loughborough, and now living in Florida. The car was sold in 1954 to a John Dalzell of Melbourne, Derbyshire. The final instalment in the tale comes from Coventry, where a reader tells us that his father sold a Lagonda of a similar type, similarly dismantled, about 45 years ago.

Motor historian David Culshaw was also a member of the Loughborough College Motor Club during his college days in the early 1960s. He remembers meeting none other than Raymond Mays on 14 October 1960; and he recalls 'fantastic club events' at the pre-Wheatcroft Donington circuit, then still being used as an army dump. The club president, college lecturer Geoff Duce, used to bring his Rolls Royce Phantom, reg. ALP 178. One of the vice-presidents was Bob Gerard. Someone else had a works Peerless, reg. 704 EBH. David Culshaw remembers crewing on rallies and treasure hunts in John Critchley's 1941 Cadillac, HJK 708, which reputedly had once belonged to Greta Garbo, and in Noel Payne's rare Renault 750 convertible, RTG 252. Other crew members were Marie McNamee and Joan Dexter, and they once managed a 2nd place despite their car giving only 21 bhp.

Marauder

Searching out the last three Marauders

" *Over the last 25 years I have been tracing the histories of the 15 Marauder sports cars built between 1950 and 1952. When I started, only seven survivors were known, but now there are twelve – a fitting tribute to their build quality. But I wonder if any of your readers can help me piece together the histories of the missing three – whether or not they have survived. They are: LOF 269 (chassis no. 11002), originally supplied by J. W. Gethin to a Mr Harper of Lapworth, Solihull; FHE 437 (chassis no. 11012), last heard of in the Sheffield area in the late 1960s having been involved in an accident; and FCT 707 (chassis no. 11013), which is believed to have been owned by a Mr Scarborough in the Sleaford area, again in the 1960s.* "

The prototype 1950 Marauder, reg. KAC 313, which his family has owned since 1952, is still in the possession of an Arundel reader. The car was the brainchild of Rover engineers George Mackie, Peter Wilks and Spen King. It was based on Rover 75 P4 running gear and a shortened P4 chassis, with some P4 body panels and the rest made first by Richard Mead of Poplar Road, Dorridge, and later by Abbey Panels. The company address was Marauder Car Company Ltd, Common Lane, Kenilworth, Warks. There's a fairly full story in the 1998/99 edition of *The Daily Telegraph Book of Motoring Answers*, pages 164–5, where a similar appeal was made using what details were known at the time, though the reg. MPC 300, given for chassis no. 11002, is now known to have been incorrect. Any readers with information, please write to Ian Glass, 'Tirionfa', Bodfari Road, Llandyrnog, Denbigh, Clwyd LL16 4HP, tel: 01824 790280.

Marseal

From Marseel to Marseal

" *In about 1927 my father owned a car called a Marseel. It was a two seater with a dicky and a polished aluminium body. I have never since seen or heard any reference to this make of motor car and would be very pleased if you could give me any information about it.* "

This was a project by Captain D. M. K. Marendaz, one that preceded the car to which he gave his name. He was the 'Mar', and his co-sponsor was 'Seel' (from Seelhaft). The cars were a 1,247 cc side-valve 9/26 of 1919; a 1,496 cc side-valve 11/55 of 1920/23; a brief experiment with a 1,754 cc ohv six; a 1,498 cc side-valve 10.8 HP of 1921; a 1,247 cc side-valve 11/27 of 1924/25; a 1,496 cc side-valve 12/40 of 1924/25; and, finally, a 1,368 cc side valve 11/40 of 1924/25. After that, Marendaz went on to produce his own cars which looked very much like miniature Bentleys. Culshaw & Horrobin give the make half a page in *The Complete Catalogue of British Cars* (ISBN 1-874105-93-6), and our other old friend, Nick Baldwin, in his *A–Z of Cars of the 1920s* (ISBN 1-870979-53-2), tells us the name was changed from 'Marseel' to 'Marseal' after Seelhaft left in 1923. Most cars were bodied by Lawson or Hancock and Warman. Marendaz himself raced one painted blue and white which he nicknamed 'Blancmange'.

Mercedes Benz

Exhausted Mercedes

" *I wonder if you could assist me in identifying a car I rode in during my youth. It was a Mercedes, the year was around 1920, and the car's owner was Captain Philip Walker, then of The Drive, Benrhydding, near Ilkley, West Yorks, and later of Weston Manor, West Otley, West Yorks. My father was vicar of the parish at that time. As I remember it, the car had a large exhaust running the length of the body, about three-quarters of the way up and with the same huge diameter along its entire length. The car was certainly an open tourer type and probably a two-seater. The engine was reputed to be an 'aero engine' and very powerful. It's noise was very long and very loud. At night it could be heard on a road three miles away on its way home. The noise was louder and slower than any Bentley. I was told that only 20 were imported.* "

It's entirely possible that this car was one of the three famous Grand Prix Mercedes that came first, second and third in the 1914 Grand Prix driven by Lautenschlager, Wagner and Salzer. Mercedes had gone all out to win this race and their 4,483 cc cars with four valves and three spark plugs per cylinder, giving maximum power of 115 bhp, were far in advance of their competitors. Of course, war broke out a few weeks after this victory and, intriguingly, one of the cars was marooned in London. Graham Robson in his *Encyclopaedia of Classic Cars* tells us that this car was speedily confiscated by the authorities and eventually studied closely by Rolls Royce, which freely admitted that its aero engines drew heavily on the technology of the Mercedes unit. If the Mercedes you rode in was, indeed, the commandeered 1914 Grand Prix car, then you are privileged to have been driven in a real piece of history.

MG

Luxurious MG

" *Could you tell me anything about a large four-seater MG drophead coupe, reg. MG 5640? All I know is that my father bought it second-hand in the mid-1950s and that he disposed of it after a short time because of a broken stub axle. I have never seen another like it.* "

This is an MG 1.5 litre VA 'Foursome' Tickford drophead coupe built between 1936 and 1939, priced £335 rising to £360. It had a 1,548 cc Wolseley-based four-cylinder engine and, with sluggish acceleration to a top speed of 81.82 mph (with the windscreen down), wasn't quick. The SA and WA with larger 2,322 cc and 2,561 cc six-cylinder engines looked similar but did not have front mudguard cutaways. 'MG' is a Middlesex registration, blocks of which were obtained by MG agents University Motors who had a branch there. To find out if the car still exists, contact the MG Car Club, PO Box 251, Abingdon, Oxon OX14 1FF, tel: 01235 555552. Middlesex 'MG' registration records have been lost.

New MG T-types

" I used to have an MGTD in the 1950s and a year or two back saw a car transporter full of what looked like 'new' LHD TDs. Is there a company manufacturing them? If so, could you please let me have details? "

Naylor Brothers (the well-known MG T-Type parts specialists, now part of Moss Europe) built a replica TF using reproduction parts with a 1,700 cc 'O'-type ohc Morris Ital engine and a coil sprung rear axle. The car was in production from 1985 to 1986, but, at £12,500, was more expensive than a genuine restored TF. The venture failed in 1986 and was taken over by Maurice Hutson, who relaunched it as the Hutson TF and also offered it in kit form. On page 132 of Chris Rees's *British Speciality Cars* there's a picture of Margaret Thatcher at the wheel of one. For MG T-type parts, Naylor can be contacted on 01274 594071. Naylors and Hutsons have a strong following and a thriving

Car Club. Anyone interested in joining should contact Freda Taylor, Airedale Garage, Hollins Hill, Shipley, W. Yorks BD17 7QN, tel: 01284 787539. The nice thing about these cars is that they were as faithful a replica of the original TF as 1980s Type Approval would allow.

Screen Magnette

" *I own a 1957 MG Magnette ZB and am naturally interested in all ZAs and ZBs. ITV recently showed an old black and white John Mills film, entitled* The Vicious Circle, *which was made in 1957. Starring in the film was a very smart Magnette ZA, registered 954 DMK. I am now trying to find out if the car still exists. It is not on the MG Car Club Z register. The film was based on a Francis Durbridge thriller entitled* The Brass Candlestick. *In the mid-1950s the BBC produced its own version of this, and that, too, starred a Z-series MG saloon.* "

It is correct to use the term 'starred' because in the story the murder weapon was found in the boot of Dr Latimer's MG saloon. The BBC production was a serial written by Durbridge. The film shown on ITV was made by Romulus Productions, was directed by Peter Rogers, and also starred John Mills, Derek Farr, Noelle Middleton, Roland Culver, Wilfrid Hyde Whyte, Mervyn Johns, Rene Ray, Lionel Jeffries and Lisa Daniely. I can tell you a story of another ZA Magnette, this one registered 53 EMM. It was the summer of 1966 and I was on holiday with my parents staying at a beach hotel by the name of 'El Sombrero', about 3 kilometres north of Calafell in Spain. The hotel staff were English catering students, and four of them had arrived in a grey ZA Magnette, which was put off the road by a truck and rolled. Among the hotel guests were a group of Ford workers from

Dagenham and a group of BMW workers from Munich. As you can imagine, this made watching the 1966 World Cup final quite interesting, but no grudges were borne and, on the incentive of a crate of San Miguel provided by the hotel's Armenian owner, the car workers all got together with scaffold poles and car jacks to straighten the MG out. Afterwards, a Spanish bodyshop installed new glass and painted the car white with an offset blue stripe.

Microplas

The mystery of the Microplas

" *I have just acquired for restoration something that was described to me as a 1953 Microplas. I cannot find any information about the model. The car has leafspring suspension all round and 8-inch drum brakes, while the engine is a large side-valve unit that looks to be non-original. The car, registered CGK 737, has been in a barn for the past 18 years. I would be grateful for any information.* "

This is a Microplas Mistral 'special', distinguished from the earlier Microplas Stiletto by the twin vents behind the front wheels. The Mistral body was built to fit the 7ft 6in Ford chassis by Microplas Ltd, James Estate, Western Road, Mitcham, Surrey, and was used as the prototype shell for the Fairthorpe Electron Minor. Apart from the body, nothing much will be standard, but the 'large' side-valve engine might have come from a Model A or B Ford or, more likely, from a WW2 Ford Jeep. You will get a lot of help and support by joining the Fairthorpe Sports Car Club, c/o Richard Disbrow, 16 The Close, Blandford Forum, Dorset DT11 7HA, tel: 01258 454879.

A reader from Oxted later wrote, 'I can clear up the mystery of the Microplas. Microplas was started by two friends and myself in, I think, 1952. We were keen members of the 750 Club and the original purpose was to make bodyshells for 750 and 1172 specials. We were joined by another friend, who was building a special powered by one of Archie Butterworth's flat-four engines (not one of the swing-valve versions). He needed a body, and I designed the shell which became the Mistral – the side vents were to mate up with ducts from the air-cooled engine. As far as I know, the car was never completed. As well as Fairthorpe, we also sold shells to AFN and to Morgan. The Mistral-bodied Frazer Nash was the one driven by Ken Wharton which crashed and burned out in one of the Ulster TTs. In 1956 we sold a mould to a company in New Zealand which was thinking of building a sports car there. I went out to NZ late in 1956 to help with the project, and we built a prototype based on a simple two-tube chassis with swing-axle front end and a properly located live rear axle. Power was initially provided by a Ford 100E engine with an Elva overhead inlet valve conversion. This competed in several local races and was quite successful during 1957. I returned to England in 1958 after we had improved the shell with proper doors and an optional hardtop. I believe that some 15 or 16 kits were sold and, by sheer chance, I stayed with one of the customers during a return visit to NZ some six years ago. Microplas went on to build boats and other mouldings, including the fairings used on the Vincent Black Knight motorcycle. With regard to the Fairthorpe, we were initially involved with 'Pathfinder' Bennett who was trying to produce a Microcar – the Fairthorpe Atom. These were very basic, with motorcycle engines. His son, Torix, carried the name on to more successful cars. One further point: the first TVRs had bodywork based on two Mistral front ends.'

Mini

Minivan

" *I would like to know how much I could expect to pay for a second-hand Minivan in good condition. There seem to be so few on the road these days, which is such a pity.* "

In really good, concours condition, £3,000-plus. Have a look in *Mini World* magazine and consider joining one of the Mini owners clubs (tel: 01543 257956, 01384 440060 or 01582 769549).

Home for Mini found

" *I am pleased to tell you that the Friends of Nuffield Place (the former home of Lord Nuffield) have agreed to display on loan your Southampton reader's 'one-owner' 1960 Mini, 8472 CR, to join a 1952 Morris Minor, MJK 648, and a 1949 Wolseley Eight, BUD 650.* "

Nuffield Place is open to the public ten times a year, on the second and fourth Sundays of each month from May to September, entry £3, OAPs £2, Children 50p. Built in 1914, the house retains the majority of the furniture and contents acquired by Lord and Lady Nuffield after they took up residence in 1933, and is still decorated in 1930s style. The house is signposted off the A4130 from Henley on Thames to Wallingford, between Nettlebed and The Crown public house. Tel: 01491 836654.

MMC

MMC for me

" *In 1909, my late uncle H. V. Flatow drove an MMC car. He was one of the earliest motor engineers in Leeds and was trained at Bradford Technical College. He later had a garage and repair shop in Mount Preston, Leeds. I have a photograph which is inscribed on the back: '1900 MMC 2 cyl 8–10 HP chain drive to rear wheels. Detachable head, automatic inlet valves. Photo taken in 1909 in Delph Lane, Leeds.' Could you tell me anything about the car?* "

MMC began as H. J. Lawson's The Great Horseless Carriage Co. Ltd of Coventry in 1897/98 (see 'Leon Bollee', above). It became The Motor Manufacturing Co. Ltd, Coventry, between 1898 and 1907, then upped sticks and moved to Clapham where it remained for its final manufacturing year, 1907/08. H. J. Lawson had grandiose plans to build cars and commercial vehicles in large numbers. His first cars which were not merely assembled Leon Bollee three-wheelers were rear-engined, and engineer George Iden's 1896 prototype (before the company was registered) had large wire wheels. The early front-engined cars, prior to your uncle's, looked almost identical to contemporary Panhards and Daimlers. The 8 HP model is listed as having had a 1,684 cc side-valve engine with a bore of 90 mm and a stroke of 130 mm. The later 10 HP had a 2,041 cc side-valve twin.

Morgan

Winter warmer?

" *No mystery about the JAP Morgan three wheeler, reg. JJ 9032, owned by my father in the mid-1930s. What does puzzle me is a boyhood memory of*

my father's assertion that, when the weather was very cold, he covered the exposed overhead valve tappets with treacle tins stuffed with grease-soaked cotton waste. I'm no mechanic, but could this story be true? **"**

Yes, but only while the car was parked. The reason was to prevent surface condensation on the exposed valve gear from freezing up. 'JJ' was a London County Council registration, first used in November 1932.

Auntie's wasp

" *My aunt drove around in a windowless, bright yellow three-wheeler which she called the 'Wasp'. With so little protection against the elements, she needed a fur coat, hat and boots.* **"**

With no windscreen she must have caught a few

wasps between her teeth in her Morgan 'Sporting'. It was built around 1912, and later fitted with electric lighting. There's a £2.25 'Shire Album' book about these by Ken Hill (no. 327), and the enthusiasts' club is the Morgan Three Wheeler Club Ltd, c/o E. Eyes, 280 Commonwealth Way, Abbey Wood, London SE2 0LD, tel: 0181 311 7282.

Morris

Publicity vehicle

" *As an old OAP now, I remember my first four wheels being a Morris 8 van, built in 1935, with those lovely old oval rear door windows. So much happened in my life when I enjoyed my old £20 van. I dearly wish to see one again and have advertised, but to no effect. Can you help?* "

By sheer coincidence, the following mailbag contained a letter from a reader from Ferndown whose father, a baker in Oxford, persuaded Morris Garages to put a small van body onto a Morris 8 chassis. Sadly, this made do with louvred vents rather than oval rear windows. It had an early example of the personalised number plate: JO 3537. 'JO' stood for Jacksons of Oxford, and '3537' was Jacksons' telephone number.

Something fishy

" *I was interested to see the letter (above) about oval rear windows in Morris 8 vans. I've just completed the restoration of a 1935 fish van back to its original condition.* "

This is a charming restoration and it would be

nice to see some more old commercials restored to their original livery. There is now a magazine, *Classic and Vintage Commercials*, published by Kelsey Publishing Ltd, for those who are fascinated by these vehicles (from newsagents, or phone 01959 541444). From the same stable comes *Bus & Coach Preservation Monthly* and *Tractor & Machinery*.

Man of two Morrises

" *My first car was a 1930 Morris Minor saloon, for which I paid the princely sum of £14 in 1938. One memory is that the handbrake clamped onto the driveshaft and, if applied while the car was in motion, caused a 'Brocks' Benefit' fireworks effect which gave my girlfriends some cause for alarm. Later I had a 1925/26 Morris 'bullnose', which I sold prior to going overseas. It ran well and had the useful feature of a mechanical headlight dipping mechanism controlled by a lever. It also had a window winder with a jointed handle which could be folded away to prevent it jabbing into one's leg. I sold it to someone in the Bournemouth area in the 1960s. Is there any possibility that either of these cars is still in existence and, if so, is it possible for me to find out where?* "

Records of 'HW' Bristol registrations from 1904 to 1964 are still held at Bristol Record Office, 'B' Bond Warehouse, Smeaton Road, Bristol BS1 6XN, tel: 0117 922 5692, but 'YM' London registration records were destroyed after computerisation in 1974. Clubs that may be able to help you find the cars are: the Morris Register, c/o Donald Moore, White Cottage, Jasmine Lane, Lower Claverham, Bristol BS19 4PY, tel: 01934 832340; the Bullnose Morris Club, c/o Richard Harris, PO Box 383, Hove, East Sussex BN3 4FX; and the Morris Cowley & Oxford Club, c/o Derek Andrews, 202 Chantry Gardens, Southwick, Trowbridge, Wilts BA14 9QX, tel:

01225 766800. Cars like the original Minor still crop up at classic car auctions.

Minor rarity

" *I have recently finished rebuilding a long-chassis Morris 8 Calshott, reg. MU 5741. I am told only seven were ever built by Stewart & Arden, before they were bought up by Henley's who have destroyed all records. From new, each car was fitted with a guarantee plate incorporating a cast facsimile of the owner's signature. This has been lost from my car and I would dearly like to find it, plus any other information your readers can supply me with.* "

Pre-1974 'MU' Middlesex registration records have been destroyed. But there's quite an interesting history to that body. It was constructed in a brand new, purpose-built factory in Acton, set up by R. I. Musselwhite and V. E. Freestone in 1931 to revive the Cunard coachbuilding company. Almost as soon as it opened for business, it was taken over by Stewart & Arden, who used it to make batch production specials for Morris, Rover and Wolseley. Would any readers with information about MU 5741 please write to John Seddon, 16 Brooklyn Avenue, Flixton, Urmston, Manchester M41 6PF. Readers interested in the history of British coachbuilding should buy the *A–Z of British Coachbuilders 1919–1960* by Nick Walker, Bay View Books, ISBN 1-870979-93-1, price £24.95.

Morris Minor (postwar)

Mystery prices

" *After the war, having saved up enough money to buy an MM outright, I placed an order for one in 1948 and eagerly anticipated delivery within a fortnight. To my acute disappointment I found there was a long waiting list due to the Labour government's 'Export or Die' restrictions on home sales, and it was a further two years before I got it. By that time the price had gone up by £200 and I had to borrow in order to pay for it. I forget what I had to pay, but I have an idea that it was around £500. Do you have any information about the price of these great little cars in 1950?* "

The 1948 launch price of the two-door series MM saloon was £358. By 1950, the price of the two-door saloon and convertible had risen to £383. But by 1951, a hike in purchase tax to an eye watering 56 per cent had pulled it up to £519-10s-0d, though the ex-works price was £333. Also in 1951, a four-door version with American-market raised headlights (later adopted for all Morris Minors) was added to the range at £569-5s-7d. (For your extra £50 you also got an interior light, ashtrays, two windscreen wipers and front door check straps.)

Classic choice

" *I will retire in August and have £5,000 or so to spend on a classic car to enjoy during my retirement. The contenders I have lined up are: a Morris Minor 1000 because of its understandable technology and active supporters club; an MGB GT automatic, for similar reasons; or a Triumph Dolomite 1850HL automatic or Sprint. I would value your opinion as to the durability and running costs of these cars.* "

I think you'll get the most out of a Morris Minor, preferably an updated convertible 'Tourer' model. Order a copy of the magazine *Morris Minor Monthly* and you'll soon get an idea of the potential both for working on the car and for enjoying it at events during spring and summer weekends. The friendly club is: Morris Minor Owners Club, PO Box 1098, Derby DE23

8ZX, tel: 01332 291675; website: http://www.MorrisMinorOC.co.uk. It's also well worth buying John Pressnell's definitive book, *Morris Minor: Exploring the Legend*, published by Haynes, ISBN 1 85960 429 3 (I did). Though faster and with equally good owners clubs, MGBs and Dolomites are not as much fun to work on. But whichever you go for, enjoy the car. Please don't get hung up on obsessive 'concours' restoration and things like cleaning the inside of the exhaust tail-pipe with a toothbrush.

Not the real thing

" *My daughter will be getting married later this year and has reluctantly decided to sell her beloved Morris Minor. We would value your advice as to the best way of doing this and what price range she should expect. The car is a 1967 1,098 cc convertible fitted two years ago with a reconditioned engine. It has been regularly serviced and has an MOT to September. She paid £5,000 for it six-and-a-half years ago to a specialist who had converted it from a two-door saloon and resprayed it Trafalgar Blue. The outer bodywork is now in need of some attention, but otherwise the car is in good condition and in daily use.* "

This is not a collector's piece due to its lack of originality, but because Tourers are attractive in the spring it should still fetch more than an original saloon in the same condition. It should photograph well, so try the photo ads in *Classic Car Weekly* and *Practical Classics* (01733 465430). Ask £2,250 (but be prepared to take £1,750), state whether or not it has been modified to take unleaded petrol, and be sure to state that it is a Tourer conversion or you'll just annoy prospective customers. Those readers who want to check if a Morris Minor Tourer they are thinking of buying is a genuine Tourer need to check the Vehicle Identification Number on the embossed plate under the bonnet. For early cars up to late 1950s build, if the second prefix letter is a 'C', it's an original convertible. If the second letter is a 'B' it used to be a 2-door saloon. For later 948 cc and 1,098 cc Minors you need to check the third prefix letter after the letters 'M' and 'A'. 'T' is for Tourer (convertible). '2S' is for two-door saloon, while simply 'S' is for 4-door saloon. Many thanks for this information to The Morris Minor Centre in Bath, tel: 01225 315449, and to Bob at Morri Spares in Epping, tel: 01992 524249. A specialist dealer in genuine Morris Minor Tourers is Canterbury Convertibles on 01277 20306.

Motorcycles

Dual-control Lambretta

" *I am trying to trace the history of a Lambretta LI 125 cc Series 3 training bike, registered 122 BRK. The rear handlebars do not steer, but are fitted with a rear brake and clutch control, presumably so that a pillion seat driving instructor could retrieve the situation if the learner got into trouble. I know the bike started life in and around Croydon in South London in 1964, and may have been used by the RAC until 1967. It then reappeared in Newton Abbott in Devon in 1971 and I have a cover note stating 'used in connection with the RAC/Auto Cycle Union and West of England Motor Club Training Scheme'. It must have been vanned or trailered there because its 1971 MOT states a mileage of 498 and the mileage is still only 535. What happened to it between then and now?* "

Norman Hands, who worked for Lambretta Concessionaires in the 1960s, tells us that this dual-control scooter was one of a number of demonstration models kept for loaning to motoring correspondents. It lay around at the company's Purley Way premises for some time. He thinks it is possible it was donated to the RAC/ACU training scheme (training took place in public carparks and school playgrounds) and that Freddie Hawken, the then Lambretta agent in Newton Abbot, may have been involved in its presence in the West Country. Another possibility is that it came into the possession of Lambretta collector Mike Karslake, who originally lived in Essex but who moved to Northlew in Devon and established a Lambretta museum in a barn. Sadly, he died a few years ago, and his wife was forced to dispose of the collection. A reader from Daventry has another example of the dual-control Lambretta, registered 111 BRK, which was supplied for use by the RAC/ACU Training Scheme in Sheffield. This machine has not been used for twenty years and its owner now wishes to dispose of it, tel: 01327 260303.

A break from the Norm

" *I own a 1950s Norman Nippy 50 cc single-cylinder autocycle in need of an overhaul. Could you tell me something of the company's history, what the autocycle may be worth and where I can get it serviced?* "

Hugo Wilson's *Encyclopaedia of the Motorcycle* (ISBN 0-7513-0206-6) tells us that this Kent bicyclemaker started building the 98 cc Villiers-engined 'Mobyk' in the late 1930s. Post-war models included off-road competition motorcycles, and had engines from 98 cc to 249 cc. In 1958, Norman bought the rights to make a Sachs-engined 49 cc moped from the defunct German maker, Achilles, and re-named it the Norman Lido. The company was taken over by Raleigh in 1961, and production of the Norman

Lido ended in 1963. I have no idea what the bike may be worth, but the National Autocycle and Cyclemotor Club should be able to help with this and with finding a restorer. The most recent address I have for the membership secretary is David Freeman, 81 High Road, Trimley, Felixstowe, Suffolk IP11 0TA.

Orpington

Like the hen, but not 'buff'

" *Have you ever heard of a car by the name of the 'Orpington'? It was built by Messrs Milroy and Smith of Orpington, Kent, launched at the Motor Show, and featured in* The Autocar *during November 1920. Our milkman was taken to school in one, and he told us it was a two-seater with a dickey seat at the rear.* "

Milroy and Smith had a garage repair business in Orpington and were agents for Willys Overland cars. But they also built their own, initially using components from the Model T Ford and a smaller, more tax-efficient 1,505 cc side-valve Coventry Simplex engine. It did not have the Model T's transverse spring suspension. M&S marketed it as 'The Businessman's Light Car', but did not do much business once Morris began to undercut the market. There's a picture on page 424 of Culshaw & Horrobin's *Complete Catalogue of British Cars 1895–1975* (ISBN 1-874105-93-6) and on page 142 of Nick Baldwin's *A–Z of Cars of the 1920s* (ISBN 1-870979-53-2).

Panhard-Levassor

ES 2

" *Through your column I hope to help a friend trace a venerable motor car, last heard of at a museum in Cheddar Gorge. It is a Panhard et Levassor, registration ES 2, imported from Paris in 1902 by a Colonel Murray Thriepland of Dryburgh Abbey House. It was laid up at Dale House, the Caithness home of the Thrieplands, from 1910 to 1938, when it was brought to a garage at Greenlaw, Berwickshire where the proprietor, W. W. McDavid, was friendly with the Thrieplands. In 1938 it was prepared and entered for the first Veteran Car Rally in Scotland (part of the Empire Exhibition) by R. R. Young, the father of my friend, who subsequently owned the County Garage, Greenlaw. Before World War Two broke out, the Panhard went once again to Caithness, then returned to Greenlaw in 1946 and was completely overhauled. R. R. Young then drove it on many Border rallies during the 1960s and early 1970s, and it completed a London to Brighton run in 1969. At some time in the 1970s, the Panhard, then valued at £5,000, went to The National Motor Museum and was there for two years. For a subsequent unknown period of time it was at a museum in the Cheddar Gorge, but is no longer there. Are you able to help trace the Panhard? Apart from being of great sentimental value to a friend, it would appear, if still intact, to be of considerable historical importance in the veteran car world.* "

I suggest you contact the following: Les Amis de Panhard et Levassor GB, 'La Dyna', 11 Arterial Avenue, Rainham, Essex RM13 9PD, tel: 01708 524425; Panhard et Levassor Club GB, c/o Martin McLawrence, 18 Dovedale Road, Offerton, Stockport, Cheshire SK2 5DY, tel: 0161 483 8262; Veteran Car Club of Great Britain, c/o Margaret Golding, Jessamine Court, 15 High Street, Ashwell, Herts SG7 5NL, tel: 01462 742818, fax: 01462 742997.

Posh Panhard sought

" *My father, Norman Pritchard, opened Pritchard's Pratts Garage at Aintree in 1919. It was the first garage between Liverpool and Preston, and his first customer was Mrs Topham of Aintree Racecourse. On 29 August 1931, I accompanied my father to The Torquay Carriage and Motor Co. Ltd, where he purchased for £50 a Panhard et Levassor straight 8, then the property of Viscount de Barbe who had been advised by his doctor to cease driving. The prototype of this model was driven at Brooklands by George Eyston, who broke many records in 1929. My father's car had a solid aluminium chassis and two-seater body, spoked wheels with knock-off hub caps, an oak tool chest, and a Smith's 8-day clock (both of which I still have). It was finished in grey with blue mudguards. It could reach 80 mph in 3rd gear and did 10 mpg. My father sold the Panhard, together with the business, in 1944, but I would dearly love to know if it survived and its whereabouts.* "

Nick Georgano tells us that the Panhard 35 CV straight-eights with bored out 7.9 litre engines had a long career in record work, which did not end until 1934. In 1929 the chassis alone of a 40–50 HP straight-eight was priced at £1,200, so your father must have been a shrewd negotiator.

Tigre by name

" *Having seen the latest retro-styled Audi TT, VW Beetle, BMW Z1, Ford Thunderbird and Daimler-Chrysler Cruiser, I am prompted to write and ask about a car that stopped for me while I was roaming France between 1967 and 1971. It was a Panhard Tiger or Tigre and gave me a ride I will never forget. It went at 200 kph and it sounded like a sewing machine. The nutcase behind the wheel was a French stunt driver.* "

The top car stunt outfit of the time was Equipe Remy Julien. Does this name ring any bells? Two Panhards were available with the flat-twin 845 cc 60 bhp Tigre engine – the four door PL17 and the good-looking 24CT coupe. One of these would really be pushing it to hit a genuine 125 mph. But maybe you hitched a lift in a DB Panhard Tigre, designed for competing at Le Mans in the Index of Performance. That would certainly do 200 kph.

Peugeot

Racing 'Bebe'

" *As far as I remember, my late father's first motorised transport was an Indian motorcycle, circa 1918, but he recalled once sitting in a racing Baby Peugeot at, perhaps, 15 years of age. The car may have belonged to his brother-in-law, Alex McGregor, who was some years his senior and something of a 'racey' character, much loved by his nephews for his largesse and his ill-performed conjuring tricks at Christmas parties.* "

Designed by Ettore Bugatti, the Peugeot Bebe of 1912 to 1920 predated the Austin 7 as the first proper four-wheeled car-in-miniature. It had a sophisticated twin-cam 'crossflow', but side-valve four-cylinder 855 cc engine. It could be that Alex McGregor was into handicap racing at Brooklands. The car couldn't have done much racing between 1914 and 1918, though. Roger Ramage of Brooklands Museum may well have some records of the car having competed there (tel: 01932 857371 or 01932 859000).

Pick

From cars to cauliflowers

" *An extract from my local paper provides a history of an almost forgotten make of car built in Stamford over a period of 25 years. For the complete history I would refer you to* A History of the Pick Motor

Company by Michael Key, published and obtainable from Paul Watkins of Adelaide Street, Stamford. John Henry Pick was born in Gas Lane, Stamford, in 1867 and became a blacksmith by trade. In 1896 he saw an opportunity in bicycle sales and started J. H. Pick & Co., Cycle Agents, offering up to 150 bicycles from stock by 1899. In March of that year, he organised a two-day event, one of the exhibits at which was a motorcycle built by The Motor Manufacturing Co. of London. This gave him the idea of starting to produce his own motor cars. The first of these was road-tested in 1900 and had the unusual feature of a pair of tiller-steered bicycle front forks suspending the front wheels. By 1903, eight different body designs were offered, and the firm moved from its Gas Lane premises to St. Martins, where his factory also doubled as Stamford's first garage. The firm finally went into voluntary liquidation in 1925 after an unsuccessful attempt at producing 30 HP agricultural tractors. "

Pick feature on page 328 of Culshaw & Horrobin's *Complete Catalogue of British Cars 1895–1975*, and eight models are briefly described. When the firm started making larger models in 1908, the name was changed to 'New Pick', reverting back to 'Pick' in 1923 when they attempted a sporting 3.6 litre side-valve model which proved to be too old fashioned compared to the contemporary Vauxhall 30/98 and the 3 litre Bentley. Nick Baldwin also describes this car in his *A–Z of Cars of the 1920s* (ISBN 1 870979-53-2), telling us: 'In 1925 Jack Pick turned his back on the motor trade and became a vegetable grower and greengrocer.'

Renault

Alive and well?

" *I bought a 1927 Renault 8.3 HP, reg. KO 4010, for £60 in 1952 with only 7,400 miles on the clock and the original beaded tyres. The hood cover was in its original (though congealed) wrapping and had never been used. The car had right-hand drive, a magneto start, and a giant single transverse spring which created an alarming angle when cornering at speed. I sold it for £85 in 1956. Do you think it is still alive and running?* **"**

The KJ-Type 6 cv was launched in France in 1923 with a 952 cc motor and three-speed gearbox. But in 1926, Renault followed Citroën's example and established a UK assembly plant at Acton. In the UK this model was designated 8.3 HP, cost £219, and gave 50 mph with 45 mpg. To find out what happened to it, try the Renault Freres Club for pre-1940 Renaults, c/o Pam Mills, 54 High Street, Durrington, Salisbury, Wilts SP4 8AQ.

Riley

Back-seat driver

" *My late father had a curious three-wheeler car in which the driver sat behind the passenger over the single rear wheel. It was talked about for many years, and the cushion from the front seat languished in the family toolshed. I have a vague memory that it was called a Rexette.* **"**

The Rex Motor Manufacturing Company of Birmingham made a 'Rexette' tricar in 1905/06 which sold for £105. It was very similar to the second type of Riley Popular Tricar, built between 1903 and 1907 with a 517 cc engine and a steering wheel rather than handlebars, and you can see one of these at the Heritage Motor Centre collection at Gaydon. It was designed by Stanley Riley, and the price was £85 new.

Riley Deauville

" Can you give me any information about the Riley Deauville 14 HP? I think that the brakes were adjusted from inside the car. All I can recall is that the car we had was 4 or 5 years old in 1935. "

The model was the 14/6, launched in 1928 with a 1,633 cc, six-cylinder, twin high-set-cam engine, which developed 50 bhp with one carburettor and a bit more with three. Top speed was over 70 mph. From 1930 there was also a Light Six version on a 114-inch wheelbase. The RAC HP rating worked out at 13.52 HP. Other body styles included the Stelvio saloon, Alpine saloon, Sportsmans coupe, special tourer, Alpine tourer, Kestrel saloon, Lincock coupé, Lynx tourer, Ascot DHC, Gamecock sports, Edinburgh saloon, Edinburgh limousine and Winchester limousine, so the chassis certainly took a fair old line-up of bodies. The 14/6 stayed in production until 1935, when it was replaced by the 1,726 cc 15/6.

Why Deauvilles are so desirable

A reader from Halstead then wrote to tell us, 'The Riley 14/6 Deauville you mentioned is an extremely rare car, for two reasons. The bodies of the 14/6 Deauville and 5-Seat Tourer were built by Hancock & Warman Ltd of Coventry, who had a disastrous fire at their Stoke factory in 1931 leading them to cease trading and Riley to withdraw the Deauville and the 5-Seat Tourer. The 14/6 Edinburgh and Winchester saloons or limousines continued until 1933/34, and the Stelvio until 1935. But all "big sixes" were at risk of losing their bodies to become racing "specials". I am happy to say that the Deauville sold by Brooks on 23 July is to be preserved, that I have a Deauville of my own, and that one other is thought to remain in a dismantled state somewhere.'

A reader from of Billington wrote to say he is helping to restore a Riley Stelvio, reg. PO 5441, owned by the Havillands for 40 years. He also tells us they owned a Deauville, reg. PL 8617, until it was sold to my Halstead correspondent, above; that another Deauville lies dismantled in Scotland, and he confirms that the third known survivor, GO 8596, recently purchased at the Brooks auction, had been sold to save its near-unique body from 'big six' special builders.

Rumbling Riley

" *Following the references to Rileys in your column over recent weeks, I wonder if my 12 HP 6-cylinder 1,458 cc Lynx, reg. NJ 808, would be of interest. I owned it from 1946 to 1957. It had three SU carburettors and, though originally equipped with a Scintilla Vertax magneto, by the time it got to me the ignition had been converted to coil with a manual advance and retard in addition to the centrifugal unit in the distributor. The problem with the engines of these cars was the three-bearing crankshaft with its water-cooled central bearing. In the winter this could easily freeze, leading to a cracked casting, as had happened during a previous ownership of my car and which had never been satisfactorily patched up. Every morning, my first job was to drain the water from the sump. The other problem with my car was the dynamo, which was at the front of the engine and driven directly by the crankshaft. A ball bearing in it had broken and jammed, then rotated in its housing, making a noise and creating such tremendous heat that the solder in the commutator melted and was centrifugally sprayed like aluminium paint. Eventually I gave the car away with a failed big end bearing, but if anyone knows of its survival I would be very interested.* "

This model, using a small-bore version of the 'six' in a stretched 'Nine' chassis, only ran from 1933 to 1935, when it was replaced by the more robust four-cylinder 1,496 cc 1.5 litre – an engine type which then lasted for 20 years. The Special Series triple carb engine was £60 extra. Barrie A. Gillies is the specialist in 1930s Rileys (tel: 01189 744772), so I checked with him as to whether NJ 808 had survived. Sadly, the Riley Register had no record of it, and the reason is highly likely to have been that water-cooled centre main bearing. A reader from Romsey later wrote of another 12 HP six, AMV 41, this time with the Lincock 2+2 coupe body, which he owned from 1955 to 1959. His only had a single SU carb, later modified to twin SUs without much success. The Riley Register is run by J. Clark, 56 Cheltenham Road, Bishops Cleeve, Cheltenham, Glos GL52 4LV, tel: 01242 673598, website: http://www.uk-classic-cars.com/ rileyregister.htm.

The life of Riley

" *I am trying to trace the life of a 1935 Riley Imp which has the unique design feature of smooth wing edges. What I do know is that it was purchased in 1951 in Yorkshire by a decorated American airman by the name of Simmons. (He was a navigator and his heroism included flying his aircraft back to the UK while injured, after the pilot died of his injuries.) Simmons took the car back to Houston, Texas, in the late 1950s, where the ENV pre-selector gearbox was dismantled following problems and remained in that state until Simmons died in the 1980s. I brought the car back to the UK and had it restored on behalf of Simmons's daughter. Though I am a member of The Riley Register and own a Riley Imp with standard wings, I have not been able to trace any history of this car prior to 1951. Only 100 or so Imps were built and, as far as I know, this is the only one with smooth-edge wings. Do any of your readers remember it and, in particular, its original registration mark?* "

Can anyone help? The car's chassis number is 6027678. If so, the telephone number to call is 0181 360 6535.

Rolland

Rolland rarity

" *My father drove his Rolland-Pilain car in the 1920s. Do you know anything of this marque?* "

Nick Georgano tells us that, though François Pilain set up Rolland-Pilain in Tours in 1906, the firm's greatest period of expansion was after World War One. Post-war models included the 2.2 litre 14/16 of 1921, which had front-wheel brakes, overhead valves and a detachable cylinder head. Even more ambitious was the 2 litre twin-cam straight eight GP car of 1922 with desmodromic valves, roller bearing crankshaft and four-wheel hydraulic brakes. Your father's car must have been one of the luxurious 4 litre straight eights introduced in the mid-1920s and costing £1,400 on the UK market. Some were fitted with smart wires, but others frequently had ugly artillery wheels. The title of Nick Georgano's definitive three-volume work (to be published in 2000) is the *Beaulieu International Encyclopaedia of the Automobile*.

Rolls Royce

No way to treat a lady

" *I have taken great interest in the fascinating life history of a 1924 Rolls Royce 20 HP, XW 3905, once used as a mobile cinema of all things, and would like to trace the missing part of its early history. With the help of Peter Baines of The Rolls Royce Enthusiasts Club I have established that it was delivered by Paddon Bros to C. H. Runge of Kippington Court, Sevenoaks and Westbourne Terrace, London on 21 November 1924 as a Barker Tourer. In 1936 it is thought that the car was owned by F. J. Brodribb of 15 Belvedere Drive, Wimbledon Hill, London SW19. In 1941 it was owned by Vyvyan Symonds, FCA, FCIS, of Devonshire House, Boutport Street, Barnstaple who, though an accountant, was quite a lively chap. During the war he may have sold it to Eric Gill, who owned the Candar Hotel, Ilfracombe. Then, in 1948, it was apparently seen with a tripod crane in the rear passenger compartment pulling a tractor out of a mire. In 1952 it was found by Dennis Knight in the showroom of Tilley & Bowers of Portland Street, Ilfracombe, fitted with an ash-framed, asbestos-clad van body. Mr Knight used it from 1952 until 1955 to carry the two Bell & Howell projectors, a Briggs & Stratton generator, a screen and the rest of the paraphernalia of his mobile cinema, visiting such venues as Woolacombe, Combe Martin, Chulmleigh, Hatherleigh, Dolton, Witheridge, Bardworthy, West Buckland School and Winkleigh. The car was very reliable, gliding up Codden Hill 'like a bird' despite the great weight she was carrying. But by 1955 she had started to use oil and lose power and was sold back to Norman Bowers. He then sold his garage business to John Cracknell, who turned the car into a pick-up and used it as a recovery vehicle until he eventually lost patience with the poor pulling power of its worn engine. In 1965, he sold it to Gerald Hickman of Old Bideford Road, who restored the bodywork in the style of a Barker Tourer and used it for wedding hire. In 1986, Arthur Miles of Builth Wells bought it and continued to use it for weddings, and when he died it was inherited by his son, Lee Miles. The car now lies dry-stored but partly dismantled and buried under old tractor parts and oil drums. It would be nice to see it rescued and restored to its original state. In the meantime, can any of your readers fill in the missing parts of its early history from 1924 until 1952?* "

Can anyone help? In particular, can anyone tell us of its fall from grace from Barker Tourer to asbestos clad van?

A London reader wrote to tell us of a Rolls Royce 20 HP garage truck in the livery of Anderson's Garage, which he spotted outside the ABC Cinema at Hulme, Manchester, in 1975, registered ON 5230, and which Geoff Browne, former editor of *Classic Car Weekly*, later identified as belonging to saxophonist Johnny Roadhouse. Johnny bought the 1926 car in about 1970, so was probably involved in a gig at the ABC in Hulme when it was seen parked outside. The car had originally been fitted with a body by Birmingham coachbuilder Flewitt, but was written off in the late 1940s and turned into a garage hack. It's now red in colour and still looks much the same, but 77-year-old Johnny is about to start restoring it and hopes to fit it with a more appropriate body. The Rolls Royce Enthusiasts Club confirmed the chassis number as GCK-26, originally sold on 21 July 1926.

Rosengart

Cider with Rosie

" *During a recent holiday abroad I discovered a vintage car in a neigh-bour's barn. Although it requires a little tender loving care, it seems to be intact except for its back axle. Neither the owner nor myself know any-thing about the automobile's history and ask if you could please help us. The car is a Rosengart and was registered in France prior to the Second World War (the headlights are white, not yellow). It is a right-hand drive, registration number 563 B 17, and the engine number is 00515. How much would the car be worth in its present condition and are replacement parts still available?* "

Rosengarts were built at Neuilly-sur-Seine from 1928 to 1937, and at Paris from 1937 to 1955. Early 1930s models, such as the LR4 (of which this is an example), were Austin Sevens built under licence, differing mainly in styling, rad-iator shell and fittings, so you should be able to get help from The Pre-War Austin Seven Club, c/o Steve Jones, 1 The Fold, Doncaster Road, Whitley, near Goole, E. Yorks DN14 0JF, tel: 01977 662828. As it stands, with its back axle off, it won't be worth much. £500 to £1,000 at the outside. But, as you say, the hard bits to replace, such as the nice headlights and radiator grille, are all there and intact, and the restoration of a small car like this is always easier than for a large car.

(I suggested this would be a nice project for an Austin 7 enthusiast to take on, and one from Torquay did exactly that, keeping the car in France.)

Rover

'This Sportsman's Life'

" *I am trying to trace the early history of my pale green Rover P2 12 HP Sportsman saloon, registered BFS 850. I have the registration book covering the period from 25 March 1960 to 20 December 1976, but nothing before or after. It was first registered on 16 September 1937.* "

Would readers with any information please phone 01722 322463. 'FS' is an Edinburgh registration and records from 1921 to 1948 are held by The Kithead Trust, De Salis Drive, Hampton Lovett, Droitwich Spa, Worcs WR9 0QE, tel: 01905 776681. I'm surprised that the Rover Sports Register, c/o C. Evans, 8 Hilary Close, Great Boughton, Chester CH3 5QP, website: http://www.uk-classic-cars.com/rsr.htm, hasn't been able to turn anything up.

75 alive

" *Having driven a 1959 Rover 90 P4 for about ten years from 1963, I was astounded by the Rover 75 displayed on the front page of 'Telegraph Motoring' on 6 February 1999. My memory tells me that the height-to-length ratio in the picture is wrong, and I wonder if it has been 'tweaked' to approximate it to that of the new Rover 75. I have a Blackfriars Guide to new and used cars from 1962 which lists the length of a 75 as being the same as that of a 90. The guide states that the original 75 began its life in 1949 but came in at least three versions, of which only the last was designated P4.* "

You've got a bit mixed up here. The original '75' was the P3 of 1948/49, which was an 'Auntie' Rover development car for the independent front suspension and inlet-over-exhaust-valve six-cylinder engine to be used in the P4 75. The

P4 was launched in 1949, exactly as per the illustration in 'Telegraph Motoring' and derived its low rear deck line from contemporary American Studebakers. This reduced the boot space, so in 1954 the car was re-styled with a boxier boot and three-piece wraparound rear screen. The re-styled body then continued for all P4 derivatives up to the 123 bhp 110 model, the last of which were built in 1964. The new Rover 75 is a comfortable and pleasant car to drive, particularly in CDI form, and sits in the market almost exactly where the P4 did during the 1950s and 1960s.

Speed Pilot

" *Way back in 1954 I was the proud owner of a 1934 Rover Speed Pilot motor car. It had a sloping back aluminium body, air-inflated leather seats, wire spoke wheels, six cylinders, three SU carburettors and a three-lamp cluster on a chrome frame. To this day, I have not seen a similar car either on the road or in a magazine.* "

There's a photo of a 1933 Speed Pilot coupe on page 172 of Sedgwick & Gillies *A–Z of Cars of the 1930s*. This has notchback bodywork, but the Carbodies-bodied 'Speed 14' of 1935 had a beautiful sloping-back saloon body, and the three-light arrangement was a feature of 1935 Speed 14s, as seen in *Classic & Sportscar* of November 1984. Your 1934 car may have been a development model, or the lights may have been added later. The Speed Pilot was the first Rover with an underslung frame, so was much lower than previous models, and the triple-carb 1,577 cc ohv six could get it up to 80 mph. Some were fitted with 2,565 cc triple-carb sixes, were designated 'Speed 20', and were good for nearly

90 mph. Only 204 Speed Pilots were built, which explains why they are a rare sight today. But there is a Speed 14 with the same unusual lighting arrangement at The Heritage Motor Centre, Gaydon, Warks, tel: 01926 641188.

Russon

Bedfordshire microcar

" *In the early post-war years, after forming a dislike for a certain 3-wheel minicar which he said was 'hopeless' (and which then became pretty successful!) my late father, Douglas Russell, formed 'Russon Cars Ltd' with the construction of a mini four-wheeler in mind. It was to be named the 'Russon' (I was the 'son' part). I think I can date this fairly accurately to about 1948 or 1950 and, at the time in my late teens, I had lots of fun driving the various chassis around the Chiltern Hills while running-in the 250 cc Excelsior Talisman two-stroke twin that buzzed the thing along. My recall is that we produced two prototypes: the first, very box-like and later rebodied as the production prototype; the second, later remanufactured into the 'final production unit'; and thereafter about a dozen production units, some of which I recall delivering on trade plates to such places as Lake Windermere, Colchester, Sleaford, Harrow, Chatham and somewhere in South Wales. I think one went to a hospital in Belfast and another was shipped to Karachi. After about 14 cars, capital shortfall precluded further production and the company was sold to Air Vice Marshall Don Bennett (of 'Pathfinder' fame) to re-emerge much modified as the Fairthorpe Atom. Also, I was led to believe that the styling of the Austin Healey Sprite may have been influenced by the Russon. The question is, 50 years on, do any Russons survive and, if so, where?* "

This expands on the listing of the Russon in both Culshaw & Horrobin's and Georgano's Encyclopaedias. There is a photo of a Russon (HMJ 263) in Georgano's book which verifies that the styling of the front does pre-date the

Sprite and even the TR2, though not the Crosley Hotshot. Georgano tells us that the car had a wide, roomy three-seater body, tubular frame and independent suspension all round, that the prototype had a 197 cc J.A.P. engine, but that production cars all had the 250 cc Talisman. Interesting that it grew into the fibreglass-bodied Fairthorpe Atom coupe of 1955/57. This was available with B.S.A. engines of 250 cc, 350 cc and 650 cc, the last of which was reasonably nippy. But apparently it lacked the creature comforts that the buying public was coming to expect from cars such as the Morris Minor and the Austin A30. It was superseded in 1957 by the front engined, bewinged 'Atomota', but this, too, failed in the marketplace. Meanwhile, from 1956, Bennett and his son had also been building their lightweight Electron sports cars in which comfort was not the priority, and this is how the company 'took off', so to speak. The Register of Unusual Microcars should know if any Russons survived (c/o Jean Hammond, School House Farm, Hawkenbury, near Staplehurst, Kent, tel: 01580 891377).

Rytecraft

Slow, slow, slow-slow, slow

" *I was fascinated to see the Rytecraft Scoota Cars which were used to illustrate Malcolm McKay's article 'Life After Unleaded' in a recent 'Telegraph Motoring'. There were several versions, one of which had a pointed 'fin' back like a Brooklands racer, and I actually raced one of these. But my main reason for writing is that I created the ultimate low-emission Rytecraft by converting one to electric power in 1946. Power was provided by 15 2-volt traction batteries made by the D. P. Battery Co. They took up so much space there was only enough room left for a driver. But it*

had a maximum speed of 20 mph and a range of up to 40 miles. I regis-
tered it as an 'Attenborough Special' and used it quite a lot. I am now 92
and bought a Porsche 928 S4 eight years ago, but my wife wrote it off. I
now stick to my much more sedate Volvo 940 turbo and expect to continue
driving it until my 100th birthday. "

Rytecraft Scoota Cars were 'launched' by The British Motor Boat Manufacturing Co. Ltd in 1934 and originally had a 98 cc Villiers engine which gave them a top speed of 15 mph. In this form they were often used as fairground dodgem cars, as well as children's toys and driver training vehicles. A boost to 250 cc and a three-speed gearbox brought the top speed up to 45 mph. The late Jim Parkinson drove a 1935 98 cc model registered BUC 515 round the world in 421 days in 1965/66. 1,500 Rytecrafts were built, and production ended in 1940, but a few cars were assembled from parts after the war.

Salmson

Monsieur Hulot's holiday car

" *Jacques Tati's 'Monsieur Hulot's Holiday' features a fascinating little car. I wondered if you would be able to identify it, and perhaps some of the other 'classics' seen at the beginning of the film? Also, can you tell me when and where the film was made?* "

Monsieur Hulot's car is an early four-cylinder Salmson, probably dating from around 1921/22, with non-standard rear bodywork and what looks like an extra-flexible chassis. The first car to overtake it was a Hotchkiss or a Delahaye, then we saw a Nash convertible, a Chausson bus, a Peugeot 203 and one car I couldn't identify. The first car to pass the sleeping dog was a

Ford Vedette V8. Next we saw a Citroën Traction roadster, a Mk IV Jaguar and finally an older Citroën or Fiat, the window of which was used to frame the small boy's excitement at reaching the beach. The film was released in 1953, and the location was the Hotel de la Plage at St Marc-sur-Mer, a district of St Nazaire between St Nazaire itself and La Baule. Readers report that the hotel is still there, looking much the same, but since interiors were shot at Studios Boulogne Billancourt, Paris, don't expect to go there and find exactly the same twanging swing-door in the dining room. Jacques Tati's first postwar movie was '*Jour de Fete*' (1948) about a postman, his third was '*Mon Oncle*' (1956), and one of special appeal to car enthusiasts was 'Traffic' (1970) which charts the progress of a Hulot-designed Renault R4-based camping car to the Amsterdam Motor Show at the Rai. I bet Mr Bean watched a few of these films as a lad.

Scott

Getting Sociable

" *My uncle owned an unusual three-wheeler in around 1930. It had two wheels in line, rather like a motorcycle combination and, according to my mother, 'it was rather unstable'. Have you any idea what it was?* "

An easy one, for once. Your uncle's strange conveyance was a Scott Sociable (you had to be to travel in it). There's a picture of one on page 474 of Culshaw & Horrobin's *Complete Encyclopaedia of British Cars 1895–1975* (ISBN 1-874105-93-6) and Giles Chapman gives the low-down on page 72 of his book *Cars that Time*

Forgot (ISBN 0-75252-083-0). It was built by the famed motorcycle manufacturer in Shipley, Yorkshire, and was originally intended as a gun carrier for the First World War. But after defence chiefs gave it the bullet it was launched on the civilian population in 1919. It had a two-cylinder two-stroke 580 cc watercooled engine mounted on the driver's side, so unless he had a fat passenger it was inherently unstable on right-hand bends. The advent of the Austin 7 (a proper miniature car) killed it off. 110 were built and the Bradford Industrial Museum has one on display at Moorside Mills, Eccleshill, Bradford, West Yorks BD2 3HP, tel: 01274 631756.

Scout

Scouting tips

" *Could you enlighten me on the history of a Scout motor car that my mother bought around 1922? It had a huge high body with acetylene headlamps, and must have been a brute to drive. It was followed swiftly by a Singer 10 purchased in 1924, reg. MH 2272.* "

Two firms announced cars by the name of Scout in the first decade of the century. One was Stephens Brothers of Stoke on Trent, but, though listed as a maker of cars from roughly 1905 to 1907, no record of them having produced any can be found. It's far more likely that your mother's Scout was built by Dean & Burdon Brothers of Salisbury, which became Scout Motors Ltd in 1908. A 1908 14 HP, 20 HP and 30 HP are all depicted on page 266 of Culshaw & Horrobin's *Complete Catalogue of British cars 1895–1975*, now in reprint, ISBN 1-874105-93-6. Scouts did well in the West

Country but after the First World War the firm's fortunes declined and its subsequent models were basically pre-war designs.

Singer

The Kaye Don connection

" *In the early 1930s my wife's family owned a car referred to as a 'Kaye Don Model', but the make is forgotten. There could have been a 'B' on the hubcap, and I wonder if it might have been a Brough Superior?* "

A reader from Iver Heath phoned to say that the 'B' was in fact an 'S' and the car was a Singer Kaye Don Special, identical to one his father owned in the 1930s. This had a British Racing Green body with black mudguards and black roof, green leather seats, thermostatic radiator shutters and 'India' red-band tyres. He vividly remembers helping his father to remove the 'Kaye Don' script from the rear mudguard. David Freeth, chairman of the Singer Owners Club, is in the process of restoring a similar car (possibly the same car) and would welcome any further information from readers on 01920 830517. Mike Worthington Williams and David Culshaw were also quick to point out the car's Singer and Kaye Don origins, but confusion could arise because there were three Kaye Don Singer Specials based on the 2,160 cc seven-bearing OHV 'Silent Six' model. The standard six-window saloon had a Singer Grille and single rear-mounted spare, while a more elab-orate six-window saloon had a C. F. Beauvais-designed body with 'vee' screen, split radiator grille, low-set headlamps and twin side-mount-ed spares. But the 'Continental' coupe was entirely different, with a standard Singer radiator shell, close-coupled four-window bodywork, a top-hinged luggage trunk and twin spares on the rear.

Kaye Don himself broke many endurance records, was the first to lap Brooklands at more than 140 mph (in the 4-litre Sunbeam 'Tiger'), and earned a Gold Star for track racing at Brooklands. The Tiger's sister car was the Sunbeam 'Tigress', in which Don set a world record for 200 kilometres at 120.91 mph on 23 September 1929. Despite eighteen valiant attempts, driving his Sunbeam 'Silver Bullet' at Daytona Beach in 1930, mostly in adverse conditions, Don failed to break Sir Henry Segrave's World Land Speed Record of 231.44 mph in the Napier 'Golden Arrow'. Besides giving his name to Singer Specials, Don had a factory in Acton, building Ambassador motorcycles (transferred after the war to Ascot), and his company U.S. Concessionaires also imported Pontiacs from the USA from 1935.

In July 1934, Kaye Don was jailed in the Isle of Man for the manslaughter of celebrated MG mechanic Frank Tayler on 30 May 1934. It had been raining, and Tayler had been working all day on Don's MG K3, entered for the 'Mannin Beg' race, while Don enjoyed the hospitality of his hotel. When the car was finished, Don insisted on taking it for a practice run on unclosed roads, crashed, and Tayler was killed. Though MG K3s then went on to finish 1st, 2nd, 3rd, 4th and 5th in the race itself, Don's fatal crash effectively ended his motor racing career and may explain the removal of his name from the rear mudguard of the car described in the letter above. Kaye Don died in 1981. The Kaye Don Bugatti 'Tiger II' is on display at The Brooklands Museum.

SS

Survivor of the original 549

" *I am in the process of restoring an early SSII, registration JD 2345 and originally finished in primrose and black. I would be very interested if anyone who knows any of the history of this car would get in touch. I can be contacted on 01803 842353.* "

The first series of SSIIs were built for only one year, 1932, and were fitted with a 1,005 cc two-bearing side-valve engine from the Standard Little Nine, mildly modified to bring the power up from 22 bhp to 28 bhp. According to Sedgwick and Gillies' *A–Z of Cars of the 1930s*, this was enough to propel the cars to a 60 mph top speed. *The Light Car & Cyclecar* and *Motor Sport* both gave the car favourable write-ups. Only 549 were built. 'JD' was a West Ham registration, but unfortunately records are thought to have been destroyed.

More roadworthy SS

" *Two SSs passed through my life, but both were the larger SSIs with six-cylinder Standard engines. The first was a 1934 model, registered CMV 199, which my father brought home in 1938 and ran for four years. It arrived in grey with red wire wheels, but had to be sprayed camouflage mud brown because of his war work on airfields. As a 12-year-old, I lusted after the car, but it was 13 years later before I was able to buy one. Mine was a 1935 'saloon' registered AWK 228, and though she had none of the steering shimmy problems of the SSII, she was, shall we say, a tad sluggish. The 64 bhp from the alloy-headed twin-carb six wasn't really enough to shift two tons at any sort of speed. The mechanical brakes weren't much cop either, with a worrying sheer if applied forcefully. And with something like ten feet of car in front of the driver, you really needed someone to 'see you out' of a tight corner. Another drawback was the back seat which consisted of two deep buckets either side of the diff – absolutely hopeless for the purpose back seats are intended for. But apart from that, she was a great success and I missed her when I was posted abroad.* "

Your car may have been a 2,143 cc 'SSI 16', with about 53 bhp, or a 2,663 cc 'SS1 20' with up to 68 bhp, depending on the source of the information. The larger engine with an ohv conversion went on to power the SS90 of 1935 and the 102 bhp SS100 of 1936–1940. But the real one to have was the 125 bhp 3.5 litre SS100 of 1938–1940. The closest I ever got was polishing a black one that was on sale for £325 at Sports Motors in Orpington High Street in 1959. The man to tell you more about SSs and whether your cars have survived is Anthony Lake, who runs the SS Register of the Jaguar Drivers Club, 29 Greenhill Road, Sandford, Avon.

As a separate endeavour, Graham Bull is building up a register specifically of SS 90s and SS100s: 2.5 litre side-valve, 2.5 litre ohv and 3.5 litre ohv. Contact him at Camberley Marine and Sports Cars Ltd, tel: 01252 614163, fax: 01252 629298.

Standard

Cypriot Standard

" *While I was stationed in Limassol in 1957, I came upon a car which had been 'liberated' from dense undergrowth. I believe the new owner took the car back to the UK at the end of his National Service. I have often wondered what it was and whether it is still in existence. Can you help?* "

It's a C. F. Beauvais-designed Standard Avon, built between 1933 and 1935. A reader from Cardiff wrote to tell us that the car had been purchased from an English Government official in Cyprus in 1939 when war broke out. The purchaser was a rich merchant by the name of Savas Hajikyriakos, who used it until his death in 1955. Another two-door Avon Sport coupe was purchased by another merchant, Elias Nicolaou, in similar circumstances, and he too used it until his death in the 1950s.

Studebaker

Long, low and Loewy

" *Can you name the streamlined Studebaker of the early 1950s? I think it was the most beautiful car I have ever seen.* "

This is Raymond Loewy's stunning Studebaker Commander Regal Hardtop Coupe, originally introduced for the 1953 model-year. With its excellent aerodynamics, and the help of a supercharged flathead six, it set a lot of land speed records for its class on the Bonneville Salt Flats, and was sometimes fitted with a Cadillac V8, as per Felix Leiter's 'Studillac' in one of the early '007' books. By 1955 it had grown an ugly chrome 'mouth-like' grille and finally became the befinned Studebaker Silver Hawk, Studebaker Golden Hawk and Packard Hawk, which could be had with Studebaker's own 289 ci McCulloch supercharged V8. Loewy's next brilliant effort for Studebaker was the equally advanced glassfibre Avanti, which continued in independent production at South Bend, Indiana, long after Studebaker/Packard closed down. Quentin Willson does full justice to the 1958 Packard Hawk and 1963 Studebaker Avanti in his book *Classic American Cars* (ISBN 0-7513-0473-5). Studebaker Owners Club UK, c/o Doug Priston, 5 Kingsway Manor Lodge Road, Rowlands Castle, P09 6AZ.

Stutz

America's first Le Mans entry

" *In the late 1920s to early 1930s I worked for Warwick Wrights specifically on the American Stutz cars, for which they were importers. These had either six- or eight-cylinder engines and the models were designated 'M Type', 'Blackhawk' and the supercharged 'Bearcat'. Just before going into liquidation, Stutz introduced a model designated 'DV32' which was a twin ohc straight eight with four valves per cylinder. Innovative features of all these Stutz models included: a 'No Back' cam and roller mechanism which prevented the car going backwards unless in reverse gear; an ignition switch which activated a gear selector lock; 'one shot' chassis lubrication; a vacuum pump attached to the oil pump which cut off fuel supply via the Autovac when the oil level was low; a Purolator oil filter; and a manually operated exhaust muffler by-pass. Frank Lockhart was a land speed record contender in a modified Stutz until he was killed on Daytona Beach after hitting a patch of soft sand.* "

Frank Lockhart drove a Stutz Black Hawk Special fitted with two ice-cooled, supercharged 8-cylinder 1.5 litre Miller engines in 'V' formation at Daytona in 1928. After a one-way run at 203.45 mph, the car hit soft sand, rolled, and Lockhart was flung out and killed. But the 200 mph barrier had already been broken in 1927 by Henry Segrave's two-way run in the 1,000 HP Sunbeam at an average of 203.79 mph. Stutz had more success at Le Mans in 1928 when their car, driven by Dick Watney, finished second to Barnato and Rubin's Bentley, and in 1929 when they were fifth to the victorious Bentley team. Norman Barrs of the Stutz Club will be very interested in talking to you (Osborne

House, 111 Bartholemew Road, London SW5 2BJ, tel: 0171 485 1540).

Sunbeam

Team Hartwell Rapier

" *I have a Sunbeam Rapier, first registered VTK 508 on 5 December 1959 at Exeter, which was one of the Hartwell of Bournemouth Rapier team cars. It was also raced at Silverstone (driver: R. Payne). Is it possible to obtain any data about the racing and any action pictures?* "

The Sunbeam Rapier began life in 1956 with a twin-carb 76.2 x 76.2 mm 1,390 cc 'R.67' Hillman Minx engine giving 62 bhp. By 1957, power was up to 67 bhp, overdrive on 3rd and 4th gears was standard, and the model's competition career had begun. (I polished a few of these for Ron at Sports Motors in Orpington High Street in 1958/59.) In 1958 it gained a longer-stroke 1,494 cc 73 bhp engine, sprouted sharp wings at the back, and was given a distinctive grille. Your car, the 1960 model-year version, gained an extra 5 bhp by increasing the compression ratio from 8.5:1 to 9.2:1, which means it won't like 'premium unleaded' even if you sort out the valve seats. For Silverstone pix, try the British Racing Drivers Club, Silverstone Circuit Ltd, Northants NN12 8TN, tel: 01327 857271. Check with *Motoring News* and *Autosport* to see if they have anything in the archives. And grub around the old magazine stalls at Classic Car Autojumbles. I presume you have already exhausted the obvious sources of Hartwells and the Sunbeam Rapier Owner's Club (01725 511140).

Teal

Teal appeal

" *You once mentioned that the kindest thing to do with a rusting Morris Marina was to donate its running gear to a breathless but much loved Morris Minor, thus enabling it to go and stop sufficiently well for modern traffic conditions. But there is an alternative, which is to use the bits of a Marina 1.8 or Ital 1.7 to build a Teal Bugatti Type 35 lookalike (I won't use the term 'replica' for obvious reasons). The resulting conversion is quite a head-turner.* "

Teals can also be built with Teal-manufactured double wishbone coil over shock-absorber front suspension and Granada disc brakes. Power can come from many sources, including 'B' series, Nissan 1800 cc and Fiat twin-cam 'fours', Triumph 'sixes' and even Jaguar twin-cam sixes up to 4.2 litres (Teal Cars, 'Omega', Shaftesbury Road, Bisley, Surrey GU24 9ER, tel: 01483 799277, email: TealCars@aol.com). Unlike some 'replicas', these cars do look good, and I've seen them sell at classic car auctions for between £7,517 and £11,329, including commission.

Thornycroft

Thorny question

" *I am researching the life and times of Frederick Bernard Fowler, who was a notable early aviator and also a motorist of some repute before the 1914–18 war. He founded the Eastbourne Aviation Company in 1911 and established an aerodrome, flying school and factory which built some 260 aircraft before and during the war. Fowler served in the RNAS during the war and was the first man to take off in a land plane from the deck of a naval vessel. Of more interest to you, perhaps, he served his engineering apprenticeship with Vickers Son and Maxim between 1901 and 1905 for whom, it is said, he drove the Thornycroft 20 HP car in*

Scottish and Irish reliability trials. I can find no reference to Thornycroft cars in reference books. **"**

Thornycroft takes up page 313 in Culshaw & Horrobin's *Complete Catalogue of British Cars 1895–1975* (in reprint, ISBN 1-874105-93-6). The Heritage Centre at Gaydon actually has a 1904 20 HP model on display. The 20 HP was quite an advanced car for its day, with a 3,558 cc ohv four-cylinder engine and shaft drive. The Gaydon car has a shell-type radiator, but 1903-model 10 HP and 20 HP Tornycrofts had tube-type radiators.

Triumph

Getaway car

" *In 1957 I purchased a 1939 Triumph Dolomite for £80 and I loved it. It was dark green in colour, one of the last 70 produced, and it was first registered in 1940. It was not in bad condition, although there was a fair bit of corrosion as it had been neglected. But the woodwork inside shone and the engine was strong and powerful. In the mad days of my early thirties I used to hurtle down the East Lancs road and once clocked over 90 mph. The car never failed to start and was a constant source of admiration as I roared around England. But the engine ran hot. In the summer I was constantly in a sweat and drinking water. I was once stopped by the police for drinking while driving shirtless in Banbury. They thought I was drunk until I showed them the Lucozade bottle full of water. How I wish I had stored the car away instead of selling it to a young man for £80. It came to a bad end. Several weeks after the sale there was a ring at the door. It was the police. I was asked if I had sold the car. Had I received the money and did I have a receipt? All was in order. I was then told by the detective, 'The car was used as a getaway vehicle in a bank robbery. Your customer was the driver. After the villains jumped into the car, he shot off without noticing a bus, smashed into it and the engine was pushed back and broke his legs. We got the lot of them, but had to make sure he had not stolen the car.' He then gave the*

address of the scrapyard where the car lay. Sadly, the glorious 'waterfall'
radiator grille was shattered and as it had been cast in some unknown
metal I knew it was irreplaceable. Maybe you can tell me some more
about the model. **"**

Yours was the bigger Walter Belgrove-styled
Dolomite 16 and one of the last true Triumphs.
To have clocked 90 mph on the flat, it must have
had the 1,991 cc ohv 'six' under the bonnet. Club
is the Pre-1940 Triumph Owners Club, c/o Jon
Quinney, 2 Duncroft Close, Reigate, Surrey RH2
9DE, tel: 01737 247218.

Sting in its tail

" *In the early 1950s I had a Triumph Scorpion, which I think dated from*
1933. Its registration was KV 1901, it had a six-cylinder engine, push-

button starter and a spare wheel on the back. I ran it for a couple of years, then sold it in Bedford in 1954. If any of your readers can supply its history before and after my ownership I would be much obliged. "

The Scorpion was a 12 HP 1,203 cc side-valve 'six', typical of the early 1930s, with coachbuilt body in various styles. Late models like this had four-speed gearboxes, hydraulic dampers and semi-elliptic springs. 'KV' Coventry registration records from 1921 to 1963 have been preserved at City Archives, Mandela House, Bayley Lane, Coventry CV1 5RG, tel: 01203 832418 (there may be a small charge for access). The club is the Pre-1940 Triumph Owners Club, c/o John Quinney, 2 Duncroft Close, Reigate, Surrey RH2 9DE, tel: 01737 247218. If any reader would like to help my correspondent with his researches, they should write to J. Corwood, 14 Antony Drive, Moulton, Northwich, Cheshire CW9 8DF.

Vauxhall

First Vauxhall

" *Please could you give me some information about an early car, reg. A 1452? I believe that the car was a Vauxhall and there is a photograph of it being driven by my father near The Spaniards on Hampstead Heath prior to the First World War. Can you give me any information that might be revealed by the registration? If not, can you tell me where I can obtain such particulars?* "

I'm almost certain that the car would be a 1903 Vauxhall 5 HP, the very first Vauxhall model to be built. They must have been good, because apparently no less than forty still survive. The Vauxhall Heritage Centre has one (the Heritage Centre is behind Griffin House on Osborne

Road, Luton, Bedfordshire, but is only open to the public once a year). The registration number, A 1452, shows that this was of course the 1452nd car registered by the London County Council. 'A' was current from January 1904 until April 1905, and encompassed earlier, previously unregistered cars.

Reader J. S. Huggins supplied further information about A 1452. He has a bound volume of *The Automotor Journal* which includes 12 pages about the car, including some beautiful illustrations. And he sheds some light as to why the car was pictured at The Spaniards on Hampstead Heath. It seems that the owner and principal shareholder of The Vauxhall Ironworks was Percy Kidner, who lived in Hampstead, so it may well have been that my correspondent's father, shown in the car, was a friend and neighbour.

Vinot et Deguingand

Mystery road-racer

" *My family had a purpose-built garage known as The West Yorkshire Motor & Garage Co., from 1915 to 1990. It was situated in Settle on the A65, and since that town had a population of just 2,000, the business appears to have been a great act of faith. It went bust twice before 1915 when my family acquired it, and it once housed a racing car.* "

A reader from South Croydon tells us that the racer was a 1908 Vinot et Deguingand 42 HP, built for the 1908 TT race in the Isle of Man and driven by Yorkshireman Roland Outhwaite carrying the number 23. It was one of a team of three cars, but retired after only seven laps and was unclassified. More information about the car and the race can be found in *TT Pioneers* by

Robert Kelly, published in 1996 (172 pages, 300 photos and illustrations covering the races between 1904 and 1922, and still listed by Mill House Books at £15.99 + P&P, tel: 01205 270377).

Vulcan

Very early Vulcans

" *I helped to organise the Vintage event at Southport which commemorated the Vulcan marque on 27/28 June 1998. I am now engaged in researching the early history of the Vulcan car and its founders, the Hampson brothers. It has been suggested that they came from Bolton and may have produced a prototype before setting up their first factory in Yellow House Lane, Southport. Can you put me in touch with anyone who knows the early history of the Vulcan?* "

The entry in G. N. Georgano's *Complete Encyclopaedia of Motorcars 1885–1968* helps. He wrote: 'Vulcan private cars stemmed from experiments conducted in the 1897–99 period by the brothers Thomas and Joseph Hampson. A belt-driven single-cylinder voiturette with lateral radiators was shown in 1902 (the "early effort" has lateral radiators), being replaced a year later by a 6 HP car with armoured wood frame, mechanically operated inlet valves, and shaft drive. It was listed at only £105 and was soon followed by a 10 HP twin, also T-headed, but with a steel frame, selling for £200.' There's much more if you can manage to get hold of a copy of the book. It appears that the move from Yellow House Lane to the Haweside Street works occurred in 1906. David Culshaw goes into more detail about the large number of models from 1903 onwards in his *Complete Catalogue of British Cars 1895–1975*, while a reader from Bringsty tells us, 'In the mid-1950s I bought AW 432, a two-cylinder 'L'-head Vulcan two-seater, at a country house auction near Wellington in Shropshire. The car was complete apart from its original lamps. With the help of friends I restored it and since then it has been in the ownership of Derek Day of Shipston on Stour. The steel-reinforced wooden chassis was only used in 1903, but AW 432 has one and was dated by the VCC as 1904. This Vulcan is the only one to my knowledge which is eligible for the London to Brighton run, but if there are others I would be pleased to hear about them. AW 432 has a good reliability record, having made it to Brighton every year since 1956 except for once when it was loaned to a non-mechanically minded friend who failed to get over the finishing line due to a broken spring in the distributor, which could have been fixed in minutes.'

Willys

Willys Knight

" On a recent walk in North Wales I noticed in a farmyard an old back axle onto which a farm trailer had been mounted. It was massively constructed and carried two original artillery-style 26-inch wheels with wooden spokes. The small multi-sided hub caps bore the letters 'WK' in their centres, and around the edges 'Willys Knight'. Can you shed any light on their origin? Would this be the same Willys that produced the wartime Jeep? If any readers are interested in the whereabouts I should be pleased to provide details. The axle appeared to be in good condition and one of the tyres was still holding pressure. "

The Willys Knight was an American car with a 4 litre Knight double-sleeve-valve four-cylinder engine (Willys Overland took over Edwards-Knight). The history of the company is incredibly complicated, but in 1920 an assembly plant was established in Stockport, Cheshire, and the Willys Knight marque was launched in the UK in 1921. The UK Willys-Overland-Crossley company collapsed in 1933, but the American firm continued, did indeed series-produce the wartime Jeep (along with Ford) and after the war amalgamated first with Kaiser, then with Rambler, and was finally taken over by Chrysler – which is why Jeeps are currently known as Chrysler Jeeps. If any Willys Knight restorer needs a back axle, please write to H. R. Sadler, 'Bronawel', Forge, Machynlleth, Powys SY20 8RN.

Wolseley

Halfpenny Wolseley

" *I would dearly like to trace a Wolseley car, registration SA 3430. The body of this car was originally built by my grandfather, James Reid, in 1906 for another car and transferred to the Wolseley in Aberdeen in 1910. It then passed through various Aberdeen owners before being purchased by my grandfather. Its proudest moment was starring in 'Pygmalion' at Her Majesty's Theatre, Aberdeen, where it was driven by my uncle, William Reid, who at the time detested driving it. At one stage he even sold it to students for a penny, then bought it back for a halfpenny. However, my other uncle, Edwin Reid, liked driving it and drove it from Aberdeen to Glasgow, thence to Edinburgh, and back to Aberdeen, on a rally in 1954. In the 1960s the car passed to a younger William Reid who has since died. Does anyone know what happened to it?* "

A reader from Ashford wrote: 'I am pleased to be able to throw some light on the whereabouts of the 1910 Wolseley 12/16 (reg. SA 3430). It is now painted yellow and I have seen it occasionally in vintage car rallies in Kent over many years, the last time at the Detling Showground in August 1996. I have a feeling it was once in the Dargate Museum collection, near Faversham, though it was not in the Sotheby's sale catalogue when the museum's contents were auctioned off in 1989.'

From wool to Wolseleys

" *My mother's father (Lt. Col. Arthur Turner) had a Wolseley car which he kept in the coach-house of his residence, Birchfields, at Aston, Birmingham. I know he must have purchased it before 1909.* "

It's a Wolseley 10 HP Tonneau, designed by Herbert Austin and built at Adderly Park in Birmingham. It was one of the most popular British designed and built cars of the day, cost £360, and several hundred were built. You can see a 1901 example at The Heritage Motor Centre, Gaydon, which also has an 1896 Wolseley Tri-car, an 1899 Wolseley Voiturette and a 1904 Wolseley 6 HP two-seater on display. Wolseley's former and concurrent business was the manufacture of automated sheep-shearing equipment, which led to many of the company's cars also being exported to Australia and Canada. Any enthusiast of early Wolseleys will enjoy Charles Neville's *Wolseley Cars in Canada 1900–1920*, available at £14.95 + £1.50 p&p from Thelma Waddilove, Regalia Secretary, The Wolseley Register, 45 Larkfield Lane, Southport PR9 8NN.

Father and daughter team cars

" *I wonder if it is possible to trace any information on two cars my father had in the 1930s. The first was a black Wolseley Daytona sports car, registered AJJ 507, in which I toured with him just before my 17th birthday all round England, Wales and Scotland. I could drive by the time we returned. The second car was an MG Magnette, twin carburettor, twin petrol fillers, racing green, bought from Norman Black for £400. We joined the Brooklands British Racing and Sports Car Club around 1937/38, using this car to flap round the course. I remember doing 100 mph off the banking with my father urging me on, but I did not make the average for the course. The club badge from the car is number 2642, which seems fairly early and may help with the dates. We only wore linen helmets then! Although I have two photographs of the Wolseley I have none of the MG. I think he called it the 'Beetle', because of its shape, but I cannot recall its registration. Not much to go on, I'm afraid, but I would love to know what happened to the cars. We had so much fun in them. Now somewhat disabled, I can no longer drive, but I remember it well.* "

The Wolseley Hornet Special Club may be able to tell you what happened to your E W Daytona, a 12 HP model capable of 75 mph (c/o club historian Roger Banks, 'Taliesin', Heath Road, Horsell, Woking, Surrey GU21 4DT, tel: 01483 769058). For the Magnette, try the MG Car Club, PO Box 251, Abingdon, Oxon OX14 1FF, tel: 01235 555552; and also try the Brooklands Museum, tel: 01932 857381, which keeps comprehensive archives and may have the registration on file. Twin carbs means your Magnette won't have been supercharged. I think it was probably one of the later 'N'-series cars which had between 57 and 73 bhp. K1, K2, K3 and N-Type Magnettes are worth a fortune nowadays, especially genuine K3s.

CLASSIC CAR CLUBS*

A30/A35 club

" I wonder what happened to 'VCE 255', a grey Austin A35 van registered in Cambridge. I purchased it new, free of purchase tax, in 1959 and installed a back seat conversion but did not cut out the rear windows. It is the same sort of van as James Hunt's (registered GDX 249E) which has the window conversion, and if the present owner so wishes I can supply him free of charge with an original van floor which I still have. I wonder if Hunt's van had the optional 'high compression' (8.3:1) engine. To avoid delivery delay, mine was the standard 7.2:1. Back in 1959 I traded in a 1954 Austin Somerset, for which I got £385 in part-exchange. Since the van cost £350, it was almost a straight swap after the cost of the rear seat. I sold the van in 1964 for £187. "

One of my first jobs was driving an A35 van for Midland Counties Ice Cream in and around Scarborough in 1967. But I got the really quick version, with a 48 bhp, 1,098 cc Morris Minor 1000 engine. The thing would do 20, 40, 60 and 80 mph in 1st, 2nd, 3rd and

---

* Club details are also found under 'Buying & Selling' and 'Classics and Nostalgia'. Note that every issue of *Practical Classics* magazine carries an up-to-date list of clubs and addresses.

4th gear respectively, and its tall narrow body made it excellent for nipping through gaps in the holiday traffic to get the ice cream to various hotels and holiday camps before it melted. To find out if 'VCE 255' has survived it's worth contacting the Austin A30/A35 Owner's Club, c/o Barbara Scott, Ardberg Farm Cottage, Ardmory Road, Ardberg, Isle of Bute PA20 0PG, tel: 01700 505745.

Austin Healey Sprite

" *I would dearly like to trace two British Racing Green Austin Healey Sprites I once owned. The 1959 Mk I was registered '10 BTA', and the 1964 Mk III was registered 'ADV 1B'.* "

Your first port of call should be the Midget & Sprite Club, c/o Nigel Williams, 15 Foxcote, Kingswood, Bristol BS15 2TX, tel: 0117 961 2759.

Allegro

" *Could you please help me? I have an Austin Allegro purchased in 1977. It has a very low mileage, and I wondered if there are any museums, clubs, collectors or Austin enthusiasts who would be interested in it?* "

I'm now getting at least a letter a week from people trying to offload Allegros. The standard advice is to try advertising in *Quartic*, the magazine of the Allegro Club International, 20 Stoneleigh Crescent, Stoneleigh, Epsom, Surrey KT19 0RP, website: http://www.uk-classic-cars.com/allegro.htm. But selling this way can be a long drawn-out process, so its also worth trying a £20 photo ad in *Classic Car Weekly* or *Practical Classics* (tel: 01733 465430). I have to warn you that, without an unleaded cylinder head conversion, these cars have very little value.

Ford 100E

" *A 15-year-old boy who lives off the beaten track in Norway is hoping to restore a 1950s Thames 5 cwt van. The van cost him £45, plus a bite from the eccentric ex-owner's guard dog. Can you provide any references to help us trace parts and an instruction manual?* "

Try these: Ford Sidevalve Owners Club, c/o Mike Crouch, 30 Earls Close, Bishopstoke, Eastleigh, Hants SO50 8HY, email: menear@ easynet.co.uk; Small Ford Club, c/o A. Carter, 115 Woodland Gardens, Isleworth, Middlesex TW7 6LU, tel: 0181 568 3227; Pre-67 Ford Owners Club, c/o Alistair Cuninghame, 13 Drum Brae Gardens, Edinburgh EH12 8SY, tel: 0131 339 1179.

Classic Fiesta?

" *I have a 1982X Ford Fiesta 1.1L with only 30,000 miles and no rust at all as it has always been garaged and not used in the winter. I have looked at* Practical Classics *and* Classic Fords *magazines and found a wide variation in the possible value of the car. Bearing in mind the need to have new exhaust valves and seats sometime this year and the lack of modern refinements, I wish to change the car either by selling for cash now and buying again at the end of the summer – or trying for the best part-exchange deal I can do at the end of the summer. Can you advise me on a course of action? Where would I get the best price for this somewhat 'odd' car?* "

Original square-front Fiestas are on the cusp of shifting from scrap to neo-classic. They were, after all, Ford's first attempt at a modern small front-wheel-drive car built at minimum cost. I've seen a few in astonishingly good condition, but most have such severe structural rust they simply aren't worth saving and scrap merchants actually charge £30 to take them away. At auction, the best square-front Fiestas are currently making around £325. Yours sounds like it might be worth saving and could be worth £300–£500 to an enthusiast. Talk to the Ford Fiesta Club of GB, c/o Mrs S. Church, 145 Chapel Lane, Farnborough, Hants GU14 9BN, tel: 01276 35422; website: http://www.fiestacentre.com.

Ford Escort Mk I

" *I purchased my Ford Escort 1300XL 4-door, registration 'OGN 196M', direct from Ford in May 1974. At the time I was serving with the Commonwealth War Graves Commission in Italy, and I used the Escort there from May 1974 until 1977 when I returned to the UK. I then left again in March 1984 for Athens, taking the car with me, and remained there until July 1997. From this it will be seen that the car has not been used on salted roads and remains in very good condition. Before leaving Athens, the engine was overhauled and the suspension renewed. As I am now 83 years old, I have decided to sell the car. I have been told that I might obtain a good price because of the good condition and comparatively low mileage of 95,000. I would be grateful for any advice you could give me and the price I might expect.* "

First, make contact with The Ford Escort Mk I Owners Club, c/o Larry Cross, 1 Port Lane, Colchester, Essex CO2 1JF, tel: 01206 799595. *Practical Classics* put a top value of £1,350 on this model, so if there's no luck with the club it would be a good idea to use a photo ad in *Practical Classics* and/or *Classic Car Weekly* (tel: 01733 465430), stressing the car's salt-free life. If there really is no rot whatsoever, you'll have no trouble selling the car, as a completely rust-free original Mk I is increasingly hard to come by. (The other Mk I Escort club is the Ford Escort 1300E Owners Club, c/o Steven Ramek, 93 Thorkhill Road, Thames Ditton, Surrey KT7 0UQ, tel: 0181 339 0572.)

Ford Cortina

A reader from Etchingham wants a valuation of his a 1965 Cortina 1500 Mk I automatic in two-tone grey, which has covered less than 1,500 miles and is in as-new condition. Its ultra-low mileage and condition could make the Mk I worth £3,000–£4,000 (a 1975 Ford Escort van with 477 miles made £2,625 at H&H Buxton last November). A reader from Martock wishes to sell her late husband's 1970 Cortina Mk II 1,300 estate car in Ermine, which she describes as immaculate and has covered 48,900 miles. This is probably worth £1,750–£2,000. Both owners should get in touch with the relevant Cortina club for an expert model-specific valuation. These are: Mk I Cortina Owners Club, c/o Karen Clarke, 6 Hobson's Acre, Gunthorpe, Nottingham NG14 7FF, tel: 0115 966 3995; email: 106553.456@compuserve.com; Cortina Mk I & Ford Owners Club, c/o Helen Pearson, 30 Oban Close, Adswood, Stockport SK3 8RW, tel: 0161 612 1361; Ford Cortina Mk II Owners Club, c/o L. Willis, 7 Underdown Road, Herne Bay, Kent; and Ford Cortina Owners Club, c/o Simon Sellers, 1 Brathay Place, Fleetwood, Lancs FY7 8DJ, tel 01253 878567.

Ford Capri

" I have a Ford Capri which I bought new in January 1981. It is a 1.6GL automatic, has always been in a garage, is in excellent condition, and has just passed its MOT. Mileage is 39,000. Between last August to this, I only drove it 350 miles and, since I am 77, I think it is time to give up driving and sell the car. Please could you tell me what it is worth? "

Probably about £1,500, but a near-perfect 85C Capri 2.0 Laser with just 14,000 miles sold for

£3,282 at H&H Classic Car Auctions in Buxton on 22 July 1998. For your car I think your best bet is to ring around the clubs. There are at least eight Capri clubs, all with their own club magazines or newsletters. Those I have the phone numbers for are: Capri Club International (01789 400455); Capri II Register (01707 336343); Capri Enthusiasts Register (0161 762 9952); Capri Collection (01203 360441); Southern Capri Club (0181 367 0310).

Ginetta

" *Form time to time you have supplied club addresses to readers and this has been most helpful. Could you help me with an address for the Ginetta Car Owners Club? I have a 1971 G15 which I stripped down completely to rebuild, but then my health deteriorated and I would prefer to dispose of the car as an on-going project rather than simply scrap the parts.* "

Ginetta Owners Club, c/o David Baker, 24 Wallace Mill Gardens, Mid-Calder, West Lothian EH63 0BE, tel: 01506 883129.

Jensen to go

" *Could you provide me with the current name and address of the Jensen Owners Club? As the executors of a relative's estate, a solicitor and myself have to dispose of a 1975 Jensen GT 1,973 cc, in immaculate condition, with a genuine mileage of 6,428 and a personalised number plate. The deceased owner was a member of the Jensen Owners Club, but so far I have been unsuccessful in contacting anyone on the telephone number I have. There are also at least £2,000-worth of spares which were purchased when Jensen closed their Kelvin Way site. Any help would be appreciated.* "

Jensen Owners Club, c/o Brian Morrey, Selwood, Howley, Chard, Somerset TA20 3DX, tel: 01460 64165; The Jensen Club, c/o Caroline Clark, 45 Station Road, Stoke Mandeville, Bucks

HP22 5UE, tel: 01296 614072, email: jensen-club@btinternet.com. It's also worth contacting Martin Robey on 01203 641951, as his company is now the principle UK source for later Jensen Interceptor and Healey parts.

Lanchester

" *My father owned a Lanchester, reg. 'AV 7723', during the 1950s and sold it some years later to my aunt, who sold it on after a year. At the time he lived at West School House, Ellon, Aberdeenshire and originally obtained the car from a colonel who lived on a nearby estate. The car had a pre-selector gearbox and fluid flywheel. Can you find out what happened to it?* "

I'll point you in the right direction. First: The Daimler and Lanchester Owners Club, PO Box 276, Sittingbourne, Kent ME9 7GA, tel: 07000 356285. Second: 'AV' Aberdeenshire registrations were issued from September 1926 to January 1938. Records from 1921 to 1948 are held by The Kithead Trust, De Sallis Drive, Hampton Lovett, Droitwich Spa, Worcs WR9 0QE, tel: 01905 776681.

MG T-Type

" *I took my driving test in a car we christened the 'Lincoln Imp' in Gainsborough, Lincolnshire, in 1960 when I was seven months pregnant. It was a green MG T-Type, reg. 'AJW 159', and the examiner approved of my practiced hand flourish as I started her on the starting handle. He also passed my five-point turn, necessary in a very narrow street, but I had to drive above the thirty limit to get the car into top gear. Soon after, during a camping holiday in the Lake District, the engine started to give trouble and eventually blew up in protest at the top of one of the higher hills. Our only recourse was to take the brake off and coast down the hill where, to our relief, we found a garage. Ten minutes later, we had swapped the 'dead' MG for a 'live' Ford Anglia and were on our way again. As our*

daughter was born a fortnight later, this turned out to have been a timely switch, but I often wonder what became of the 'Lincoln Imp'. **"**

There is club specifically for these cars which is the MG Octagon Cat Club, c/o Harry Crutchley, 19 Hollins Business Centre, Rowley Street, Stafford ST16 2RH, tel: 01785 251014. He will be able to put you on to the club's registrar of surviving 'T'-types.

Clubman clubs

" *Until April 1998 I was driving a 20-year-old Mini Clubman automatic which is in very good condition and has covered just 31,028 miles. However, as it needed a new gearbox and a repair to the exhaust system, I decided to buy a newer car. I now need to sell the Mini Clubman and was wondering what I could get for it?* **"**

The value of the car depends on the true condition of the body. Someone might want to restore it as a Clubman Automatic, use the body to restore a 1275GT, or use it as the basis of a Mini special. In its present state it could be worth £500, but if it has any rust its value could be as little as £100. The best place to advertise is *Mini World* magazine (order a copy from your newsagent). Or get in touch with one of the Mini Clubs. These include Club Mini Classics c/o Phil Kershaw on 01582 769459; the Club Mini Classics 1275GT Register, c/o Colin Banks on 01244 390605; National Mini Owners Club, c/o David Hollis on 01384 440060; British Mini Club, c/o C. Cheal on 01543 257957, website: http://www.brochure.org/moc; and Mini Seven Racing Club, c/o Mike Jackson on 0121 707 5881.

Morris/Austin/MG 1100

" *I have an Austin 1100 which I wish to dispose of. The particulars are: first registered 1 February 1967, reg: 'HWH 371E', mileage: 23,864; one lady driver from new; MOTs from 1974 to 1979; car always garaged. Can you possibly give me any idea of its value and if anybody would be interested in it?* "

As a non-runner, the car has very little value. But if it can be economically recommissioned, MOT-tested and put onto a SORN to retain its registration (it should already be on the DVLA records) you might be able to realise more than you paid for the car in the first place. One avenue is the 1100 Club, c/o Steve King, PO Box 3326, London N1 1QD.

Opel Monza

" I would like to sell a full Vauxhall/Opel Workshop Manual for Monza, Royale and Senator models from 1979–85. It is in five volumes, plus a microfiche sheet. It cost me £150, but has saved me many times that amount. I have tried advertising in Exchange & Mart to no effect, and I wrote to the owners club at an address in Northwood Hills, Middlesex, but received no reply. What next? "

The Autobahnstormers has a new secretary: David Waddington, 19 Olivers Drive, Witham, Essex CM8 1QJ, tel: 01376 516034, email: dwgsi24v@aol.com. You could also try the Vauxhall Royale Opel Monza Owners Club International, c/o Martin Yardley, 71 Polmear Park, Par, Cornwall PL24 2AU, tel: 01726 815749; email: cgodfrey4@aol.com.

Peugeot

" I have a 1982 Peugeot 504GR with 55,711 miles, all MOTs available, used for towing my caravan. I am now 78 and giving up caravanning, so wish to sell this car. Please let me know if there is a Peugeot Classic Car Club. The car is rust-free and has never let me down or failed to start. What would be a fair price? "

Between £750 and £1,250, but there really isn't much to go on as I have never seen one at a Classic Car auction and don't see them at the part-exchange sales I attend. The membership secretary of Club Peugeot UK is Peter Beale, 49 Upper Green, Tewin, Welwyn, Herts AL6 0LX, tel: 01778 422274.

Renault 4

" I have a late-registration Renault 4 which is in very good condition. Unfortunately, for medical reasons, our main car must be an automatic *and so the Renault is rarely used. Rather than leave it to stagnate in the garage we would like to see it used, as the car still has some sentimental value to us. Do you have any details of a Renault 4 Enthusiasts Club where I might find someone interested in cherishing this out-dated but interesting and very practical car?* "

The address of the Renault Owner's Club is: c/o J. Cowgill, 89 Queen Elizabeth Drive, Beccles, Suffolk NR34 9LA.

Society of Elves

" *I have been offered a 1962 Riley Elf which is in very good condition, has covered just 40,000 miles driven by two owners and is still in its original paint. It has a current MOT certificate. What would you advise on the price I should pay? And is there a Riley Elf Club?* "

Before you pay a high price for this car you need to be certain it is in perfect condition, with no rot in the sub-frames. Though this is the less desirable 850 cc version, its year of manufacture makes it one of the first. Classic auction prices are all over the place, from around £950 to £3,850, but *Practical Classics* magazine values a good, clean example at £2,250. The club for these is Club Mini Classics, c/o P. Kershaw, 18a Douglas Road, Harpenden, Herts AL5 2EW, tel: 01582 769549.

Rover P6

" *My 1974 Rover 3500 automatic has been taxed every year since new, but has been very little used for the past 15 years and the total mileage to date is only 70,700. The car is in pristine condition and is greatly admired, but now, at eighty-six years of age, all our present day needs are met by our Polo. I would like the Rover to go to a caring owner, but have no idea of its worth, or how best to find a buyer. I would be grateful for your advice.* "

This model is known as the P6, and Rover's innovative monocoque design was much admired. There are two enthusiasts clubs: P6 Rover Owners Club, c/o M. Jones, 48 Upper Aughton Road, Birkdale, Southport PR8 5NH, tel: 01704 560929; and Rover P6 Drivers Club, PO Box 1477, Walsall WS5 3XY, fax: 01922 648133. Either may know of a member looking for a car or will allow you to advertise in its magazine. Another possibility is to try a Classic Car Auction (listed at the end of 'Buying and Selling'). Yet another is to put the car in a photo ad in a magazine such as *Practical Classics* or *Classic Car Weekly* (tel: 01733 465430). Going by your description, I'd ask £3,500.

Rover SD1

" *I shall be grateful if you will kindly advise me how best to dispose of – and at what price – a Rover SE 3500, 'A'-registered, in excellent condition with guaranteed 50,000 miles, purchased as the agent's ex-demonstrator and owned by me ever since.* "

By 1983, these cars were debugged of the sort of problems which beset them in the seventies. The SD1, most desirable of which is the 190 bhp 'twin plenum' Vitesse, has featured in a number of classic car magazines (for example, the 'Buying Guide' in *Classic & Sportscar*, October 1997 issue). You're most likely to find a good home for it by contacting Rover SD1 Club, PO Box 255, Woking, Surrey GU21 1DJ, tel: 01483 888432, or the oddly-named Rover SD1 Mania, c/o Tom Willis, 59 Third Avenue, Enfield, Middlesex EN1 1BU, tel: 0181 482 7387. If the clubs can't help, try a £20 photo ad in *Classic Car Weekly*, tel: 01733 465430.

Singer Vogue

" *You have mentioned the Singer Owners Club in connection with older Singers. But there is also the Association of Singer Car Owners which has registers catering for later models, right up to the last Arrow-bodied Singer Vogues. The membership secretary is Anne Page on 01923 778575. If memory serves me right you may not be overly fond of the pre-Arrow Vogues, but two of our members have made me feel quite humble by their enthusiasm for the cars and their determination to fly the flag for old British cars. They also improve them as they see fit, and the red and white 'two-tone' finish gives the cars a cheery transatlantic look.* "

The 1961–67 Vogue would not be my choice. But I'll defend the right of anyone to preserve cars like this as part of our heritage. For people who like them, old cars also represent the perfect retirement project, second only to gardening.

SS Register

Not as sinister as it seems, the Jaguar Drivers Club has a register for early SS models. Anyone with questions, or especially with information, please write to Anthony Lake, SS Register, 29 Greenhill Road, Sandford, Avon. And Graham Bull is building up a register specifically of all SS 90s and SS100s: 2.5 litre side-valve, 2.5 litre ohv and 3.5 litre ohv. He can be contacted at Camberley Marine and Sports Cars Ltd, tel: 01252 614163, fax: 01252 629298.

Swift

" *I have the opportunity to purchase a 1937 Swift four-door, four-cylinder car with a soft top. It is in a totally dismantled state but I am told it is complete. Some refurbishment has been done but a great deal of work remains. Can you give me any idea of what I should be prepared to pay for it? And is there a Swift Owners Club?* "

The Swift Club (c/o John Harrison, 70 Eastwick Drive, Great Bookham, Leatherhead, Surrey KT23 3NX, tel: 01372 452120) caters for English Swifts from 1901–31, when production ended. I would guess that the dismantled car is most likely to be a late 1920s model. I only have one Swift on my auction data bank, which was a 1923 12 HP tourer in good running order sold by H&H Classic Auctions in Buxton on 24 September 1997 for £10,058, including commission (tel: 01925 730630). The club will be better able to advise what to pay for your basket case.

Toyota

" My wife and I recently gave up driving due to our age and health. Reluctantly, we have now decided to part with our car as there is no point in simply leaving it covered up in the garage. It is a 1978 2.0 litre Toyota Cressida four-door saloon, and is in remarkable condition with a mere 47,000 miles recorded from new. It really does 'run like a Swiss watch'. I was hoping that, with the increased interest in Japanese 'classics', there may be someone out there who would cherish it. At what sort of price would you value it, and how best to sell? "

This will be the RX30 model 18R engine built from 1976 to 1980, and my New Zealand Shell Guide tells me that it needs a VSRP additive plus 'Superunleaded', or at least 96Ron Lead Replacement Petrol to continue running in the UK after 1 January 2000. No one yet knows precisely what the effect of the withdrawal of leaded petrol will be in the UK, but in New Zealand many older cars are happily running on high-grade unleaded with an additive. Your best market for the car would be the Toyota Enthusiasts Club run by Billy Wells, 28 Park Road, Feltham, Middlesex TW13 6PW, tel: 0181 898 0740. You could try advertising it in a photo ad in *Classic Car Weekly* or *Practical Classics* (01733 465430). A 35,000-mile 74M Corona Mk II made £1,806 including premium at an H&H Classic sale on 24 September 1997, so your car could be worth around £1,500 to a real enthusiast for the marque.

Vanden Plas

" *I own a 1974 Vanden Plas 1300 which has covered just 16,100 miles and has been stored in my well-ventilated private garage since 1977. Because of alterations to the house I now need to dispose of this car and seem to remember the existence of a Vanden Plas club. Do you have the address? And would you be able to put an approximate value on the car?* "

These are in short supply in the UK because a few years ago they became a fashion item in Japan and many were exported. This market has now collapsed, but your car may still be near to unique and could be worth up to £3,000 depending on the amount of recommissioning work needed. Clubs worth contacting are: Vanden Plas Owners Club, c/o Nigel Stephens, The Briars, Lawson Leas, Barrowby, Grantham, Lincs; and the 1100 Club (all 1100 and 1300 variants), c/o Steve King, PO Box 3326, London N1 1QD.

Vauxhall Cavalier

" *Can you please help me? I have a red 1977 2.0 litre Limited Edition Vauxhall Cavalier Sports Coupe in beautiful condition with a full history of services and MOTs. My problem is that I am 81 years old, and five months ago I fell and broke my left arm and wrist so can no longer drive my lovely car. I would therefore like to sell it and obtain an automatic. How will I get the best deal in selling it?* "

These rear-wheel-drive Opel/Vauxhall models were very good cars and were responsible for restoring Vauxhall's fortunes in the 1970s. The company's own Heritage Centre in Luton might be interested. Speak to Bernard Ridgeley or Ray Cooper on 01582 426527 and they will find out if there is any possibility of Vauxhall itself buying your car back. Also speak to the Vauxhall Opel Drivers Club, c/o Elizabeth Morphew on 01362 691144, and the Opel Manta Owners Club (your car is a rebadged Opel Manta), c/o Richard Miller, 186 Norman Place Road, Coundon, Coventry CV6 2BU.

Victor

" *An old friend of mine has standing in his drive a 1969 Vauxhall Victor Estate 3300, reg. VYD 450G. It has a straight-six engine and for its age looks to be in remarkably good condition. Since it has now been there for several years and is in the way, he wants to get rid of it, but feels it may be worth more than just scrap.* "

This was a bit of a monster based on the handsome 'coke bottle' FD Victor with a 3,294 cc 123 bhp GM straight six. It was known as the 'Ventora' in saloon form and as the 'Victor 3300' with the estate body. Have a word with the Vauxhall Victor Owner's Club, c/o Mike Knowles, 27 Northville Drive, Westcliff-on-Sea, Essex SS0 0QA; website: http://www.uk-classic-cars.com/vauxhallvictor.htm; and the Vauxhall Owners Club, c/o Roy Childers, 51 Greenbank, Melbourne, nr Royston, Cambridge SG8 6AS: website: http://www.uk-classic-cars.com/vauxhallowners.htm.

VW Corrado

" *Did you know that there is also a club specifically for Corrados? The VW Corrado Club of Great Britain now has 440 members, and at the last event we attended we managed to field 140 Corrados.* "

Great car, particularly the VR6, so this should be a good club. Potential members should write to Chris Rochford, 20 Melford Drive, Macclesfield, Cheshire SK10 2TW, tel: 01625 511783 (eves & wknds). Membership fee is £15.

Wolseley/Ambassador 'Wedge'

" *I read that a reader had sent you some Wedge-related items, and you mentioned the demise of the old club. In fact, a new club was formed in June 1997. We have 65 members to date, and eleven cars attended our first national rally at Billing Aquadrome.* "

Any interested readers should contact P. Maycroft, Princess and Ambassador Owners Club, 26 Castlehall, Glascote, Tamworth, Staffs B77 2EJ. These cars are cheap: I saw one sold for £1 at a part-exchange auction in April 1999.

COOLING SYSTEM

Rusty rad

" On 12 July I purchased a Peugeot 306 XLDT which had been first registered six months previously. The car had travelled 8,000 miles when I bought it and has now covered 28,000 miles. All services have been done by the book. When I went to start the car the coolant warning light came on and I discovered that the radiator was empty. I took the car to a local garage which found that the radiator was useless due to corrosion. A new radiator has now been fitted at a cost of £285, but a 'goodwill' claim for the refund of this cost has been refused by Peugeot. I feel this is most unfair and would appreciate your advice. "

First find out when the car was built in relation to when it was first registered by checking the month and year stamps on the plastic components. The problem may be due to the car sitting around in a compound for a year or so before it was put on the road. Alternatively, the engine may have lost its coolant (for whatever reason) and the coolant was replaced with nothing more than water. Since all engines are corrosion batteries, and since they rely on corrosion inhibitors in the coolant not to corrode, this is the most likely reason why your radiator rusted through. If I'm right, your dispute is with the selling dealer, not with Peugeot. Corrosion inhibitors in MEG coolants only last two to three years and in MPG Trigard coolants up to four years. Switching to Trigard is a very sensible piece of preventative maintenance, but be warned that when refilling your car's XUTD engine it is vital to avoid airlocks.

Core of the problem

" *In July 1998 I acquired an 998 cc Mini Clubman automatic with an 'S' registration suffix, which had been in our family since new in 1978. It had not been driven for eight years, but has recently been fully overhauled and is now in good order. It has just 14,000 miles on the clock, which we know is the genuine mileage. In an effort to keep costs down, the person who did the overhaul advised me that the radiator was 'tender' but did not appear to be leaking and therefore had not been changed. Now that the car is being regularly driven, it is losing coolant at a steady rate. The temperature gauge shows 'normal', the fanbelt and radiator cap are tight and there is no leakage at any of the hoses. The only clue I can find is that when the coolant falls to the level of the top of the radiator core, the surface is covered in bubbles, perhaps indicating head gasket leakage. As I see it I have three alternatives: have the head gasket checked by 'pressure testing'; change the radiator; do nothing and wait until it gets worse. What do you suggest? Finally, I notice that Mini Sport of Padiham, Lancs, is supplying 'lead-free' exchange cylinder heads for Minis at an exchange cost of £140 (tel: 01282 778731). Since it would be necessary to remove the head to replace the head gasket, do you think this would be a good idea?* "

Yes, even if the head gasket is not the cause of the problem. Ron Hopkinson (01332 756056) also does unleaded exchange 'A' Series heads with the important extra benefits of being gas-flowed and fitted with new valve springs at £175. Another very likely culprit of the leak is a rusted-out block core plug, inconveniently at the rear bulkhead-facing side of the engine, and a very common problem with transverse 'A' Series engines. This is so difficult to get at that it may well mean an 'engine out' job, but lift the car on a garage ramp and you should be able to check for the leak from underneath. Also remember, since your AP autobox shares its oil with the engine, the oil and filter need to be changed at least every 3,000 miles or every six months, whichever comes first, or you could be in for transmission trouble.

A loss to explain

" I have a beautiful motor car that gives me numerous opportunities to read Haynes manuals, speak to mechanics and part with vast sums of money. The car is a 'J'-registered 2.9 litre TVR S3 (non-cat) and it loses approximately one litre of coolant every 100 miles. The head gaskets were replaced 18 months ago and there is no sign of milky emulsion in the oil. I cannot find any crystalline deposits indicating where a leak may be coming from. I do not see any steam escaping from the system nor any coolant dripping onto the floor. And, when the temperature indicates 90° centigrade, the electric radiator fan comes on as it should. The TVR agent has twice pressure-tested the system and given it a clean bill of health. I have replaced the thermostat, but I also tested the old one and found that it opened at 85–90° centigrade. In the past, I have seen coolant overfilling the expansion tank and dripping onto the floor. The agent improved matters by putting a pressure cap on the expansion tank. I admit, I don't know if the water pump is working effectively, but assume it would have been tested by the agent. The coolant must be going somewhere and obviously the less coolant in the system the hotter the engine gets and the greater the risk there is of overheating. Any suggestions? "

Fernhurst Motor Co. (01428 656377) is a good TVR agent not far from you, so I plumbed them for a few suggestions. First they were worried that the head gaskets had been replaced as this is an unusual requirement on the old Ford V6 lump. It could be that the block and heads were not faced properly when this work was carried out and they suggest using a gas analyser to test for CO_2 in the header tank. Other likely reasons are stone damage to the radiator matrix creating constrictions in the flow or airlocks in the heater system.

Blowing its top

" *Though I must obviously defer to Fernhurst's vastly superior specialist knowledge of TVRs (see 'A loss to explain' above), I had a similar problem with an 88E Escort 1.6CVH and can offer a solution which may apply to other cars. I found that the steel insert of the small bore expansion tank hose connector on the thermostat housing was so badly corroded it had become totally blocked. As a result, the coolant was boiling and the steam created was forcing the coolant back down the cylinder head and block to the expansion tank from which it was being discharged.* "

This is a useful analysis that may help many owners of older 'cooking' models with a tendency to boil. But there is a fair chance that the corrosion would never have occurred in the first place if the coolant had been changed before the corrosion inhibitors in it degraded. With ordinary MEG coolants, this process takes about two years and with environmentally friendly MPG 'Trigard' coolants it takes about four years.

DISABLED DRIVERS

(SEE ALSO 'ALTERNATIVE TRANSPORT')

Width restriction

" *Further to your helpful remarks about able-bodied people parking in spaces allocated to the disabled, there is another point you could have made about these spaces. Besides being closer to the destination, they are also much wider, enabling us to open our doors wider so we can actually get out of our cars. If we try to park in a normal space we may not be able to get out of our cars. I am pleased to see that Welcome Break motorway services now display signs beside spaces allocated for the disabled warning that non-disabled badge holders will be clamped.* "

While I'm no fan of private clamping operators, I think they can be justified in these circumstances as long as they remain on hand to release the offending vehicle on payment of a fee and quickly clear the space for a disabled person.

Service with a scooter

" *I have been delighted to discover that Hankins (Garage) Ltd, the Proton agent in Alresford, Hampshire, now keeps an electric scooter and wheelchair for the used of disabled customers while their cars are being serviced. Alresford is a charming town and is, of course, on The Watercress Line. The thoughtfulness of this agent has turned a dreary chore into a pleasure. Alresford is also much more accessible than it used to be since the Blackwater Valley Bypass was completed.* "

Hats off to Hankins of 45 West Street, Alresford, tel: 01962 732601. Proton's PR agency later informed me that all Proton agents were planning a similar service to the disabled. This begs the question why other franchised agents can't offer a similar service where their garages are situated within a scooter ride of a town centre or some other important destination.

Complicated problem

" *Following a road traffic accident I am permanently confined to a wheelchair. I now have a daughter of two years and am expecting another baby soon. At present I drive a 1993 Toyota Corolla two-door hatchback. This suits me because I can slide from my wheelchair into the driver's seat, cantilever the passenger seat forward, recline the driver's seat, then lift the wheelchair over my reclined body into the rear footwell behind the passenger seat. With the arrival of the new baby I will need a four-door hatchback in which I can perform the same operation. Can you think of any?* "

My first reaction was to refer you to the various organisations best able to advise you, which include: The Disabled Driver's Association, Ashwellthorpe, Norwich NR16 1EX. tel: 01508 489449; The Disabled Drivers Motor Club, Cottingham Way, Thrapston, Northants NN14 4PL, tel: 01832 734724; The Royal Association for Disability and Rehabilitation (RADAR), 12 City Forum, 250 City Road, London EC1V 8AF, tel: 0171 250 3222; and The Federation of Independent Disabled Motorist Clubs National Mobility Centre, tel: 01743 761718. Then a Peugeot delivery driver arrived outside my house in what may be the perfect car for you. The new Peugeot 206 hatchback not only has lever-operated 'instant recline' seats, the five-door version can be ordered with an 'Adaptable Passenger Seat'. The squab of this folds forward to reveal a hidden storage compartment and the backrest can then also be folded forward in the same way as the back seats of some estate cars. If that doesn't quite work for you, you may also be able to buy a front passenger seat from a two-door 206, which cantilevers forward. I should add that the 206 is a sweet little car with lots of other thoughtful touches and, like the 306, is British-built in Coventry.

Shopmobility

" Have you ever given any thought to the subject of electric three- and four-wheeler 'mobility' scooters? Having progressed from more than 80 years of driving real vehicles to one of these I found it a real eye-opener. Mine has a maximum speed of six mph, but I understand I may use it at up to four mph on the public footpath. Kerb ramps are obviously essential and these are 99 per cent okay in Windsor, but the odd one per cent can be dangerous, particularly if one's eyesight is poor. From four mph to eight mph one is required to use the public highway, and on dual carriageways an orange flashing light must be used. The carrying capacity is limited and excludes large bags of potatoes. But many shops encourage one to use the scooter inside. Mine cost less than ten per cent of the price of a car, does not condemn me to pay 84 per cent of the petrol pump price in tax, costs just £40 a year to insure, incurs no road tax and travels 20–30 miles on a single battery charge. Parking on double yellow lines is ignored by traffic wardens, so no £50 penalties. I can see these scooters becoming popular – and maybe even a pest! "

We were alerted to a mobility scooter price scam last year, and anyone thinking of buying one should first contact the British Healthcare Trades Association on 01732 458868. (See also 'Mobility Mugging' in the Alternative Transport section.) As for Road Traffic laws, Class 2 invalid carriages of less than 113.4 kg unladen are restricted to 4 mph and can be used on footpaths. Class 3 invalid carriages must weigh less than 150 kg unladen, can do up to 8 mph, but are restricted to 4 mph on the footpath. Extra requirements of Class 3 scooters are that they must have a speed indicator and a horn, must not be wider than 0.85 metres, and must not be driven by anyone under the age of 14. The yellow flashing light is a good idea for use on all roads with speed limits over 20 mph, not just dual carriageways.

DISPUTES WITH GARAGES

Registration scam?

" *It is my custom to renew my new car every three years. This gives me trouble-free motoring, a three-year warranty, no MOT to worry about, inclusive AA/RAC pan-European cover, etc. The problem I have is with the registration of the car I took delivery of on 1 February 1998. As the dodge had been tried on the previous two cars (which I managed to stop in time), I specified quite emphatically that I wanted it taxed and registered on 1 February. When I collected it, sure enough the new disc expired on 31 January 1999, but when the registration document arrived from Swansea it showed that the dealer had registered it in January. It appears obvious that he wanted to get an extra sale in January and he had not properly responded to my complaints – merely that it is normal practice to register a vehicle in the previous month. To me, that's poppycock. It seems I am now faced with a worse residual value and an earlier MOT if I still own the car. Your comments please.* "

1 February 1998 was a Sunday and both Vehicle Registration Offices and Post Offices are closed on Sundays. Alfa Romeo, Fiat and Nissan now offer instant automated registration and taxing of new cars, and this service is available for 60 hours a week 8 am to 6 pm Monday to Saturday, but even they would have had to register and

tax your car on Saturday 31 January in order for you to drive it away the next day. However, had you delayed registration and taxing of your new car until Monday 2 February, it could have been registered as a February car and the only real reason for the dealer registering it before this date would have been to achieve a monthly sales target on which a bonus depended. Any residual loss of value between January and February is negligible, but there would be a significant value difference between a February and a March registration because of the March prefix letter change.

New car, old battery

" *My wife purchased a Citroën ZX in February this year under the Citroën Hallmark scheme. It had been first registered in March 1997, had completed 10,000 miles, and she paid an additional £298 for a two-year extended warranty. On 10 June the battery failed. I was aware that the warranty excluded batteries, but when I went to replace it I was told that the battery in the car had a charge date of August 1994, indicating that it was five years old. I naturally assumed that the battery had been swapped at some time, so I confronted the Citroën agent which offered to fit a new battery at the full retail price of £72. I asked the agent to raise the matter with Citroën UK, but was told that Citroën stated it was normal practice to fit a four-year-old battery to a new car. I find this difficult to accept.* "

So do I. One of four things has happened. At some time during its life the car sat around for a long time, the original battery lost its ability to hold a charge and was replaced by an older battery that worked. (Check the true build date of the car from the date stamps on the plastic components.) Or the first owner substituted the original battery when he part-exchanged it. Or a trader got his hands on the car between the first owner and the Citroën agent and he swapped the battery. Or the Citroën agent swapped the battery while the car was in stock.

'Compensation' claimant

" *I took my six-year-old left-hand-drive Renault Savanna to the local Renault agents for a 30,000-mile service, its first for a year. The bill came to £295.52 (but this included £183.30 for three new tyres so the bill for the service itself was £112.22). When I got the car home, I found that the radio no longer worked as it had before the service. It worked for ten minutes, then bleeped and failed to respond to the controls. I attempted to claim compensation from the garage and from Renault UK, but to no avail. Two months later, the car developed a serious braking fault. I took the car back to the garage where the rear drums were removed and the wheel cylinders were found to be leaking. These were renewed but, after having been replaced, the garage phoned to ask for authorisation to replace the master cylinder as well, which was also found to be faulty. On collecting the car, I paid the invoice of £266.67 under protest. I feel that the agent's failure to spot this potentially life-threatening problem at the service put our lives at risk, that the garage has failed in its Duty of Care, and that I should be refunded the full £266.67. How I go about proving my case against the garage?* "

This reader wrote to me in two stages: first about the radio, then the brakes. The problem with the radio is most likely to be an earthing fault – easily checked externally, but if the earth cable has become detached inside the unit it will require a visit to a car audio specialist. Nothing done during the service could have caused this fault. Regarding the brake failure, he had clearly opted for the cheapest possible service, which consists of an oil and filter change, fluids check and general visual inspection with no dismantling involved. In my view, such a service should be carried out every six months rather than every year, and standard-fill brake fluid and MEG coolant should be changed every two years

(Renault recommends a brake fluid change every three years). There is no evidence that this had been done, so it's reasonable to expect the old, contaminated brake fluid to start causing problems. He could also have asked for the brakes to be dismantled and inspected, whereupon any problems could have been spotted and rectified. But he didn't. So it's the reader's skimping on servicing that has cause his problem and he has nobody but himself to blame. Renault also recommends a timing belt change at five years or 72,000 miles. If the reader ignores this as well, he could be faced with a bill for a new engine in the not-too-distant future.

Small car, big bill

" We recently put my wife's 28,000-mile 'L' reg. Micra into the Nissan agents for a service, MOT and repair to a slipping clutch. After reading in your column the potential damage caused by a broken timing chain, we also enquired about having that replaced. At first the receptionist thought the car had a timing belt rather than a chain but, having checked, told us it did indeed have a chain and this never gave trouble. The agents later rang back to tell us that a brake wheel cylinder was leaking, which would cost £50 plus labour and VAT to replace, that the clutch would cost £260 plus VAT, and that the timing chain would need doing at the horrendous cost of £630 plus VAT. We had the service and MOT done for £146 inclusive, but went elsewhere for the rest. A very reliable local garage did the clutch for £149 all-in, said the brake cylinder was not leaking and that the timing chain had a barely perceptible 'tick'. Replacement of these two items should not even be considered. I expect franchised agents to be expensive, but because of the intimidating print in the warranty document I use them for the warranty period. But it strongly looks like this one went well over the top. Don't agents realise that incidents like this can rapidly change a loyal, regular customer into a 'never again' new car buyer? "

Sixteen-valve Micras are good little cars with an enviable reputation but two Achilles heels. The first was the clutch on early models which was not up to the task of city use and led to many being changed to more robust units under warranty. The second is the timing chain. In theory, this should never need touching but the tensioner can sometimes give trouble. This is a pig to get at, which explains the horrific estimate. The best way to avoid timing chain trouble is the traditional way which is to have the oil and filter changed every six months rather than every year. It is particularly important in a car that does a low mileage mostly of short runs because the condensation this creates inside the engine gets no chance to evaporate and contaminates the oil.

Engine bill blow

" *In April 1998, I spent £1,210.65 on an extremely thorough franchised agent service of my four-year-old Audi 80 2.6E automatic. The service included replacing the gearbox ATF and brake fluid and reassembling the oil pump which had developed a leak. Then in October 1998 the oil pump failed and the engine seized. The cost of a replacement long engine and installation amounted to £5,077.56. I wrote to Audi Customer Service, and in return I received an offer of a 25 per cent reduction in the cost of the parts as 'a gesture of goodwill'. This does not seem much in the circumstances. What do you think?* "

If you took this further, your problem would be one of proving that negligence by the agent who rebuilt the oil pump actually led the engine to seize. The agent would counterclaim that you must have ignored the oil warning light, which tells you to stop as soon as you can and switch off the engine. Unless you suddenly lose oil pressure at high speed, it is usually possible to stop and switch off an engine before lack of oil pressure leads to damage. You cannot expect to

be able to 'limp home' with the oil warning light on. So my advice would be to accept Audi's goodwill offer. Remember, Audi was under no obligation to make this offer. Any dispute you had would always have been with the agent that rebuilt the oil pump which failed.

Lost service book

" I recently paid top money (over £2,000) for an 80,000 mile 'A'-registered VW Golf Mk I Driver. My main reason for paying this price was the fact that the car came with a full VAG service history showing that services had been carried out every 6,000 miles. I then took the car in for another service and the agent lost the service book. My questions are: what is the value of the car now, without its service history? Do I have any redress against the garage which lost it? "

Depending on its true condition, without its service history the car is now worth between £500 and £1,000. So I'd ask the garage which lost the service book to either buy the car from you for what you paid, or pay you £1,000 for losing the service book, or look a bit harder and find your service book. The garage clearly failed in its Duty of Care towards the customer, and if it doesn't willingly put matters right, speak to the Trading Standards Office which covers its locality.

Four engines in nine months

" *I bought a 1990 'G'-registered Proton 1.5SE LE from a garage in Chesterfield on 7 April. The recorded mileage was 74,098. Eleven days later, at 74,466 miles, the oil warning light came on. I stopped immediately and the car was returned to the garage. I was told that the oil pressure relief valve had failed, the engine was replaced and I paid £100 for a warranty on the replacement engine. On 22 July, at 77,688 miles, the oil warning light came on again. I stopped immediately and the car was delivered to my local garage. They told me the reason was that the oil pressure relief valve had failed again, a new engine was needed and, because the so-called warranty had a £150 limit, I was forced to shell out £1,160 for the fitting of a replacement engine from API. On 25 September, at 80,309 miles, the same thing happened yet again. API came out to inspect the engine, and fitted a third replacement free of charge. Then, on 18 September, at 81,896 miles, the same thing happened yet again and, to their credit, API fitted yet another replacement engine, again free of charge. I have been told that there is a fundamental flaw with the oil pressure relief valves of these Mitsubishi/Proton engines. Is there any way I can get my £1,160 back, possibly by invoking the Sale & Supply of Goods Act?* "

There is something strange about the copy V5 registration document you sent me. It states that the car was registered to the Chesterfield garage on 6 April, then to you on 7 April. For this reason, I suggest that you get in touch with the DVLA, find out the name and address of the one previous recorded keeper who owned the car from new, and ask him what the mileage was on disposal. If you find this was higher than the mileage on the invoice, then contact Chesterfield Trading Standards so that criminal proceedings can be taken against the garage. But remember, if this puts the garage out of business, you won't stand much change of getting any compensation. There is no problem with 8-valve 1.5 litre engines fitted to UK-market Protons and earlier model Mitsubishis apart from oil drain-down caused by the fitting of incorrect oil filters which lack anti-return valves. However, there can be a problem when Japanese-market Mitsubishi 'Jet' engines are used as replacements. These engines have emission-reducing compressed air jets into each combustion chamber which don't work in European conditions and necessitate the jets being blanked off. They also have an oil pressure relief valve which can be prone to sticking. So the second time API replaced your engine they modified the oil pressure relief valve so that it will not stick again, provided the correct oil and oil filter is used.

Service fit-up?

" Isn't it about time that the Office of Fair Trading looked into the unholy alliance that exists between car manufacturers and their agents in the matter of annual services? A great many owners, including me, continue to take their cars to the garages from which they purchased them, probably deluded by statements such as: 'only your official dealer has the special tools and services required to provide you with safe and reliable motoring'. Basically, of course, we know that this is largely bull, as the average annual service requires little in the way of special tools and services. We know too that our car will be put through a rigid system, irrespective of its particular requirements, and at considerable cost. Indeed, *much of the work done will come under one of the following headings: (a) probably didn't need doing; (b) could be, and probably has been, done by the owner; (c) covered by the MOT inspection. I have a 'K'-registration Volvo 440. Last summer my garage rang to say I was due for a 60,000-mile service. I had only done 27,000 miles, but I know about short journeys causing extra wear and tear, though I am not entirely convinced by it. My car was collected 'free' at about 8.30 am and at about midday the garage rang to say that the work had been completed. When I received the bill, the charge for labour alone was £181, plus £9 for replacing a tail bulb and exhaust mount. Now, even if work had commenced on my car the moment it arrived and had only been completed when they rang me, that works out at nearly £60 an hour. And what did I get for it? Well, they had replaced the camshaft drive belt which, given the mileage, probably didn't need doing. Apart from that, the usual run of things: changed the engine oil, topped up the battery, changed the brake fluid, oiled the hinges, checked the brakes and tyres and so on. Not a lot for nearly £200.* ”

Though the OFT is investigating franchised garage servicing costs, this letter gives no grounds for complaint. The the owner of a seven-year-old car has a free choice of taking it to an independent garage for servicing. The Volvo agent he consigned it to clearly has menu servicing which absorbs the cost of the car being collected from and delivered to his home (a time-consuming task requiring two drivers each way, or leaving transport at the customer's address). The garage has changed the car's timing belt which, if not done at this age, would have stood a 50/50 chance of snapping before his next service and wrecking his engine. The high labour cost could be because one fitter did this work while another carried out other parts of the service. And it has conscientiously checked everything, possibly saving the reader from a fixed penalty for driving with only one tail lamp operational. He paid a fair price for this level of service.

DRIVING ABROAD

Headlamp converters

A number of readers and manufacturers replied to my appeal for headlamp protectors and beam deflectors, in particular for the 'old' BMW 5-Series, the lights of which are not switchable from left to right dip. Signam Limited make a useful range of 'Smoothy' light protectors which are available from accessory shops. If you can't find them, call the company on 01926 417300. (Signam also makes number plates.) With some new cars such as the Ford Focus, dropping the beams to their lowest load-compensating setting can be enough to make sure you don't dazzle oncoming motorists when driving on the right.

Travel cover for older cars

" On 9 July I went to my local AA office to renew my 5-Star annual overseas insurance and was told it had been withdrawn and that the vehicle age limit had been cut to 11 years for those with any months left on their policy. Can you tell me who still covers older cars on an annual basis? "

Annual AA overseas cover is only available for cars less than 11 years old, and only to AA members. Others who cover older cars on an annual basis are General Accident Direct: cars over 10 years old £133.72 (0800 121007); Green

Flag: cars 10-15 years old £290, cars over 15 years old £435 (0800 400638); Mondial: cars 10–15 years old £143.96 (0181 666 9352); and RAC: cars over 11 years old £143.50 for members and £155 for non-members (0800 550055). Norwich Union 'Private Car Club' insurance policies actually include European breakdown cover for any age of car at no additional cost.

Which grade?

" *While on holiday in France recently, I noticed that French garages were offering two grades of unleaded petrol. I am embarking on a drive through France, Switzerland and Italy soon and would appreciate your advice on which grade of fuel would be most suitable for my 'P' reg. Nissan QX.* "

Usually the grades are the same as they are here: 95Ron 'Premium' unleaded and 98Ron 'Superunleaded'. But two great advantages of driving on the continent are that petrol is neither taxed nor profiteered on as heavily as it is in the UK, and the price difference between 95Ron and 98Ron is no more than a few centimes. With high performance cars, Super gives you better mpg, better performance and lower emissions. Other cars such as Fords are designed to run on 95Ron.

It tolls for thee

" *Your readers should be warned that, in common with Switzerland, Austria now imposes a toll for the use of its faster roads. Vignettes, costing the equivalent of £3.50 for ten days, are available from the automobile clubs and filling stations at the border and at post offices and tabacs. The fine for running without displaying a yellow vignette is the equivalent of £55, payable by credit card. The civilised Austrian police even have credit card terminals in their cars.* "

Thank you for the warning.

DRIVING CONDITIONS

Parking adjudication

" *Last August you advised me to approach the London Parking Appeals Service to mediate on a parking ticket I had received from Camden Council. I am delighted to report that the adjudicator referred to his 'Parking Attendant's Handbook', decided the ticket was completely unjustified, and cancelled the penalty.* "

Good. Other readers parking in areas controlled by London Councils should be aware of this service, which should, in fact, be offered as soon as they dispute any parking penalty in London other than on a 'Red Route'. The address of the London Parking Appeals Service is PO Box 3333, London SW1Y 4XP, tel: 0171 747 4700. If your car is towed away or clamped in London, call Vehicle Trace on 0171 747 4747 (24 hours).

M62 Junction 12

" *Recently I had to travel from York to Sale, near Manchester, to attend a funeral. I used to live in the area, so know it quite well. I would normally turn from the M62 to the M63 at Junction 12. However, on this occasion, when looking for the M63 signposted Sale and Altrincham, all I saw was*

M60 Manchester Airport. I thought it must be a new junction and carried on, then, realising my mistake, turned off at Warrington and made my way back to Sale on the old roads. While this was inconvenient for me, it might have been a disaster for someone else, resulting in the last-minute lane changes which cause tragic accidents. Surely, when the designated number of a road is changed, the junction signs should explain this with words along the lines of 'formerly M63'. "

This is a good point. Locals cotton on to such changes within days, but drivers returning to an unexpected change could easily be caught out. Several 'count down' motorway signs would help. It would be interesting to know if there have been any accidents at this junction since the sign was changed.

The curious case of the Copse Hill chicanes

A reader from Coombe Hill alerted us to some strange roadworks on nearby Copse Hill, London SW20. So I went, I saw, I photographed. This wide road is subject to a 30 mph limit, but the downhill incline between the Atkinson Morley hospital and Coombe Lane always made it difficult to stick to the limit without continually braking. So what the planners have done is install a series of chicanes. Unfortunately, they have used vertical kerbs six to eight inches high at the exits of these chicanes. Because I'd walked the road to take photographs before I drove it, I was well prepared. But, even at 30 mph, two of the exit kerbs have the potential to wreak serious damage to the front suspension of any car which hits them. So, though the chicanes may have served the planned object of slowing traffic on Copse Hill, the high cost of this could be a subsequent accident elsewhere due to suspension damage inflicted by the kerbs. I asked to hear from anyone who had hit any of the kerbs or bollards. I also welcomed any justification the planners were able to offer for the design and execution of these seemingly dangerous road works.

I had an interesting response. From what I could gather, the chicanes were installed in late 1997 or early 1998, and by Summer 1998 had been the cause of around 100 damage-only accidents and at least one involving personal injury. As a result, a review was held during Autumn 1998 and some of the chicanes were re-sited, but not the double chicane on the uphill stretch which, in my view, is the most dangerous of the lot. An extremely vicious high-kerbed island, 'almost in the middle of the road', to quote a Wimbledon reader, juts out from the nearside, followed all too quickly by a second island, forcing the driver to steer very accurately to avoid hitting them in clear conditions, never mind in blinding winter sunlight, snow, ice, rain, fog, darkness or any combination of these conditions. This particular chicane was responsible for £388.60 of damage to a brand new car, and also caused severe damage to the tyres of more than one Wimbledon driver, one of whom has suffered no less than three blowouts from striking the kerbs on the Copse Hill Chicanes. It is arrogantly 'anti-car' and plain dangerous to install double chicanes with high vertical kerbs in what appears to be a deliberate attempt to damage cars. If Merton Council wishes to continue its traffic calming experiment with chicanes it must, at the very least, replace the vertical kerbs of the islands with chamfered edge kerbs so that the kerbs themselves do not cause unnecessary damage to car tyres, wheels and suspension.

As a result of public pressure, not least from the residents of Copse Hill itself, a public meeting was held in Christchurch Hall, Copse Hill at 8pm on 12 January 1999. According to reports, hundreds of Wimbledon residents attended. In their words, 'there was a huge amount of opposition…the whole room was seething with anger'. The hall in which the meeting was held could not contain the numbers who turned up to protest. Merton Council officials explained to the residents that it had been allocated a traffic calming grant and had only limited time to spend this. That is why the project was rushed through, why it was so badly designed, and why residents were not adequately consulted before the car-damaging double chicanes were installed. The council was only officially aware of eleven accidents on Copse Hill since the chicanes were installed, because the hundreds of tyre, wheel and suspension-damaging incidents caused by the unforgiving kerbs in the middle of the road were not reported to the police. Opposition is obviously so great (further reports of car damage keep flooding in) that is seems likely the council will be forced to replace the Copse Hill Chicanes with a more vehicle-friendly form of speed control.

Engine flood damage

" *My daughter recently drove her Vauxhall Cavalier 1.7TD through flood water (no warning signs) and suffered catastrophic engine damage as a result of water being sucked into the engine through the car's low-set air intake. A new engine has been priced at £4,350 fitted, including VAT, with an allowance of £450 if the seized engine is not too badly damaged. Please warn your readers of this danger.* "

I have, several times. The warning was repeated

on page 580 of the previous edition of this book, and here it is again. Particularly vulnerable are old-shape Renault Espace TDs, and Citroën Xantia TDs, which have not been raised on their suspension to lift the intake above the flood water. The incompressibility of the water drawn into the combustion chambers either bends the con rods or blows the head gasket. Petrol engines with low set air intakes can also be affected. A bit of good news is that this reader's daughter can get a fully reconditioned Isuzu diesel engine for her Cavalier for £1,550 + VAT from API on 0500 830530. The price includes all gaskets, a 12-month/12,000-mile warranty, and even the special running-in oil. This is a much better bet than spending £4,350 on an engine for a car which is only worth £4,000 tops.

Motorway speed limit

" *Further to your timely warning about a speed limits review, I have written to Lord Whitty, Transport Minister, DETR (National Speed Review). The text of my letter is as follows: 'In your review of speed limits, I suggest that if a limit is considered necessary on motorways, it should not be lower than the French limit of 130 kph/85 mph. Lower limits encourage bunching, boredom and inattention. In your publicity you persist in promoting the slogan, "speed kills". This is a fallacy since speed, per se, does not kill. It is the relationship between the circumstances and the speed which is critical. We have to accept in modern life the risks associated with speed otherwise we would not travel by air or high-speed train. I would also put it to you that strict enforcement of speed limits has more to do with revenue generation than with road safety. There is a growing body of opinion which would wish the same levels of surveillance and successful prosecution be applied to thugs and thieves as is applied to generally law abiding motorists who may inadvertently exceed unrealistic speed limits. A review of camera positioning would prove my point. I am pleased to say I do not have a personal axe to grind. Our existing motorways could best be improved by adoption of the following: Strict enforce-*

ment of keeping to the left (except while actually overtaking); Positive sep-aration of carriageways, perhaps by an earth bank, so as to eliminate crossover accidents, dazzle and rubbernecking; The provision of street lighting throughout the network; More research into the problems of spray and poor visibility. Kindly acknowledge receipt. Should any of the points I raise not be part of the review, please pass them on to the appropriate department and give me the relevant details. "

Bravo. Anyone advocating the opposite approach – such as lowering the motorway speed limit or rigid enforcement of the existing one – must hold themselves responsible for the national gridlock and economic collapse which will surely follow. And, of course, for choking pollution because, though a car travelling at 90 mph emits more pollution than one travelling at 50 mph, cars stuck in traffic jams emit far more pollution than either. The only way for our road network to successfully cope with the volume of traffic is for each vehicle to complete its journey faster. A car that completes a 300-mile journey in four hours is on the road for a third less time than a car which completes it in six hours. A car that completes the 300-mile journey in eight hours effectively takes up twice the amount of road-time as the four-hour car. If all vehicles take twice as long to complete their journeys, they effectively double the amount of traffic on the roads.

Lies, damn lies...

" In the past you have remarked on the use of bogus statistics to justify various road traffic laws, and this has prompted me to remind you of what was probably the most blatant use of fiddled statistics in motoring history. I refer to the figures originally used to justify the 70 mph speed limit, which was made law in 1967 by Labour Transport Minister Barbara Castle. It followed an experimental 70 mph limit introduced the previous

year. The idea was put forward by a Department of Transport advisory committee which normally had 12 members, but on the day the idea was mooted, at just 24 hours notice, only four of these were able to attend. The late, great Jim Clark and representatives of the RAC and AA (the origin of which was a club to warn members of speed traps) were notable by their absence. At the end of the 12-month 'experiment' Ms Castle used a statistic that road deaths were 20 per cent down on the previous 12 months to justify making it law. In fact, they were only 0.58 per cent down (a figure more likely to be explained by the increased wearing of seat belts). The 20 per cent improvement was on an anticipated rise in road deaths for 1966–67 which never actually took place. Though some form of motorway speed limit is undoubtedly needed, there has always been doubt that 70 mph was the right choice. **"**

On the date the 70 mph limit was imposed it meant little hardship, because most traditional British family cars of the time could not cruise at much more than 70 mph anyway. Imposing the 70 mph speed limit thereby held back progress in car design and the net result is that Britain no longer owns its motor industry. Remember, in 1967 BMW was still a small company using the unrestricted autobahns to breed its mile-eating 1500–2800 cc saloons. Now BMW cars are coveted throughout the world and the company owns the last British car manufacturer to be sold into foreign ownership.

Traffic harming measures

" *As long as motorists can prove negligence of the council in failing to comply with whatever government guidelines refer to the particular measure, if their cars are damaged by traffic calming measures they may be able to successfully sue the council through the Small Claims Court. I did, and won.* **"**

The DETR has issued so many Traffic Advisory Leaflets, it has had to issue an index to them.

The latest at the time of writing is TAL 4/99, 'Traffic Calming Bibliography', available free from the Traffic Advisory Unit, Zone 3/23, Great Minster House, 76 Marsham Street, London SW1P 4DR, tel: 0171 676 2478. Once you know which leaflet you need, you can order it and can set about checking whether the traffic calming measure which damaged your car conforms to the guidelines. Readers might also want to obtain Leaflet 2/93, 'The Highways (Traffic Calming) Regulations 1993', from Network Customer Services (Operational Strategy), tel: 0171 921 4531. It's interesting that in Holland, the founder nation for successful 'traffic calming schemes', kerbs at chicanes are angled so they do not damage vehicle tyres, rims or suspension.

A reader from Hertford Heath writes of a ludicrous 'traffic harming' measure in his village. Apparently there is a one-way chicane on Hailey Lane where traffic approaching in each direction is posed to give priority to the other. The result is either gridlock, or drivers accelerating at each other in vain attempts to get through. My correspondent obtained the relevant Traffic Advisory Leaflets, only to find that Regulation 25 (4) of the Traffic Signs Regulations and General Directions 1994 does not prevent the use of 'give way' signs at either end of the obstruction. So he wrote for clarification and received a reply stating, 'The proposal is to include in the Traffic Signs Regulations and General Directions, presently being revised, clarification that the road marking to Diagram 1003 (Give Way marking) cannot be used at both ends of a chicane or similar. The exact wording is still being discussed.'

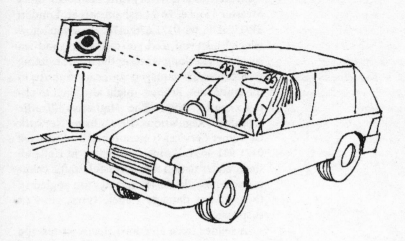

You're being watched

" *In motoring around the country I detect a new form of surveillance appearing alongside roads. These are dark blue posts, the size of small lamp posts. Some have new sensors or cameras mounted on top; some just one; others none (yet). With the sensors come two vertical rods, perhaps antennae. Can you tell us more?* "

These are part of the new 'Trafficmaster' system designed to monitor traffic jams and provide advance information to drivers. Originally, we were told that Trafficmaster would only release part of the number plates of any vehicles caught on camera. But, of course, the system can be used for surveillance purposes and probably it eventually will be.

Congestion question

" *It was odd to read Andrew Baxter's suggestion that councils should have greater powers to fine utilities for creating congestion by spending too much time digging up roads. Odd because, in the same paper, it was reported that Leicester Council is deliberately creating congestion to deter motorists from visiting its town centre. What is going on? Diverting traffic will not cure pollution, nor will more buses. It merely creates more pollution as people make unnecessary journeys trying to find somewhere to park in order to use public transport which usually takes a roundabout route and does not always take them precisely where they want to go. "*

Too right. Anything that slows traffic down increases pollution by forcing vehicles to spend more time on the roads with their engines running. The faster and more direct each vehicle journey can be, the more efficient we will be as a country and the less pollution we will all suffer. That's why we urgently need to get rid of pointless one-way systems and parking restrictions, and to raise the motorway speed limit to at least 85 mph.

Great driving roads

" *I am looking forward to purchasing my first new car next year, probably a 3-Series BMW, and will be taking it on a touring holiday from the South of England up to and around Scotland and the North. I am very interested in knowing of any recommended books on the subject of 'great driving country' or the like, with beautiful countryside, few vehicles and adventurous roads to enjoy the first few thousand miles and a holiday at the same time. "*

Sandfords, the map shop in London's Long Acre, should be able to sort you out with something. But a word of warning. No such book is likely to be up to date on the proliferation of Gatso and Truvelo speed cameras. The A68

North of the Border, which used to be a great driving road, is now festooned with them. Of course, locals know exactly where the cameras are, so the only drivers the Gatsos get are visitors to Scotland, which is a nice welcome likely to put a dampener on any touring holiday. You also run the Gatso Gauntlet on the A1 into Scotland. Strangely enough, this proliferation of Gatso cameras is not making these roads any safer. Since the first cameras were installed, there have been more than 50 deaths on the A1 between Newcastle and Edinburgh.

DRIVING COURSES*

NOTE: 'Pass Plus' is a course of six post-test lessons aimed to familiarise a new driver with aspects such as night and motorway driving not covered in the driving test. Courses are available with BSM and other approved driving instructors and the cost is usually offset by a discount offered by most insurers on the new driver's first year's cover.

- Driving Development, 61 Holly Bank, Ackworth, Yorks WF7 7PE. Tel: 01977 612094.

- Ecôle de Pilotage Winfield, c/o Winfield Motorsport, PO Box 839, Ascot, Berks SL6 7SB, tel/fax 01344 876169. (Advanced Racing Driving Techniques, including 'trail-braking'. Possibly the best racing driving school in the world. Techniques taught in Formula Renault cars at the Paul Ricard Circuit, South of France. First two days: £700; next two days £660.)

- Defensive Driving Consultants, Litton House, 52–56 Buckingham Street, Aylesbury, Bucks HP20 2LL. Tel: 01296 398783.

- AA Driving School, Head Office, Basingstoke. Tel: 01256 20123 (press office).

---

* Driving courses/skid training/circuit courses listed in alphabetical order of office address.

- Road Safety Services Ltd, 162 Eversley Road, Bexley Heath, Kent DA7 6SW. Tel: 01322 337523.

- RoSPA, Edgbaston Park, 353 Bristol Road, Birmingham B5 7ST. Tel: 0121 248 2000. (Defensive Driving Courses. RoSPA 'Advanced Drivers' are re-tested every 3 years.)

- Lancs County Council Road Safety Office. Tel: 01772 264472. (Lancs Road Safety Office runs £10 Skid Control Courses at its Road Safety Training Centre, Ewood, Blackburn. Tel: 01722 254868.)

- Bill Gwynn Rally School, Turweston Aerodrome, Westbury, Brackley, Northants NN13 5YD. Tel: 01280 705570; fax: 01280 701691.

- Brands Hatch 'Earlydrive' and all circuit courses, tel: 0990 125 250. Circuit itself, tel: 01474 872331. (Basic track course in BMW 318i and single-seater, £85 – highly recommended for learning braking and gear changing disciplines; skid control courses, £59.)

- Defensive Driver Training Ltd, Business & Technology Centre, Pound Road, Old Bury, W. Midlands B68 8NA. Tel: 0121 552 8844.

- Club 89 Trackdays. PO Box 89, Attleborough, Norfolk NR17 2QS. Tel: 07000 89 89 89; fax: 01953 457989. (An excellent club providing on-track instruction, rides with British Touring Car Championship drivers, and the chance to drive your own car on racing circuits throughout the UK.)

- Motor Safari, Milestone Inn, Milestone Trail Park, Ruthin Road, Bwlchgwyn, Wrexham LL11 5UT. Tel: 01978 754533. (Half-day off-road courses from £89.)

- Cadwell Park, Lincolnshire. All circuit courses, tel: 0990 125 250. Circuit itself, tel: 01507 343248.

- System Advanced Driver Training, 62–66 Lowther Street, Carlisle, Cumbria CA3 8DP. Tel: 01228 515914.

- Forest Experience Rally School, Tony and Christina Higgins, Carno, Montgomeryshire SY17 5LU. Tel: 01686 420201.

- Castle Coombe Circuit, Chippenham, Wilts SN14 7EX. Tel: 01249 782101. (Skid pan courses from £49.50.)

- Peak Performance Management, The Stables, Walton Lodge, Chesterfield, Derbyshire S42 7LG. Tel: 01246 568953.

- Institute of Advanced Motorists, IAM House, 259–365 Chiswick High Road, London W4 4HS. Tel: 0181 994 4403.

- Croft Circuit, near Darlington, North Yorkshire. Tel: 01327 320326. (Silverstone Driving Centre courses in single-seaters from £85.)

- 'Drive and Survive' skid control courses, Crowthorne, Berks. Tel: 01344 751117.

- Jim Russell Racing School, Donington Circuit, Donington Park, Derby. Tel: 01332 811430. Also Jonathan Tait Skid Control, Donington Circuit, Donington Park, Derby. Tel: 01332 811430.

- The Cardrome, Upper Rainham Road, Hornchurch, Essex. Tel: 01708 471340. (Off-road 'real road' system where youngsters of below driving age can learn to drive safely, in safety, from £9.)

- Road Sense Ltd, Royal Highland Centre, Ingliston, Edinburgh EH28 8NB. Tel: 0131 333 3000.

- Driving Services, Portside House, Lower Mersey Street, Ellesmere Port, Cheshire L65 2AL. Tel: 0151 355 2873.

- Driving Management Ltd, Midlands Skid Pan, Fradley, near Lichfield, Staffs. Tel: 01264 771074.

- Peter Gethin Driving Courses, Goodwood Motor Circuit, Goodwood, Chichester PO18 0PH. Tel: 01243 778118. (Single-seaters, also rides in Ferrari F40: 3 laps, £50.) Goodwood Skid Control courses. Tel: 01903 691810.

- Harrow Driving, Cycling and Road Safety Centre, Christchurch Avenue, Harrow, Middx HA3 5BD. Tel: 0181 424 1993. (Eight-session driving course for 16-year-olds – three theory, five in-car, £80.)

- Drive & Survive UK Ltd, The Maltings, Bridge Street, Hitchin, Herts SG3 2DE. Tel: 01462 441844.

- Under Seventeens Car Club, 59 Coleridge Close, Hitchin, Herts SG4 0QX. Tel: 01462 457813. Membership Secretary: Eileen Simpkin, 51 Deerhurst Chase, Bicknacre, Chelmsford, Essex CM3 4XG. (Sponsored by BP Oil.)

- Autodriva Driving Instructor Training Courses by Margaret Stacey, in preparation for the ADI Parts 1, 2 and 3. Margaret Stacey, The Mount, 53 Heanor Road, Ilkeston, Derbyshire DE7 8DY. Freefone: 0500 555757.

- AA Training Services, AA College, Widmerpool Hall, Keyworth, Notts NG12 5QB. Tel: 0121 5017389.

- Phill Price Rally School, Coed Harbour, Llangunllo, Knighton, Powys LD7 1TD. Tel: 01547 550300. (RAC MSA approved.)

- Road Skills, Hill Rise, Canada Crescent, Rawdon, Leeds LS19 6LT. Tel: 0113 250 1756.

- Paul Ripley Driving Courses, Paul Ripley Promosport, PO Box 2, Horsforth, Leeds LS18 5UE. Tel: 0113 258 5194.

- Driving Management Ltd, Skid Control Course, Lichfield. Tel: 01264 771074. (Also at Thruxton Circuit.)

- British School of Motoring Head Office, London. Tel: 0181 540 8262 (press officer Leslie Miles). BSM 'Masterdrive' two-hour course at £49 to check and brush up observation skills.

- Formula 1 Driving after ARDS instruction at Mallory Park, from £599; Ferrari Driving after MSA instruction at circuit on Presswold Hall airfield, Leicester, from £175; Rally Schools at Presswold Hall and Enstone (Oxon). Tangerine, Millennium Business Centre, 3 Hudson Road, London NW2 6DW. Tel: 0181 208 3333.

- Everyman Driving Centre, Mallory Park Circuit, Leicester LE9 7QE. Tel: 01455 841670.

- City of Manchester Road Safety Unit. Tel: 0161 234 4480.

- DriveTech, 32 Beechingstoke, Marlow, Bucks SL7 1JH. Tel: 01628 473537.

- Fusion Centre, Millbrook Proving Ground, Bedfordshire. Tel: 01525 404918.

- Drive Alive UK, Rowan House, 26–28 Queen's Road, Hethersett, Norwich NR9 3DP. Tel: 01603 259989.

- Aintree Racing Driver's School, 1 Fairoak Court, Whitehouse, Runcorn, Cheshire WA7 3DX. Tel: 01928 712877. (ARDS approved. Prices: £95–£155. Courses at the Three Sister's Circuit, Wigan.)

- Chris Birbeck International Rally School, Manx Lodge, Low Farm, Brottom, Saltburn, Cleveland. Tel: 01287 677512. (Half day: £99; full day: £160; weekend course: £300.)

- Snetterton, Norwich. All circuit courses, tel: 0990 125 250. Circuit itself, tel: 01953 887303.,

- James Pritchard Associates, 3 Bolts Close, Old Marston, Oxford OX3 0PP. Tel: 01865 241854.

- London Rally School (Oxford area). Tel: 01869 278199. (Half days £95; full days £180.)

- Drive It All Rally Driving Courses, The Rally & Off Road Driving Centre, Church Enstone, Oxfordshire OX7 4NP. Tel: 01608 678339.

- PGL Adventure Holidays, Alto Court, Penyard Lane, Ross-on-Wye, Herefordshire HR9 5NR. Tel: 01989 764211. (Offers 'Grand Prix' children's holidays in which they learn to handle go-karts, trials bikes and ATV Quads at Borreatton Hall, Shropshire and Myerscough College, Lancs from £259; 'Motocross' children's holidays on trials bikes and Quads at Beam House, Devon, Dalguise, Perthshire and Tan Troed in the Brecon Beacons, from £249; Driver Awareness Courses of six half-day sessions of theoretical and practical instruction in dual-control cars at Court Farm, Herefordshire, The Bluecoat School, West Sussex, Moreton Hall, Shropshire and Myerscough in Lancashire, from £289.)

- Rally Drive International Rally School, Kings Street, Sancton, Yorkshire YO4 3QP. Tel: 01430 827430.

- Silverstone Driving Centre, near Towcester, Northants NN12 8TN. Tel: 01327 320326 (info); 01327 857788 (bookings). Silverstone Rally School. Tel: 01327 857413.

- Driver Education Centre, Canute Road, Southampton SO14 3FJ. Tel: 01703 333058.

- Oulton Park, Tarporley, Cheshire. All circuit courses including Earlydrive, tel 0990 125250. Circuit itself, tel: 01829 760301.

- Cadence Driver Development, 59 The High Street, Tetsworth, Oxon OX9 7BS. Tel: 01844 281440. (Advanced car and motor-cycle driving courses, skid control, high-performance and defensive driving, anti-hijack, corporate days.)

- Driving Dynamics, 19 Town Street, Thaxted, Essex CM6 2LD. Tel: 01371 830496.

- Driving Management Ltd, Thruxton Circuit, near Andover, Hants SP11 8PW. Tel: 01264 771074. (Skid control courses.)

- Ian Taylor Motor Racing School, Thruxton Circuit, near Andover, Hants SP11 8PW. Tel: 01264 773511.

- SAGA Group Car Confidence Courses, Centrex Centre, Telford, Shropshire. Tel: 0800 300 500. (Basic 7-night residential course: £399; Advanced course £499. Reduced-price rail or coach travel to and from Telford can be arranged.)

- AGS Formula 1 Driving, Circuit du Luc, Hyeres/Toulon, Var, France. UK agents, Wildside Adrenalin Sports. Tel: 0181 366 1766. (Cost: at least £1,000.)

- Tunbridge Wells 4x4 Driving School, 23 Pennine Walk, Tunbridge Wells, Kent TN2 3NW. Tel: 01892 514389. (Courses £69 and £99.)

- Advanced Tuition and Skid Training, Hanger 1, Hurricane Way, North Weald, Essex CM16 6AA. Tel: 01992 522287.

- High Performance Course (John Lyon), HPC Ltd, 21 Church Street, Wellesbourne, Warks CV35 9LS. Tel: 01789 841229. (Prices from £125.)

- Brooklands Auto Project, c/o Paul Jobson, Elmbridge Area Youth Office, Public Library Building, Church Street, Weybridge, Surrey KT13 8DE. Tel: 01932 840986. (Pre-driver training for 15/16-year-olds over four Sunday mornings, price £20.)

- BSM Qualified Driver Training, 81–87 Hartfield Road, Wimbledon, London SW19 3TJ. Tel: 0181 545 1350.

- Corporate Driver Training Ltd, Elnup House, 6 Sherington Avenue, Wigan, Lancs WN6 8AT. Tel: 01257 422331.

- Professional Driving Instructors Group, High Wycombe. Tel: 01494 813064. (Day course for 16-year-olds on Bovingdon aerodrome.)

- T.I. Rally School, The Airfield, Seaton Ross, York YO4 4NF. Tel: 01759 318820. (Half-day courses from £95, full days from £129.25.)

Local driving schools recommended by readers

- Birmingham: Graham Birchall. Tel: 0121 456 4244.
- Kenilworth: Brian Snook. Tel: 01926 852206.
- Wembley, London: Neil Wallace. Tel: 0181 902 9498.
- Hampshire: Adrian Dobson (disabled driving instructor). Tel: 01264 736262

Advanced motorcycle road riding

- BMF Rider Training: 01825 712896.
- Cooper Bike Training: 01633 374782.
- Institute of Advanced Motorists: 0181 994 4403.
- Highway Rider Training: 0121 742 2936.
- Newcastle Rider Training: 0191 276 1972.
- Open Road Advanced: 01375 382124.
- Roadcraft: 01489 896041.
- Shire Training Services: 01480 464689.
- Road Runner: 0114 278 9943.

Motorcycle track days

- Circuit Breakers: 0181 330 3351 and 09733 61858.
- Honda Britain Performance Riding School: 01455 251800.

- Kawasaki Riders Club: 01652 680060.
- No Limits: 01952 606777.
- Redline: 01244 680000.
- Ron Haslam Racing Academy: 01332 883323.
- Speed Freak and James Witham: 0161 487 2222.
- Track Attack: 01332 810048.
- Track Time Promotions: 01384 278387.
- Yamaha Race Schools: 01507 343555.

DRIVING TIPS AND LAW

Radar warfare

" *The Queen's Bench has ruled that the use of radar detectors is not, and never was, illegal under the Wireless and Telegraphy Act 1949. Your comments please.* "

K. Mark Hughes, a former police officer, who publishes the *Hughes Guide to Traffic Law for the Enforcement Officer* and the *Hughes Guide to General Police Duties*, wrote to clarify the legality of radar detectors.

Section 5(b)(1) of the Wireless Telegraphy Act 1949 states: 'It is an offence for a person to use any wireless telegraphy apparatus with intent to obtain information as to the contents, sender or addressee of any message which the person using the apparatus is not authorised to receive.' This may be used to prosecute people listening to police radio frequencies. But on 28 January 1998 it was adjudged in *R* v *Knightsbridge Crown Court* ex parte *Foote* that to use a passive radar scanner which does not reflect or jam a carrier wave does not constitute 'receiving a message' and is not therefore in breach of Section 5(b)(1) of the Wireless Telegraphy Act 1949.

However, Section 13(1) of the Wireless Telegraphy Act 1949 states: 'It is an offence to use any apparatus for the purpose of interfering with any wireless telegraphy.' The maximum penalty for such an offence is six months imprisonment, and using a device designed to jam or reflect carrier waves is just such an offence. Because the police cannot immediately distinguish between a passive detector and an active jammer, they may seize any detector as evidence of an offence under Sections 19 & 32 of the Police and Criminal Evidence Act or Section 79 (3) of the Telecommunications Act 1984, and, if they manage to prove it has elements which can actively jam, it may be liable to forfeiture under Section 80 of the Telecommunications Act 1984.

A jammer is therefore clearly illegal, but if you have a passive detector which has its own 'anti-detection-of-use' circuitry, this too might fall foul of Section 13(1) and land you in jail.

Hughes Guide to Traffic Law For the Enforcement Officer is available from Motorvation Consultants Ltd, price £15 (annual update service £8), PO Box 3250, Milton Keynes MK6 3ZT, tel: 01908 676008. Currently, the best radar/laser detector seems to be the Bell 855E from LE Concepts, tel: 01388 835835. My Cobra Trapshooter is close to useless.

Radar prosecution

A press release from Northamptonshire County Council Trading Standards Office tells of a successful prosecution of TBS Industries Ltd for incitement to commit a crime by advertising its product in *Auto Express* magazine and for contravention of the Trade Descriptions Act by selling a product that does not do what it claims to do. The company was fined a total of £3,000, with £1,300 costs awarded to Northamptonshire County Council. The advertisement on the inside front cover of the magazine stated: 'NO MORE SPEED TRAPS. JAM THEM. The unique Mirage 2001TM Speed trap Jammer is not a detector. A radar detector can only notify you that a ticket is on the way unless you can brake faster than the speed of light. By contrast, this patented device *guarantees* to JAM and render your car totally invisible to all major speed traps including photo radar. WARNING: It is not illegal to own this radar jamming device but its use may contravene the 1949 Wireless Telegraphy Act.' In fact, if it worked, its use would contravene Section 13(1) of the Wireless Telegraphy Act 1949.

'Straight-on' understeer

" *I have driven rear-wheel-drive cars for over 50 years, and my wife's small front-wheel-drive car for 15 years. Abroad, some years ago, I decelerated slightly in a front-wheel-drive car on a slight curve and promptly slid onto the verge. On inspection of the road surface, the stone was slippery and polished. Last winter, on a snow-covered road at a right-angled bend in my wife's new front-wheel-drive car, I slowed to 10 mph and gently steered to the right, but instead the car continued straight ahead. To avoid the hedge bank, I straightened up and quickly stopped in the farm lane ahead. In a rear-wheel-drive car I have always been able to correct any skid, but have been told that in the above cases I should have accelerated.* "

What you should have done is dip the clutch and steer in the direction the car is skidding. When you lift off in slippery conditions in a front-wheel-drive car, 'engine braking' can cause the front wheels to lose adhesion. (This is why Saab 96s were equipped with freewheels.) Dip the clutch and you lose the resistance caused by engine braking and stand a better chance of regaining steering control. Any skid control instructor will tell you this. At speed there are occasions where a bit more power might pull you out of an understeering situation, but racing instructors prefer novices not to try this.

Speed cameras

" *Many speed camera signs create a dangerous situation in themselves in that a stranger to the area has to take his eyes off the road to look for a corresponding speed limit sign which is either non-existent or hidden in foliage. Often the driver can only rely on the flow of traffic in order to guess the limit. As local drivers know precisely where the cameras are, they tend to speed until they reach a suitable braking distance just before the cameras, giving a false impression of the limit and also creating a potential pile-up from the knock-on effect of their sudden braking. There is no doubt that fixed cameras have little to do with safety but are merely a means of increasing fine revenue and potential road rage.* "

As an occasional user of the A40 Western Avenue I find much to agree with in this. Speed limits change from 70 to 50 to 40 then back up to 50 then 60, then down to 30 as you approach London. The same is true of the South Circular. What is needed for all limits over 30 and less than 70 is a reminder every 50 metres, as in mainland Europe. The police say that speed cameras are sited at accident black spots, but the truth is this is rarely the case. They are far more likely to be sited at the best revenue-earning sites. 'Operation Victoria' is now ambushing Lancashire motorists with a vast increase in camera installations. The name came from the Australian state which is infamous for speed camera abuse. After the state's roads were blanketed with the devices, an internal police report leaked to the media dismissed the idea of placing speed cameras at accident blackspots, stating: 'Insufficient numbers of motorists would be booked, making the camera of little fund-raising benefit.' Any reader who wants to become active in opposing heavy-handed policing designed only to increase revenue from fines would do well to join The Association of British Drivers, PO Box 19608, London SE19 2ZW, tel: 07000 781544.

Rules or cooperation?

" On one recent evening, it took me half an hour to drive a quarter of a mile. There had been no accidents, no road works, no traffic light troubles, no obstructions. My miserable rate of progress was due entirely to bad behaviour by other drivers. The trouble occurred when I had to cross a main road at traffic lights. One side of the main road was choc-a-bloc with traffic and, when the lights changed to green, we could not cross the junction for cars from the main road stuck half way across it (it wasn't a box junction). My suggestion is, why not apply the box junction rule, 'Do not enter the junction until your exit is clear', to all traffic light junctions? If a new law is require it could be phrased, 'It is an offence to stop in the path of any other stream of traffic entering the carriageway from either side.' This might help prevent total gridlock. "

Government policy seems to be to create gridlock in towns so that cars owned by town dwellers become nothing more than status symbols, placed outside houses as a guide to the owners' wealth and sense of style. They want us to buy cars, and pay the huge taxes on them (or there would be a £30 billion net tax revenue shortfall), but they don't want us to use them. Surely a better answer is to confound the anti-car lobby with a spirit of cooperation among car owners. Strangely enough, this already exists among most parents on the school run in my area. Cars are beckoned out of side-roads into the inevitable slow-moving queues and we all seem to get the daily ritual done remarkably painlessly. If any eco warriors start grumbling about me taking the kids to school by car (total seven miles), my answer to them is as follows. By 8.15, when I start the run, I've already done an hour's work, with another ten to twelve hours to do, and I simply can't afford the time to prat around with bicycles, public transport or walking. I also want my kids delivered to their schools fresh, not knackered after carrying a 50 lb bag of books and sports kit several miles to school.

Shuffle steering

" Not being obsessive about 'the correct way' of doing anything, it troubles me to watch learner drivers performing the useless charade of 'pumping' the wheel from hand to hand while engaged on another manoeuvre deserving their entire attention. Even without PAS, which is increasingly available on small cars, modern steering is light and predictable and will never, ever 'kick back'. Its carefully designed geometry renders this two-handed play-acting a pointless and counter-productive distraction, which should have no part in modern roadcraft. The driving test of the 1930s was almost certainly drafted by a senior civil servant (probably born in the 19th century) who had himself learned to drive during the First World War or shortly thereafter, when steering was heavy and both hands were needed to control the vehicle. It looks, and is, far safer to have total fluency in control of the wheel and thus the car, and I would substitute 100 per cent concentration on car control and positioning, and especially on never cutting corners. "

The IAM book *Pass Your Advanced Driving Test* tells drivers, 'Steering movements should be made by feeding the wheel through your hands'. Of course, the IAM allows greater arm movement than the silly 'push–pull' you describe, drawing the line only at actually crossing arms. *Roadcraft (The Police Driver's Handbook)* is rather more flexible and does suggest 'rotational steering' (which involves crossing arms) when necessary. Common sense dictates we should all hold the wheel with both hands as much as possible, but how we brace those hands and where we hold the wheel will depend on the many and varied circumstances in which we find ourselves and on the lightness of the car's steering.

Asleep at the wheel

" *Some years ago I fell asleep at the wheel – and fortunately got away with it. I don't want it to happen again. Would it be a luxury, or a real safety factor, to buy a car with air conditioning? My near-miss was on a warm, sunny afternoon on a journey of only 28 miles.* "

'Keeping cool' obviously does help a driver remain alert and also helps to prevent 'road rage'. But there are several other causes of 'falling asleep' at the wheel apart from tiredness and the boredom of keeping to ridiculously low speed limits. One is carbon monoxide poisoning due to a leaking exhaust manifold or a system joint which is no longer gas-tight. If this leak occurs before the exhaust reaches the car's catalytic converter, the 'cat' will not have had a chance to 'convert' the poisonous CO to non-poisonous CO_2. Another cause is alcohol, not necessarily imbibed immediately before the journey, but taken at any time in the previous 24 hours. You may think that delaying a journey until the evening will clear out the effect of a bottle of wine at lunchtime. But in fact you will probably be hung-over, your judgement will be clouded and you will be in no fit state to drive.

CO_2 and alcohol are a particularly deadly combination. Remember also that, if your car is running on cruise control and you fall asleep, the speed you have selected could be the speed at which you crash. Without cruise control, if you drop off, you tend to take the pressure off the accelerator and the car will lose much of its speed.

Running-in a diesel

" *In August I will take delivery of my first new car, a diesel. I would be very grateful if you could give me any information about running in a new diesel engine.* "

The best way to run one in is 'don't'. Diesels that are lightly driven or driven in too high a gear during their first 10,000 miles tend not to 'loosen up'. As a result they deliver poorer performance, use more fuel and burn more oil than a diesel which has seen plenty of different levels of engine revs during its early life. The engine will probably come with a special cocktail of 'running-in' oil in its sump, so changing that prematurely for the wrong oil may also be detrimental. Do not switch to fully synthetic oil or use any oil additives until the engine has done at least 10,000 miles and preferably 15,000 miles. Once the engine is run in, don't push the oil changes beyond 5,000 miles even if it's a TDI with stipulated 10,000-mile oil change intervals.

We've got your number

" *You are right that police forces are increasingly imposing £20 fixed penalty fines for non-endorsable offences such as sounding a horn after 11.30pm and carrying illegible number plates. They're even tougher in the London area because every time a driver is stopped and fined, the offence is logged on the Police National Computer. After three number-plate offences, the DVLA is informed, and has the power to withdraw the registration mark and replace it with a 'Q' plate. That's why you rarely see valuable cherished registrations with script faces in the London area.* "

This penalty has now been extended nationwide, but, of course, it is only a deterrent to those with valuable cherished registrations. It doesn't deter owners who adopt script faces for ordinary registrations in an attempt to confuse speed cameras.

Illegal emergency wheel?

" *I always thought it was illegal to mix tyres of different types or sizes on the same axle. On the Volvo S40 and V40, the 'spare' is a smaller size than the normal road wheel and, if used, there are restrictions on speed and length of journey. What is the legal position for these smaller size 'spare wheels'.* "

They are exempt from the normal rules as long as their use is for emergencies only. Though the tyres look smaller, they have the same rolling circumference as the standard tyre. But they are at much higher pressure and do not dissipate heat as well as standard tyres, which is why there are restrictions on speed and length of journey. They also don't brake as well as standard tyres, so always leave extra room in front of you and be prepared for a much longer 'emergency stop'.

Starting to drive again

" *I am a recently widowed mature lady who returned to the UK's South Coast from Spain a year ago. My Spanish driving licence expired at the same time and, though I had not held a British licence for 14 years, to my surprise and delight the DVLA has issued me with a current licence. Life is pretty grim in sheltered accommodation, so in order to get out and about I am investigating the possibility of running a small car. I have up to £900 to spend, but am worried about what the tax and insurance is likely to cost and the likely running costs of the car which I would use two to three times a week for journeys within a 30-mile radius. As I am used to left-hand-drive, would a left-hand-drive car make more sense? Would it be cheaper than a right-hand-drive car in the UK?* "

After a 14-year absence it would be a wise precaution to brush up on The Highway Code and take some lessons from a local driving school to match your skills to UK conditions. You should also contact some good insurance brokers such as ABM on 0181 681 8986, Rauch & Stallard on 01702 348261 and Age Concern Insurance Services (Motor Department) on 01245 351540, to establish the cost and viability of insurance. 'Tax discs' are currently free for all cars first registered before 31 december 1972. The Left Hand Drive Place specialises in LHDs (tel: 01256 461173) but, living on the South Coast, you may be lucky enough to find a small car which has seen very little use on sale for very little money.

Automatically dangerous

" *I feel it is time someone spoke out of the dangers of automatic cars, particularly in the hands of retired people. I could list six fatal accidents connected to these cars, and I was involved in one which involved smashing along the side of a parked car, bucking and rearing like a horse. Don't tell me automatic cars are safe. The driver of the car was shocked out of her wits and quite unable to understand what she had done or not done. Other people have not been so lucky. One elderly driver a couple of months ago backed out of his drive in Peacehaven, then swept past his own house and straight over the cliff. Automatic cars are dangerous unless the driver knows about cars and has swift reactions, not dulled by retirement or stress.* "

Quite right. The dangers of out-of-control automatics is a subject I have brought up and returned to continually. In my view, the only way to remain fully in control of an automatic car is to drive 'two-footed' (left foot on the brake, right foot on the accelerator). Whatever happens, you are then in a position to stop the car quickly using the footbrake. But, and it's a big but, some drivers either don't have the brain and foot coordination to do this, or they are prevented by a physical disability. That's why there is no specific rule which can apply to every driver.

Back-door identity cards

" *I think your readers should be made aware of a sneaky means being used by the DVLA to persuade elderly motorists into adopting the new photocard driving licences. As you know, any driver over the age of 70 must renew their driving licence every three years. When the reminder ar-*

rived for mine, included with it were forms for a 'photocard' licence, but nowhere did it say that this is not compulsory. I feel very strongly that this practice might well cause unnecessary anxiety and expense to elderly licence applicants. "

A new rule came in on 1 July 1999. From this date, anyone holding a paper driving licence who needed to change the details on it or replace it for any reason has had to replace it with a photocard licence using the new application form D750. Anyone who returned their paper licence to the DVLA for any changes to be made will have been sent a photocard driving licence application form D750R. I changed my paper licence for a photocard in early 1999 anyway, because I like to carry a means of identifying myself. But the necessary verification of photographs and documentary proof of your identity for a photocard licence can prove onerous. The cost of a photocard driving licence is £11 and the form D750 can be obtained by phoning 01792 792 792, Monday to Friday 8.15 to 16.30, or from any main post office. The DVLA warns that processing can take a minimum of three weeks.

Slowness kills?

" *I agree with your correspondent that the police should enforce the rule 'Keep to the left unless overtaking' (see ' Motorway speed limit' in the Driving Conditions section). This was always 'The First Rule of the Road'. Earth banks between opposite carriageways of new motorways also make sense. But I can't agree with your 'bravo' to the suggestion that the motorway speed limit should be raised to 85 mph. You will appreciate that if we are to achieve anything in the interests of accident prevention it is essential that we agree on the basic fact that 'Speed does kill'. I learned to drive 75 years ago, and I still drive.* "

I'm happy to comply with 'Kill your speed' notices at the entrances to villages, because that's what I do anyway whether there is a posted speed limit or not. But on fast A and B roads, dual carriageways and motorways, speed doesn't kill. Mistakes kill, and we're all more likely to make them when we're bored or otherwise inattentive, which is exactly what tends to happen to us when we drive too slowly. The other fact is, most business drivers already regard 80–90 mph as the normal speed for motorway travel. They have to, because they simply don't have the time to travel more slowly. Many people who retired ten or more years ago have no idea how much harder everyone has to work these days just to stay employed. Every hour wasted unnecessarily on the roads is an hour lost forever. Efficient use of motorways depends on a significant proportion of the traffic travelling at well over the 70 mph speed limit. The DETR admits that its enforced variable speed limit experiment on the M25 reduced average speeds on the section from 56 mph to 50 mph. That has forced the average driver (of trucks and vans as well as cars) to spend 12 per cent more time on this section of the motorway. Enforce the 70 mph national motorway speed limit to the same degree and the average time drivers are forced to spend on their regular journeys will rise by at least 12 per cent. If you spend 1,000 hours on the motorways every year, this will increase the time you spend on the road by *at least 120 hours*. But because of the congestion and huge tailbacks this will cause on motorways such as the M1, the true average increase in journey times could rise to 50 per cent or as much as *twenty-one extra 24-hour days* on the road for a 60,000-mile-a-year driver.

Stopping distances

" *As a former police officer and driving instructor, I fully agree with you about the over-simplicity of the slogan 'speed kills'. Like much of the 'Highway Code', it is often instructive to look at the opposite of what is written. I always taught pupils that stopping distance is the distance within which one cannot stop even when one wants to. The only question is, what speed you will be down to when you hit whatever obstacle comes into your path. Unfortunately, the figures given in the present Code are the self-same figures given in the first edition published in the 1930s and have not been adjusted to take account of improvements in cars and roads. The figures are for cars with drum brakes, probably cable-operated and without servos. The formula for working them out is to square the speed, divide by 20 and add the first figure. For example, 30 x 30 = 900; divide by 20 = 45; add 30 = 75. The 'thinking distance' is based on a reaction time of 0.67 of a second. Many good drivers can react as quickly as 0.4 of a second. Finally, drivers cannot measure distances in feet, for example the 345-foot thinking and stopping distance, as given in the 'Highway Code'. But most drivers can estimate 115 yards with reasonable accuracy.* "

The 'Highway Code' braking distance from 70 mph remains at 82 yards. On 26 March 1998 on BBC 'Top Gear', Jeremy Clarkson demonstrated true braking distances using vehicles as diverse as a 1960s Ford Anglia and a Lexus GS300. The Anglia stopped in 81 yards; the Lexus in 46 yards. On 1 June 1999 on Channel 4's 'Driven' programme, Mike Brewer stopped a Vauxhall Zafira, a Renault Megane Scenic and a Ford Focus estate from 70 mph in less than 58 yards. But the fact is, at 70 mph you are travelling at 34.2 yards a second. In a reaction time of 0.4 of a second you will travel 13.68 yards. In a reaction time of 0.67 seconds you will travel 22.91 yards. (At 85 mph these distances increase to 16.62 yards and 27.85 yards.) If you're fiddling with your radio or talking on your mobile phone, your reaction time could be 2–3 seconds. And this takes no account of the difference in braking performance between your car and the car in front. Always try to leave a lot more distance between you and the car ahead. And if you have to brake suddenly, keep an eye on your mirror because you may need to use up some of that cushion to give room for the car behind you to brake. The other advantage of leaving a big cushion of space in front is to give yourself a better chance to swap lanes if the cars in your lane begin to concertina into each other.

Coded messages

" The new 'Highway Code' enshrines the myth that one third of accidents are caused by speed. This is refuted by both a 1994 AA Cambridgeshire survey of the causes of 7,590 non-motorway accidents, which showed that six per cent were caused by inappropriate speed, and TRL Report 323, which studied the causes of just under 6,000 accidents and found that seven per cent were caused by inappropriate speed. This same TRL Report showed that, of the fatal or serious injury accidents involving pedestrians, the pedestrian was to blame in 85 per cent of cases. This also contrasts with the January 1999 DETR TV advertising campaign which strongly suggested that drivers, and speeding drivers in particular, are to blame. "

The TV campaign you refer to would have been a very good one to exhort drivers to 'Stay Alert or You'll Kill Someone'. To assert that breaking the speed limit alone killed the young woman in the ad was naive. In the same vein, I have to take issue with your words, 'the pedestrian was to blame in 85 per cent of cases'. Who cares who's to blame if someone is lying dead? Whatever speed we choose to drive, we should always remain alert to anticipate other people doing stupid things, in particular pedestrians taking chances crossing the road. Under the Road Traffic Act 1998, the new 'Highway Code' is evidential. What this means is, if you have an accident which is clearly not your fault, but you are not conforming to the letter of the Code at the time, this could be used against you in civil or criminal proceedings.

Mascots

" Are three-inch-high mascots mounted 12 inches from the foot of the windscreen illegal? "

Regulation 53 Road Vehicles (Construction and Use) Regulations 1986 states: 'No mascot, emblem or other ornamental object shall be carried by a motor vehicle in any position where it is likely to strike any person with whom the vehicle may collide unless the mascot is not liable to cause injury to such a person by reason of any projection thereon.' Since a modern car bonnet and windscreen are designed to provide a cushion for any pedestrian the car should hit, a three-inch mascot mounted 12 inches from the screen could easily pluck out an eye or penetrate a skull. Exemptions are motor vehicles first used before 1 October 1937 and vehicles which comply with EEC 74/483 or ECE Reg. 26.01. These cover sprung mascots such as the Mercedes star and the Rolls Royce 'Spirit of Ecstasy'.

Fine the lane hogs!

" I hesitate to suggest even more law enforcement than we already have. But we are all familiar with available lanes on motorways and dual carriageways being reduced by drivers failing to keep to the left-hand lane unless overtaking (New Highway Code Rule 238). Instead of using

unmarked police cars to catch public-spirited drivers getting out of every-one else's way by doing a sensible 80–90 mph, why not equip these cars with video cameras so they can film the lane hogs they come up behind, then issue them with a simple fixed-penalty ticket? No need to be too draconian to get the message across, but a £20 fine and no endorsement should be enough to persuade most drivers to drive in the correct lane and help free up the road system for the rest of us. "

Not a bad idea. The sort of lane hogging you describe is not a specific offence and, as far as I can ascertain, is not covered by the Fixed Penalty System. But it is behaviour which could be interpreted as 'driving without due care and consideration for other persons using the road', and this is an endorsable offence carrying three to nine points. As you suggest, lane hogging should be listed as a specific example of a lesser, non-endorsable offence of 'driving without due consideration'. I'd far rather the police raised revenue in this positive way than by fining public-spirited drivers who spend as little time as possible on the roads thus leaving more space on them for the rest of us.

Direct action

" *After the latest fuel tax increases, motorists now pay £35 billion a year in tax, yet are hassled and harried from every direction and still seem to take it all without a murmur. Far too much publicity and credence is given to the tiny anti-car minority when motorists should be the single largest pressure group. The Countryside Campaign frightened the Government with one march. If motorists got together, we could make that look like a picnic. The AA and RAC have abrogated their role of championing motorists in favour of commercial enterprise. I have received literature from the Association of British Drivers and, while I support their causes, they don't seem to be organising any direct action, which is what is needed to make the politicians sit up and take notice – as the lorry drivers have found. The difficulty is galvanising the support that*

I am sure exists. I am willing to put a lot of effort into organising an 'Action Day' if you can put other like-minded people in touch with me. "

It has taken three years for the Brits to wake up to the way they are being ripped off by UK car 'list prices', but they are now, finally, voting with their feet and may also be in a mood to complain about paying over 400 per cent tax on unleaded petrol, then being fined and having their livelihoods threatened for trivial speeding offences. Anyone who wants to get in touch with this reader should write to A. Endicott, The Lodge, Erwarton, Ipswich IP9 1LQ. Please enclose an SAE.

EPHEMERA

Bookworms

Though the information was in the last two books, readers continue to ask how they might dispose of old motoring literature. The answer is to try the following, all of whom take stalls at various events and 'autojumbles' throughout the year (remember, most have day jobs so it's better to call them in the evenings): Kenneth Ball Autobooks Ltd, tel: 01273 84500; Eoin Young, tel: 01483 283311 (summer only); Anton Spencer, tel: 0181 337 7452; Peter Davidson, tel: 01295 810853; Graham White, tel: 01243 771961; Alan and David Burden, tel: 01923 246668; Les Wilson, tel: 01270 812410; David Ellnot, tel: 01524 762271; Andrew Currie, tel: 01276 477201; and Alan Riley, tel: 01327 351203. Don't expect magazines from later than the 1960s to be worth much, though. The dealers who attend 'automobilia' events are not very interested in them because of the sheer weight they would have to carry around. Some shops which deal in collectible motoring literature are Chaters Motoring Booksellers of 8 South Street, Isleworth, tel: 0181 568 9750; The Vintage Motorshop of Batley, tel: 01924 470733; Collectors Carbooks of Woburn, tel: 01525

290088; Simon Lewis Transport Bookshop, Lydney, tel: 01594 843151; John Knowles of Great Ellingham, Norfolk, tel: 01953 452257; Pooks Motor Bookshop of Rothley, Leicestershire, tel: 0116 237 6222; and Ray Roberts's 'Wheels, Wings and Water' of Whiston, tel: 01785 712232. But don't expect them to come and collect. To advertise, try *Practical Classics* and *The Automobile* magazines, both of which have a Motoring Literature classified section.

Armchair journeyman

" *There are many collectors of old road maps, most of whom go for Ordnance Survey products. I am something of an oddity in that I collect maps once issued by petrol companies. These are not generally sold by motoring ephemera specialists, so to boost my collection I would like to make your readers an offer. For every old petrol company road map they send me in good condition, I will make a donation to the MacIntyre Charitable Trust (registered charity no. 327052). Overseas petrol company maps will be particularly welcome.* "

Seems fair enough. Maps to: Ian Byrne, MacIntyre Petrol Map Appeal, 17 Medland, Milton Keynes MK6 3BH.

Old magazines

" *I have a large box of motoring magazines, mostly* Motor *and* Autocar *covering the Earls Court Show numbers from 1950 into the 1960s, and also some bound volumes of the* Motor Review Road Test Annual *and bound volumes of similar vintage* Sporting Motorist *magazine. Are these worth anything? If so, how much? And where should I advertise them? I would prefer to dispose of them on a 'buyer inspects and collects' basis.* "

Advertise in the 'Assortments' column of free reader services in *Practical Classics* magazine. This is also good for advertising old spares and classic 'swaps'. Alternatively, tote the mags along to any of the autojumble events in your area during the summer and offer them to a stallholder. Again, *Practical Classics* lists upcoming events. By far the biggest is the Beaulieu Autojumble in May and September (ticket hotline: 01590 612888; information: 01590 612345). You could even take a stand, but please don't expect to sell many of your magazines from a stand at a single event. Don't expect more than £1 a copy for the mags, or £2 a copy for the Motor Show reviews.

Mystery books

" Just a line about Mike Hawthorn's books. He definitely did write at least two boys' 'adventure style' books about 'Carlotti', a young Italian racing driver. One, Carlotti Joins The Team, *I read as an adult and thoroughly enjoyed, but I can't remember the title of the other. Mike Hawthorn also wrote a very interesting autobiographical work about his Grand Prix career. I found that very good indeed and wish I could find a copy now. Each starting grid was shown as a full-page plan and it was rather sombre to see how many drivers were deceased even when Hawthorn himself was still alive. Hope you can find copies and even time to read them. "*

There are mixed opinions on this. Some people agree that Mike Hawthorn wrote the books, but others think they were 'ghosted'. For possible sources, see the list of shops and dealers under 'Bookworms' above.

That's the spirit

" I have in my possession a two-gallon petrol tin embossed with the Shell logo, stamped '5/-' and marked 'Aviation Spirit'. I believe it is about 100 years old and is a collector's piece. Have you any information on who and where the collectors are so I could pass this tin on to one of them? "

Avid collector M.M. of Bampton tells us that these cans were date-stamped, usually with the month and year of manufacture. (The date stamp may be hidden in the inside of the base plate flange.) Because, prior to the mid-1920s, most petrol was sold in cans rather than pumped directly into motor vehicle or aircraft tanks, a deposit was payable on the can. Before the Second World War, the deposit was 3 shillings; after WW2 this rose to 5 shillings, then to 6 shillings, then to 8 shillings. (This would make my correspondent's can, stamped 5/-, post-war and only half as old as he thought it was.) M.M. tells us that clean, undented cans which are still fuel-tight are worth £18–£20 and that most collectors would blanch at paying more than £25. But some very rare cans will fetch up to £300.

Who's the horn-blower?

" *I have an ornament that was made from a car radiator mascot reputed to have come from a Rolls Royce. It doesn't look familiar, so can you tell me anything about it?* "

Thankfully there is one in the Automobilia section on page 320 of the 1997/1998 *Miller's Collectors Car Price Guide*. It's identified as a silver-plated bronze entitled 'La Renommee', designed by Emile Peynot for Ballot who used it from 1922–28. In good condition with its original radiator cap, auctioneers Brooks estimate its value at £1,375–£1,450. But there were many reproductions and, without the correct radiator cap, their value is considerably less. Other books covering mascots are: *Automobilia* by Gordon Gardiner and Alistair Morris (ISBN 1-85149-293-3) and *Automotive Mascots* by

David Kay and Lynda Springate (ISBN
1-901295-42-7).

Original brochures

" *I am looking for the large landscape-format brochures used to launch
the E-Type Jaguar and the MGB. I have tried various bookshops and autojumbles all to no avail.* "

The friendly and very helpful chaps at Chaters
Motoring Bookshop of Isleworth (0181 568
9750) put me straight on to two brochure
specialists: Andrew Currie (01276 477201) and
Pooks Motor Bookshop (0116 237 6222).
Obviously whether they will have exactly what
you want and how much it's likely to cost you
will depend on the scarcity of the brochures.

FUEL AND EMISSIONS

Lead-free results

The Federation of British Historical Vehicle Clubs announced the results of lead-substitute testing at MIRA on 20 March 1999. The cylinder heads tested were a series of unmodified BL 'A' Series mounted on the same 'A' Series block. Tests included 50 hours at 3,800 rpm and 20 hours at 5,500 rpm. Of ten 'lead substitutes' and two fuel line 'catalysts' tested, those pronounced adequate for normal use were: Millers VSP Plus, Red Line Lead Substitute, Superblend Zero Lead 2000, and Valvemaster. Some of the others gave 'acceptable protection at medium engine speeds' (i.e. below 3,000 rpm). *No fuel tank or fuel line 'catalysts' passed the test.* A word of warning was given: mixing lead substitutes can cause very serious engine damage, so, once you have settled on an additive, do not mix it with anything else and do not mix it with 'Lead Replacement Petrol' which may contain a different additive. The Petrol Retailers Association feels that the most effective additive is phosphorous (Valvemaster, STP), but Shell LRP,

Texaco LRP and Superblend Zero Lead 2000 contain potassium, Redline and Wynns use sodium (which can damage turbochargers); while Millers VSP Plus is manganese-based. Millers has put its product to a six-month test in ten 1.3 litre Austin Maestros which showed that, without treatment, the valve seats would have failed after just 622 miles. A treatment of 8 mg per litre was adequate for normal use but allowed valve seat recession at motorway speeds. A treatment of 36 mg per litre gave valve seat protection as good as leaded four star. Lead Replacement Petrol is likely to be 97Ron and not suitable for many high-performance cars. But owners of classics with relatively low compression ratios will have the option of running on cheaper 95Ron Premium Unleaded plus an additive, while owners of high-performance classics will be able to run on 98Ron Superunleaded, either with an additive if their valve seats are relatively soft or without any additive at all if they have already had hard chrome-steel exhaust valves and valve seat inserts fitted to their heads. I have ridden in older modified Jags with up to 300bhp that run far better on Superunleaded than they ever did on 97Ron four star. Valvemaster: 01908 372611; Superblend: 0116 291 1700; Red Line: 01732 866885; Millers: 01484 713201.

Dirty vehicle ban

" Delegates from 70 local authorities recently attended a meeting called by 'ALTER' (Alternative Traffic in Towns). The objectives are to create Low Emission Zones in areas of high vehicle pollution such as town and city centres, and all 70 local authorities are now required to set start dates for compliance. As from these dates, the only vehicles allowed into the central areas will be those powered by LPG, CNG or electricity. Complying will *not be as onerous as many people think. There is now a standard conversion of the Perkins 180 diesel engine for buses and trucks, enabling them to run on LPG at a slightly increased consumption rate, but using a fuel which is half the price of diesel. Conversion costs of cars and vans is typically £800–£1,200 and approved conversions to cars less than one year old qualify for a 75 per cent 'Powershift' grant. UK LPG is wellhead gas, rather than refined from crude oil, and current estimates are that there is enough under the North Sea to last 40–60 years. There are now 221 LPG filling stations in the UK; there should be 400 by the end of 1999, and by the end of year 2000 there should be 800. The latest LPG filling station information is available on two websites: http://www.lpga.co.uk and http://www.autogas.lpg.com. "*

Accepted, this letter came from an LPG installation specialist. But the following list shows no grace or favour: Autogas 2000 of Thirsk, tel: 01845 523213; Gentrac Systems Ltd of Chandlers Ford, tel: 01703 254744; Key Autogas of Leicester, tel: 0116 2608813; Marine Ecopower Ltd of Lymington, tel: 01590 688444; and LPG Auto Power UK of Bradford, tel: 01274 729425. The LP Gas Association (tel: 01425 461612) can also supply an up-to-date list of outlets and LPGA accredited converters whose conversions qualify for the 75 per cent Powershift grant. The Natural Gas Vehicle Association, tel: 0171 388 7598, can supply a list of CNG 'Gas Stations'. Since emissions are low, taxes are low, and it's the favoured fuel of John 'Twojags' Prescott. Availability of LPG is rapidly expanding. Vauxhall has launched an LPG Vectra and a CNG Combi van, while Volvo has introduced a CNG bi-fuel S70/V70 which qualifies for the Powershift grant, bringing the cost down to just £311 + VAT over and above the price of a standard S70/V70.

Superunleaded economy

" *I agree with your views about using Superunleaded to gain extra fuel economy. I have been able to achieve an extra nine per cent mpg on average with that type of petrol in my Honda-powered 1990 Rover 416GSi. However, it tends to surge suddenly at approximately 3,000 rpm (regardless of the type of petrol I use), and a proprietary injector cleaner only seems to work for one tankful of fuel. What do you suggest?* "

Switch to Texaco CleanSystem 3 Superunleaded. I know it works because, after running on it, and without being re-tuned, my 13-year-old Jetta GTi passed its exhaust emissions test with just 79 ppm HCs. This made complete nonsense of the extra tax formerly imposed on Superunleaded because it was supposed to contain more benzene than other petrol. In 1997, the average benzene content was 2.9 per cent compared to 2.3 per cent for ordinary unleaded and 1.9 per cent for Four Star. It is now less than 1 per cent for all petrol. Any benzene tailpipe emissions are contained in the HCs, so if Super reduces tailpipe HCs from a permitted 1,200 ppm to 79 ppm it effectively reduces average benzene emissions as well. This explains why the Government could justify reducing the tax on Super to just 2p more than Premium, and why Super should now cost no more than 78p a litre. If the surging of your Rover 416 persists, it could be due to a fault with the electronic ignition igniter which is the one problem that seems to develop with these engines.

Automatically thirsty?

" *I recently purchased a three-year-old 30,000-mile Ford Mondeo 1.8 automatic and the car is fine in every respect except its fuel consumption. In urban use I get no more than 18–19 mpg. The garage which sold me the car has tested and checked everything, so is this sort of heavy consumption usual? I drive with no more than the lightest of touches on the accelerator. The figure for the 'urban cycle' with this car is supposed to be 26.6 mpg. What can I do about this?* **"**

If your driving includes large numbers of short runs of less than five miles from a cold start then you can expect relatively heavy fuel consumption. The Ford Mondeo goes through a three-stage warm up cycle from cold, automatically increasing the richness of the mix and the engine speed until the fuel injection sensors judge that the engine has reached a high enough temperature to allow it to run leaner and more economically. The old 'urban cycle' did not include cold starts, nor spending a significant proportion of urban running at idle in a traffic jam. The current 'urban cycle' is more realistic and includes cold starts.

Diesel additives

" *I am in the process of buying a two-year-old Peugeot 306 turbodiesel. I have never owned or driven a diesel car before. I am now being advised by many 'helpful' friends to used fuel additives. Are they a good idea, and if so, why? What names should I look out for?* **"**

Miller's Dieselclean Plus seems to be the best. It contains detergent to keep the injectors and fuel system clean, a cetane improver to provide better combustion, and a lubricity enhancer to help preserve the distribution pump. For a list of outlets, call 0800 281053.

Emission missive

" *On 22 April 1998, while driving my 'G'-registered Escort along the A5117, I was diverted by police into a vehicle inspection point. After a* *brief check, I was told that my exhaust was exceeding the permitted limit of 3.5 per cent CO. The measurements I was given were 5.636 per cent CO and 703 ppm HCs. My car was issued with a delayed prohibition notice and I was told I had ten days to get a new MOT, take the new MOT to a main police station, get a discharge of prohibition document and send that document to the Vehicle Inspectorate. I then took the car to an MOT testing station where the emissions were measured as 1.43 per cent CO and 209 ppm HCs. No adjustments had been made to the engine, which was hot on both occasions. Surprised by this, I then took the car for two further emissions tests at two other MOT testing stations. One gave a reading of 6.4 per cent CO and 700 ppm HCs and the other 2.5–3.5 per cent CO and 200 ppm HCs. Even for an old Escort, these results seemed so at variance I felt it called into question the accuracy of the gas analysers being used. Sure enough, the roadside test gas analysers had not been calibrated since 17 November 1997 and were not due to be re-calibrated until 18 May 1998 – a six-month gap during which time they could have been dropped, banged, contaminated or otherwise rendered so inaccurate they should never have been used as the basis for a roadside emissions test.* ”

On the face of it, this is very worrying. Either the testing is totally inconsistent or the carburation of your car is, which is very likely with an Escort of this vintage. There was one way to find out. I got in touch with the Vehicle Inspectorate to ascertain if the gas analysers which had been used for your roadside test were found to be incorrect when they were re-calibrated on 18 May. The answer to this question turned out to be an Official Secret. But the accuracy of roadside emissions tests has now been brought into question.

Burning issue

“ *I was reading about a whole family that tragically perished when their car caught fire after overturning. I can't help thinking that unleaded petrol is more flammable than the leaded variety and would like your comments on this theory, as cars seem to catch fire more often since unleaded petrol was introduced. I think that my wife and I will be all right, however, as we both run Citroën diesels.* "

You're partly right in that diesel is less volatile and therefore far less likely to erupt into a vehicle fire than petrol. So, apart from the benefits of economy, that's another good reason for running a diesel car. But the main reason why cars burst into flames is not the petrol but the fuel system. Mid to late 1980s fuel injection had electric pumps and no safety shut-off valve, so if a car crashed and the fuel line was severed, fuel would continue to be pumped out. By the time catalytic converters (which require fuel injection) became universal, this danger had been recognised and safety shut-off valves have been installed in the fuel lines ever since.

Clean diesels

" *My company car is coming up for renewal and, since I cover around 35,000 miles a year, I am likely to target a VW Passat TDI 110 estate. The economy and low CO_2 emissions of this engine are not in dispute, but the puffs of smoke every diesel seems to put out occasionally remain cause for concern. Is it possible to run a clean diesel, or should I switch to petrol?* "

Make sure you order a TDI 115, which replaces the TDI 110. Then use City Diesel from Sainsbury's, City Diesel from Tesco within the M25, Shell Pura diesel, or Elf ultra-low-sulphur diesel, which should be available everywhere. The 2p a litre tax break on this fuel pays the increased refining costs and you will see very little exhaust smoke, even during a cold start.

From rot boxes to valve stems

" *The reason why non-stainless steel rear silencers on catalysed cars corrode prematurely is not simply un-evaporated condensation from short run use. It is that some types of catalytic converter release hydrochloric acid vapour if the car is driven for short runs during the first few thousand kilometres of its life. Now a question: can you tell me if it is true that low-sulphur fuels are giving rise to sticking exhaust and inlet valves?* "

The refining process used to remove sulphur from diesel fuel can also remove its inherent lubricity and can lead to premature wear in the diesel pump if a lubricity additive such as Exxon's Paradyne 631 is not added to the fuel. (Low Sulphur 'City Diesel' contains Paradyne 631; Shell Pura also contains a lubricity additive.) A problem of unleaded petrol is that engines miss the dry lubricating effect of lead. As well as protecting valve seats, this had the effect of preventing tars and gums from adhering to valve stems, leading to the 'sticking valve' problem experienced in some mass-market 16-valve engines. The cure is a petrol with adequate detergent content. However, because many motorists insist on using the cheapest petrol available which conforms to the relevant 'British Standard' and may not contain adequate detergent, manufacturers have been forced to increase the lubrication of valve stems in 16-valve engines by the engine oil.

Seven-mile-high pollution

" *Car manufacturers are exhorted by environmentalists and governments to cut the amount of pollution produced by vehicle exhausts. The public is encouraged to make fewer car journeys and to use mass public transport. But what is being done to reduce air traffic and the pollution caused by aircraft? In fact, the opposite seems to be happening with new airports and increases in global air traffic planned. Could you explain to me what happens to the thousands of tons of kerosene burned daily at high altitude? Surely this has a more disastrous effect on the ozone layer than the £5 worth of petrol I use in a week?* "

Well, yes. The question had to be asked. The best answer I have heard is that one 747 crossing the Atlantic once creates more atmospheric pollution than 40,000 vehicles travelling the length of the M1 from London to Leeds and back. That said, the trend is towards larger, more fuel-efficient aircraft that pollute less per passenger mile.

More fuel you

The Petrol Retailers Association have written to say that, rather than take up tankage with a Lead Replacement Petrol in service stations not currently selling Superunleaded, their preferred option for 2000 onwards is to use Super-unleaded and Premium unleaded supported by a phosphorous-based additive sold separately. That would then cover the octane needs of engines separately from their valve seat protection needs. Owners of unleaded-tolerant engines needing Super would not need to buy the additive, while owners of older cars with low compression ratios could run them on lower grade, cheaper Premium unleaded together with the additive. Though no additive is as effective as lead in increasing the octane of petrol, preventing valve seat recession and lubricating the 'hot' end of valve stems in their guides, all the worldwide research findings gathered by the PRA clearly indicate that phosphorous is more effective than the alternatives of potassium, sodium and manganese. The difference in fuel cost between Premium and Super is only about 1p a litre, so if Super sold better, its price could be reduced considerably. From 1 October 1999 the difference in fuel duty between Premium and Superunleaded was reduced to 2p, so the pump price of Super should not be more than 78p a litre. The few pence more than Premium should be offset by the extra fuel economy and lower emissions when used in in high-performance, high-efficiency engines.

They must be choking

" *I have viewed with some considerable consternation and irritation the aspects of the Government and media claims levelled at the car and the motorist regarding health, pollution and global warming. I would therefore like to see an honest comparison between public transport (including aircraft), commercial vehicles and privately owned cars for their polluting effects. What I mean by this is average private mileage and pollution units for cars and likewise for all other forms of transport, because all must pollute to some degree. It would be very surprising to me if it were still weighted against the British motoring public. I also feel that having to depend on public services to effect one's daily tasks and life-support necessities would be mind-blowing, considering how many people would want to travel on the same bus at the same time. The bus which comes ten minutes earlier or ten minutes later isn't good enough for me, nor, I think, for anyone else in this lifestyle we have created. I await with interest any genuine comparisons and comments.* "

Attempting to reduce CO_2 by taxing cars has been likened to trying to lower sea levels by handing out drinking straws. 96.5 per cent of all CO_2 emissions are naturally sourced from animal respiration (D. S. Schimel (1995) *Global Change Biology*, 77–91). Of the remaining 3.5 per cent of CO_2 emissions, only about 13 per cent comes from cars. So all tax on fuel can ever do is attempt to reduce a maximum of 0.5 per cent of all CO_2 output. A reader from Cheltenham takes these arguments a stage further by proving that climate change is governed by the earth's orbit, axial tilt changes, the sun's varying output and tectonic activity. Vehicle CO_2 emissions are irrelevant to climate change. The purpose of 'CO_2' tax on cars is to raise taxation revenue. It is not, and cannot be, to reduce 'global warming'. If world powers really want to stop CO_2 emissions affecting the atmosphere they should plant more trees and stop the burning of rainforests in Indonesia. The 1997 forest fires in Kalimantan and Sumatra emitted more CO_2 than the whole of Europe, and at the same time destroyed billions of trees which naturally absorb CO_2.

Consumptive Micra

" *I bought an 'L'-reg. Nissan Micra 1.3 from a Nissan agent in October 1997. It was one owner with 11,000 miles on the clock and I traded in my 'E'-reg. Vauxhall Nova 1.3. I was disillusioned with the petrol consumption of the Micra about the town and, as the engine appeared to be running fast, I took it back to the agent to be checked. It was pronounced 'correct according to manufacturer's standards'. I continue to be unhappy with the fuel consumption of 26–28 mpg around town. My Nova did far better than this with the same engine size. Your comments, please.* "

This is the price of emissions legislation. To protect its catalytic converter from misfires while the engine is cold, your Micra goes through a cold running phase which involves an enriched mixture and higher engine revs than at normal warm idle. It is, of course, very wasteful of petrol. So, if most of your journeys are of less than five miles, the engine will never warm up enough for the ECU to weaken the mixture and lower the revs. The official 'Extra-Urban' fuel consumption figure for a Micra 1.3 is 34 mpg and, while this involves some cold running, it is not a figure for an engine that is run cold for most of the time.

Unleaded conversion

" *We own a 1986 Mini Mayfair that has covered 51,000 miles and is used as a second car at the rate of 6,000 miles a year. We have been told to take various options ranging from an engine rebuild costing £400, to the fitting of a filter in the fuel line at minimal charge, to doing nothing and continuing to use leaded petrol until supplies cease towards the end of the year. Any guidance you give would be appreciated, as we have no intention of disposing of the car.* "

There are numerous trial and error possibilities, including various types of 'lead replacement petrols' using additives which are not compatible and cannot safely be mixed. Because Mini gearing is relatively low, keeping engine revs below 3,000 rpm is not an option, so the only safe course of action is to stump up for a properly modified cylinder head. The best specialist (and the most helpful) I have come across is Ron Hopkinson, 850 London Road, Derby DE24 8WA, tel: 01332 756056. Prices for exchange lead-free heads for 'A' Series engines, complete with new hardened exhaust valves, hardened valve seats, new valve guides and new valve springs are from £175 + VAT. ('B' Series heads and Spitfire/Midget 1500 heads are £195 + VAT.) If your local garage removes the old head, stores the car and fits the new one, a total bill of £400 would be reasonable.

Cheap and nasty petrol

" *My 'D'-registered Volvo estate car developed a problem a couple of months ago in that the engine continued to turn and shudder for a few seconds after the ignition was switched off. My garage man said the reason could be the 'cut price' 4-star unleaded petrol I had been buying from a local supermarket, citing an example of another Volvo owner who had been using the same petrol whose fuel system became clogged up with impurities and who successfully claimed £90 from the supermarket in compensation. I then switched to Esso and within two tankfuls the fault had disappeared completely. I suspect that drivers are unaware that, though the grade of petrol has to conform to a British Standard, the quality of the petrol is not the same. Perhaps you could find space to warn your readers about this.* "

I have, many times. The fact remains that some cut price petrol does not contain an adequate amount of detergent to keep fuel systems clean of tars and gums. The reason for the running-on is that some of these gums have carbonised and the carbon glows red in the combustion chamber, acting like a spark plug after you switched off. In my experience, Texaco CleanSystem 3 Super has the best detergent package of any pump petrol, and Shell Super isn't bad either.

Poor petrol

" *Further to your Volvo-owning reader's experience (see 'Cheap and nasty petrol' above), cheap petrol may not even make economic sense. My Citroën XM 2.0SEi had been running on supermarket petrol for two years and developed a 'hesitation' at low speeds, coughing a little. I changed to Elf (our nearest branded service station) and immediately not only cured the problem, but petrol consumption for local work improved from 23.5–25 mpg to 25–27 mpg and on long runs from 30 mpg to 32 mpg (calculated brim to brim). Despite a higher pump price, the overall cost of petrol was thus marginally reduced.* "

I can well believe it. The supermarket petrol you were using obviously had little or no detergent content and this was allowing the fuel system to foul up. Once you started using petrol with a detergent additive, not only did it clean out your fuel system, the inevitable result was better economy.

Jetta propelled

" *I have a 1987 Jetta GTi 16v which has done 140,000 miles and has given me over 11 years of trouble-free motoring. I am now worried that when 4-Star 98Ron petrol disappears from our forecourts at the end of the year my car will become obsolete, as it seems it cannot be modified to take unleaded petrol. Do you have any advice for me and any fellow owners?* "

The VAG 1.8 16v engine was built to run on leaded or unleaded 98Ron petrol. Because most '4-Star' was 97–98Ron in the UK, it has often had to settle for that (but it doesn't like Shell 'low lead' 4-Star). You should find it will run better than ever on 98Ron Superunleaded, which is the petrol it was designed to run on in the first place. As from 1 October 1999, tax cuts should mean that the price of Super will come down to 78p per litre. Your alternative is to fit a K-Star 'Millennium' chip which reduces the octane requirement of K-Jetronic 16-valve engines to 95Ron, but if the difference in price between Premium and Super is reduced to less than 5p a litre, the £200–£300 outlay may not be worth it. K-Star, Milford Microsystems, Milford House, Oddington, Kidlington, Oxon OX5 2RA, tel: 01865 331552. Fitting and mapping specialists are AMD, Oxon, tel: 01865 331226; TSR, Somerset, tel: 01278 453036.

GEARBOX AND CLUTCH

Diesel automatics

" Which do you think is better to drive: a petrol automatic, or a diesel automatic? "

Diesel automatics have become more numerous and far better than they ever were in the past. An advantage is that, with peak torque lower in the rev range than a petrol car allied to a torque converter, they can pull a very tall top gear. Good examples include the VW Passat TDI 110 automatic; the equivalent Audi A4 TDI 110 automatic; the Mercedes C250TD auto and E300TD auto; the Citroën Xantia TD auto; and the Vauxhall Astra DI auto, though, with more limited torque, this particular car pulls a relatively shorter top gear of about 24 mph per 1,000 rpm.

I'll try to list all the diesel automatics I know of in alphabetical order: Audi 80TDI, Audi A4TDI, Audi A6TDI, New BMW 320TD, BMW 325TD, BMW 325TDS, BMW 525TD, BMW 525TDS, Citroën ZX Avantage and Aura D to 1996, Citroën Xantia LXD and SXD to 1996,

Xantia 1.9TD auto, Citroën XM 2.1TD (but not 2.5TD), Ford Granada TD, Ford Scorpio TD, Land Rover Discovery TDI, Range Rover TDI and TD six, Mercedes Benz 190 2.0D and 2.5D, Mercedes C Class 220D, 250D and 250TD, Mercedes E Class 300D and new E Class 220CDI, Mitsubishi Shogun 2.8TD, Old Nissan Primera D (not turbo), Peugeot 605 2.1TD, old Renault Safrane 2.5TD Executive, Suzuki Vitara TD, Vauxhall new Astra DI, Vauxhall Omega TD, VW Golf Mk III Ecomatic (very rare), VW Golf Mk IV TDI 90, VW New Passat TDI, VW Sharan TDI 110, VW Caravelle Multivan 2.4SD, Volvo S70TDI. Though they're relatively expensive, a Mercedes is likely to be the longest lasting. My personal choice would be an E220CDI auto.

Selecta selection trouble

" *In April 1995 I bought an 'M'-registered Fiat Punto Selecta with 7,401 miles on the clock which had previously served as a hire car at Gatwick airport. I'm extremely pleased with it, except for one thing. From time to time, when I come to a halt, the selector lever will not move from neutral to drive. This happens when the engine is revving more quickly than usual. I'm at a loss to understand why the engine revs should vary. As far as I can see, my driving habits are regular. My garage mechanics tell me they cannot understand why the lever should jam, but suggests that when the problem arises I should wait until the revs drop. However, they never do. Can you throw any light on this, please?* "

Do not in any circumstances, ever use force to move the gear selector lever. With a catalysed car, the engine management system sometimes increases engine revs to protect the 'cat' from petrol which would have remained unburned at lower revs. This often causes problems for drivers of automatics who do not habitually drive two-footed. But, to prevent 'creep' while stationary in 'Drive', the Punto Selecta also has a complex electromechanical dog clutch which locks as revs rise. If you force it into 'D' while the clutch is locked due to high revs, you could wreck both the clutch and the CVT transmission. Make sure the automatic transmission fluid level is always up to the mark and top up if necessary. And have both the ATF and ATF filter changed at least once a year.

More CVT troubles

" *Four years ago I bought a new Nissan Micra CVT automatic. The gear change was a bit stiff, which I put down to the car being new. But last year it got much worse and I took it back to the supplying agent for advice. I was told the car needed a new magnetic clutch, and remedial work to the gearbox which had been damaged as a result. Though the car had done less than 5,000 miles, it was out of warranty and I would have to pay the cost of approximately £1,200. I then consulted my local garage which has looked after the car. They took it to an automatic gearbox specialist who said the engine management computer had a fault and would require a new torque converter. We also approached Nissan who said the problem was the result of me driving with my hand on the gear lever and revving the engine while the car was stationary. Have you ever heard of this problem with Micras? What worries me is, if I pay up, the same problem may occur again, landing me with even more expense.* "

Apart from the CVT in the Volvo 440/460 1.8 (quite rare) and the Honda Civic 1.6i (very rare), the Micra's CVT seems to be the most reliable of this type of box, and Fords and Fiats the least reliable. Like the Fiat Punto, your box has an electromagnetic clutch operated by sensors which can sometimes play up. As a general rule of thumb, if the change into gear ever feels stiff, you should seek help from your dealer immediately and not force it or you are highly likely to damage the gearbox itself. The other essential with CVTs is to check the ATF (gearbox oil) level at least every week and if it drops below the minimum to immediately top it up with the correct ATF fluid. (Buy a bottle from the agent.) Follow this advice and, once your gearbox is repaired, you should not have any further trouble.

Erratic automatic

" *My daughter has a 'top of the range' 1992K Renault 19 1.8 automatic that has been regularly maintained in accordance with the manufacturer's recommendations by Renault agents. The automatic gearbox has now failed at a mere 56,000 miles and is going to be very expensive to replace. Is it reasonable for an automatic gearbox to fail at this mileage? I would have thought that a good quality car, properly maintained and looked after, should give around 100,000 miles of trouble-free motoring – or am I living in Cloud Cuckoo Land?* "

Lexus AS40E and GM4L-30E autoboxes, as fitted to Carltons and Senators, are good for well over 100,000 miles, and Mercedes autoboxes also last well. But not many others do and the quickest way to kill them is never to change the automatic transmission fluid. When faced with gearbox failures, most franchised agents immediately quote for a new exchange box, which costs the customer an arm and a leg. What you need is an automatic transmission specialist such as Trevor King on 01372 728769. Explain the symptoms and he'll work out if the problem is electronic or hydraulic, and he should be able to repair and recondition your existing box for a fraction of the cost of the new one. King Automatics is at Epsom, not far from Croydon, but if readers want to find a specialist more local to them, call The Federation of Automatic Transmission Engineers on 0585 228595.

Automatic solution

" *I have a 'G'-registered Vauxhall Cavalier automatic which is still giving me good service despite having run for 106,000 miles. A couple of years ago it developed a fault with the transmission. After a few miles driving, second gear would cease to operate. It would still change from 3rd to 4th, but would not return to 1st, nor would it change automatically out of 1st. The local Vauxhall agent diagnosed a '2/3 solenoid fault' and estimated a repair cost of £800–£1,400. A local automatic transmission specialist was more helpful, but wanted to charge £260 to remove and test the gearbox valve block. That afternoon, I opened the bonnet and gave the gearbox a long stare. I noticed a number of cable looms which looked as if they might have something to do with the gearbox, so I disconnected them one at a time, gave them a good wiggle, sprayed them with WD40 to drive out any moisture and reconnected them. You have probably guessed that when I drove the car again, the fault had disappeared and my only problem was deciding what to do with the £1,000 or so I had just saved.* "

Checking the connectors is a good tip, but I also expect that any honest garage would do this before committing to an expensive and possibly unnecessary repair. Better to quote high and then give the customer a nice surprise than to quote low and come back with a final bill that gives him a heart attack.

Holding the gears

" *I have a VW Passat TDI 110 diesel automatic estate car, and while I agree it is a superb motorway cruiser, there is a different story to tell about town. The problem is that the car holds second until 38–40 mph, which makes it tiresome and unnecessarily noisy to drive around town. Presumably the electronics and valving could be modified to make this more acceptable, but I am seriously considering changing the car because it is so irritatingly unsatisfactory to drive. Diesel Car magazine made the same point in the June 1998 issue, stating that the Citroën Xantia TD automatic was much better in this respect.* "

I read the article in *Diesel Car* and have driven both the Xantia and the Passat. While it's true that the Xantia can sometimes be made to change into 3rd at 30 mph, it doesn't do this every time and the normal change speeds can be close to those of the Passat. The trouble is, you can't have everything. A diesel, even one with a flat torque curve such as the TDI 110, still has a relatively narrow rev band where both torque and bhp are healthy. Lose a gear ratio, as you do with a 4-speed auto, and compromises have to be made. What both VW and Citroën have done is run relatively high ratios, so 2nd is more like the 3rd of a 5-speed box, 3rd more like 4th and, pulling between 28 and 39 mph, 4th is like a stepped-up overdrive 5th. If you messed around with the valving and the electronics, you'd end up with a very sluggish car.

Automatic self-destruct

" *In August 1997 I acquired a 96N Ford Scorpio 2.0 litre Ultima automatic estate which has now done 42,000 miles. It recently started slipping out of 4th when travelling at speed on a feathered throttle. I have been advised that this is due to failure of the clutch plates and my local Ford agent suggests that the most effective solution would be a replacement box at a cost of £1,500. After discussing this with Ford Customer Care I was told it is a known problem and I was offered 60 per cent of the cost as a goodwill gesture. I also run a nine-year-old Carlton GSi 3.0 litre automatic, which has now covered 150,000 miles and has never been any trouble at all. On this basis, and that of numerous fault-free Mercedes and Volvo automatics I have run in the past, I would not have expected to attend to the Scorpio gearbox until at least 100,000 miles, by which time I would have sold the car so it would not be my problem. What should I do with the Scorpio once it has been repaired? Sell it or keep it?* "

The Carlton has one of the better automatic boxes. The Scorpio doesn't, and failures are common usually at around the 60,000-mile mark. When King Automatics rebuild these boxes they modify them slightly to give them a longer life (01372 728769). But, since Ford has offered 60 per cent of the cost of a new box, you're probably better off with a manufacturer replacement. Whether to sell or keep the car is another matter. Even though the used market is flat, demand tends to hold up quite well for Scorpio estates, especially during the holiday season, and you should be able to get £10,000 for it. But a seasonal warning – if used for towing a caravan, these boxes can overheat unless an automatic transmission fluid cooler has been fitted.

Clutchless change

" *A few months ago 'Telegraph Motoring' ran an article about a conversion of manual gearboxes to a type of automatic, avoiding the use of the clutch pedal – similar to the Renault Twingo's 'Easy' system, but possible to transfer from vehicle to vehicle. Please will you supply the name, address and telephone number?* "

I think you are referring to the TUV-approved Vehvac AutoClutch, which employs a button on the gearshift knob and an electric motor to dip the clutch for you when you want to change gear. The product is AutoClutch, from Vehvac Ltd, Fircroft Way, Edenbridge TN8 6EJ, tel: 01732 868080.

Another clutch of clutch failures

A spate of readers has suffered premature clutch failure on cars as diverse as VW Polos, Citroën ZXs and Peugeot 306s. (Previously, it was VW Golfs and old-shape Rover 200s/400s.) Many complain of the first clutch failure in 40–50 years driving. Assuming the clutches themselves are not faulty, the most likely reason is failure of the self-adjusting mechanism in the cable. (VW has now scrapped self-adjusting cables.) The other possibility, no offence intended, is that as we all get older and stiffer, we may not be aware that we are dragging the clutch, touching the pedal while driving along or failing to fully disengage the handbrake. But if your clutch has failed at less than 30,000 miles and the car has a self-adjusting clutch cable, I'd like to hear about it in order to try and work out if there is any pattern here. (If you're not sure whether the car has a self-adjusting clutch cable or not, ask your garage.)

Automatic dipsticks

" *A different sort of 'dipstick' problem has occurred with automatic Volkswagens. In 1992 I purchased a new VW Golf Mk III automatic, the gearbox of which was fitted with a dipstick and the handbook of which recommended a regular change of automatic transmission fluid. In 1994 I purchased a new Golf Mk III estate: same dipstick, same recommendation. In 1996, I purchased a third, only to find no dipstick and no recommendation to change the ATF. I queried this and was told that the 'gearbox is sealed for life'.* "

Same goes for the ZF boxes fitted to non-supercharged Jaguars and the same explanation is given by Jaguar (supercharged Jags are fitted with Mercedes S600 gearboxes). When gearboxes are 'sealed for life', you have to ask, 'what "life"?' By preventing routine checks and discouraging regular oil changes, it could be as short as five years or 60,000 miles. Readers have complained of some non-VW automatic gearboxes failing at 30,000 miles, so if that's their design life it's logical for manufacturers not to fit them with dipsticks.

Minor modifications

" *I would very much like to own a Morris Minor Traveller but, as I only have a driving licence for automatics, I am not sure if this is possible. Was the Traveller every produced as an automatic? Would it be possible to convert one?* "

No, and yes. But it will mean fairly major modifications to the Minor. The easiest is to use the 1,275 cc engine and three-speed automatic gearbox from a Marina, and the technical department of the Morris Minor Owners Club will be able to advise you about this (MMOC, tel: 01332 291675 – nice, helpful people). Alternatively, Bob at Morri Spares (01992 524249) is gathering information about alternative conversions such as an adaptation of the Ford V4, plus automatic box from the Corsair. Minors have been fitted with anything from Fiat twin cam engines to the complete chassis and engine of a Ferrari Tipo 555 'Supersqualo'. Gary Bezer's Series II Traveller sports a supercharged Rover V8 and Rover autobox.

Broken boxes

" *The gearbox of my 1995 'M'-registered Peugeot 306 failed at only 25,900 miles. I bought the car, which had previously been registered to Peugeot itself, on 23 February 1996 with 10,000 miles. I find it astonishing that a major component such as this, which one would normally expect to last the life of the car, has failed at such an early stage. Repairs cost me £523.11.* "

Three other readers complained of premature gearbox failure in the same week's mail. The box of a 1996 Clio failed at 15,000 miles, but was covered by the extended warranty (though, of course, clutch replacement wasn't). The gearbox bearings of an 'M'-reg. Laguna became noisy at 33,000 miles, necessitating £595 of work, while the gearbox casing of a 1994L Renault 19 RTD cracked after four years and 83,000 miles. It is always a good idea to have the gearbox oil of a modern car changed after the first year's use. If any shards of metal, rust or dirt are lying around in the oil, this will get them out and prevent them from gradually damaging the bearings, gearbox casing or the gears themselves.

Surging automatics

" *I can suggest a reason why some cars with automatic gearboxes may surge when manoeuvring: air conditioning. While the car is at speed on a hot day, the rush of air helps to keep the engine and interior cool. But as soon as the car slows right down, engine and interior temperatures rise and the air-conditioning pump has to cut in to keep to any pre-set level. To compensate for power lost to turning the pump and to prevent the engine from stalling, the ECU will increase engine revs slightly, and this is sometimes enough to engage 'Drive' when the driver has all feet off the pedals.* "

Good point. This is most likely to be felt in a low-powered automatic fitted with air conditioning, but is not a universal trait.

GIZMOS AND TOOLS

(SEE ALSO 'TOWING')

Acoustic parking

" *I am trying to locate an electronic car reversing aid which warns a driver of unseen obstacles in the path of a reversing car. I am told such a product exists, but no motoring store appears to stock them. How reliable are these devices and where can they be obtained?* "

Auto Express magazine tested a range of these devices in issue 535. The one they rated best was Autosonics Backminder, at £175 for the kit (01259 217004). Next best, scoring four stars, was Ultrapark 2000 at an expensive £346 (Laver Technology, tel: 01279 436080). Next, with three stars, the Cobra ParkMaster at £151 for the kit (01923 240525). Equal fourth, and also with three stars, were the much cheaper £86 AlliGator (Western Brands, tel: 01242 570227) and the Proximeter at £170 (0171 345 5050). Another product which uses coloured lights as well as 'beeps' was originally designed for reversing caravans. It is made by Brigade Electronics, is called the 'Backscan RI–OS',

costs around £200 fitted and worked well when fitted as an optional extra to a Ford Scorpio I tried. Brigade Electronics can be contacted on 0181 852 3261.

Click Clean body wipers

" *Some time ago I bought one of these, and I find it invaluable for removing water after washing the car. Half a dozen strokes clears 95 per cent of the water from the roof; three or four strokes clear the bootlid and bonnet; a couple of downward strokes clears each of the doors. It saves time and preserves wash leathers. But I have not been able to find one recently. Do you know if they are still made and, if not, can any manufacturer be persuaded to make them again?* "

A reader from Sproatley eventually came to the rescue on this, recommending the 'First Pass Auto Dry Blade', which is made in the USA and is available from Allapatah Enterprises, PO Box 348, Twickenham, Middlesex TW1 1UG, tel: 0181 891 0201. He tells us, 'It is an easily held blade by virtue of its chunky grip, is 12 inches in length, and I am delighted with its performance on both flat and curved surfaces.' Another, from Epsom, found the Polco Water Wiper, with its thick, 'specially developed soft blade', to be ideal for dispersing water without leaving run marks. Price £4.75 from Autoparts of High Street, Thame, though other accessory shops should have it.

Ring of confidence

" Here's a useful little last minute Christmas present for anyone thinking of buying a car in the New Year. Use the 'Motor-Ring' just once to find undisclosed filler, fibreglass or aluminium mesh hidden in the bodywork and it will have paid for itself many times over. The subtle design of a finger ring with a magnet instead of a gemstone allows all such checks to be made surreptitiously under the eyes of the vendor. "

I wore one at an auction the day it arrived, just to see if it worked, and, like any weak magnet or magnetic paint thickness tester, it sticks to good steel but not to aluminium (or to 'gob', 'clag', or 'pudding', depending on where in the country you're checking out a dodgy car). The price is £9.99. Teslec also makes a pentop sized electronic 'Ferristor' filler finder at £14.99 which can locate even a thin layer of filler between paint and steel. Teslec Ltd, New Springs, 90a Blackburn Road, Whittle-le-Woods, Chorley PR6 8LG, tel: 01257 271105.

Magic roundabout

" Your readers may be interested in our revolutionary turntable. It means they can drive into a short driveway, then turn the car in its length

so they can safely and legally emerge 'front first'. It can also be used at restricted driveway corners, inside a garage which is wide enough to accommodate the width of the car, and in many other places where access is restricted and the surface is level. **"**

Readers have asked about turntables many times before, but this is the first one to come in at prices from £4,000 for one of 3.5 m diameter turned by hand. More information from Car Parking Solutions Ltd, PO Box 15, Alresford, Hants, tel: 01962 733716 or 01705 522017.

GOOD GARAGE GUIDE

In Summer 1996 we ran a reader's story about the difference between big garages in Britain and small garages in France. I felt that the contrast was more likely to be between bad garages and good garages generally, so I asked for readers' recommendations. The first 100 or so came in thick and fast, and have continued to do so. The result is this updated list which now reaches into the far corners of the land.

Remember, the list is based purely on readers' recommendations (plus four from me). Inclusion is not a guarantee of quality, competence or good value, and neither The Daily Telegraph *nor me can accept any responsibility for the consequences of taking a car to any of the garages listed. Nevertheless, many of the testimonials I have received were fulsome in their praise, so if you are looking for good service, this list may be a good start.*

- ABBERLEY: Alan Hole, P. Owen & Sons Ltd, Motor & Agricultural Engineers, The Abberley Garage, Abberley, Worcestershire, tel: 01299 896209.

- ABERDEEN: Harpers of Aberdeen. Main workshop, tel: 01224 697772. Rapid Fit (open 8–6 Mon, Tues, Wed, Fri; 8–8 Thurs; 8–5 Sat; 10–4 Sun), tel: 01224 663232. (Good, helpful, Ford franchise.)

- ABERGAVENNY: Abergavenny Autos, Monmouth Road, Abergavenny, Monmouthshire, tel: 01873 852712. (Reliable Renault franchise.)

- ABERYSTWYTH: Anthony Motors Ltd, Aberystwyth, tel: 01970 624444. (Good Mazda agents.)

- ALDEBURGH: Chris Copeman, Copeman & Son Engineering, Hazelwood Farm, Aldringham, Nr Aldeburgh, Suffolk, tel: 01728 830640 (mobile: 0860 614518).

- ALTON: Neil Carpenter, Farringdon Industrial Centre, Alton, Hants, tel: 01420 587 403.

- AMERSHAM: T and F Motors, White Lion Road, Amersham, Bucks, tel: 01494 765286.

- ANDOVER: Chris Monaghan and Martin Dix, Intech GB Ltd, Unit 12 B, Thruxton Industrial Estate, Thruxton Circuit, near Andover, Hants, tel: 01264 773888. (Service and repair specialists for Japanese 'grey' imports from Honda Beat to Lexus 'Soarer' Coupe.)

- ASHBOURNE: Hulland Ward Garage, Main Street, Hulland Ward, Nr Ashbourne, Derbyshire, tel: 01335 370209.

- ASHTON-UNDER-LYNE: Quicks, tel: 0161 330 0121. (Ford Agent with longstanding customer loyalty.)

- AYLESBURY: Ivor Miles, Churchway Garage, Churchway, Haddenham, Aylesbury, Bucks HP17 8HA, tel: 01844 291263.

- AYLESBURY: Lodge Garage (Aylesbury Mazda) Ltd, Bicester Road, Kingswood, Aylesbury, Bucks HP18 0QJ, tel: 01296 770405.

- BALLATER: J. Pringle, Victoria Garage, Ballater, Grampian AB35 5QQ, tel: 013397 55525.

- BEDALE: John Gill Ltd, Bedale, N. Yorks, tel: 01677 423124. (Daihatsu dealer and general repairs.)

- BEXHILL-ON-SEA: Peter Johnson, Motor Engineer, Unit 3, de la Warr Mews, Station Road, Bexhill-on-Sea, East Sussex TN40 1RD, tel: 01424 224169.

- BEXLEYHEATH: Paul at PDQ Car Services, Bexleyheath, Kent (best to phone first for directions), tel: 0181 303 1618, mobile: 0831 138463.

- BILLINGHURST: Geoffrey Sizzy (Automobiles), Wisborough Green (Nr Billingshurst), West Sussex, tel: 01403 700661. (Independent Peugeot specialist – sales, service, very good after-sales service.)

- BIRMINGHAM: R. Newman, Motor Engineers, rear of J. H. Hancox Ltd,) Alcester Road, Portway, Birmingham B48 7JA, tel: 01564 824996.

- BIRMINGHAM: G. & B. Clements, Baldwins Lane Service Station, Baldwins Lane, Hall Green, Birmingham B28 0XB, tel: 0121 744 5453.

- BOGNOR REGIS: Middleton Garage, 169 Middleton Road, Middleton-on-Sea, Bognor Regis, tel: 01243 58276. (Very helpful Fiat franchise.)

- BOSTON: Mick Barsley, Barsley Motor Engineers, 78 High Street, Boston, Lincs, tel: 01205 355396.

- BOURNEMOUTH: Horizon Motors, tel: 01202 294341. (Honda agents.)

- BRIDGWATER: Tim Stiles Racing, Units 5 & 6 Transform Estate, Wylds Road, Bridgwater, Somerset TA6 4DH, tel: 01278 453036. (VW/Audi performance modifications at reasonable prices and labour rates.)

- BRIDGWATER: Stogursey Motors, High Street, Stogursey (8 miles from Bridgwater near Hinkley Point power station), tel: 01278 732237. (Car, van and motorcycle repairs and MOTs.)

- BROADWAY: Alan Aston Motor Engineers, Childswickham, Nr Broadway, Worcs, tel: 01386 852311.

- BROMLEY: Ted and Neil Craker, The Vehicle Test Centre, 107 Southlands Road, Bromley, Kent BR2 9QT, tel: 0181 460 6666. (Very well equipped and sensibly priced servicing workshop/ MOT test centre, with two 'rolling road' brake testers and full diagnostic equipment.)

- BURTON-ON-TRENT: Peter Sharp, European Car Specialists, Parker Street, Burton-on-Trent, tel: 01283 540414.

- BUSHMILLS, CO. ANTRIM: James Wylie Auto Repairs, 40A Ballyclough Road, Bushmills, Co. Antrim BT57 8UZ, tel: 012657 32096. (Citroën specialist, as well as other makes.)

- CAERLEON: Autotech, Panthir Road, Caerleon, Gwent NP6 1NY, tel: 01633 423717. (One of the semi-official Autotech chain of independent BMW specialists.)

- CANTERBURY: Ashford Road Service Station, Chilham, Canterbury, Kent CT4 8EE, tel: 01227 730223.

- CANTERBURY: Hewitt Motors Ltd, Rhodans Town, Canterbury, Kent, tel: 01227 464386.

- CARDIFF: Continental Cars (Cardiff) Ltd, tel: 01222 542400. (Mercedes franchise; treats elderly drivers with extra consideration.)

- CARNFORTH: The Mountain Family, Lune View Garage, Melling, Carnforth, Lancs LA6 2RB, tel: 015 242 21457.

- CARNFORTH: Mill Brow Garage, Kirkby Lonsdale, Carnforth, Lancs, tel: 015 242 71248.

- CASTLEFORD: Castleford VW Spares, Methley Road, Castleford, W. Yorks, tel: 01977 518254. (VW/Audi servicing and parts.)

- CASTLE CAREY: Moff Motors, Castle Carey, Somerset (near Castle Carey station on Shepton Mallet Road), tel: 01963 350310. (Independent dealers with good after-sales service.)

- CHANDLERS FORD: Hendy Lennox, Chandlers Ford, Hants, tel: 01703 483100. (Good, helpful Ford agent.)

- CATFORD: Gilbert's Motors, tel: 0181 698 7067. (Honda agent prepared to repair expensive components rather than replace them.)

- CHELMSFORD: Mr & Mrs John Plumb and son Steve, Central Garage, Latchingdon, Nr Chelmsford, Essex, tel: 01621 740284.

- CHERTSEY: Speedtest, Unit A, Gogmore Lane, Chertsey, Surrey, tel: 01932 568921. (Honest, straight servicing and MOT centre. Good with Citroëns and Renaults.)

- CHESSINGTON: Mole Valley TVR, Chessington, Surrey, tel: 0181 394 1114. (Good TVR dealer – two recommendations.)

- CHESTERFIELD: Bridgegate Ltd, Chesterfield, tel: 01246 208681. (Very helpful BMW agent, even for older models.)

- CHIPPENHAM: David Giddings, 14 Brook Street, Chippenham, Wilts SN14 0HN. Ex-Directory. (Specialist cars including Alfas and Jensens.)

- CHISLEHURST: Paul and Tony at PDQ, 1a Albany Road, Chislehurst, Kent, tel: 0181 295 0121 (BMW and Jaguar specialists).

- COLWYN BAY: Meredith and Kirkham, Colwyn Bay, tel: 01492 515292. (Rover agent with longstanding customer loyalty.)

- CREWKERNE: Misterton Garage, Misterton, Crewkerne, Somerset, tel: 01460 72997. (Ford retail dealer – good for servicing and repairs at reasonable prices.)

- CWMCARN: Bijou Motor Services, rear of 99–101 Newport Road, Cwmcarn, Gwent NP1 7LZ, tel: 01495 271033. (Citroën specialists.)

- CROWBOROUGH: John Cottenham, Care's Garage, School Lane, St Johns, Crowborough, East Sussex TN6 1SE, tel: 01892 653519. (VW.)

- DARWEN: Brunswick Street Garage, Darwen, Lancs, tel: 01254 762300. (Mercedes Benz-trained independent MB specialist.)

- DAVENTRY: Dave Carvell Cars, Staverton, Nr Daventry, Northants, tel: 01327 300739.

- DERBY: Citrognome, Great Northern Road, Derby, tel: 01332 345869. (Citroën specialists.)

- DORCHESTER: Loders, Dorchester, Dorset, tel: 01305 267881. (Good franchised Audi dealer service.)

- DORCHESTER: Old's Jeep, Dorchester. (Good franchised Chrysler dealer service.)

- DORKING: Steve Bradstock, The Coach House, Beare Green, Dorking, Surrey, tel: 01306 713424.

- DRUMNDROCHIT: J. E. Menzies & Son Ltd, Lewiston Garage, Drumndrochit, Inverness, tel: 01456 450212.

- DUBLIN: Walden Motor Company, Parnell Street, Dublin, tel: 00 3531 873 0400; email: cars@walden.ie. (Ford agent with longstanding customer loyalty.)

- DURHAM: Volksparts, Langley Moor, nr Durham, tel: 0191 378 0284. (German car specialists – Audi, BMW, Mercedes, VW.)

- EASTBOURNE: Visick Cars Ltd, Birch Close, Lottbridge Drove, Eastbourne BN23 6PE, tel: 01323 722244.

- EAST HORSLEY: Philip Stonely, The Body Workshop, Forest Road Garage, Forest Road, Effingham Junction, Surrey KT24 5HE, tel: 01483 284805.

- ELVANFOOT: South of Scotland Coachworks, Elvanfoot, Lanarkshire (adjacent to A74M), tel: 01864 502236. (General repairs and service.)

- EMSWORTH: Lillywhite Bros Ltd, 40 Queen Street, Emsworth, Hants PO10 7BL, tel: 01243 372336.

- ENFIELD: Stephen James, London Road, Enfield EN2 6JJ, tel: 0181 367 2626. (Friendly BMW agent with sensibly priced servicing.)

- EPSOM: King Automatics, 'The Chalk Pit', College Road, Epsom, Surrey KT17 4JA, tel: 01372 728769 . (Automatic transmissions of all types, including CVTs.)

- EPSOM: Kwik-Fit, 166 East Street, Epsom, Surrey, tel: 01372 739955. (Replaced a reader's tyre valve free of charge.)

- EPSOM: Drift Bridge Garage Ltd, Reigate Road, Epsom, Surrey, tel: 01737 360111. (VW agent.)

- EXETER: Volkswagen Services, 11 Coombe Street, Exeter, Devon EX1 1DB, tel: 01392 493737. (VW servicing.)

- EXETER: Carrs of Exeter, tel: 01392 823988. (Good Mercedes and Porsche service.)

- EXETER: Reg and Paul Stephens, Snow and Stephens, King Edward Street, Exeter, tel: 01392 256552. (General car repairs.)

- EXETER: Rockbeare Motor Services, Rockbeare, Exeter EX5 2DZ, tel: 01404 822410. (General car repairs.)

- EXETER: Best Tyres, Verney Street, Exeter, tel: 01392 411100. (Low prices, good service and excellent for suspension alignment.)

- EXMOUTH: Karl Brigham, KB Auto Services and Repairs, Victoria Way, Exmouth, Devon, tel: 01395 223330.

- EXMOUTH: Bentleys Garage, Chapel Hill (High Street), Exmouth, Devon, tel: 01395 272048.

- FAREHAM: Peter Cooper, Fareham, Hants, tel: 01329 288233. (Good, helpful VW franchise.)

- FERRING: John Cooper Garages, Ferring, West Sussex, tel: 01903 504455. (Very helpful Honda franchise.)

- FINCHAMPSTEAD: Cresswells, California Crossroads, Finchampstead, Berks, tel: 01734 732201.

- FORRES: Pedigree Cars, Forres, Morayshire, tel: 01309 672555. (Citroën garage.)

- FRENCHAY: Frenchay Garage, Frenchay Common, Frenchay, Bristol BS16 1NB, tel: 0117 956 7303.

- GARSTANG: H. and J. Kitching, Hornby's Garage, Lydiate Lane, Claughton on Brock, Garstang, Lancs, tel: 01995 640229.

- GRAVENHURST: Chris Case, Town Farm Garage, Campton Road, Gravenhurst, Beds, tel: 01462 711017.

- GUILDFORD: A. H. Autos, Unit 11, Foundation Units, Westfield Road, Slyfield Green, Guildford, tel: 01483 303942. (VW/Audi specialists.)

- HARROGATE: Mr Greenwood, Western Garage, Valley Mount, Harrogate, N. Yorks H62 0JG, tel: 01423 502902.

- HARROGATE: Nidd Vale Motors, Harrogate. (Vauxhall agents.)

- HEMEL HEMPSTEAD: V. P. Autos, Hemel Hempstead, Herts, tel: 01442 68163.

- HENLOW: Alan Turner, Henlow Car Centre, Henlow, Beds, tel: 01462 814668.

- HERSHAM: Colin Marshall or Keith Rhoods, Wheelbase Garage, 43 Queen's Road, Hersham, Surrey, tel: 01932 252515 or 01932 252881. (VW/Audi specialists.)

- HERSHAM: Sunbury Coachworks, Unit R3, Lyon Road, Hersham Industrial estate, Hersham, Surrey, tel: 01932 254057. (Good bodyshop offering excellent Autocolor paint finish at reasonable prices.)

- HEXHAM: Fred Almond, Haugh Lane Garage, Haugh Lane, Hexham, Northumberland, tel: 01434 60 4163 or 0836 532999.

- HOLMFIRTH: M and M Engineering Services, Clarence Mills, Holmbridge, Holmfirth HD7 1NE, tel: 01484 687706. (Citroën.)

- HOLT: Eddy Lynton, Academy Garage, Castle Street, Holt, Clwyd LL13 9YL, tel: 01829 270781.

- HOUNSLOW: Franco Motors, 29 Vine Place, Hounslow TW3 3UE, tel: 0181 570 3798.

- HYTHE: Auto Pat, 3 Hardley Industrial Estate, Hardley, Nr Hythe, Hants, tel: 01703 804163.

- ILFORD: Whichford Rover, 404 Eastern Avenue, Gants Hill, Ilford, Essex IG2 6NW, tel: 0181 554 8888. (Rover dealer, fixed faults on recently purchased used cars at no charge and without question.)

- ILKESTON: Dave's Motors, West Street, Ilkeston, Derbyshire, tel: 0115 9441 886.

- JARROW: David Ellis, Jarrow Coachworks, Curlew Road, Jarrow, Tyne and Wear, tel: 0191 4892715, mobile: 0860 424813.

- KIRKWALL: A. T. S., Kirkwall, Orkney. (Tyre specialists and general servicing.)

- LANGPORT: J. A. Scott, Langport Motor Co., Westover Trading Estate, Langport, Somerset, tel: 01458 251100. (Citroën specialist.)

- LEAMINGTON SPA: Brian Ricketts, tel: 01926 451545. (VW/Audi.)

- LEAMINGTON SPA: Midland Autocar Co., Russell Street, Leamington Spa, Warks CV32 5QB, tel: 01926 421171. (General repairs and service.)

- LEAMINGTON SPA: Bull Ring Garage, The Bull Ring, Harbury, Leamington Spa, Warks CN33 9HR, tel: 01926 61275. (Excellent local garage.)

- LEDBURY: R. and J. Mathews, Blacklands Garage, Canon Frome (near Ledbury), Hereford and Worcester, tel: 01531 640374.

- LEEDS: David Wood, 11 Primley Park Road, Leeds LS17 7HR, tel: 0113 268 1815, mobile: 0780 858 0859. (VW/Audi.)

- LEEDS: IVC (Independent VW/Audi Centre), Globe Road, off Water Lane, Leeds LS11 5QS, tel: 0113 242 0875.

- LEEK: Andy Jackson of A&C Vehicle Services, Ball Haye Road, Leek, Staffs, tel: 01538 398227. (VW/Audi.)

- LEIGHTON BUZZARD: Tom Goodman Motors, Comptons Yard, Grovebury Road, Leighton Buzzard LU7 8TS, tel: 01525 375972.

- LEWES: Morris Road Garage, Western Road, Lewes, East Sussex, tel: 01273 472434. (Independent Bosch fuel injection specialists.)

- LICHFIELD: Central Garage (Lichfield) Ltd, Queen Street, Lichfield, Staffs, WS13 6QD, tel: 01543 262826. (BMW and Mercedes.)

- LINCOLN: Riccardo Emiliani, Lincoln, tel: 01522 531735. (Helpful Honda agent.)

- LISKEARD: Ken Rowe, Rowe's Garage Ltd, Dobwalls, Liskeard, Cornwall PL14 6JA, tel: 01579 320218. (Citroën franchise.)

- LITTLEBOROUGH: J. Stanton, Stantons Motor Garage, Brookfield Mill, Canal Street, Littleborough, Nr Rochdale, Lancs, tel: 01706 370166.

- LIVERPOOL: Orlando Heeson, Landers Autos, 19–22a Cathedral Road, Liverpool L6 0AT, tel: 0151 263 4913.

- LIVERPOOL: Philip Walker, Dudlow Motor Company, Menlove Gardens West, Liverpool, tel: 0151 722 2396.

- LLANGOLLEN: Kenrick's Garage, Market Street, Llangollen, North Wales, tel: 01978 861381/861382. (Friendly local garage with excellent and reasonably priced 'rescue' service.)

- LOANHEAD: Stewart McLennan Garage, 44 Lawrie Terrace, Loanhead, Midlothian EH20 9ET, tel: 0131 440 0597.

- LONDON E5: Tony, D. A. M. Car Repairs, 1–8 Broadway Mews, Clapton Common, London E5 9AF, tel: 0181 800 7121.

- LONDON N4: G. Horscraft, Supertune Motor Engineers, 2A Beatrice Road, Stroud Green, London N4 4PD, tel: 0171 272 7678.

- LONDON N4: Nick Sandamas, G&N Garages Ltd., 54–58 Wightman Road, Harringay, London N4 1RU, tel: 0181 340 331. (Independent Saab specialist.)

- LONDON SE6: Gonella Brothers, 9–13 Catford Hill, Catford, London SE6, tel: 0181 690 0060. (Alfa, Fiat and Lancia specialists.)

- LONDON SW2: Hearn Bros Ltd, The Hill Garage, 94 Brixton Hill, London SW2, tel: 0181 674 2888.

- LONDON SW17: Carpenters Garage, 69–71 Bickersteth Road, Tooting, London SW17, tel: 0181 672 4891. (Small, family run independent garage and MOT testing station.)

- LONDON W8: ACE Cars of Kensington, tel: 0171 938 4333. (Specialises in older Saabs: 900, 99, 96.)

- LONDON W12: AC Automotive, 247–251 Goldhawk Road, London W12, tel: 0181 741 9993. (American car parts and servicing.)

- LOWER BASILDON: Les Allum, Allum Auto Services, Reading Road, Lower Basildon, Berks RG8 9NL, tel: 01491 671726.

- LYMINGTON: Dory's Garage Ltd, Sway Park, Station Road, Sway, Hants, tel: 01590 683432. (Citroën specialists.)

- MAIDENHEAD: Delta Motors, tel: 01628 675064; contacts: Jerry Houdret – sales; Roger Towers – parts. (Renault agents.)

- MANCHESTER: Derek Boardman, Units 12–25, Morton Street Industrial Estate, Failsworth, Manchester, tel: 0161 681 0456. (VW/Audi.)

- MANCHESTER: Westron, 7 Nell Lane, Manchester M21 8UE, tel: 0161 881 1061. (Citroën suspension specialists.)

- MALVERN: Denver Davis, The Station Garage, Thorngrove Road, Malvern, Worcs, tel: 01684 574088.

- MERSTHAM, John Witty, Witmun Engineering, 67 Nutfield Road, Merstham, Surrey RH1 3ER, tel: 01737 644828. (Citroën specialists.)

- MIDDLESBROUGH: Dave Stott Motors, Charlotte Street, Middlesbrough, tel: 01642 224805. (Independent Citroën specialists.)

- MORETON-IN-MARSH: N. E. Repairs, Hospital Road, Moreton-in-Marsh, Gloucs, tel: 01608 650405.

- NEEDHAM MARKET: Richard Robinson, Robinson's Motor Engineers, Debtrac Centre, Needham Market, Suffolk, tel: 01449 722240.

- NEWTON ABBOT: K. Tapper, Decoy Motors, Unit 10 Silverhills Road, Decoy Trading Estate, Newton Abbot TQ12 5LZ, tel: 01626 68701.

- NORTH SHIELDS: John Gallagher, Collingwood Garage, North Shields, tel: 0191 296 2888.

- NORWICH: Peter Whitley Motor Services, 7 Low Road, Drayton, Norwich NR8 6AA, tel: 01603 860154.

- ORPINGTON: Chelsfield Motor Works, Court Lodge Farm, Warren Road, Orpington, Kent BR6 6ER, tel: 01689 823200.

- OULTON BROAD: John Pope, Pope Brothers, Station Garage, Bridge End, Oulton Broad, Lowestoft, tel: 01502 573797.

- OXFORD: North Oxford Garage Ltd, 280 Banbury Road, Oxford, OX2 7EB, tel: 01865 319000. (Helpful BMW franchise.)

- OXFORD: Motor World Mitsubishi, Oxford, tel: 01865 722444. (Mitsubishi agent offering excellent after-sales service.)

- PENARTH: Bernard Cody, Motor Engineers, Station Approach, Penarth, Mid Glamorgan, tel: 01222 704293. (RMI, VBRA, AVRO and MOT testing station.)

- PENRHYNDEUDRAETH: Dafydd Williams, Garreg, Lwyd, Penrhyndeudraeth, Gwynedd, LL48 6AW, tel: 01766 770203. (Second-hand Twingos, servicing, advice and 'hard to get' parts.)

- PENZANCE: Autostop Service Centre, Longrock, Nr Penzance, Cornwall, tel: 01736 330300. (Excellent, non-franchised service and repair garage.)

- PERIVALE: AC Delco, 19 Wadsworth Road, Unit 14, Perivale, Middx, tel: 0181 810 4595. (American car parts and servicing.)

- PETERBOROUGH: Brian Pitts, 'The Complete Automobilist', 35–37 Main Street, Baston, Peterborough PE6 9NX, tel: 01778 560444.

- PETERHEAD: Harpers of Aberdeen, Rapid Fit (open 8–6 Mon, Tues, Wed, Fri; 8–8 Thurs; 8–5 Sat; 10–4 Sun), tel: 01779 474849. (Good, helpful, Ford Rapid Fit centre.)

- PEWSEY: Stevens Cars, Nicol's Yard (rear of Post Office), Pewsey, tel: 01672 563330.

- PLYMOUTH: Simon Rouse, Peverell Garage, Weston Park Road, Peverell, Plymouth, Devon PL3 4NS, tel: 01752 266099.

- POOLE: Connellys, Ashley Road, Upper Parkstone, Poole, Dorset, tel: 01202 738700.

- POOLE: Grand Parade Motors, Poole Road, Poole, Dorset, tel: 01202 763361. (Good Vauxhall agent.)

- PORTHCAWL: John Rogers, Station Hill Garage, Porthcawl, Mid Glamorgan, tel: 01656 786705.

- PORTMADOC: The Glanaber Garage, Borth-y-Gest, Portmadoc, Gwynedd, tel: 01766 512364.

- PRESTON: J. C. and M. Davis, Garstang Road Garage, Garstang Road, Pilling, Preston PR3 6AQ, tel: 01253 790322. (General repairs, but good with diesels and Citroëns.)

- PRESTON: I. J. Woodburn, Unit 4 Garage, Langley Lane, Goosnargh, Nr Preston, Lancs, tel: 01772 861126. (Reliable independent BMW specialist.)

- READING: Clever Cars Ltd, Prospect Mews, Prospect Street, Reading, tel: 01734 576405. (Citroën specialists.)

- RIPLEY: Colbourne Garages Ltd, Portsmouth Road (old A3), Ripley, Surrey, tel: 01483 224361. (Oldest established UK VW agent, still good.)

- SADDLEWORTH: Greenfield Service Station, Chew Valley Road, Greenfield, Saddleworth, Nr Oldham, Lancs, tel: 01457 873700.

- SANDERSTEAD: Steven Pengelly, Vorne Motorsport, 145 Limpsfield Road, Sanderstead, Surrey, tel: 0181 651 5344.

- SEVENOAKS: Antwis Engineering, Vestry Industrial Estate, Otford, Nr Sevenoaks, Kent, tel: 01732 450386. (Very good with BMWs.)

- SHEFFIELD: Bridgco Garage, 160 Broad Oaks, Sheffield 9, tel: 0114 2441775.

- SIDCUP: Steve King, Kings Auto Services, 313–315 Blackfen Road, Blackfen, Sidcup, Kent SA15 9NG, tel: 0181 298 9225.

- SOUTHAMPTON: E. and J. Jarvis, Motor Engineers, Onslow Road, Southampton, tel: 01703 229297.

- SOUTHAMPTON: Hilton Motors, Bond Road Garage, Bitterne Park, Southampton SO18 1LH, tel: 01703 555600. (General service, repair, sales garage and automatic transmission specialist.)

- SOUTH MOLTON: Andrew Geen, Geen's Garage, South Molton, North Devon, tel: 01769 572395.

- SOUTHSEA: John Skerratt, Owl Motor Services, Richmond Road, Southsea, Hants, tel: 01705 736393.

- ST ALBANS: Godfrey Davis St Albans, 105 Ashely Road, St Albans, Herts AL1 5GD, tel: 01727 859155. (Good Ford servicing facility capable of correctly diagnosing problems.)

- STEBBING: Bob Rains, Drakeswell Garage, Bran End, Stebbing, Essex, 01371 856391.

- STOCKPORT: Chris or Stewart, Tenby Garage, Lavenders Brow, Churchgate, Stockport, Cheshire SK1 1YW, tel: 0161 480 5075.

- STOCKPORT: The Dave Arnitt Citroën Repair Centre, Arthur Street, Reddish, Stockport, tel: 0161 432 0636. (Citroën specialist.)

- STOCKPORT: General Motors, Cooke Street, Hazel Grove, Stockport, tel: 0161 483 3883. (Independent Audi/VW specialists.)

- STOCKTON: Shearborne Engineering, Preston Farm, Stockton-on-Tees, tel: 01642 677744. (Independent Jaguar specialists.)

- SUTTON, SURREY: G. B. Autos, 271 Gander Green Lane, Sutton, Surrey SM1 2HD, tel: 0181 641 1999. (Independent Volvo and air conditioning servicing specialists.)

- SUTTON COLDFIELD: G. Chamberlain & Sons, Four Oaks Garage, Lichfield Road, Four Oaks, Sutton Coldfield, W. Midlands B74 2UH, tel: 0121 308 0309.

- SUTTON COLDFIELD: Dave Buckland, D. J. Buckland (Motor Engineer), rear of 162 Birmingham Road, Wylde Green, Sutton Coldfield, tel: 0121 355 7634 (out of hours, tel: 0121 350 6881).

- SWINDON: Fish Bros, Elgin Drive, Swindon, Wilts SM2 6DU, tel: 01793 512685. (Several recommendations: Fiat, Alfas Romeo and Mitsubishi franchise – good at diagnosing unsolved faults on Alfa Romeos.)

- TAUNTON: Paul Lyall, Fairwater Garage, Staplegrove Road, Taunton TA1 1DF, tel: 01823 277268.

- WADEBRIDGE: John Smith, Old Forge Garage, St Miniver, Wadebridge, Cornwall, tel: 01208 863323.

- WANTAGE: Paul Rivers, Hillcrest Garage, Reading Road, West Hendred, Nr Wantage, Oxon OX12 8RH, tel: 01235 833363.

- WANTAGE: T. A. Collins, Motor Engineers, Denchworth Road, Wantage, Oxon, tel: 01235 768321. (Volvo specialist.)

- WARRINGTON: Dave Roundell Services, Milner Street, Warrington, Cheshire, tel: 01925 635958.

- WARRINGTON: School Lane Garage, 19 School Lane, Hollins Green, Warrington, Cheshire WA3 6LJ, tel: 0161 775 3179 and ask for Chris. (Independent VW specialists.)

- WELLINGTON: Grants Repairs, Mantle Street, Wellington, Somerset, tel: 01823 662067. (Independent BMW specialist – chief mechanic Trevor Klimpke.)

- WEOBLEY: John Simpson, Whitehill Garage, Weobley, Hereford HR4 8QZ, tel: 01544 318268.

- WEST BROMWICH: The Sun Garage Company, Sandwell Road, West Bromwich, West Midlands B70 8TG, tel: 0121 553 0296.

- WESTCLIFF-ON-SEA: J. Harold Penny of Westcliff on Sea. (Ford agent with longstanding customer loyalty.)

- WEST MALLING: B. Butler, The Saab Sanctuary, 'Almandene', Woodgate Road, Ryarsh, West Malling, Kent ME19 5LH, tel: 01732 872722.

- WESTON-SUPER-MARE: Howards Citroën (tel: 01934 644644) and Howards Rover (tel: 01934 643434) both of Hildersheim Bridge, Weston-Super-Mare BS23 3PT.

- WESTON-SUPER-MARE: Howards Nissan (tel: 01934 416454), Herluin Way, Weston-Super-Mare BS23 3YN.

- WESTON-SUPER-MARE: Howards Peugeot (tel: 01934 636049), Searle Crescent, Weston-Super-Mare BS23 3YX. (Howards are franchised agents for Citroën, Rover, Peugeot and Nissan, all – very unusually – in the same town.)

- WEYBRIDGE: S. S. Motors, 16c Hanwell Lane, Weybridge Business Park, Weybridge, Surrey KT15 2SD, tel: 01932 821555. (Mercedes specialist run by Mercedes-trained ex-franchise service manager.)

- WEYBRIDGE: Dagenham Motors (Weybridge), Wintersalls Road, Byfleet, Surrey, tel: 01932 332933. (Good official Ford service agent.)

- WEYMOUTH: Tyre & Exhaust World, Weymouth, tel: 0345 419937. (Friendly, honest and values its customers.)

- WINDERMERE: Keith Donnelly, Oldfield Road Garage, Oldfield Road, Windermere, Cumbria LA23 2BY, tel: 015 394 46710.

- WINDSOR: New and Son, West End Service Station, Dadworth Road, Windsor, Berks, tel: 01753 862078 and 851685.

- WOLVERHAMPTON: Roger Williams, Oxley Service Station, Fordhouse Road, Wolverhampton, tel: 01902 787386.

- WOKING: Colbourne Garages Ltd, 76 Maybury Road, Woking, Surrey, tel: 01483 722415. (Oldest established UK VW agent, still good.)

- WORTHING: Rod Denton, Denton Motors, 1–3 Park Road, Worthing, West Sussex, tel: 01903 233790.

- WRAYSBURY: George Williams, Lakeside Garage, 48 Welley Road, Wraysbury, Middlesex TW19 5JD, tel: 01784 482158.

- YEOVIL: Eastside Garage, Lufton Trading Estate, Yeovil, Somerset, tel: 01935 31412. (Citroën specialist.)

- YEOVIL: Auto Wizard, Penhill Trading Estate, Yeovil, Somerset, tel: 01935 410532.

- YEOVIL: Douglas Seaton Ltd (Ford franchise with longstanding customer loyalty.)

- YORK: John Galley Motors, Pocklington Industrial Estate, Pocklington, York, tel: 01759 303716. (VW/Audi.)

- FRANCE (CHERBOURG): Garage Pichard, 124 Rue du Val de Saire, Cherbourg 51000. (Rover agent.)

- SPAIN (VALENCIA): Imperauto, Valencia, tel: 342 06 22. (Land Rover.)

HORSES FOR COURSES

Wants a Bentley

" I would like to drive or own a Bentley for a couple of years prior to my having to pack up driving. Can you give me some idea of the right model to buy for economy, price, value and residual value? I thought that a Bentley would be a comfortable and enjoyable ride for a few years. Is it a sensible car to purchase? "

How much have you got? How much can you afford to lose? Are you talking about a new Bentley, a late Bentley, a 1960s Bentley, a 1950s Bentley, a 1930s Bentley or a genuine 1920s W. O. Bentley Bentley? Obviously you need to avoid the latest BMW-powered Bentley Arnage, which is a bit of a camel. But no such worries with the old Cosworth-built 6.7 litre V8 because VW bought Cosworth in order to secure supplies of these (and promptly sold off the racing engine division to Ford, which suited everyone). In my experience, Turbo Rs tend to plummet towards the £10,000–£20,000 bracket, then stay there. In terms of investment, you'd be far better off with something like the wonderful 1956 Bentley S1 Continental sold by

BCA Blackbushe at their evening classic sale on 15 June 1998 for £48,987 inclusive of commission and VAT. Or, if you're really keen, you can pick up a 1920s W. O. Bentley 3.0 litre from around £50,000 and stand a very good chance of getting your money back. For up-to-date auction information, subscribe to *Classic Car Weekly* (via your newsagent) and 'The Collector's Car Auction List' (tel: 0181 534 3883 for credit card subscriptions, or 0336 424800 for a faxback at 50p per minute). Remember, annual tax on a post-1972 6,750 cc Bentley could soon be £675.

£3,500 car

" *My 24-year-old daughter is learning to drive and wishes to buy her first car. She has £3,500 maximum to spend. Her priorities are: reliability (she is a doctor), good driving seat support, PAS, manual gear change, engine size no more than 1.4 litres. She is not worried about street cred.* "

I think the best car to meet all your criteria for the money is a Fiat Punto 75 SX. This has an excellent, fully-adjustable driving position (courtesy of the Ergonomics Group at Loughborough University), is tough and reliable, but may or may not have PAS, which was an extra (it doesn't desperately need it). Problem areas are rear brake adjusters giving too much front brake bias, worn rear suspension pivots, and misrouted rear window washer hoses. Properly maintained, the 'Fire' engines in these cars are good for 200,000 miles and the bodies are electro-galvanised so don't rust unless accident-damaged.

Pandering to a daughter

" *My 17-year-old daughter recently passed her driving test, and for her first car she has in mind a Fiat Panda because they are cheap to buy and run. However, she has now been told by many self-styled 'experts' that the Fiat Panda is Britain's most unsafe car. Is this correct? Can older Pandas that run on leaded petrol have their cylinder head valve seats attended to so they can run on unleaded petrol?* "

I don't know where 'Britain's most unsafe car' came from. It is true that a pre-1990 pre-galvanised Panda can rust like an old fridge in a pond. But all pandas will run on unleaded (though early 998 cc Fire models will need to have the ignition retarded to run on 95Ron unleaded). The other day an 'H'-reg. Mk II Panda actually caught my eye. It was the 'Sergio Tacchini' designer model in metallic blue with bight green seats. It had the excellent 999 cc Fire engine (good for unleaded and runs to 200,000 miles plus), it had the revised Mk II suspension and, despite having obviously been left outside for most of its life, there wasn't a scrap of rust to be seen. This should be around £1,000 as a private sale and sells for around £650 at auction. At that money it would be a very good buy.

Ladder-van

" *I am setting up a small painting and decorating business for which I need a smart new small car or van. The only selection criterion I have is that the vehicle must be able to carry a ten-foot ladder safely. I have seen a Fiat Punto van and a Fiesta van, but I want to make sure I have checked all the options. I am looking to obtain the van on contract hire to keep my capital free, so should I opt for the maintenance or the non-maintenance package?* "

Go for either the Citroën Berlingo with special

'ladder flap' rear doors, or the Renault Kangoo with ladder flap. I like the Berlingo because of its numerous other advantages, such as the folding passenger seat which becomes a table and also hides a usefully big cubby hole for items you want to keep hidden. But the Kangoo has a passenger seat which folds to extend the load platform. Yes, go for the full maintenance contract. Also register for VAT *before* you take on the van, then you can claim back the VAT on the rental payments and on the maintenance element of the contract.

Miniature automatic

" *Can you recommend a reliable automatic that will fit the extremely restricted amount of space in my garage? At present I am driving a manual Fiat Cinquecento. Several years ago I had an automatic Mini which proved to be a disaster.* "

Fiat recently announced a 'Citymatic' version of its cute Seicento which, as you know, replaced the Cinquecento. This is not a true automatic because you shift the gears. But it has an electronically controlled automatic clutch, so there are only two foot pedals. It also has electro-hydraulic power steering and the UK price is £7,120 on the road. The Seat Arosa and VW Lupo 1.4 automatics are true automatics. Daihatsu also does an automatic version of the Move and Hyundai offers both semi-automatic and fully-automatic versions of the Atoz. The tiniest automatics I know of are the old two-speed 796 cc 1986–92 Suzuki Alto, the 469 cc Aixam diesel microcar, the 505 cc Ligier Ambra diesel microcar, the Microcar Virgo and the Swatch Smart car (for suppliers see the Alternative Transport section).

£12,000 to spend

" My son will soon have £12,000 available for a new or nearly-new 5-door hatchback for family use, preferably a 1,600 cc. It will be used daily, annual mileage about 12,000, and he plans to keep it for at least five years. He is interested in the Ford Focus, the Astra and the Rover. Any comments on the pros and cons of these or any alternatives would be much appreciated. "

The brilliant Ford Focus is the best car in this class and has an electro-galvanised body guaranteed not to rust through for 12 years. If you can't get a new one from a Ford agent for £12,000, go to Motorpoint of Derby who were advertising new Focus 1.6 Zetecs for £11,999 (01332 347357). However, if he can stump up the extra, he'd be well advised to go for the 1.8 rather than the 1.6 because the 1.6 doesn't quite have enough puff to pull a family and their luggage along due to a tall 5th gear. If he's prepared to undergo the hassle of shopping in Europe, *What Car?* magazine's excellent import guide (free with the June 1999 issue) tells him where he can get a Focus 1.6LX for £10,495.

Capri 2.8i replacement

" *My elderly Ford Capri 2.8i is now becoming troublesome and I seek your advice over a replacement. Top of my list is the handsome Honda Prelude (92–96 model), but I am doubtful about its sombre interior and dreadful dashboard. Second is the Calibra – not so attractive, but the interior is streets ahead. Third is the Rover 220 Coupe, but this too comes with a depressing black interior and very hard seats. Fourth and fifth are the Audi Coupe and the VW Corrado – both probably too expensive and again usually dark inside. Under the headings 'driveability', 'performance', 'reliability' and 'maintenance' I would be very interested to know your views. Points out of ten perhaps?* "

Here's how I rate your choices under your categories (I have assumed all these cars have the most powerful engines available):

	drivability	performance	reliability	maintenance
Prelude	8	9	9	8
Calibra	5	8	5	8
Rover	3	7	5	7
Audi	6	7	7	7
Corrado	10	10	7	7

Soft shoe Shuttle

" *I share your enthusiasm for the Honda Shuttle MPV. I bought a 2.3iLS version a year ago. It is tremendous value for money with aircon, ABS and automatic transmission as standard for just over £18,000. It is superb to drive, with comfortable seats and excellent visibility; performance with the 150 bhp 2.3 litre engine is sparkling yet economical (I have averaged 29.3 mpg from new); it carries seven adults in comfort with room for a reasonable amount of luggage; the rear seats fold away into the floor and the middle row folds forward snugly, so there is no need to risk a hernia lifting seats out. Yet the model is almost universally unknown. Many in the trade have never heard of it. I understand that Honda doesn't advertise it because it is imported and therefore subject to quota restrictions. What a pity. Those who drive Sharans, Espaces, etc. don't know what they're missing.* **"**

The widely advertised CRV is also subject to quota restrictions. It must be more profitable.

Shuttle shuffle

" *I wish to replace my 1989 old-style small Honda Shuttle 1.4 litre and, since Honda has chosen to discontinue this model, I cannot find a small hatch or estate car with similar space inside. Any suggestions?* **"**

Daihatsu Grand Move, Fiat Multipla, Mazda Demio, Mercedes A Class, Mitsubishi Space Star, Renault Megane Scenic, Vauxhall Zafira.

Time to de-Volvo

" *I have a 93K Volvo 850GLT 2.0 20v automatic which has covered 41,000 miles. As I am in my early 70s, I would very much like to own a more luxurious car before I 'shuffle off this mortal coil'. I have in mind a Jaguar XJ6 3.2 auto, a BMW 528 auto or a Mercedes E230 auto. My cash limit would be £12,000–£15,000, plus the part-exchange value of the Volvo. Fuel consumption will not be a problem due to my comparatively low annual mileage. Which of the cars I desire could I expect to purchase?* **"**

The Jag, for a lot of reasons. Despite the fact that Jaguars from 1995 model-year onwards are the most reliable ever built, prices are now quite sensible and your money will go further. I've even seen lumpy ones below £10,000 at auction. And, though Mercedes aren't as hard-riding as they used to be, the Jag is a lot more luxurious than the Mercedes E230. It's also as 'British' as a British car gets these days.

More micros

" *I saw a tiny new car in the north of Mallorca, where it was being used in a small village with narrow streets. It sounded as if it was powered by a lawnmower engine and I couldn't help thinking it would make a perfect city car for the UK. Does anyone know what it is and if it can be purchased in the UK?* "

It's a JDM Titane, a smart-looking 8-foot-long two-seater hatchback, powered by a 523 cc Yanmar diesel engine, built by JDM Simpla Constructeur, 12 rue Paul Langevin – BP 19 – 49241 AVRILLE CEDEX, tel: 0033 2 41 21 13 59, fax: 0033 2 41 42 71 98. (See the Alternative Transport section for microcars being imported to the UK.)

Fortifying an over-40

" *What sort of car would you recommend a 40-year-old man to buy to help alleviate that mid-life crisis? I have in mind something sporty like an MG but don't want to spend more than £7,000.* "

A Mazda MX5 1.8. But be careful the car isn't really a grey-imported Mazda Eunos Roadster from Japan. Some of these are seriously dodgy and may even have been cloned (more than one on the same registration, to overcome SVA quotas). A proper check by Automobile Buying Services (tel: 0345 419926) is in order to make sure that all is what it seems.

How classy is 'A' Class?

" *I am retiring from my NHS consultancy post soon and, with my lump sum, feel I can treat myself to a new or 'nearly-new' car. I'd like a smallish car, automatic, four side-doors with a bit of style and status and enough room for luggage, plants, etc. At the moment I am considering a new Golf, but am intrigued by the Mercedes 'A' Class as I am unlikely to meet any elks on my journeys. Have you any advice on this car? Or should I consider a larger Mercedes or BMW? I am female, value comfort more than acceleration, and am prepared to spend up to £18,000.* **"**

The 'A' Class is a very clever little car because, though shorter than a Ford Ka, the interior space is the equal of a 'C' Class and you certainly don't feel like you're driving something tiny. The seats are comfortable. The driving position is fine. The £500 optional automatic clutch is also the best I've come across and very easy to get used to. Though UK prices start at £14,490, your £18,000 will get you into a top model such as an A160 Avant Garde with full length 'Armadillo'-like sectional sliding sunroof, aircon and enough nice touches to make you feel you're driving something special. It was re-engineered to cope with sudden manoeuvres – whether to avoid an elk, a dog, a child or another car – and these modifications are successful in normal driving conditions. But the car is far less happy on twisting mountain roads with sudden tight corners and hairpin bends, and it moves about a bit in strong winds on the motorway. Not dangerously, but enough to keep you alert. The steering is also less than wonderful about the straight-ahead, largely due to the column feeding through two universal joints from the right-hand side of the car to the left -hand side of the steering rack. With these reservations, it is a genuinely innovative car and deserves to carry the status of the three-pointed star.

Sitting comfortably

" *I suffer from degenerative narrowing of the cervical spine. I wear a surgical collar for much of the time and always when in a car. However,* *the jarring of suspension causes much discomfort and pain. I currently drive a BMW 730iSE automatic. I would like to change to something like a Mercedes coupe, but I need a soft ride and seating, so what would you suggest? Could a Mercedes coupe be modified to give a softer ride than standard?* "

Forget the coupe and go for a new Mercedes Benz S320, which is far better value at £49,145 on the road. The new S Class is the best saloon car in the World and has 'AirMATIC' suspension which can be set to whichever type of ride you prefer. Make sure you run through the option list before ordering and specify £950 'Comfort' seats with £366 Orthopaedic backrests. Far better to go for a car which is designed to offer a comfortable ride from the outset than to try what might be dangerous modifications to a car which isn't.

Low depreciation estate

" *My husband and I will soon be reaching retirement age and are contemplating replacing our 'L'-reg. Peugeot 205 Junior. We feel that a small estate car with a maximum engine size of 1.6 litres would meet our needs best for jobs such as the weekly shop and visiting the local rubbish tip. One requirement would be power steering, and a vehicle with good residual value is a must. What do you suggest?* "

The Dutch-built Mitsubishi Space Star, which is a short, tall estate built on the Carisma/Volvo S40 floorpan and prices of which start at a reasonable £11,195 on the road, with a three-year unlimited-mileage warranty. You sit about 6 inches higher than in a conventional car, and all models have height-adjustable drivers seats and steering wheels; slide-forward 2/3-split fully-folding and semi-reclining rear seats; a protected and low loading rear sill; and a three-point centre rear seatbelt. It's exceptionally easy to get in and out of and to park, so is ideal for elderly drivers. High-speed cornering isn't a strong point, but it's not designed for that anyway, and even the 84 bhp 1.3 litre version is easily capable of cruising at sales rep speeds on the motorway.

Perfect Prairie

" *May I say what a pleasure it is to be the owner of a Nissan Prairie Mk 1? The 'one box' MPV is in vogue and one manufacturer extols the virtues of sliding rear doors. Another emphasises the unique versatility of sliding, removable rear seats. But it was all done years before in the original Prairie. After nearly forty years of motoring I can honestly say that the Prairie has been the most enjoyable, reliable and economical vehicle I have ever driven. Its layout allows me to use it as a conventional car. And, on my trips as a stallholder to clock fairs all over the country, it swallows everything from cases of wristwatches to grandfather clocks. Mine has done 120,000 miles and remains in excellent condition. I put this down to three things. One: it has always had Castrol premium engine oil, changed well before the suggested service mileage. Two: it has always been looked after by John Coleman and his team of experts at Fakenham Nissan Centre, Norfolk. Three: Nissan produced in the early 1980's a well-thought-out, futuristic and durable design.* "

All good points. But with such a huge hole in either side due to the lack of door-pillars, the Prairie offers no side impact protection whatsoever, and to prevent these vehicles going banana-shaped it is essential to keep them entirely rust-free.

'Japanese reliability' from the Brits

" *I recently read that, of the Japanese-owned car plants in the UK, the only one to achieve the traditional standards of reliability that we've come to expect from Japanese cars is Nissan's Sunderland plant. My Sunderland-built 'D'-reg. Bluebird 2.0SLX has now covered 115,000 miles with few signs of age other than a replacement gearbox. However, I recently called for a minicab, and up rolled a similar car to mine, but with 212,000 on the clock, with all but the last 5,000 on the original engine. I have just bought a new 2.0 litre Primera estate from the same Sunderland plant. What price 200,000 miles from this one?* "

The 'J'-reg. Primera 2.0SLX minicab that took me to Gatwick in January had done 155,000 miles and was still as smooth as Des Lynam. The 2.0 litre chain-cam Primera engine is virtually bulletproof but, like any engine, repays frequent oil changes and regular use. It's more likely to clock up 200,000 miles without trouble in four to six years than it is in eight to 12 years.

CTI

" *I currently own a Peugeot 205CTI, which is getting a bit long in the tooth. This car has been the most enjoyable I have ever owned, with sparkling performance and handling and a thoroughly practical soft top. I would like to replace it with a newer 205CTI and would like answers to the following questions, please: (1) When was the last year the CTI was sold in the UK? (2) Was the CTI ever sold in the UK with the 1.9 engine? (3) Was it sold with power steering and, if so, does this adversely affect the handling? (4) Is there any other four-seat convertible that might offer me the same amount of fun per pound spent?* "

1. 1994 (1993 production). But best to buy 92J so it can be legally de-catted.
2. From October 1991, but the 1.9 was strangled by an emissions kit and a catalytic converter to deliver 105 bhp instead of 130 bhp.
3. PAS was optional from June 1989 and doesn't hurt the handling, but you do lose some steering feel.
4. A late 1800 cc Mk I Golf GTi cabrio, which is stronger, lasts better, has a glass rear screen, but isn't as alive to drive as the Pug.

Calibra replacement

" *I am about to replace my third Calibra, but now that the model is out of production what do you suggest I replace it with?* "

A Peugeot 406 Coupe. Its faultless Pininfarina lines make it the most universally applauded coupe currently on the market. It seats four in even more comfort than the Calibra. It's much easier to reverse-park. It has a decent sized boot. And, though the 3.0 litre version can be a bit of a handful, the lighter 2.0 litre 16v steers and handles almost as well as the Peugeot 306 GTi-6. It's a far sharper car than your Calibra. The neighbours may even think you've gone and bought yourself a Ferrari 456.

2.1 to HDI?

" *I am contemplating changing my 1997P Peugeot 406 LX 2.1DT estate for the equivalent new model with the new HDI high pressure direct injected 'common rail' engine. My motive for change is that the new engine has better low-speed performance and fuel consumption, according to the official literature. However, before doing this, I would much appreciate your comments on the advisability of making this change in view of the fact that the HDI engine is new and untried. Also, is there any other vehicle I should consider?* "

I had this engine in a Citroën Xantia in November 1998. Despite filthy weather and some fairly high speeds, it averaged 52.9 mpg in the hands of two different drivers. Driving at similar speeds, but in better conditions, I averaged 40.96 mpg in a Xantia 2.1TD and 43.46 mpg in a 406 2.1TD, so would reckon the HDI to deliver around 25 per cent more miles to the gallon. The very precise fuel delivery system gives much more progressive power and torque delivery than the 2.1TD, without any 'turbo surge', so it isn't exciting to drive but it is smooth and quick. The French have had it for two years now, which is plenty of time to iron out any bugs. The other obvious contender is the VW Passat TDI 110, or TDI 115 Estate. And, depending on the deal on offer, it may also be worth considering a Mercedes C250TD Estate, or the new 'common rail' direct-injected C220 CDI.

2 + 4 + dog

" I currently drive a beautiful, but battered and, at 181,000 miles, worn-out Peugeot 505 Family Estate. I need to replace it with a new car that will swallow four children under six using bulky car seats, a large dog and a pushchair. However, I want a car, not a mini-bus, and with the advent of MPVs nobody makes cars with three rows of forward facing seats and a big boot – or do they? What can I spend my £26,000 on? "

You're right. Nobody does make what you want, so you're going to have to bite the bullet and buy either an MPV or a big 4x4. The best MPV for your purposes is a Renault Grande Espace because, unlike some other large MPVs, the rearmost seats are separately removable, so one child can sit alongside a suitable cage containing the dog. And even with all seven seats in place there is enough room behind the rearmost seat for a folded pushchair.

6-seater 4x4

" My partner and I have four children between us, with two children aged 11 and the others aged 8 and 4. We want to transport all of us in one vehicle, rather than in two as we are currently doing. We're not too keen on 'people movers', and would prefer a 4x4 (e.g. Discovery, Frontera, etc.) which could legally and safely accommodate us all.

Ideally we would be looking to get something second-hand (three to four years old perhaps) within the £10,000–£12,000 price bracket. I would also use the vehicle for business, with a total annual mileage of around 30,000. Please could you tell us which makes and models of vehicle would best fit our requirements? "

While you should get 30 mpg plus out of a Discovery TDI doing 30,000 miles a year, the enormous extra burden of four-wheel-drive and the extra servicing costs don't make sense for this type of mileage. Unless you need four-wheel-drive because you live up a muddy track or get snowed in during the winter, it's better to forget the idea and plump for a sensible MPV such as a Renault Espace TD or a Synergie/Ulysse /806 TD or a Mitsubishi Space Wagon. As more come onto the market, you might also find a Galaxy/Alhambra/Sharan TDI within your price range, or, best of the lot, a Honda Shuttle.

Galaxy, Alhambra, or what?

" *We are a family of two adults and three rapidly growing children. In a moment of great daring we test-drove a Ford Galaxy, which supplied a satisfactory combination of seating comfort and luggage space, plus two spare seats for taking grandparents with us on outings. We have heard that the engines of MPVs are pretty much identical, but we like the look of the Galaxy and the Seat Alhambra. Our budget is under £15,000. Do you have any comments that would persuade us in any particular direction?* "

£15,000 buys a new Kia Carnival 2.9TDI 16v, which has three rows of seats in Voyager 2-2-3 configuration and comes with a three-year warranty. Second-hand Galaxys, Alhambras and Sharans are thicker on the ground than any other recent MPVs, but if you can find a 7-seater Honda Shuttle 2.3iLS for your £15,000, that's the one to go for. Sold as the Odyssey in the USA, it's the most reliable MPV in the world and comes with the benefits of air conditioning plus an excellent 4-speed automatic transmission as standard. But it will only do about 28 mpg compared to a Galaxy TDI's 38 mpg. Do your shopping after the holiday season rather than before or during it, and you can expect to save about £2,000.

Most economical

" What are your suggestions, please, for the most economical three-door hatchback, both in terms of price and mpg for regular round trips of 60–100 miles? "

Has to be the Seat Arosa or VW Lupo 1.7SDI. Owners prepared to keep below 60 mph can expect up to 70 mpg. Prices start at £8,495 for the Arosa and £9,295 for the Lupo, including VED, registration tax and a three-year warranty.

Thrilled to Ibizas

" Early last year I felt it was time to replace my Peugeot 205Gti, and I sought your advice. My requirements were for a small, narrow car for the lanes in our area, yet one powerful enough for the 1-in-3 pass at the head of our valley and suitable for Voluntary Social Care Service, mostly taking elderly people shopping and to the doctor. You recommended a Seat Ibiza TDI and, after 66 years driving experience, I have been most impressed. Thank you very much. There is just one snag. My wife (who calls the car 'Sophie') likes the Ibiza so much that she and it go missing several times a week. "

Another satisfied customer. The reasons for this particular recommendation were the Ibiza TDI's impressive torque, its tidy handling, and its frugal consumption of fuel (even I got

55 mpg). For these virtues, its slightly gruff nature is easily forgiven. There is now a new range of Ibizas with much improved suspension, nicer interiors and a better range of engines, including a TDI 110 and a 156 bhp petrol turbo. Readers seem to like Seat dealers as well.

Same, but bigger

" *I am thinking of replacing my 16-year-old VW Polo with a new car in the autumn. As it is to be a family car I want something larger, at least Golf/Escort size. Can you suggest a make and model that you think will give me the same reliability, durability and longevity as the Polo? My budget is £16,000–£18,000. I would also be interested to know if you think the market is such that I ought to be able to get a discount from a franchised agent.* "

At first I thought VW Golf Mk IV TDI 110. In everyday driving, it's as quick as a GTi 1.8 20v Turbo, but stretches its fuel at least 50 per cent further. It's also very eco-friendly, emitting a mere 131 g/km CO_2, so should be one of the cheapest cars of all in terms of annual VED from October 2000. But then I drove the new SEAT Toledo TDI S 110. This is less money at £15,885, including aircon and 15-inch alloy wheels. It has a stiffer four-door body and different suspension settings, so steers and handles better without compromising ride comfort. It has a long-life galvanised body guaranteed not to rust through for 12 years. And It comes with a 3-year unlimited-mileage mechanical warranty. If past VAG products are anything to go by you will have to make a few repairs and replacements as the years go by, but if I was picking an Escort-sized car to last me 16 years, I'd go for the Toledo. The downsides: though the boot is big, you have to post your luggage through a narrow opening; and UK supplies are going to be very short, so discounts are unlikely. But for what you get for your money, this car is sensibly priced by UK standards and should hold its value well.

Last car

" *I am proposing to change my car, currently a Renault Clio RT 1.4, for a similar or slightly larger car. My annual mileage is below 5,000 with a fair number of short journeys. I am considering another Clio, a Peugeot, Fiesta or something a bit larger such as the Rover 200 or Renault Megane. Reliability is a vital feature, particularly as it might end up with my wife as a widowed and elderly driver. Would a diesel be a good choice, and have you any recommendations as to make?* "

The Skoda Felicia keeps coming close to the top of the Top Gear/J. D. Power Customer Satisfaction Surveys. The best Skoda Felicia for your requirements is the VW-engined 1.9 litre diesel which has power steering as standard, costs £8,504 on the road with a year's VED and a three-year warranty. There is now a Haynes manual for these cars. A new Felicia based on the next-generation VW Polo floorpan arrives in 2000.

Long-termer

" *From the vast array of cars available today, can you suggest a current equivalent for our Saab 99? We seek a high-quality, durable and robust car. Our specification includes the ability to carry a family of four in reasonable comfort for long journeys on all types of road, to negotiate our farm's somewhat rough tracks, and to tow a one tonne load if required. The list of electronic and motorised features is nowhere near as valuable to ourselves as highest quality of basic original design and longevity. Many people have suggested a 'Discovery'-type vehicle, but from our experience the supposed failings of a standard car are far outweighed by the gains in ride and handling. With ever greater emphasis on secondary safety, one should not overlook the primary safety aspects of good handling and manageable acceleration. A modern Saab 9-3 is aimed at a different market from that intended for the 99 when it was launched almost thirty years ago. The only potential vehicle we have found is the Subaru Legacy, but we have reservations about long-term underbody corrosion when looking in the cluttered wheel arches. At almost 14 years old, 220,000 miles, near 30 mpg, virtually nil oil consumption and minimal corrosion, we consider our Saab 99 underrated and a very hard act to follow. What would you recommend?* "

Either a Skoda Octavia TDI 110 4x4 estate or a Subaru Legacy 2.0LX Classic Estate. Legacys don't offer the fuel economy of a TDI, but I know of Subarus which have done 600,000 road miles. Other possibilities are a VW Passat TDI S 115 bhp, a Seat Toledo TDI S 110bhp, a VW Bora TDI 110, a VW Golf Mk IV TDI 110, or a VW Golf Mk IV TDI 115 6-speed estate. All are galvanised.

250,000-mile Cavalier

" *Can you recommend any car today which offers the same performance and dependability as the Mk III Vauxhall Cavalier 2.0 litre? I have had four: two 1988s and two 1990s. All clocked up over 120,000 miles and one did 250,000, all on the same engines and clutches. None were 'officially' serviced, other than having timing belt and oil changes, and none ever saw the inside of a garage. It is getting harder now to buy low-mileage examples and I find the interiors of the post-Autumn 1992 facelift models cheap and tatty by comparison.* "

A recent German TUV report may provide the best answer. The lowest percentages of mechanical defects in cars up to three years old were found in the Subaru Legacy (1.2 per cent), the Toyota Carina E (1.6 per cent) and the Mercedes C-Class (1.8 per cent). In cars up to seven years old, the lowest percentages of defects were found in the Toyota Camry (3.1 per cent), the Subaru Legacy (3.3 per cent) and the Toyota Carina (3.5 per cent). Top Gear/J D Power Customer Satisfaction Surveys also put Subarus at the top of the tree. But running to the kind of mileages you do, it's going to be hard to avoid failures of items such as the now-compulsory catalytic converters which were not fitted to your Cavaliers.

Desert Stormer

" *I intend to move and work in Dubai this autumn, hopefully for a few years, and was advised that, to take advantage of the off-road opportunities that exist there, I should buy a four-wheel-drive vehicle. What would you choose? I have no idea of a budget, except that fuel costs are negligible. I would also used the vehicle to commute a 20-mile round trip each day on high quality metalled roads.* "

The brawniest and best 4x4 in the world is a Toyota Landcruiser 4.2 GX TD Amazon (201 bhp, 317 lb ft torque, optional active suspension). But don't reckon on the Dubai specification conforming to EU Type Approval if you were planning on bringing it back to the UK.

Drab Trab

" *I would like to buy a second-hand Trabant. Would you please advise me where I should look to find such a car and are there any particular points that I should be aware of?* "

If you were an impoverished East German farmer with little more than a couple of potatoes to rub together, then the Trabant would have been the car for you. It was simplicity itself, with a 594 cc two-stroke engine that ran on almost anything (as long as a generous dollop of oil was added) and a body made of textile and plastic fibres over a flimsy tubular steel frame. The very last of the Trabbies were fitted with 1,043 cc VW Polo engines. The main thing to look out for is that the vehicle has never been UK registered and now cannot be because it lacks the correct documentation and is, effectively, an 'illegal immigrant'. There is a club: the Trabant & Wartburg IFA Club UK, c/o Dave Milne, 23 Kings Well Court, The Causeway, Seaford, East Sussex BN25 1WE, tel: 01323 873007. A trustworthy dealer in Trabants and other oddities is Alan's Unusual Automobiles of 56 Lechlade Road, Faringdon, Oxon SN7 8AQ, tel: 01367 240125 (visits by appointment only).

Omega commendation

" *I have just taken delivery of my second Vauxhall Omega 2.5 TD automatic estate. I cover about 16,000 miles a year and regularly tow a five-metre caravan both in England and abroad. The Omega is a gem. The BMW six-cylinder diesel engine is superb. The weight of the car is ideal for stability, either with a full complement of passengers or towing, and the fuel economy is quite outstanding. These cars are grossly underrated and if one purchases, as I did, a 'nearly-new' example with a jolly good saving on the list price, from a reputable dealer, the driving pleasure can last for years. Incidentally, I purchased this and my previous Omega from Nidd Vale Motors, Harrogate, with whom I have no connection other than to recommend them highly for their customer care and exemplary service.* "

Forty-three other readers then added their opinions of Omega ownership. Most popular model was the 2.5 V6 CDi. Likes include reliability, comfort, interior space, roadholding, brakes, performance, reasonable fuel economy. Dislikes are strange gear ratios in the MV6 model, intrusive engine noise in diesel versions, lack of interior storage space, first-year depreciation (better bought 'nearly-new') and the pre-'gas discharge' headlights. Problem areas included radios, air conditioning, handbrake, sunroof, engine slow running, door locks, automatic gearboxes (especially when used for towing), timing belt failure, immobiliser and ABS.

Cavalier to Vectra?

" *I have owned my 'J'-reg. Cavalier L hatchback for most of its life. It has given excellent service and been totally reliable, as were my previous three Cavaliers, and they all worked hard. My natural choice of replacement is a low-mileage Vectra, but the 'Top Gear' lot keep slagging them off. Are they being fair? If they are, what alternatives do you recommend?* "

Unless it's an 'Li', your Cavalier is pre-cat, so doesn't have that built-in problem and will be cheaper to run long-term than a catalysed Cavalier. The Vectra is quite nice looking but it wasn't a revolutionary change from the Cavalier in the way the Mondeo was from the Sierra, and doesn't drive significantly better. Not only that, clutch replacement, which could take as little as half an hour on a Cavalier, can be as much as seven hours work on a Vectra due to the extra dismantling involved (about the same as for a Mondeo). In fairness, GM has listened to the criticisms, progressively improved the Vectra over the years, and brought out a Mk II Vectra in early 1999. Expect to pay between £8,000 and £9,000 for a year-old 2.0 litre example – but I'd go for a Mondeo.

Getting loaded

" *I have finally given in to the taxman and decided to forgo my company Volvo in favour of either a VW Sharan 110TDI or a Passat TDI 110 estate.*

Self-levelling suspension does not appear to be an option on either of these and VW says that their vehicles don't need it. I load my V70 up at the back with huge bike racks, stack windsurfers on the roof and tow boats, and the optional self-levelling works brilliantly to keep the car on the level. Should I be concerned if I buy a VW without it? "

You should be more concerned about the way you load your vehicle, and so should every reader. Self-levelling or not, an unduly high load which severely raises the car's centre of gravity will make the car unstable and dangerous. Putting any kind of heavy weight on top of a tall vehicle such as an MPV or a tall 4x4 such as a Discovery is very risky. Loading an estate car load area to roof height impedes rearward vision and, unless the load is restrained by a very strong luggage guard, could result in rear-seat passengers being decapitated after a heavy impact. If you want to carry five passengers and a lot of luggage, an MPV is far better than an estate car because the same load will only come up to the bottom of the rear window height rather than fill the entire load area. Always load a vehicle with the heaviest items as low and as much within the wheelbase of the vehicle as possible. The police are rightly paying a lot more attention to overloaded private cars than they used to. Readers have praised the Sharan's £235 dealer-fitted 'handling kit' which lowers the suspension, greatly reducing body roll, and its ability to carry bicycles inside the vehicle. However, readers have had a few quality problems with early Galaxys, Sharans and Alhambras – all of which are assembled at the same plant in Portugal. The most annoying fault on older models is failure of the cable-operated bonnet pull.

Economy with an 'i'

" *My eight-year-old VW Golf GTi 8v has done 123,000 miles, has achieved an overall 43 mpg and is still on the original front discs. Although I never abuse my vehicles, I don't exactly pootle around either. My problem is what to replace it with, since I can think of no comparable car which will give the performance and economy of my non-cat Golf.* "

If you have been getting 43 mpg out of a Golf GTi, you'll see 60 mpg from a Golf Mk IV TDI 110 and you certainly won't be disappointed by the performance.

Ten-year car

" *I am retired and will shortly be using the last of my capital to buy a replacement for my 'F'-registered Sierra Estate. It will need to be a smaller, second-hand family car costing around £10,000, and will have to live outside for the next ten years. I have been happy with the Sierra, which still runs well at 117,000 miles, and I would gladly keep it if only the bodywork had not started to admit water around the window seals. What replacement do you recommend?* "

Dr H McArthur has written a book which, among many other things, explains precisely why Sierra doors rust in the manner you describe. The title is *Motor Vehicle Corrosion Prediction and Prevention on Vehicles (1950–Present Day)* available from Dr McArthur at 18 Rawlins Close, Woodhouse Eaves, Loughborough, LE12 8SD, tel: 01509 890607, price £10 inc. p & p. A reader I met at an auction had a pretty good idea of what you should buy. He went for an 18-month-old, 16,000 mile VW Golf CL TDI Estate, for which he paid £9,700. I had warned him that it was probably a trader's car, that it would have been a better buy with a sunroof, and, if he went for it, not to bid more than

£10,000. In the event, he came away happy with a car which will provide pleasant, economical and very practical motoring for at least ten years. And, of course, if it has a full VAG service history, an 18-month-old Golf will come with the balance of the manufacturer's 36-month warranty. If you want to be even more certain of avoiding rust, take a look at an Audi A4 or Audi 80, both of which have galvanised bodyshells.

'Classic' 480

" *I recently purchased a second-hand Volvo 480ES 1.7i. The car has covered just over 100,000 miles. I am tidying it up and in the process I've discovered that the 480 was quite an exclusive car and fairly advanced when originally launched. Various people have informed me that it will become a classic. What is your opinion of the car, and do you know of a 480 Owners Club for parts and information? Which is the best engine and do you think this car is a better buy than a 360 GLT? My 480 suffers body roll in fast bends. I am told this is due to the poor condition of the rear shocks. Was the 480 generally a good-handling car?* "

Most owners love this model but, because of early build-quality problems, one magazine dubbed it 'the coupe from hell'. The part-galvanised bodies resist rust well, but the clips under the rubber window seals in the doors do tend to cornflake quite badly. On balance, the 1.7 litre Renault engine is probably the best, as early 2.0 litre models suffered severe oil consumption while high-mileage turbos tend to smoke. The power steering's a bit light, but the back should not roll severely, so your shocks are probably in a severe state of shock. The 480 is unusual enough to become a minor classic, eventually. Most collectible is the 1994 480 GT Limited Edition, of which only 250 were built in RHD. I have no record of a 480 club, but there are two

Volvo clubs: Volvo Enthusiasts Club on 01872 553740. and Volvo Owners Club on 01705 381494. Is it better than a 360 GLT? Of course it is.

The 'big' issue

" *I am 17 and am looking for a car. I need something reasonably small and easy to drive, with good fuel consumption and low insurance premiums. The problem is, I am 6ft 4in with long legs and have found all the usual cars too small. I simply don't fit into a Fiesta, a Micra, a Citroën ZX or a Nova.* "

Among newer cars, check out the current VW Polo, the VW Lupo and the Seat Arosa SE. If these are too expensive, you may think this ridiculous, but it's worth taking a look at a Mini or an Austin Metro. Quite a few tall people find that the strange driving position of these cars allows then to spread their legs out and suits them very well.

6ft 4in and 5ft 3in

" *I am 6ft 4in tall and weigh 15 stone, so the smallest car I can manage with any degree of comfort is a Ford Mondeo 1.8LX. My wife is 5ft 3in and much prefers her Corsa. We now intend moving closer to town and rationalising our transport down to one car. Assuming we sell both the cars we have, what do you suggest?* "

Rising in size from small to 'upper medium', the cars with the best range of seat adjustment are: Seat Arosa SE, VW Lupo, VW Polo GL, Fiat Punto ('SX' spec up), Fiat Bravo and Fiat Brava (all models), New Seat Toledo, Skoda Octavia, VW Golf Mk IV, VW Bora, Ford Mondeo with electric driver's seat, Rover 75 and the current VW Passat.

IMPORT/EXPORT

HONEST JOHN'S STEP-BY-STEP GUIDE TO
IMPORTING A CAR FROM EUROPE

1   Get the relevant Government booklets and forms. First phone the
    DVLA on 01792 772134 and ask for the pack on personal imports.
    This includes a booklet, 'How to Import a Vehicle Permanently into
    Great Britain', Form V100, which explains registering and licensing
    procedures and gives a list of Vehicle Registration Offices, and Form
    V55/5, which is an application form to licence a vehicle in the UK for
    the first time. (Alternatively, phone the DETR on 0207 676 2094,
    write to DETR VSE1, Zone 2.01, Great Minster House, 76 Marsham
    Street. London SW1 4DR, or visit the DETR website at: http://
    www.roads.detr.gov.uk/vehicle/vse1/index.htm.) Then phone your
    local VAT enquiry uniy listed in the telephone directory under
    'Customs & Excise' and ask for the 'VAT Notice 728 Pack' which in-
    cludes a form, Appendix D, 'New Means of Transport – Notification
    of Acquisition'. (The Customs & Excise numbers 0171 864 3000 and
    01304 224372 have both become overwhelmed with enquiries, so
    don't bother to try them.)
2   Decide which makes and models you are interested in and obtain
    the UK brochures for these cars. Then phone each manufacturer's
    UK customer helpline, say you have one of their cars and ask for a
    current list of continental service dealers.
3   Choose the car and specification you want, then start phoning.
    When you find a receptive dealer, fax the exact specification of car
    you want and ask for a quote, to include temporary registration

and export plates. The best countries to buy in are likely to be Holland, Belgium, Germany and France. Remember, if you buy in Europe, you will be buying a Europe-spec car with RHD as an extra. Other things, such as a radio, tinted glass, alarm/immobiliser and seven seats in an MPV may be extras too.

4   Order your car from the dealer offering the best combination of price and delivery date. Delivery could easily be six to eight months for a car such as a VW, Mercedes Benz of Alfa Romeo. You will be asked to pay a deposit of between 10 and 30 per cent on receipt of order, either by credit card, Switch or international bank credit transfer. Make sure the dealer faxes, emails or posts you a receipt for this and a confirmation of your order.

5   Decide on whether you are going to gamble on Sterling rising or falling against the currency in which you will be buying the car. If you gamble on Sterling rising, leave your funds in a high-interest Sterling account. If you gamble on Sterling falling, open a foreign Currency Call Account at your bank. This is a deposit account in a foreign currency offering interest based on the much lower base rates for the foreign currency.

6   Keep in touch with the dealer by phone, fax or email to make sure your order is being processed. Within two months of the delivery date, start asking for a scheduled build date for your car.

7   Once the dealer gives you a delivery date, ask for the VIN number (Vehicle Identification Number) of the car and insure it using the VIN from the date you propose to collect it. Then organise your flight out and ferry back and a bank draft to pay for the car.

8   When you go to collect the car, inspect it carefully to make sure it complies with the specification you have ordered. Make sure the dealer gives you a Certificate of Conformity to European Type Approval (a 'C of C'), a Registration Certificate naming you as the keeper, an insurance document to prove the car was insured in the country of origin (often combined with temporary registration) and, of course, an invoice. Make sure you buy some petrol in the country of origin and keep the receipt. Keep any hotel and restaurant receipts. And keep the ferry ticket.

9   As soon as possible (this *must* be within seven days of arriving back in the UK with your new car), fill in the form 'New Means of Transport – Notification of Acquisition' which came with VAT 728 and take it,

together with completed form C55/5, the dealer's invoice, foreign registration document, the Certificate of Type Approval Conformity, your petrol receipts and any other foreign receipts to prove you have driven the car abroad, your ferry ticket, and your UK insurance certificate based on the VIN number to your nearest Vehicle Registration Office. On payment of a £25 first registration fee and either six or twelve months' VED, they will issue you with a registration number and a VED disc. The date of first registration will be the date the car was first registered in the country of origin, not the date you landed in the UK. Your V5 registration document will then be sent to you from Swansea.

10 The VRO will send form NMT, Notification of Acquisition, on to Customs & Excise, who will then send you invoice VAT 413 for UK VAT at 17.5 per cent of the cost of the car, which you have 30 days to settle. Once this is paid, you will receive a receipted VAT 413.

11 Order a set of plates. Phone the manufacturer's customer helpline number to put the car on the manufacturer's UK database for warranty purposes and in case of any recalls. Though Customs & Excise only insist you keep the purchase invoice and the receipted VAT 413 for six years as proof that VAT has been paid, it's advisable to keep *all* the documentation, including petrol receipts and ferry tickets, in a safe place to pass on to the new owner should you sell the car.

A reader-recommended Dutch broker who will do most of the work for you and still sell you a car at a sensible saving is Intercar at Brunssum in Limburg in the South of Holland (tel: 0031 45 525 3494; email: sales@intercar.nl)

The state of SVA quotas

As from 31 May 1998 (effectively 30 June 1998 after a month's 'grace'), all vehicles imported to the UK at up to three years old which do not bear an EU country National Type Approval Certificate or, if first registered after 1 January 1998, a Certificates of Conformity to European Type Approval, have been subject to a Single Vehicle Approval Test at a Vehicle Inspectorate HGV testing station.

The test costs £165 for cars or £60 for a lesser test for commercial vehicles. All non-EU-Type-Approved trade imports (vehicles for re-sale) up to ten years old have also been subject to this test. You can buy a copy of the 'Single Vehicle Approval Inspection Manual', price £25, from the Vehicle Inspectorate, PO Box 12, Swansea SA1 1BP, order code 'SVA 01'.

But the big bone of contention is a quota system whereby only 50 of each individual model may be imported to the UK in this way in any one year. Effectively, this limits the number of new and nearly new vehicles which can be independently imported from the Far East or from the USA, but has no effect on imports from Europe.

Former Transport Minister Dr John Reid had planned to lift the quota restriction in May 1999, but was opposed by non-driving Trade Secretary Stephen Byers who had been lobbied heavily by British companies officially importing Japanese vehicles and Japanese companies building vehicles in Britain. The lifting of the 50 per year quota restriction will not now take place until March 2000. From this date, the 50 cars per model quota system will gradually be replaced by a monthly total import quota, rising from 1,000 in March to 10,000 in December, allowing a total of 55,000 such imports in year 2000 and unlimited imports from 1 January 2001.

At the same time, the loophole by which individual private imports over three years old were not subject to the SVA test will be closed and all non-European imports up to 10 years old will be subject to the SVA test. The SVA test itself will 'enhanced' in terms of 'key environmental, safety and anti-theft items to apply to commercially traded vehicles'.

European imports bearing EU Certificates of Conformity will not be affected by the new rules.

Since the current number of testing stations can only cope with 20,000 SVA test appointments a year, either SVA batch testing will have to apply or testing stations and testing staff will need to increase threefold.

Of course, by the time commercial imports are freed up, the Monopolies and Mergers Commission will have reported on UK car pricing, Karel van Miert's successor as EU Competitions Minister will have made his own report into car pricing across Europe, and Sterling may have fallen sharply against the Euro, the Dollar and the Yen. In the meantime, manufacturers and importers who are able to get away with charging UK car buyers up to 52 per cent more than in other EU markets will continue to do so.

However, by Spring 1999, UK public reaction against being over-charged for cars had become so great that many oversupplied models were not selling. Manufacturers and importers were forced to let tens of thousands of cars go for as little as 60 per cent of the UK 'list price'. The choice was restricted to cars from stock, but some UK private buyers were actually buying new cars in the UK for less than they would have had to pay if they imported them from Europe. Not BMWs. Not Mercedes. Not Audis, VWs or Seats, because these cars are not oversupplied to the UK market. But the sheer numbers of cars sold at huge discounts may be enough to convince the MMC that there is no cartel operating to keep UK prices artificially high.

Importing from the States

" *I am considering bringing over a 6-seater pick-up truck from the USA. It has been owned by a member of my family since it was bought new two years ago, and its approximate value now is £10,000. Would I be liable for import duties and VAT when trying to register it here? Can anything be done to reduce such liabilities? Would the picture change if I bought a new vehicle from a dealer in the USA? I have no plans to dispose of any such vehicle for two to three years.* "

You would have to pay European import duty of 10 per cent plus UK VAT of 17.5 per cent on the invoiced purchase price plus the cost of shipping. The only way to avoid this tax is genuinely to have lived in the USA for over a year, to have owned the vehicle for over a year in the USA and to continue to own the vehicle for over a year in the UK. In either case, and if you bought the vehicle new or at up to three years old from a US dealer, the vehicle will be subject to a UK Single Vehicle Approval Test (see above). If the vehicle is personally imported and is more than three years old at the date of importation, under the rules at the time of writing, it is not subject to the SVA, but is subject to a UK MOT test. All vehicles up to ten years old (apart from motor caravans and ambulances) which are commercially imported are subject to the SVA. You need to speak to a professional importer, such as Anthony Cohen of American Car Imports (0181 889 4545), who will know from experience whether your vehicle can be made to pass the SVA, what this is likely to cost, and whether it will be within the 50-cars-a-year model quota. Leaflets on the SVA ('The Single Vehicle Approval Scheme' leaflet, SVA1, printed December 1996) can be obtained from Vehicle Standards and Engineering Division, Zone 2/01, Great Minster House, 76 Marsham Street, London SW1P 4DR, tel: 0171 271 4800. A personal import pack, including Department of Transport leaflet P12, 'How to Permanently Import your Vehicle into Great Britain', and Vehicle Registration Form V55/5, can be obtained from the DVLA on 01792 772134. The VAT notice 728 pack can be obtained from HM Customs & Excise on 0171 865 3000.

American auctions

" Do you have any information on American East Coast vehicle auctions, shipping procedures and costs? "

A good shipper is Mann Motor Ships (tel: 01703 237711) which ships from US ports Jacksonville, Charleston, Baltimore, New York and Halifax to Southampton and Liverpool, using Wallenius Lines. Mann only uses roll-on roll-off ships, but you can have a car shipped as deck cargo or fully containerised. Expect to pay between $495 and $625 to ship a 'one-off' average car between 351 and 500 cubic feet in volume. You'll also have to pay US wharfage of $75–$85 and UK wharfage of about £30. Insurance has to be negotiated with a Stateside broker. British Car Auctions head office, tel: 01428 607440, can put you in touch with ADT in the USA, while Manheim UK's head office in Leeds, tel: 0870 444 0407, can put you in touch with its parent company in the USA.

Australian car prices

" I have recently returned from a three-month holiday in Australia. Could you please explain why in Australia you can buy a Ford Mondeo (made in Belgium) with air conditioning for only £10,000 while the equivalent model in the UK costs £14,000? Also the Ford Fiesta, called the 'Festiva' in Oz, is only £5,500 compared to £7,500 in the UK. It seems to me that the UK is literally being taken for a ride with its prices versus Australia, Europe and the USA. "

UK SVA import quotas prevent independent importers bringing in more than 50 of any vehicle model which is not European Type Approved in any one year. And the fact that we drive on the left-hand side of the road makes it difficult (but not impossible) for UK private buyers and independent importers to source cheaper, Euro-Type-Approved RHD cars from continental Europe. The fleets like it this way because they buy more than 60 per cent of new cars sold in the UK, usually at even lower prices than new cars are sold for in Germany, France, Spain and Australia. But they want the private market to think that these cars are much more valuable so that private buyers will pay high prices for them once they end their lives on the fleets. If Ford and Vauxhall ended fleet discounts, both companies could probably drop their 'list' prices by 25 per cent. The joke about company cars is that company drivers pay benefit tax based on list prices, not on what the cars actually cost. Other manufacturers and importers, such as VW and BMW, like the overhyped UK market because they don't give such big discounts to fleets, and charging £3,000–£4,000 more for a car like the VW Golf in the UK brings them £2,500–£3,400 more profit.

Holden hold-up

" *I was about to buy a Vauxhall Corsa. Then my son, who until recently was resident in Australia, indicated that he could purchase an equivalent vehicle, a Holden Barina City, much cheaper there and have it shipped back to the UK with his effects. However, I wasn't prepared for the hassle I have encountered since the car arrived. At present it is at the shipping depot in Croydon and I'm having to pay storage costs. I'm having difficulty registering it and would like your advice. It took a long time finding an insurer which was willing to cover it, and only then at a high price. Now my local VRO has pointed me in the direction of the Single Vehicle Approval Scheme. Vauxhall would not give me a Certificate of Approval because the car is not built to European specification. What can I do? Is there a conspiracy afoot to prevent the importation of cheaper cars from abroad?* "

Has 10 per cent European import duty plus 17.5 per cent UK VAT been paid? Where is your son? Under the new rules, if the car is to be a personal import, the importer must have owned it in the source country. If not, you will be treated as a trader and the car will be subject to both an SVA test costing £165 and the SVA quota. See 'Importing from the States' (above) for leaflets and procedures. If the car fails the SVA test and cannot economically be made to pass it then you will have to re-export it.

Miniature Mk II

" *Would you please advise me of a company that could assist me in importing into the UK a Mitsuoka Viewt convertible? I would also appreciate any details of the car.* "

The Viewt is yet another Nissan Micra-based 'retro' special, this time aping the looks of the Jaguar Mk II. Roland Danes of Park Lane (01420 544300) tells me they are very expensive even in Japan and it's likely that the cost of landing one, paying import duty and VAT and getting it through the SVA could set you back between £20,000 and £25,000. The other problem is getting it through the SVA at all. Without carefully inspecting one and putting it through an SVA 'pre-test', even Danes (who knows more about this than anyone else) would not know if it could be made to pass – and without an SVA you can't get a Minister's Approval Certificate (MAC), so a Viewt of less than three years of age could not be UK registered – even as a genuine personal import.

FTO

" *As a replacement for my ten-year-old Toyota MR2, used only as a second car, I am considering buying a three-year-old Mitsubishi FTO 2.0 litre V6 Tiptronic from one of the various dealers handling used Japanese imports. I realise that servicing and spares may present a problem, but with an anticipated mileage of 6,000 a year and the known reliability of Japanese products I am prepared to accept this small risk. Can you answer the following questions: Do you have any knowledge of this particular car? Have you any knowledge of the agents handling these imports? Should I insist on a Single Vehicle Approval Certificate? Are there any other aspects that should concern me?* "

FTOs cost £450–£700 to get through the SVA test. Speak to Intech at Thruxton Circuit, Hants about this on 01264 773888. Intech also offers a nationwide chain of service franchises and can advise on any problems involved in running the Mivec V6 on UK petrol (non-Mivecs are okay). API can supply parts (0500 830530). Some agents who handle these cars are: Ralliart UK, 01785 220220; Park Lane, 01420 544300; Warrender of Bolton, 01257 427700; Orbis International (part of Sidney Newton PLC), 0181 965 9666; MMC International Holdings Ltd, 0181 656 1555 (website: http://www.mmc-intl.com); Intercar, 0181 203 3399; and Direct Vehicle Rental, 01902 353393. Even if the car is already UK registered, you should insist on an SVA certificate because it might be a fake 'personal import' on a dodgy MOT. You should have the car inspected by ABS Vehicle Inspections who know what to look for in Japanese imports (tel: 0345 419926). I'd also HPI the car (tel: 01722 422422) and, if you find this shows up a lot of recent UK changes of ownership, steer well clear because the car might be one of several on the same registration.

Export/import

" *I am about to take up a new job in the Netherlands and I'm intrigued by how I might use import/export rules to buy myself a cheap car. It occurs to me that I could buy an LHD Audi A4 1.8 Avant tax-free in Holland and import it to Britain, paying no UK VAT on the import. If I keep the car on Dutch plates in Britain for six months while I am in Holland, I believe I could then export the car back to Holland without having to pay Dutch import duties. Since Dutch pre-tax prices are among the lowest in Europe I ought to find myself with a much cheaper car than I would otherwise get. Am I right?* "

No. UK VAT is due within 30 days of the car being imported to the UK. You can't avoid Dutch BPM registration tax either (around 30 per cent of an A4's pre-tax price) because, even if you import the car to the UK, register it in the UK, then re-export it to Holland, BPM is still due on the value of the car on the date of registration in Holland.

Refused export order

A reader from Edgware was refused point-blank when he attempted to order a VW Passat from S. Bertou of Hoogenboom, VW/Audi agents in Rotterdam. The reason, quoted from EC Regulation No. 1475/95, was: 'The consumer's freedom to buy anywhere in the Common Market is one of the fundamental achievements of the European Community, and the Regulation reinforces this right. The consumer's right is not accompanied by an obligation imposed on dealers to sell, since it is normally in a dealer's interest to maximise its profits.' Bertou added: 'Since we think that we can get more profit out of selling this VW Passat here in the area to people who will probably service, insure and/or finance this car with us, and we have a chance that, after a few years, this car will be traded in for a new one, we won't supply you with a VW Passat.' So, essentially, while VW UK assures me that the system is in place for a UK citizen to order a VW in Holland, it remains a dealer's prerogative to refuse an order, and because Passats are hard to get, this dealer would rather sell one to a Dutchman than to a Brit for the reasons Bertou gave. I, too, was verbally refused an order for an LHD VW Golf Mk IV GTi Turbo on the grounds that 'the rules are being tested'.

Four stress-free imports

" Whilst serving in the RAF I bought three cars from Intercar at Brunssum in Holland. Intercar has been supplying cars to service personnel and civvies for 32 years and all their staff speak fluent English. Last year, as a retired civilian, I ordered another car, this time a Golf Mk IV SE TDI. I was told delivery would be eight months and I paid my 10 per cent *deposit in Deutschmarks. My email enquiries about progress over the following months were dealt with promptly, in February Intercar supplied me with the VIN number for insurance purposes, and in March I collected the car. Intercar also supplied temporary Dutch registration and the requisite Certificate of Conformity and, had I wanted them to, would have arranged overnight accommodation. I drove back via 'Le Shuttle', paid the UK VAT and registered the car with no problems whatsoever. My total saving was just over £4,000 on the UK list price. Intercar's email address is sales@intercar.nl, tel: 0031 45 525 3494; fax: 0031 45 525 9529.* "

A good deal. Readers should note, however, that this is not the same company as UK-based Intercar international (tel: 0181 203 3399).

Moving from Holland

" *Me and my partner will soon be relocating from Holland to the UK. Due to the expense of moving, house rental deposit, dog quarantine, etc., we won't have much money at first, so will bring our faithful LHD 227,000 km 1985 VW Golf 1300 with us. How long can we drive it in the UK on Dutch plates and Dutch insurance before having to officially import it? Can we pay UK 'road tax' while it is still on Dutch plates? And when we finally register it in the UK, will there be any UK garages which would consider it for a trade-in?* "

Under current EU rules, as long as the car is insured and taxed for use in Holland, you can now run it in the UK for up to a year on Dutch plates (used to be six months). But the car has virtually no value here, so it would make much more sense to take it back to Holland in ten or eleven months when you have more money, part-exchange it in Holland for a new LHD or RHD car (depending on when you plan on returning to Holland), buy that car free of Dutch BTW and BPM and import it to the UK where you will only have to pay UK VAT of 17.5 per cent (same rate as Dutch BTW). That way, because pre-tax prices of cars in Holland are on average 35 per cent lower than in the UK, you will make a big saving, but you will need to order the car well in advance, particularly if it is to be RHD.

Japanese import warning!

" *The quota limits on the original SVA legislation, imposed from the end of June 1998, have led to a mass of pseudo-private grey imports over three years old which were subject to no more than a UK MOT which, in many cases, has proved to be fake. These cars are now recirculating on the UK used-car market and may continue to do so for many years to come. An innocent purchaser could buy one and only later find that it was never capable of passing a UK MOT and could be subject to a total 'Prohibition of Use' order.* "

Too right. If buying any car which you suspect is not to UK spec, you should have it inspected by ABS Vehicle Inspections (tel: 0345 419926) and also HPI the car (tel: 01722 422422). You wouldn't be the first to find out that not only was it not to UK spec, it was actually up to four years older than the declared age on the V5.

Going Dutch

" *Buying a car in Holland does not always work out as favourable as one might think. A friend of mine living in The Hague personally checked out the export price of an RHD BMW 318Ti Compact automatic for me. UK list is £17,835. Dutch list is £12,878, plus 17.5 per cent UK VAT, which equals £15,132. However, in Holland, RHD is an extra at £323, and, after adding all the extras I wanted (a/c, sunroof, tinted glass, metallic paint, foglights, computer, armrest, passenger airbag, radio, CD, rear wiper, clock), delivery, Dutch export plates and ferry costs, plus UK VAT, UK VED and UK registration tax, the total comes to £19,175. Not so very far off the UK price, including all the extras listed, of £20,645. Buying Dutch would have cost me just 7 per cent less than buying in the UK at the full*

UK list price, and I'd have had to put down a 50 per cent deposit then wait six months for the car. Instead I went for a UK-supplied Hyundai 2.0SE Coupe automatic with mica paint, supplied immediately at an 8 per cent discount, and costing me just £16,700. **"**

This reader won't find out the true cost of his Hyundai in comparison to the BMW Compact until he comes to part-exchange it. (In Spring 1999, Motorpoint of Derby were selling new Hyundai 1.8 litre coupes for just £10,999 and 2.0SEs for £13,999.) But he makes a good point and one that needs emphasising. The Germans have very cleverly engineered their cars into being the most desirable throughout the whole of Europe. As a result, waiting lists in other European countries are as long if not longer than in the UK and, with such strong demand for their cars, there is no need for German manufacturers to give as big a discount to anyone, including the fleets, as a manufacturer with an oversupply problem. German manufacturers will always argue that buyers benefit because German cars hold their value that much better, but this will only be true as long as German cars remain the status symbols they have become in the UK.

Second-hand Euro imports

" *We are all aware of the financial advantages of buying a new car in a European country, although it does require considerable time, effort and financial planning. Is there a similar financial advantage in buying a two- or three-year-old car in Europe? If so, which is the best country? I am thinking of a small diesel hatchback or estate car.* **"**

Not worth it for the type of car you're looking at. Even in the countries where low ex-factory prices are taxed at a sensible level, such as

Germany and Spain, second-hand diesels tend to have been driven to death and could easily have 300,000 kms under their wheels. Add the hassle of left-hand drive, changing the lights and changing the speedo face and there's no advantage. But as long as Sterling remains strong against the Mark, importing a sports car from Germany does make sense. The saving on a three-year-old Porsche can be between £10,000 and £15,000. Germans generally maintain their sports cars to an extremely high standard. LHD on a track day is no handicap at all. And you can pick up a copy of 'DAZ', the huge-format German national *Auto Trader* at the airport for just four Marks.

Couldn't be simpler

" *In March, despite having read all the press coverage of the difficulties, I decided to attempt to buy a new Mercedes C200 Elegance from Germany. I looked in the handbook of my 190E and under 'Workshop Directory Europe' found the number for Mercedes Benz AG, Nunerlassung, Dusseldorf. I speak no German but on phoning was transferred to the relevant department without problem. Herr Herrwerth spoke perfect English and was delighted to help. I faxed my requirements, with extras quoted by sales code number. A few days later, I was sent an itemised* pro forma *invoice to check. To order, I was required to sign the top copy and forward this, together with a 10 per cent deposit, for June/July delivery. At the beginning of June, Herr Herrwerth telephoned to advise me that the car was about to go into production and asked if I wished to alter any of my specifications. I took this opportunity to add air conditioning. A new invoice was sent covering this and a 3 per cent discount was also shown, amounting to DM 1,750. Herr Herrwerth phoned again in mid-July to advise that the car was completed and I requested that it be kept until August so I could register it in the UK on an 'S' plate. German temporary number plates and 28 days' third party insurance were arranged at a cost of DM 580. My wife and I flew to Dusseldorf on 4 August to take delivery, having arranged fully comprehensive insurance with Norwich Union on the VIN number. I had paid for the car by bank draft, sent several days previously, but I still owed DM 330 which was waived. We were given several small gifts, including a Mercedes leather wallet, a keyring and a boxed C200 model. Herr Herrwerth had also arranged a night's accommodation in a nearby hotel, free of charge to us, which we did not take up because our schedule was too tight. On returning to the UK via the Ostend–Dover Hoverspeed, I forwarded all documents to HM Customs & Excise at Dover and after about ten days received the VAT bill and the C&E form 386 to allow UK registration. I did have to pay German VAT at 16 per cent, but this will be reimbursed once UK VAT is paid. My car and the Certificate of Conformity were inspected at a Vehicle Registration Office on 21 August, VED was paid and the vehicle was registered. In total I saved just under £6,000, having bought my DM at 3 to the pound. I had no outside assistance and Mercedes in Dusseldorf, Customs & Excise at Dover and VRO Chelmsford were all extremely helpful, making the entire process trouble-free. Based on my experience I would recommend anyone to consider purchasing a vehicle in this way.* **"**

Though Mercedes Benz UK has been reported as not being happy about trade imports of its new cars, it cannot and does not object to genuine personal imports. But again, it has to be said that the more UK buyers who purchase Mercedes in this way, the more Mercedes residual values generally will be dragged down. You can't expect to buy a car at a £6,000 saving and for the car then to be worth £6,000 more than you paid for it.

Import pre-registration service

Marjorie Maycock of Car Services Company, based at Carterton, near Brize Norton in Oxfordshire, has written to tell us of a service for personal importers that can save the cost of registering and insuring the car in the country of origin. As long as the EU supplier can supply a European Type Approval

Certificate of Conformity for the car, evidence of newness, and proof of purchase (in the form of an invoice showing the deposit paid); and as long as you can provide an insurance certificate for the car based on the VIN number, Car Services Company can pre-register and tax it for you. You can't officially use your tax disc and plates in the country of origin (and the DVLA has recently stamped down on this), but if you can persuade the dealer to deliver the car to the port of embarkation, you can use the UK plates and VED disc as soon as you arrive in the UK. Remember, this applies only to new EU-supplied cars with EU Type Approval Certificates of Conformity. It does not and cannot apply to Far Eastern imports. Car Services Company can be contacted on **01993 842399**.

Game over

" *I am a serviceman serving abroad and have taken advantage of the arrangement whereby servicemen were allowed to purchase RHD UK-specification cars VAT free, then sell them in the UK after six months. I have a seven-month-old Mercedes C200 Elegance automatic in blue/black with a/c and 4,000 miles, and engaged the services of an agency advertising in* The Daily Telegraph *to sell it at a cost to me of £146.68. I had been advised by a friend who works for 'Glass's Guide' that the guide values it at £23,000 to a private buyer and that I should get at least £22,000. It is now six weeks since I placed the car with this agency and so far there have been no offers at my bottom line of £22,000. All I have from the agency is the advice that I am asking too much, that the days of servicemen making a profit on their VAT-free cars are now long gone, that all the car is worth is £19,000, and that if I leave it any longer it will be worth less. How can this be if Mercedes agents are advertising cars similar to mine for £25,000–£26,000? I intend advertising the car in the Saturday* Telegraph. *What is a reasonable price to ask?* "

The days when servicemen could buy VAT-free RHD cars in Europe, keep them for six months, then re-sell them in the UK at a substantial profit are indeed long gone. Ask £19,750. Take the telephone numbers of all the offers you receive, and accept the highest, because that's the best you're going to get.

Getting it covered

" *For the private motorist the incentive to buy a new car across the Channel is now irresistible. But what happens when we get our vehicles back home? Are the manufacturers' warranties pan-European, and will local distributors be obliged to offer normal service facilities?* "

Buy any car within the EU and the manufacturer warranty which applies in the country of purchase applies on a pan-European basis. If an extended manufacturer warranty is purchased, this also applies on a pan-European basis. But if, for example, you bought an MGF in Singapore, the warranty which applied in Singapore might not apply in the UK. And if you bought a Subaru in Japan, the UK Subaru concessionaires are under no obligation whatsoever to honour the Japanese warranty on the car. UK franchises for European cars rarely turn away profitable servicing business of any kind and VW even asks personal importers to register their cars with its customer care department (0800 711811) in case it needs to make a technical update to the car. Mitsubishi has now trained its franchises to service grey imports from Japan. But, at mid-1999 exchange rates, if you buy a car in Europe and travel to Europe often, you will find it much cheaper to have the car serviced there rather than in the UK. There is nothing to stop personal importers purchasing mechanical breakdown insurances from OneQuote Respond on 01452 529969, Motor Warranty Direct on 0800 731 7001, or AA Personal Warranties on 0990 225600. But these are not the same as manufacturer or importer warranties because no private warranty underwriter will meet claims due to manufacturing defects already present in the vehicle when the warranty was taken out.

New 'Beetles'

" *Having owned VWs for the past 30 years you could describe me as a fan of the marque. Recently I came across an advertisement for new Beetles, imported from Mexico by a firm in Hampshire and offered for £8,500 pre-converted to right-hand-drive. Are these conversions a success and would they create any difficulties in insurance or in driving the car? How do you imagine this latest Beetle would compare with my present Polo 1.4CL, which I think is an excellent little car?* "

In case any readers are slightly confused, this letter refers to the air-cooled, rear-engined Beetles which are still in production in Mexico, and not the new water-cooled, front-wheel-drive, Golf-based 'Beetle' cult car. The company importing 1.6 litre rear-engined Mexican Beetles is Beetles UK Ltd, The Stables, Tan House Lane, Rangeworthy, nr Bristol, South Glos BS37 7LP, tel: 01454 228999. In comparison to a modern car, they drive like a 30-year-old Beetle. Before buying any such car, readers should make sure that it satisfies UK Type Approval regulations, has a European Type Approval Certificate of Conformity, or has passed a UK SVA Test. Beetles UK also imports new rear-engined LHD VW Type 2 'Bay Window' vans, for which the SVA test is not as onerous.

Euro imports via an agent

" I am considering buying a new Citroën or Peugeot through an import agent. I understand it will come with manufacturer's warranty and that it will be imported from Ireland at a very reduced price. Are there any potential problems with guarantee work or servicing on such imports? And what else should I be aware or wary of? "

First, either pay your deposit by credit card, or make sure it goes into a 'client' or 'escrow' account so it is not part of the agent's assets should the agent go bust or do a runner before your car is delivered. Second, set parameters for price and delivery date. The agent's price will be subject to currency fluctuations and you may have to wait up to six months for the car. Third, agree the precise specification in writing on the contract. Irish spec is lower than UK spec, so you need to list everything you expect the car to have. If not, a vehicle such as an MPV which you expect to have seven seats may come with five. When you have taken delivery, call Peugeot's or Citroën's customer care line and register the car's existence in the UK. Once this is done, take it to a UK Peugeot or Citroën franchise and have it checked over. This establishes a provenance for the car and will help you sell or part-exchange it in years to come. There should be no problems over the manufacturer's warranty as these are pan-European for the first year. The advantages of dealing with agents Origin Euro (new number: 0181 381 3000) and European Car Imports (0181 889 4848) are that they import cars by transporter to their own UK compounds, so the first place they are registered is the UK rather than the country of origin. They settle the VAT bill for you. And because they have the financial resources to pay for the car, you don't have to pre-pay the final amount until collection.

Out of Focus

" I have a property in Pollensa, Majorca. Because car prices here are 30 to 40 per cent lower than in the UK, I recently asked my local Ford agent to order a Focus for me in right-hand drive. The agent made enquiries, then advised that the RHD Focus must be ordered from a UK agent and shipped from the UK to Spain. Since the cars are built in Spain and Germany, this makes a mockery of EU rules. Who should I complain to? "

Under EU rules, the agent is not obliged to supply you with a car for export if he feels that by doing so he will miss out on income from servicing the car and taking it back in part-exchange in the future. Also remember that the Focus 1.6 'Trend', listed at Ptas 2,000,000, is a Spanish market 'special' in LHD only. But if the agent orders a Focus for you, Ford is obliged to supply it to you through him at a price which reflects current Spanish list price levels plus a reasonable charge for the extra cost of RHD in a LHD country. So go back to him and ask him to place the order. If he agrees, then runs into trouble, take the matter up with The EU Competitions Minister, DG IV, European Commission, 200 Rue de la Loi, 1049 Brussels.

Duty-free car cruises

" I believe that there is a ferry company organising car buying trips to Holland, but I can find no reference to such a thing in the motoring press and my local travel agent couldn't throw any light on the matter. Could you? "

Yes. Broadspeed and Stena Lines are now organising car purchase cruises to Europe at an all-in price of £299 for two cruises for two people

(to order and to collect the car) with overnight accommodation and expert help available. Call Broadspeed's 24 hour information lines on 0171 413 9940/9950/9960/9970/9980, or go to their website at http://www.car-prices.com. Book tickets by calling Stena Lines on 01233 646881. But please remember this is a 'tax dodge' and the loophole that allows it could be closed. As in Eire, Dutch pre-tax car prices are artificially low because Dutch car buyers pay 17.5 per cent BTW (VAT) plus a further variable tax (BPM) which works out at an average 30 per cent of the pre-tax price of the car.

'My friends all have Porsches...'

" *I wrote to you last September seeking advice on car purchase. Now, thanks to your comments, I am the proud owner of a new Mercedes*

E300TD with lots of extras to complement the leather interior. I had to go to Germany to pick the thing up, but saved myself £7,000 in the process. It was an adventure. It was fun. And even my local Mercedes franchise is happy to look after the car. Seven thousand thanks to you. "

The information this reader used can be found in *How to Buy & Sell Cars*, price £6.99 (ISBN 1-84119-035-7). Since then, *What Car?* magazine published the best-researched and most useful import guide I have seen with its June 1999 issue and you may be able to buy a reprint from Haymarket Reprints on 01235 534323.

Contraband diesel

" I have been going to France to pick up cheaper diesel in a 1,000 litre tank when I stock up with booze. I have been told that the diesel bit is not legal. If not, what should I do about it. "

You're smuggling. The offence is no different from filling your 1,000 litre tank with brandy because what you are doing is deliberately evading UK Customs & Excise duties. To make it legal you'd have to rig an extra tank to supply its content to the engine as a 'long range' fuel tank. But C&E will only accept a reserve tank of up to 60 litres. If the vehicle is relatively new, the mod would need to conform to European Whole Vehicle Type Approval, and if it is older it would still need to conform to UK Construction & Use regulations.

Tax-free cars

" Tenerife is a tax-free island. Yet despite this, and the fact that pre-tax Spanish car prices are already far lower than in the UK, dealers in Tenerife are still offering discounts. Your readers might be interested in a few press cuttings. To benefit in full from these prices, you would need a 'Residencia' or at least to own a property out there. "

Coincidentally, a reader from Darlington also sent a collection of clippings from Canary Island newspapers. The tax-free prices worked out as follows: Alfa 146 Junior 1.6: £6,860; Fiat Seicento: from £3,400; Fiat Punto 55 (not 60): from £3,840; Fiat Bravo: from £5,776; Ford Fiesta 1.25 16v 'Tattoo': from £4,740; Ford Focus Tddi: from £8,100; Ford Mondeo 1.8i 16v CLX: £9,112; Ford Mondeo 2.0i 16v Ghia: £11,008; Hyundai Accent 82cv: £4,780; Mazda Demio: from £6,380; Nissan Primera: from £7,204; Nissan Primera estate: from £9,635; Opel Corsa 'Top' 16v: £5,152; Peugeot 106 'Max' 1.1 litre: £4,100; Renault 5 Express Combi 1.9D: £4,900; Seat Arosa: from £4,240; Seat Cordoba 'Dream': £5,180; Seat Cordoba 1.6 Vario: from £5,868; VW Polo hatchback: from £5,160; VW Polo saloon: from £5,760; VW Polo estate: from £5,880.

Time to Twingo?

" On a recent continental holiday, I saw quite a few Renault Twingos. I understand these cannot be imported to the UK. Why is this so? It would surely fit into the under-1,100cc category which we are all supposed to be encouraged to drive these days. For a low-powered vehicle it looks remarkably presentable, without 2CV oddities, so what's the snag, I wonder? "

We have covered the Twingo quite a lot before, both in the *Telegraph* column and in the last book of *Motoring Answers*. It never fitted the under-1,100cc category because the first engines were 1,171cc and the current engines are 1,149cc. Enthusiasts have been importing them almost since they were launched. But they can't be converted from left- to right-hand drive (the only attempts resulted in failure). VCA-approved left-dipping headlights can be supplied by David Benton, Broadmeadows

Garage, Padstow Road, Wadebridge, Cornwall PL27 7LS, tel: 01208 812046 at £150 a pair delivered. Mph and kph speedometers with installation kits can be supplied by Peter Hass, Twingo Direct, HMS Ltd, TLF Unit 4, Castle Lane Industrial Estate, Melbourne, Derbyshire DE73 1DY, tel: 01332 864659 at £224.50, plus postage, plus VAT. All that then remains is to move the rear foglight over from the left to the right. It has often struck me that left-hand-drive Twingo Matics with power steering would be ideal vehicles for the disabled because they would then have a small, inexpensive, very versatile vehicle they could get out of much more safely kerb-side. Suppliers other than those already mentioned include: South: Auto Europ, c/o 7 Clementine Close, Beltinge, Herne Bay, Kent CT6 6SN, tel: 01227 769700, fax: 01227 741257. Midlands: Studio Imports UK, Alscott Park, Stratford-upon-Avon, Warks CV37 8BL, tel: 01789 450480. Wales: Dafydd Williams, Garreg Lwyd, Penrhyndeudraeth, Gwynedd, LL48 6AW, tel: 01766 770203. France: Diffusion Automobiles Calasiene, 58/60 avenue de Saint-Exupéry – B.P. 154 – 62103 Calais, tel: 00 33 321 19 15 58. Spain: Inaki Martin Dominguez, Twingos Aragon, Calle Sagrada Familia 3, 2 – esc, 3-B, Zaragoza 50 012, Spain. Tel (mobile): 00 34 09 06 02 13, fax: 00 347 623 4917 (week-days), 00 347 656 2366 (weekends). Twingo Club, c/o Dave Thornton, Renault Twingo UK Register, 30 Cranmer Avenue, Ealing, London W13 9SH, tel/fax: 0181 932 3396. Website: http://www.geocities.com/MotorCity/2090/index.htm.

INSURANCE AND WARRANTIES

Free recovery omissions

" *In December 1996 I purchased a new Chrysler Neon LX and am very happy with it. But because the 'package' included three years Chrysler Assist breakdown cover I let my own GEM policy lapse. Then I read the small print and found that Chrysler Assist does not cover me for recovery following an accident or vandalism (which is when one really needs to be covered). So I re-joined GEM.* "

Makes sense. GEM provides good, inexpensive cover, but first you have to join the Guild of Experienced Motorists. Even so, membership including breakdown recovery insurance is £46.50 a year which compares more than favourably with some of the other organisations. More from The Guild of Experienced Motorists, Station Road, Forest Row, East Sussex RH13 5EN, tel: 0645 645505.

Accident solicitors

" *I recently had an accident which was not my fault and for which the other driver admitted liability. My car was then towed to a nearby accident repairers where I was asked if I wanted the repairs done through my insurers or through one of several firms of solicitors and car hire companies whose brochures he showed me. I opted for one of these and the service I received was excellent. The repair took six weeks and I had a 'free' hire car for the entire time. My question is, do you recommend using these companies?* "

Certainly. A firm recommended by readers is Easthams Solicitors, and I spoke to Andrew Eastham to find out what can and cannot be done in such cases. First, it needs to be understood that they only get involved where the client is not at fault, where there is a genuine and recoverable 'uninsured loss' and where the third party that was responsible for the damage is properly insured. Their enquiry officers will establish this during the first telephone conversation. Depending on whether a client is 'Third Party', 'Third Party, Fire and Theft' or 'Comprehensively' insured, uninsured losses could include: loss of earnings; hire of a car or loss of use of the damaged car; repairs to the damaged car, diminution of value of the damaged car after repair; personal injuries; ambulance fees; damage to other property (such as clothes or belongings in the car); taxi fares to and from hospital; insurance excess; increase in premiums as a result of the claim; and 'reasonable expenses' (not including the client's costs of corresponding with them). Easthams Solicitors' two addresses are: Continental House, 292-302 Church Street, Blackpool FY1 3QA, tel: 01253 299222, and 10th Floor, Leon House, High Street, Croydon CR9 0TE, tel: 0181 681 5464.

'No fault' accident solicitors

Here is a list of solicitors specialising in 'no fault' accidents. I strongly advise anyone involved in such an accident to consult one of these solicitors before instituting an insurance claim, because it makes sure that you will get what you are entitled to get rather than a lesser settlement which may suit the insurers but leaves you out of pocket. The first question you must ask is, will the solicitor handle your case on a 'no win, no fee' basis? If so, get it in writing. Do not hire a car to keep yourself mobile unless it be on a guaranteed 'no cost' basis.

- Motor Accident Solicitors Society, Bridge House, 48-52 Baldwin Street, Bristol BS1 1QD, tel: 0117 929 2560.

- Kingsford Flower & Pain, Solicitors, 7 Bank Street, Ashford, Kent TN23 1BZ, tel: 01233 665544.

- Thomas Taggart & Sons, Solicitors, 27 Church Street, Ballymoney, Co. Antrim BT53 6HS, tel: 012656 62118.

- Easthams, Solicitors, Continental House, 292-302 Church Street, Blackpool FY1 3QA, tel: 01253 299222.

- Brian Camp & Co., Solicitors, No 1 Europa House, Conway Street, Birkenhead, Merseyside L41 4FT, tel: 0151 201 8080, or Freefone: 0500 122 559.

- Philip Baker & Co., Solicitors, 1st Floor, Newater House, 11 Newhall Street, Birmingham B3 2NY, tel: 0121 212 1100.

- Widdows Mason, Solicitors, 2 Princess Street, Bolton BL1 1EJ, tel: 01204 528105.

- Burroughs Day, Solicitors, Road Traffic Accident Unit, 14 Charlotte Street, Bristol BS1 5PT, tel: 0117 929 0333 (out of hours, tel: 0117 925 0334).

- John Hodge Nichols Strickland, Solicitors, 9 Queen Square, Bristol BS1 4HR, tel: 0117 9292281.

- Clarke, Willmott & Clarke, Solicitors, The Waterfront, Welsh Back, Bristol BS1 4SB, tel: 0117 941 6600.

- Steele Ford Newton, Solicitors, 1–3 Colne Road, Brierfield, Burnley BB9 5HW, tel: 01282 616446.

- Russell & Russell, Solicitors, Belgrave Terrace, 10 Manchester Road, Bury BL9 0EB, tel: 0161 764 5424.

- Marquis Penna, Solicitors, Post Office House, Elliott Street, Crook, County Durham DL15 8QH, tel: 01388 762466.

- Easthams, Solicitors, 10th Floor, Leon House, High Street, Croydon CR9 0TE, tel: 0181 681 5464.

- McArdle, Cardwell & Mitchell, Solicitors, 56 Duke Street, Darlington, County Durham DL3 7AN, tel: 01325 482299.

- Stephen Rimmer & Co., Solicitors, 28 Hyde Gardens, Eastbourne, East Sussex BN21 4PX, tel: 01323 644222.

- Tayntons, Solicitors, Clarence Chambers, 8–12 Clarence Street, Gloucester GL1 1DZ, tel: 01452 522047.

- Andrew M. Jackson & Co., Solicitors, PO Box 47, Essex House, Manor Street, Hull HU1 1XH, tel: 01482 325242.

- Stephensons, Solicitors, 26 Union Street, Leigh WN7 1AT, tel: 01942 608942.

- Quinn Melville, Solicitors, 15 Stanley Street, Liverpool L1 6AA, tel: 0151 236 3340.

- Bermans Solicitors, Pioneer Buildings, 65–67 Dale Street, Liverpool L2 2NS, tel: 0151 227 3351.

- Cotton Griffiths & Co., 880 Stockport Road, Levenshulme, Manchester M19 3BN, tel: 0161 225 5813 (not a solicitor, but a respected claims assessor well versed in 'diminution in value'.)

- Lopian Wagner, Solicitors, 9 St John Street, Manchester M3 4DN, tel: 0161 834 2324.

- Philip Shuker & Co., Solicitors, New Church House, 34 John Dalton Street, Manchester M2 6LE, tel: 0161 839 7900.

- Berry & Co., Solicitors, 2nd Floor, Building 1, Wilson Park, Monsall Road, Manchester M40 8PA, tel: 0161 205 0081.

- David Harris, Solicitors, Lloyd House, 18 Lloyd Street, Manchester M2 5WA, tel: 0161 834 2200.

- Colemans, Solicitors, Elizabeth House, 16 St Peter's Square, Manchester M2 3DF, tel: 0161 228 7393.

- Lyons Wilson, Solicitors, Dickinson Chambers, 1 Central Street, Manchaster M2 5WR, tel: 0161 834 6836.

- Sedgewick Phelan & Partners, Solicotors, Argyle House, Warwick Court, Park Road, Middleton, Manchester M24 1AE, tel: 0161 653 5299.

- Aubrey Isaacson & Co., Solicitors, 2 Scholes Lane, Prestwich, Manchester M25 1ED, tel: 0161 798 6700.

- Fennemores, Solicitors, 200 Silbury Boulevard, Milton Keynes MK9 1LL, tel: 01908 678241.

- Poole Alcock & Co., Solicitors, Mill House, 14 Mill Street, Nantwich, Cheshire CW5 5ST, tel: 01270 625478/624560.

- Hewitt Brown-Humes & Hare, Solicitors, 21 Dalton Way, Newton Aycliffe, County Durham DL5 4DJ, tel: 01325 316170.

- Nelsons, Solicitors, Pennine House, 8 Stanford Street, Nottingham NG1 7BQ, tel: 0115 958 6262.

- Innes & Company, Solicitors, 214 London Road, North End, Portsmouth PO2 9JE, tel: 01705 693052.

- Blake Lapthorn, Solicitors, Harbour Court, Compass Road, North Harbour, Portsmouth, Hants PO6 4ST, tel: 01705 221122.

- Whittle Robinson, Solicitors, 5, 6 & 7 Cannon Street, Preston PR1 1PY, tel: 01772 254201.

- Blackhurst Parker & Yates, Solicitors, 9 Cannon Street, Preston PR1 3QD, tel: 01772 253601.

- Pitmans, Solicitors, 47 Castle Street, Reading, Berks RG1 7SR, tel: 0118 958 0224.

- Atkinson & Co., Solicitors, 140A Framingham Road, Brooklands, Sale, Cheshire M33 3RG, tel: 0161 976 1921.

- Windsor Bronzite, Solicitors, 162 Millbrook Road East, Southampton SO15 1EB, tel: 01703 634555.

- Stathams, Solicitors, Hammonds Court, 22 London Road, Southampton SO15 2AF, tel: 01703 211617.

- Brignalls, Solicitors, Queensway Chambers, Queensway, Stevenage, Herts SG1 1BA, tel: 01438 359311.

- Beardsells, Solicitors, Vienna House, 281 Wellington Road South, Stockport, Cheshire SK2 6ND, tel: 0161 477 2288.

- Davies & Co., Solicitors, 2a Lawton Road, Alsager, Stoke-on-Trent ST7 2BJ, tel: 01270 873132.

- Ross Aldridge, Solicitors, 3 Rowcroft, Stroud, Gloucs GL5 3AZ, tel: 01453 766193.

- Smith Llewellyn, Solicitors, 18 Princess Way, Swansea SA1 3LW, tel: 01792 464444.

- O'Connor & Co., Solicitors, 63 Lemon Street, Truro, Cornwall TR1 2PN, tel: 01872 271919.

- Dawson Hart, Solicitors, The Old Grammar School, Church Street, Uckfield, East Sussex TN22 1BH, tel: 01825 762281.

- Frasers, Solicitors, 29 Old Market, Wisbech, Cambs PE13 1ND, tel: 01945 582664.

Insurance groups

" *I wonder if you could enlighten me as to why a standard petrol-driven Peugeot 205 is in insurance Group 5 while my 205 diesel (not turbo) is in Group 8? I find this ridiculous as diesels are not known for their lively performance. I have asked both Peugeot and the Association of British Insurers, but each vacillates and refers me to the other. Do you have an 'honest' answer?* "

Insurance groups are determined mostly by damageability and repairability because the cost of this to insurers represents 70 per cent of claims. Next comes security. Next comes the likelihood of a claim due to the performance of a car and, with very high-performance cars, the high likelihood of claims will partly outweigh any damageability and repairability benefit. This is why your 205 diesel is in Group 8, but a cheaper to repair petrol model is in Group 5. It's also why the cheaper to repair, more secure 306 diesel is in Group 4 and why the blisteringly quick 306GTi-6 is in Group 16.

Second-hand surgery

" *In discussion with a sales manager I was surprised to learn that damaged cars may be repaired with second-hand parts salvaged from other damaged cars (perhaps insurance damage write-offs). Those parts have been paid for by insurance claim settlements, yet the repairer apparently charges the customer the new part price plus VAT. If this is so, it seems to me to be a reprehensible practice. It costs the repairer labour only. If the repair is the subject of an insurance claim, it seems to me that the insurers are paying twice for the same part. This must affect the cost of insurance. Your comments would be welcome.* "

What happens is that a lot of fleet cars are insured third party only. If they are damaged towards the end of their time on the fleet, the fleet manager cuts costs by having them repaired partly with second-hand parts before sending them to auction. The insurance companies certainly don't lose by this because they sell their write-offs to auto dismantlers. Where second-hand parts are used for insurance repairs it is inevitably because the insurer has cut the repair budget to such an extent that this is the only way to repair the car with the funds allowed. Anyone who thinks that car repairers are making a fortune at the expense of the insurance companies ought to try it some time.

Premium rate, premium service

" *You will know that over the last year insurance premiums have risen quite sharply – by between 10 and 15 per cent. This makes it more beneficial to shop around just before the next premium becomes due. Each month our researchers obtain between 5,000 and 6,000 telephone quotes from all the leading insurers and most recently found a variation of £143.53 for the same cover on a Mondeo 1.6. A simple premium-rate phone call at 50p a minute will establish the lowest premium being offered by the 30 leading direct insurers and telebrokers. We will have to ask a few questions, but calls usually last around two minutes. The number is 0660 250567.* "

This seems to be a useful service, especially now that direct insurers generally are becoming less competitive than they used to be. However, readers should still satisfy themselves that the cover being offered at different rates is 'like for like' and that additional charges for overseas cover are not excessive. They should also put a good broker onto the task, such as ABM on 0181 681 8986 or Rauch & Stallard on 01702 348261, especially if their needs are in any way specialised.

Another unwarranted claim

" *I have an 'F'-registered Volvo 760 which was covered by a Mechanical Breakdown Insurance Warranty. I have it serviced every six months and every 3,000–4,000 miles. Shortly after a service, carried out at 152,734 miles by a mobile servicing operator at a cost of £84.78, I claimed under the warranty for a replacement power steering rack, for a replacement air-conditioning condenser, and for recharging the air conditioning system. The MBI company directed me to specialists for the work, which cost a total of £724.97, including VAT, but later rejected my claim on the grounds that I had not complied with the servicing schedule as laid down in the MBI policy document, and also revoked the MBI on the same grounds. I asked for clarification, but have received no reply.* "

Both power steering and air conditioning systems require regular maintenance which, on the information you supplied, does not seem to have been carried out by the mobile servicing operator. This would be grounds for rejection of a claim. I phoned the MBI company to check on its terms and conditions, but a cheerful voice told me I would have to wait in a queue and I'm afraid life's too short for that. The moral of this little story is, as always, that if you take out a Mechanical Breakdown Insurance you must make sure you comply with the terms of it to the letter or your claim is likely to be rejected. These people are in the business of making money, not giving it away.

Less is more

" I am a member of the RAC. When I renewed my membership at a cost of £215 in April, I was not informed that some member services had ceased to be covered by the membership fee. I had occasion to phone RAC Travel Information on 3 June and was told that this is now subject to a 50p a minute surcharge. I wrote to complain about this and was told that 'The introduction of the charge is designed to support new journey management products. We are having to make a charge to cover the costs involved in researching, gathering and collating much more data that will enable these new products to be made available to members.' I just thought your readers ought to know. "

Another reader wrote: 'I have just received my renewal notice for the RAC. The opening paragraph states, "Recent changes at the RAC mean you now have even more benefits as a member." Page 5, paragraph 16 of the accompanying leaflet tells me in small print that my wife is no longer covered. A telephone call to the RAC confirms that if I apply for a separate card she will be covered for the coming year, after which it will be £22 extra. Please could you alert RAC members to read the small print of the booklet very carefully?' This sort of thing might be enough to break the inertia that keeps motorists with the same rescue organisation.

'Free insurance' is not free

" *My wife recently purchased a Peugeot, taking advantage of the offer of two years 'free' insurance. However, when she came to cancel her then current 'direct' policy, she found she was not entitled to a refund because her policy was cancelled in the first year. In this situation, the insurer explained, 'the premium is re-calculated and includes a short period rate, as mentioned on page 18 of our policy booklet under the "cancellation" paragraph, of £50. Because the unused part of your premium is approximately £46, the cancellation fee wipes out any refund due on this occasion.' My point is, like most people when taking out an insurance policy, my wife did not get to see the policy booklet until she had purchased the policy.* "

Fair point. But what difference would it have made if she had? Most policies include a similar clause and when she took this one out she could hardly have anticipated she would be replacing it with a 'free' policy within the first year. It's also worth remembering that if, for any reason, you terminate a policy within the policy term after you have had an accident, you will not be entitled to any refund at all. This happened to a reader whose car was written off in the accident. He then replaced it with a different car on which his insurer would not offer him cover, so had to go to a different insurer and lost the balance of period refund.

Insurance upset

" *I was appalled to read of the insurance ombudsman's decision to uphold the claim by the man whose BMW was stolen when he left it with the ignition keys in. Any more decisions like this and we can expect our premiums to go up tenfold. I would never dream of leaving my car unlocked, never mind with the keys in the ignition. Admittedly, it's a Skoda diesel.* **"**

Too right. Traditionally, if a car was stolen with the keys left in it, that amounted to contributory negligence by the driver. And it's still quite common for lowlifes to nick 'private sales' when out on the test run. When you swap drivers, take the keys with you and only hand them to the prospective buyer when you're safely ensconced in the passenger seat. The other insurance factor about test runs, of course, is the question as to whether the other driver is actually covered to drive your car at all. If he doesn't have a policy of his own and your policy is not 'any driver', he won't be.

Old car cover

Several readers owning cars more than 25 years old have found that when they went to renew their insurance policies their cover is now restricted to Third Party, Fire and Theft only. On shopping around they have found that their own age increases the cost of cover and that 'comprehensive' can be twice the price of TPFT. There are two answers to this. One is to contact a good broker such as ABM on 0181 681 8986, Rauch & Stallard on 01702 348261 or, if you are getting on, Age Concern Insurance Services (Motor Department), Halford House, 2 Coval Lane, Chelmsford, Essex CM1 1TZ, tel: 01245 351540. The other is to opt for an 'agreed value' classic car policy through specialists such as Footman James (0121 561 4196) or Firebond (01223 566020). An ordinary comprehensive policy only gives a diminishing 'market value' for an old car, which may be a derisory amount and has nothing to do with the value you have given for it on the proposal form. But an 'agreed value' policy gives the value of the car as established after inspection by officials of the relevant classic car club (see *Practical Classics* magazine for a comprehensive list).

New for old insurance

" *Your reader whose Cavalier V6 was stolen would never have suffered the problems he encountered if he had take out a Replicar insurance policy. In the event of a total vehicle loss, Replicar covers the difference between the insurance company's pay-out and the actual cost of a replacement as originally purchased. So, if for example he bought his 94M Cavalier 2.5 V6 GLS in 1996 (when it was two years old), Replicar would cover the difference between the insurance company valuation and the cost of a two-year-old V6 Cavalier – even though his was four years old at the time of its theft. The cost for this extra cover is a mere £120, from Car Care Plan on 0113 218 0000.* "

The attached notes state, 'If the vehicle (subject to a total loss claim) was bought new, Replicar will ensure the replacement is brand new, even if the lost car was up to three years old.'

Uninsured 4x4s

" *I recently purchased a Jeep Grand Cherokee Limited 2.5 diesel, and took advantage of Chrysler Jeep's training weekend where I was taught to drive the vehicle safely off-road. Imagine my surprise when, on checking with my (direct) vehicle insurer, I discovered that the vehicle was not insured to go off road. Eventually, after speaking directly to the underwriters, cover was agreed at no extra charge. But I wonder how many 4x4 owners take their vehicles off the road without checking whether or not they are insured to do so.* "

A very good point. Their insurers can now expect a burst of telephone enquiries. Though it has to be said, very few 4x4 owners do actually take their 'off-road' vehicles off the road.

Punto warranty

" *We bought a new Fiat Punto in early October and in mid-January the two-year warranty document and two years AA cover card have still not arrived. The nice people at Fiat say, 'Don't worry, sir, it will be coming.' This delay is ridiculous. We just want to complete our file. Could you find out for us the reason for this unnecessary delay?* "

Fiat Customer Care was not aware of your complaint. The procedure is to phone 0800 717000 with the car's chassis number. If this department has no record of the car, it will refer the matter to Fiat Customer Care which will check the chassis number against those of official UK imports and if the car is an official import, will issue the relevant documents. If it is not an official import, you are not entitled to the AA cover or the extended two year warranty anyway. You will only be entitled to the pan European warranty effective in the country of origin.

Insurance reforms

" *Your readers might like to know that, as from 26 April 1999, the Woolf Reforms to the UK Civil Justice System came into effect. The aim is to make the resolution of disputes quicker, cheaper and simpler by shortening time limits, promoting earlier settlements and penalising parties for non-compliance and unreasonable behaviour. In particular, if a claim is made against anyone, that person has only 21 days to respond, either personally if they are uninsured or through their insurer, which means that any intimation of a claim must be passed to the insurer immediately. Failure to respond within 21 days could mean that the claimant can issue proceedings without worrying about the costs and in certain circumstances it could mean that no defence can be entered. After responding within the 21 days, the insurer has only three months to investigate the claim and issue an acceptance of liability or a denial supported by evidence on the behalf of the insured defendant. Your readers can find additional information on the Summit Web site at http://www.summit-insurance.co.uk.*"

A useful reminder.

Once in a 'Lifetime Care'

" *I own a caravan. In August 1997 I purchased a 'J'-registered Volvo 960 estate car for general and towing duties. I paid £10,000 and the car came with a full Volvo agent service history, qualifying it for Volvo's 'Lifetime Care' warranty. I purchased the car expecting it to last more than 18 months. But I now discover that the cylinder block is cracked, resulting in a coolant leak. I have also discovered from a journal published by Volvo itself that 'a faulty die cast process at the block supplier caused material defects which can lead to fatigue cracks. Cylinder blocks produced between nos 9151 and 9206, engine serial numbers 25000 to 52873, can be affected.' The engine number of my car is 32966. I am being quoted £4,500 to £5,000 for the fitting of a new block, to which Volvo is prepared to contribute 25 per cent under its 'Lifetime Care' warranty. I feel that because the fault is a result of a material defect in manufacture, Volvo should be prepared to contribute more.*"

I'm afraid I don't. Volvo has pointed out to you that the car had covered 112,000 miles when the engine failed and that the failure could have been due to overheating, which can easily occur when towing a caravan. As the 'Lifetime Care' brochure explains, this warranty only ever covered components for a reasonable lifetime and Volvo considers that 100,000 miles is a reasonable lifetime for an engine. In any case, its contribution is only ever for the difference between the mileage and age at which the component failed and the reasonable lifetime.

So in offering you 25 per cent it is effectively giving your engine a 'lifetime' of 149,300 miles and reimbursing you for the 37,300 miles short of that when it failed. Even though cylinder head and block cracks are a known problem with this six-cylinder 24-valve model, the car is now so old that if I was you I'd take the 25 per cent offer with good grace.

Not what it seems

" *Your readers should know that RAC cover purchased as a 'rescue package' from a direct insurer for only £35 may not be the same thing as RAC cover. When I purchased mine I was given a freephone number, but when I tried it I found it was answered by my insurer who I was told would pass on the details to the RAC. Not the speedy service I would hope for when stuck on the hard shoulder on a cold, wet night.* "

Nothing is for nothing, and a cut rate service will inevitably mean less of a service. The best of the low price (as opposed to cut rate) rescue services seems to be that offered by The Guild of Experienced Motorists (GEM), tel: 0645 645505.

Communication breakdown

" *My wife and I recently suffered a puncture from debris on the motorway. We stopped on the hard shoulder and, as we are both more than eighty years old, we were very grateful when a good Samaritan stopped to offer help. He tried to phone the AA, using the easy-to-remember number (0800 88-77-66) on our membership card, but was told by the AA that they would not accept the call. He then changed our wheel for us and we all went on our way. I protested about this to the AA, only to be told that had I read the AA book in detail I would have found an alternative number to be used with mobile phones. I just wonder how many people realise that they cannot use their mobile phones to call for help to the number on their cards.* "

Some confusion here. Every AA member can use his or her mobile phone to call out the AA. It may be that for some reason your Good Samaritan's mobile service provider bars 0800 numbers rather then charges them to his bill (0800 numbers aren't always free from a mobile). Also, though it wasn't the case here, it's also possible to find yourself outside the phone cell, in which case, the phone will tell you 'no network'. The police prefer motorists who break down on the motorway to summon help using the roadside emergency phones. But some forces stipulate that if your own rescue service does not pick you up within half an hour, you must use the official police service at a non-refundable cost of around £120.

LEGAL MATTERS AND CONSUMER RIGHTS

Your rights under the Act

The Sale of Goods Act (1979) was modified in January 1995 by The Sale and Supply of Goods Act (1994) which more tightly described what was meant by the requirement for the goods to be of suitable quality and 'fit for the purpose' for which they were sold. It states:

'Where the seller sells goods in the course of a business, there is an implied term that the goods supplied under the contract are of satisfactory quality … Goods are of satisfactory quality if they meet the standard that a reasonable person would regard as satisfactory, taking account of any description of the goods, the price (if relevant) and all the other relevant circumstances.' (This differentiates a garage or even a trader operating from home from a private vendor. A trader operating from home cannot hide from the obligations as outlined above.)

'…The following are in appropriate cases aspects of the quality of goods:

(a) *Fitness for all the purposes for which goods of the kind in question are commonly supplied.* (For example, it is reasonable to expect a Rover Metro 1.1 to operate adequately on shopping trips, the school run and leisure trips. It is not reasonable to expect it to pull a large caravan or to run all day at 100 mph.)

(b) *Appearance and finish.*

(c) *Freedom from minor defects.* (For example, it is reasonable to expect a new car to be free from minor defects such as small scratches and paint chips. It is not reasonable to expect a second-hand car to be.)

(d) *Safety.* (For example, it is reasonable to expect the brakes, steering and suspension of a new or second-hand car to be safe, taking account of the nature of the deal and the price paid. It would not be reasonable to expect an old car bought as a 'non-runner', with no MOT, to be safe.)

(e) *Durability.* (For example, it is reasonable to expect a new or second-hand car to run properly without breaking down and without falling apart for a reasonable period of time, taking account of the nature of the deal and the price paid, and provided the buyer has maintained it properly and not abused it. It would not be reasonable to expect a £200 banger to immediately be capable of a long journey.)'

But these terms do not extend to 'any matter making the quality of goods unsatisfactory...

(a) *...which is specifically drawn to the buyer's attention before the contract is made.* (If defects are pointed out to you by the vendor, you cannot later reject the car for those defects.)

(b) *...where the buyer examines the goods before the contract is made and which that examination ought to reveal.* (If you are given a good chance to inspect the car and fail to notice a very obvious fault, you cannot later reject the car for that reason. However, a professional buyer is expected to know what to look for and to inspect the car much more carefully than a private buyer.)'

The Act then defines what is meant by 'acceptance'.

'Goods are accepted where the buyer intimates to the seller he has accepted them or when the goods have been delivered to him and he does any act in relation to them which is inconsistent with the ownership of the seller. (So, start using a car as your own, without the permission of the seller, and you are deemed to have accepted it.)

'But where goods are delivered to the buyer and he has not previously examined them, he is not deemed to have accepted them until he has had a reasonable chance of examining them. (So, if you order a car on the basis of a test drive or the viewing of another in the showroom, you are not deemed to have accepted the car you ordered until you have had a reasonable chance of inspecting it.)

'The buyer is also deemed to have accepted goods when after the lapse of a reasonable time he retains the goods without intimating to the seller he has rejected them.

'The buyer is not…deemed to have accepted the goods merely because he asks for or agrees to their repair by or under an arrangement with the seller. (So if you ask the seller to put right a fault and the seller does put it right you are still not deemed to have accepted the car.)'

Case law

Rejection under the Acts

There are a number of examples of case law on this section of the 1979 Act. In *Bernstein v Palmerston Motors 1987,* the engine of Mr Bernstein's new car failed after three weeks and 120 miles. Palmerston Motors fitted a new engine, but Mr Bernstein still attempted to reject the car. When it went to court, Mr Bernstein's case failed. But in *Rogers v Parrish 1987* the buyer tried to reject a Range Rover after six months and 5,500 miles for a catalogue of faults, including defective oil seals, gearbox defects and body problems. His case was upheld on appeal by the Queens Bench. Against this, in 1995 in Scotland, the case of a buyer who tried to reject a car after ten months (and two minor accidents) was rejected on appeal. And in *Carlisle v Lane 1996,* which concerned a used Range Rover alleged to be older than indicated by the date of registration, the case failed on appeal on the evidence because the buyer was adjudged to have been told the car was older than its registration date at the time of sale. In yet another, more recent case, the buyer of a VW Polo was held not to have rejected the car, because he kept possession of it rather than returning it to the dealer he sought redress against.

Termination of a purchase contract

A more recent case, *Johnson v HWM 1997* (Kingston Crown Court), set another precedent.

Mr J, an Aston Martin Virage owner, ordered a new Virage in October 1988 during the heady days of supercar speculation. He was required to put down a deposit of £20,000 of which VAT was charged as a proportion because, unlike an 'option to buy', his deposit constituted a part-payment for the car.

In 1989 Mr J decided he would like a more powerful car, and changed his order to the Vantage model. Then, over the years (there was a very long waiting list) he began to change his mind again, and, in 1993, asked to cancel the order. HWM refused to refund his part payment and instead suggested he took a new Virage which, by that time, had been uprated.

Mr J then launched a campaign against HWM alleging that, amongst other things, the Vantage was not a full four-seater and the car was not what he ordered because the automatic gearbox of Vantage models was retro-fitted. (In fact, a Vantage is merely a highly modified Virage and shares the same body shell as the Virage which Mr J already owned.)

HMW tried to settle the matter out of court, but could not reach agreement, so the case went to court.

On 15 August 1997 the judge found for HWM. Mr J not only lost his £20,000 deposit, interest on the deposit and HWM's loss of profit, he was also ordered to pay HWM's legal costs and court fees as well as his own. The precedent set here is that, in between the time of order and delivery, a manufacturer can change the specification of the car for any reason, whether it be legislation, development, changes of parts suppliers or whatever.

Misrepresentation

C.M. of Dover had a dispute with a Mercedes salesman over the paintwork of a secondhand 300TE he purchased in October 1992. No instance more perfectly confirms my advice to avoid litigation for damages over and above a reasonable settlement offered by a dealer.

C.M.'s case hinged on the salesman's description of the car as 'an original one-owner car which [his garage] had supplied new to that owner and serviced'. The car, new in 1990, had a lot of extras to justify the price of £22,950 – partly paid by a part exchange allowance of £10,995 for C.M.'s older 300TE. But the word 'original' was important to C.M. because the newer car was in a shade of solid red, the pigment of which is notoriously difficult to match.

After two years, C.M. noticed that the paint on the nearside front wing and door had 'bloomed' to a different colour from the rest of the car. It later transpired that, early in the car's life (at fourteen weeks old), the paintwork of those two panels had been damaged by a golf trolley and they had been resprayed by the selling garage at a cost of £213.47, which included replacing the grille.

In April 1995, the garage offered to 'cut back' the bloomed paint, but C.M. declined: He demanded that the garage either took the car back and refunded the original purchase price, supplied him with a better car, or paid him £5,000. This figure was based on a perceived 'trade guide' price difference between the two cars involved in the original transaction, plus £800 'damages'.

On getting no satisfaction, C.M. issued a County Court summons for £900, representing the difference in trade value between an 'original' 1990H 300TE and one with repaired damage. The case was heard by District Judge Morling in the Ashford County Court on 12 December 1996 (*Mulloy v Darren Dawkins*). The judge agreed that the car was not 'original' and should not have been described as such – particularly where the golf trolley damage had been repaired at an earlier date by the selling garage and the information was on its records. But, in finding for the plaintiff, the judge awarded a mere £500 in damages and costs on Scale 1. This left C.M. more than £5,000 out of pocket and, though he was able to recover part of this after a Taxation Hearing, his loss was still considerable.

So, though a case of 'misrepresentation' was proven against the salesman (and may set a precedent for other similar cases), C.M. has still lost out. It could be argued that, in the circumstances, C.M.'s claims were less than 'reasonable' and the system punished him for this. But as long as the costs of legal action in the UK can outweigh any benefit, even when a case is proven, private individuals are ill-advised to take a case such as this as far as C.M. did. Unless you have money to burn, it is especially ill-advised to pursue any matter through the courts on 'a matter of principle'.

Mercedes Benz UK has taken the view that the case should never have gone to court and, according to C.M., has written to the selling garage asking it to refund to C.M. the balance of his costs as a 'gesture of goodwill'. However, since C.M. has asked Mercedes Benz UK to review the franchises of both the selling agent and another MB franchise which the agent called in as an expert witness, 'goodwill' may be a little thin on the ground.

Falling out with a restorer

If you consign a car to a restorer and then fall out with him, the relevant precedent is *Peter Troy Davies v Anthony K. Divey* (Peterborough County Court).

Troy Davies claimed that in January 1994 he took out a contract with Anthony Divey who trades as Triking Cyclecars to restore his car for a price of £1,791. He then paid £2,000 in advance, and in June 1994 he paid a further £400 to Triking Cyclecars. The plaintiff relied upon the implied condition of the contract that work would be done using all reasonable care and skill and that parts supplied would be of merchantable quality. He claimed that the defendant had failed him in each case, enlisted the help of the legal department of *Which?*, and relied on an RAC report carried out five months after he had collected the car from Triking. The plaintiff had refused to have his vehicle inspected by the RAC before he removed it from Triking's premises. After collecting the car on 28 April 1995 the plaintiff had faxed and demanded a refund of £3,301.90 on 2 May 1995. The refund was to be paid by 9 May 1995, and he later increased his demand to £4,300.

He made a claim on 30 January 1996, and issued a summons on 16 February 1996. Triking filed its defence and counterclaim on 22 March 1996, but the plaintiff did not respond to this until 12 June 1996. Action commenced in the Hitchin County Court on 21 October 1996, and was later transferred to the Peterborough County Court, a transferral which the plaintiff had opposed. After various delays, the plaintiff presented his case, but was absent when District Judge Cernik heard the defendant's evidence on 12 August 1997.

The defendant's case was that there was never a written contract. He agreed he had collected the plaintiff's cyclecar in order to look it over and give the plaintiff a general idea of what could be done within the plaintiff's available budget. He then presented a fax sent to him by the plaintiff on 1 March 1994 listing a number of 'things to be done', which stated: 'Tony, if you can give me an idea of the cost of the above I will then know how much of my budget I will have left over to do the items below. As said on the phone, I am away from the end of March/April/ May and possibly June, so there is no rush to get the job done. I suggest you look at it as one of those jobs to be done when things are a bit slack … There is no rush for the job. I don't even care if you can't start on it till your six orders are complete.' The plaintiff's fax then went on to mention other jobs he would like doing, including a complete respray, a re-trim of the cockpit surround, the fitting of a removable head, some new side pipes and stainless steel silencers and two replacement rocker box covers. He paid the defendant £2,000 as an advance, but not on the basis of any quotation. After costing the work and making a number of adjustments to what the plaintiff had requested, the defendant had quoted that he could perform a number of tasks for a price of £2,450, as long as time was not of the essence.

A first attempt to respray the vehicle was unsuccessful, due to concealed accident damage which the defendant had not found on his first inspection.

The Judge declared himself satisfied that 'at no time did the defendant agree to undertake a complete restoration' and that the 'all-important fax of 1 March referring to things to be done and other jobs that he would like to do are entirely inconsistent with a complete refurbishment. … I formed a clear impression that the plaintiff was something of a perfectionist and found it less than agreeable to have anything to do with something that was in effect a compromise. … The notice that he gave by letter of 21 April 1995 to complete the job on 24 April 1995 was clearly unreasonable. … The plaintiff did not challenge the defendant's case that the defendant had wanted an independent expert called there and then (before the car was removed from his premises). … He then commissioned his report from the RAC on 8 September which was a good five months later.'

Working from a large number of photographs taken by the defendant during the restoration, the Judge decided that the vehicle inspected by the RAC was not the same vehicle presented by the plaintiff after restoration that May. Parts were missing and wear was in evidence that would not have been possible in the five months since the restoration, during which the plaintiff had anyway claimed he had been unable to use it. As a result the Judge stated, 'I frankly find it difficult to attribute any degree of reliance upon the remainder of the Plaintiff's evidence … I believe the Plaintiff got what he paid for. What the Plaintiff did after that in the presentation of this case suggests to me an attempt to distort the true facts and mislead the Court. ... I dismiss the Defendant's counterclaim, but the Plaintiff must pay the costs thrown away by the Defendant to include the hearing on 21 April ... a total of £495.'

This seems to represent a victory for restorers working to contracts where time is not of the essence and presented with dubious claims by their clients.

Falling out over a sale 'on consignment'

Case No 96BUS188 between Richard John Leeson and Classic Automobiles of London Ltd went to trial in the Central London County Court on 13 August 1997.

In R.L.'s words, 'I had known the defendant for many years and in 1996, over a very enjoyable lunch, I agreed to allow his firm to sell a recreated Bugatti Type 40 of mine, constructed from original parts, for a net return to me of £50,000. The verbal agreement we reached also allowed me to sell the car myself at no commission to his firm on the basis of "first past the post" and I informed the defendant that some interest had already been expressed as a result of an advertisement in the Bugatti Owners' Club newsletter. Within a few days I received a call from one of the defendant's salesmen that he had an offer of £30,000 plus an Austin Healey he considered to be worth at least £20,000. I turned down this offer which was followed by a revised offer of £40,000 which I also declined. By that time, a potential purchaser I had spoken to some time previously expressed a more serious interest in the car and wanted to fly out to the UK to view it. This he did, by arrangement with the defendant's firm, and on the day he made me a firm offer of £50,000. He then expressed his satisfaction with the deal to the defendant's sales manager, and we returned to my home in Surbiton to complete the sales agreement and receipt. Two days later, I spoke to the sales manager about the sale and he told me that the car had already been sold earlier on that day to a -purchaser who took out an option on it several weeks before and had now offered the full asking price. The case went to trial and when it was heard I was totally vindicated. But, unfortunately, it was not possible to "undo" the deal between the defendant's firm and the person to whom it sold my car, so my purchaser was disappointed.

Judgement was in favour of R.L., and Classic Automobiles of London Ltd was ordered to pay him £50,000, plus interest at £5,633.44, plus most of R.L.'s costs. What this case illustrates is the absolute necessity to put all such deals and any subsequent alterations in writing, so that any dispute can be easily resolved without the enormous cost of going to court (in this case estimated at more than £100,000).

My advice

The Retail Motor Industry runs a conciliation service for disputes between its members and used car buyers where the purchase was made less than 12 months previously. (It will not become involved in disputes over new cars.) The telephone number is 01788 538316/538317, but the RMI will only arbitrate where the dispute remains private, with no involvement of solicitors, Trading Standards officers, TV or the press. Alternatively you can discuss the matter with your local Trading Standards Office.

However, my advice is to think very carefully before you engage a solicitor and try to pursue the seller for costs over and above the amount you paid for the car. Where dealers agree to a refund, they are likely to stick their heels in over such costs. When a refund is agreed, a dealer will usually ask the recipient to sign a receipt stating that the refund is 'in full and final settlement', to preclude any further claims. This is often the best you are going to get.

If you fight the dealer for costs all the way to an Appeal Court hearing, not only may you lose the refund, you may find yourself landed with £10,000–£15,000 of court and solicitors fees – on top of a nerve-wracking delay before the Appeal hearing.

Ridiculous complaints

Now and again, 'chancers' send me ridiculous complaints in the hope of trying to blackmail manufacturers into paying large amounts of money as 'compensation'. One missive came from a Bath reader who personally imported a

BMW 3-Series during the first half of 1991. It is true that early-production E36 3-Series did suffer from a few quality problems, mainly confined to cabin fit and finish, but to demand financial compensation from the manufacturer seven years after purchase seems a bit rich to me – particularly since, having purchased his 'H'-registered car in the first half of 1991, he did not take it in for its first service until May 1993. In failing to have his car serviced on time, he threw away any legal or moral right he may ever have had against the supplier. In UK law (Sale of Goods Act 1979 and Sale and Supply of Goods Act 1994), responsibility for the goods being of 'merchantable' quality, modified by the later act to 'satisfactory' quality, rests with the supplier, not the manufacturer. If you personally import a car and it develops faults outside the terms of the manufacturer's warranty which are partly of your own making, you're on your own, chum.

Nice work if you can get it

" *Further to a 'Street Legal' article by Fenton Bresler, headed 'Rich Rewards for the Cowboy Clampers', I wonder if my own experience and the release fee demanded sets any records. Several times a month I import cargoes of computers via Air France cargo handling at Heathrow. I recently left my estate car in the vehicle park at Shoreham Road, which I have done many times before over the past two years, in order to collect a shipment weighing 155 kilograms. At precisely the time my collection note was being stamped, my car was clamped by BAA's contractor, London Borough Controlled Parking Ltd, and I had to pay a release fee of £85. Since I could not possibly carry 155 kilos of computer equipment to my car parked in one of the public car parks, I have now had to transfer my inwards shipping business to an organisation which has designated parking and is outside the area covered by BAA.* "

I can beat it myself. In January 1998 I paid an employee of a security company £100 cash to release two friends' cars which had been clamped in Claygate Station car park at 10.30 at night. (Though I have warned readers to keep their eyes peeled for clamping notices at stations, it was a rainy night and the rain had washed away the times between which the parking fees applied.) The chap came out promptly to release the cars, and I just happened to have £100 in notes about my person, so, after a little argument, I coughed up, thinking that after I took photographs of the inadequate sign as proof I'd get the money back from the security company. No way, even after protracted correspondence. So I sent a photograph to South West Trains and received my money back by return of post.

Duff turbo

" *I have a 1995 'M'-registered VW Golf TDI, owned by me since new and maintained by a VW agent in accordance with the manufacturer's recommendations. A week before the 50,000 mile service I noticed excessive smoke from the exhaust, and the cause was diagnosed as a faulty turbocharger. I was quoted £848.35 for a replacement turbo. I contacted VW Customer Care and was offered free fitting as an act of goodwill. Do you think this is reasonable, bearing in mind that the total cost to me will be almost a thousand pounds including the cost of hiring a car? The main reason why I chose a VW vehicle in the first place was the company's reputation for producing reliable and economical cars. At this rate, I'll have spent the equivalent of the next ten years' servicing charges.* "

Turbo bearings and oil seals do go, mainly due to 'coking' of the oil. In my view, the stipulated 10,000-mile oil change intervals for the TDI engine are inadequate. Though a direct injected diesel is 'kinder' to its oil than indirect injection, 10,000 miles is far too long to leave any oil in any car engine and it should be changed at least every 5,000 miles or six months, whichever comes first. Irv Gordon of New York has set a new world record for mileage of 1,636,341 miles in his 1966 Volvo P1800, but, like all owners who really want their cars to last, he changes his oil every 3,000 miles.

Rover to the rescue

" *My 16,000-mile February-1996 Rover 216SLi would not start. I called the AA, who came in 15 minutes and then spent an hour on the car in heavy rain. The patrolman thought that the main computer was down, could not fix it, and towed me to a Rover agent which confirmed that the ECU was down: £516 please. I was given a Freefone number for Rover Customer Care which paid the full bill without quibble. Well done, Rover. Much appreciated.* "

And, of course, when you are due for a change, you'll be back for another Rover. I've received several highly complimentary stories about Rover's recovery service and had two favourable experiences myself.

Rental management

" *As one whose salary is paid by the taxpayer I feel obliged to 'buy British' as much as possible, even if that does mean buying cars made in Britain by foreign manufacturers. I have bought two nearly-new Rovers from the same Salisbury agent and purchased my third in February this year. I paid £14,250 for an 8,500-mile Rover 416SLi automatic described to me as 'ex-Rover management'. I did not see the V5 before buying it, because the deal included a year's VED and the agent saw to this on my behalf. Only when the V5 came back from the DVLA did I discover that the previous registered keeper had been Avis. Avis has confirmed to me that the car had been on its daily rental fleet. How would you regard this car now? Apart from the dishonesty of the Rover agent, would your valuation be any lower in the knowledge it had been a daily rental car? And if so, by how much? Would you expect me to have any greater difficulty selling it with Avis as the first registered keeper?* **"**

I have previously advised readers to assume that any car described by a dealer as 'ex-management' to be ex-rental unless offered concrete proof to the contrary. Nevertheless, if the car was described to you as 'ex-Rover Management' – and you can prove this – you were clearly misled and what you were told would amount to a false trade description. In any case, the price you paid was £2,000 more than the car was worth. In Spring 1999, Trade Sales of Slough were offering new 'T'-reg. Rover 416SLi automatics for £10,299. Speak to your local Trading Standards Office and see what back-up you can get in demanding a £2,000 refund.

'Clocking' switch

" *I recently took a longish taxi journey in a VW Sharan. The chatty driver proudly showed me a new dashboard switch he had wired in to disconnect the electronic speedometer and odometer. He said he used it 'about half the time' to 'prove' lower income-earning miles than he had really covered in case the Inland Revenue queried his tax return. Obviously, on resale, the lower mileage would also get him a higher resale price. Apparently the switch and wiring can be removed leaving no visible trace.* **"**

This is a high-tech version of 'unhooking' (disconnecting the speedo cable) and is one of the reasons why the trade downvalues well-used privately-owned cars with suspiciously low mileages. It's also why the trade favours ex-lease cars which have been on full maintenance contracts and come with computer print-outs of their entire maintenance histories. Careful scrutiny of these (looking for tyre replacements every 5,000 miles, for example) will soon reveal if the car has been 'run unhooked'.

Stupid boy

" *I have been rather stupid. I so much wanted a car of my own that I paid a £100 deposit on a 'W'-reg. Escort XR3i which was then delivered to me. It is not taxed and I can't drive it as I have not passed my test yet. I'm 17. My dad was furious when he found out and demanded the keys so that he could return it to the dealer. However, the dealer had abandoned his site and was trading under a company name anyway, so I don't know how to contact him. Now I'm stuck with a car I don't want and I don't even know if I'm the owner. My dad does not think it is roadworthy and wants to take it to the scrapyard. However, the dealer did not give me any papers at all. Help? What can I do?* "

First, lift the flap in the carpet between the front seat and the door sill to see if the VIN number stamped in the floorpan has been tampered with. If it has, and the VIN plate on the bonnet slam panel appears to have been altered or badly pop-riveted on, inform the police. If not, phone 01722 422422 with a credit card handy and spend £32 on an HPI check. If the car comes up clean, use Form V62 (from post offices) to apply for a vehicle registration document for the car in your own name, and also phone the DVLA Customer Enquiry Unit on 01792 772134 for a V890 which you need to make a Statutory Off Road Notification. (If the car is standing un-taxed, and uninsured with no MOT on a public road, an offence is already being committed.) Once you have done all this and received a V5, you can arrange to sell the car or have it scrapped. But be aware that if there is still some-thing fishy about the car, your application for a

V5 may lead to the DVLA alerting the local police stolen vehicle squad and you may lose both the car and your £32. If you have the name of the company the dealer was trading under, give it to the police and they will make a company search to get the registered addresses of the company and of its directors.

Piggy in the middle

A reader from Hull bought a new Citroën in 1996. To protect himself, he took out a three-year MBI warranty sold to him by the Citroën agent. In August 1998, having had the car overnight, the Citroën agent noticed a knock when the engine was cold-started. The engine was dismantled, whereupon the warranty underwriters had it inspected and diagnosed a manufacturing fault. Because this was present before the warranty was taken out, they refused the claim. Citroën was then asked to step in, and provided a new set of pistons and associated parts free of charge, but the car's owner was asked to pay half the total cost of the repair. Since he had taken out the warranty specifically to avoid this sort of expense he felt hard-done-by, and I agreed with him. I put his case to Citroën UK and, though it was really down to the Citroën agent for selling a mis-matched car and warranty in the first place, Citroën UK agreed to meet the repair bill in full.

Fit for the job

" *I am a freelance lighting cameraman. In the course of my work I have to travel all over the country and arrive at specific locations at specific times without fail or my non-presence delays the shoot at vast expense to the production company. Attracted by its capacity for equipment and the fact that its 10,000-mile servicing intervals would mean less time off the road, I purchased a VW Sharan in April 1997. Since then, due to various problems with the vehicle, it has been unavailable for my use on no less than ten occasions. I have sought to reject the vehicle with no success, and have also asked for compensation but have been offered nothing more than a £100 accessory voucher. What can I do, or what should I have done?* "

There isn't much you can do at this late stage. But next time you or any other reader buys a vehicle for a specific purpose, you should enter this on the purchase contract. In your case you should use words along these lines: 'Vehicle purchased specifically to transport the equipment of a lighting cameraman. Must be 100 per cent reliable and must be available for work 24 hours a day seven days a week apart from during standard garage servicing.' You are then protected not only by the Sale & Supply of Goods Act 1994 regarding satisfactory 'fitness for purpose', but also by standard Contract Law. This is not too onerous on the dealer because it merely obliges him to keep you mobile by means of loan vehicles and it gives you the protection you need.

Slower than you think

" *I purchased a Renault Scenic three months ago and found that the first long journey I made was about eight miles further than it had been in my previous car. I then checked the speedometer and calculated that it over-read by about 5 per cent. Renault contends that there is a legal tolerance of 10 per cent on these instruments. What I would like to know is: (a) where is the legal requirement covering this laid down? (b) If there is a 10 per cent error, would a warranty be honoured if servicing took place every 11,000 miles rather than every 10,000 miles? (c) If there is a 10 per cent error, can the car legally be clocked back by 10,000 miles when the recorded mileage is 100,000 miles? (d) What is the position on speeding offences when there is a 10 per cent error?* "

(a) Reg. 35 Road Vehicles (Construction and Use) Regulations 1986, plus EC Regulation (Community Directive) 97/39 and ECE Regulation 39, both of which refer to 75/443/EEC. A speedometer may not under-read, and at between 40 kph and 120 kph it may not over-read by more than 10 per cent + 4 kph (10 per cent + 2.5 mph); for example, it must not read more than 79.5 mph when the car is doing a true 70 mph. (b) Anyone who stretches oil changes to 10,000 indicated miles is asking for trouble anyway. (c) Clocking isn't illegal; only selling a clocked car is. (d) The police usually allow 10 per cent + 2.5 mph over the limit anyway, even though speedos are not legally allowed to under-read. Anyone who wants to be clear on motoring law should obtain a copy of *Hughes Guide To Traffic Law For the Enforcement Officer* from Motorvation Consultants on 01908 676008. This loose-leaf book is updated every six months.

Free masochist with every inspection

" *Over the years, whenever I buy a second-hand car, I have found it sensible to make any such purchase subject to a satisfactory AA report. At the moment I am contemplating the purchase of a 1995 VW Polo 1.4CL from a VW agent. I contacted the AA and arranged for an inspection of the car at the agent's premises. The morning of the inspection was bitterly cold and it was raining quite heavily yet, despite the weather, the AA inspector proceeded to carry out his inspection in the open in the car park. The agent told me he was happy to provide inspectors with the usual workshop facilities, including hydraulic ramps. Yet, despite the conditions, this AA engineer made no such request and proceeded outdoors, in poor light, using a trolley jack. The cost of the report was £140, including hire purchase and security checks. I do not accept that, by carrying out his inspection in the manner he did, the AA inspector acted in my best interests. I have informed the AA that I am not prepared to pay the full £140 for the*

report, but the AA does not accept my argument and unless I can prove that the engineer missed a defect the full £140 must be paid. What do you think? **"**

Pay the £140. The AA inspector may have felt he would have been compromised if he used the selling agent's equipment. And the AA's point is fair enough. You had the inspection to avoid defects. If you can prove that the inspector missed a defect, the AA will consider a refund. If you can't, there aren't any grounds for one.

Two-car Fiesta

" *We purchased a Ford Fiesta from a dealer on 18 March 1998. Six months later, when the MOT was becoming due, we were told by our mechanic that he thought it was two cars. We returned it to the dealer who had it repaired by a garage. Then, on 12 September 1998, it failed the*

MOT. We returned the car to the dealer, who had it repaired again, but the MOT station would still not pass the floor as up to the MOT standard. We then did an HPI check and discovered that the car had been an insurance damage write-off in September 1995. The dealer still refused to refund our money. We had an RAC check done on 22 October 1998, were told that the car was probably made up of three cars, and that it should not be driven on public roads. We sent a letter as dictated by a solicitor to the dealer on 14 November, giving him 14 days to refund our money, but he refused. We issued a summons on 27 November, but the dealer refuted all the claims. We are now waiting to go to court. We do not qualify for legal aid, but neither can we afford £130 an hour for a solicitor. All the official bodies we have contacted are not interested. The police will not help. Trading Standards will not help. Neither will the DVLC or the Vehicle Inspectorate. Do you know of any law or organisation that would be on our side?"

No. Presumably this has become a County Court case and, on the facts you have presented in your letter, you should stand a good chance of winning the case after presenting it yourself. Prepare a short summary, and have with you all the documentary evidence in chronological order. (You will be required to photocopy all of it for the defendant's solicitors.) The Police and Trading Standards have not become involved because they do not consider that you can provide adequate proof that a criminal offence has been committed by the dealer. It is not a criminal offence to sell a car made out of two cars; it is only a criminal offence to sell an unroadworthy car, and, due to the passage of time, you cannot prove that the car was unroadworthy on the day of sale. The lessons to be learned from this are: check the history of the car *before* you buy (HPI: 01722 422422; AA/Experian: 0800 234999; ABS: 0800 3895169) and have the car inspected (AA: 0345 500610; ABS: 0345 419926; RAC: 0800 333660; AAA Motor Vehicle Inspections, London area only: 0705 0158123; Autocheck GB

Ltd: 0181 678 7060; D S Crawford, Central Scotland only: 0131 453 4393.)

Rejection accepted

" *In January I took delivery of a new-shape Astravan 2.0 litre direct injected diesel. After 200 miles it became clear that the turbo was throwing out oil. The dealer had one unsuccessful attempt at fixing it and I then rejected the van on the ground that it was faulty on delivery. The Vauxhall agent, Burton of Bridgend (01656 648648), promptly loaned me a hire car while it fitted a new turbo to the van, then let me continue to use the rejected van until a brand new replacement arrived. How's that for service? I should add that, apart from this bit of teething trouble, the vehicle is excellent.* "

Top marks to Burton of Bridgend, which was under no legal obligation to keep you on the road while you waited for the replacement vehicle.

Mileage enquiries

" *On 2 January 1998 I bought a second-hand Renault 5 from a dealer I trusted in Worthing. The car had first been registered in November 1995 and was sold with a mileage reading of 15,568. Recently, I decided I really needed a car with power steering, so I part-exchanged the Renault 5 for a new 'T'-reg. Ford Ka on 1 March. I can't remember what the mileage was at the time, but I know it was at least 20,000 and at most 26,000. This morning I received a document from 'The National Mileage Register' run by Equifax plc asking: Date purchased? Mileage on purchase? Who I purchased it from? Date sold? Mileage when sold? And who sold to? The date and mileage questions give a choice of four tick-boxes: Exact, Approximate, Very Approximate and Not Known. The document also asks if, to my knowledge, the vehicle ever had a speedometer change. I am very worried to receive such a form. I do not believe that my car has been chosen in some sort of random check and wonder if it has been 'clocked' before I bought it.* "

Nothing to worry about. This is a standard procedure to establish a register of mileages on disposal and help to prevent inter-sale 'clocking'. If any reader receives a similar form, either from Equifax, Experian or VMC (Vehicle Mileage Check), you should answer it to the best of your knowledge and send it straight back. The new V5 vehicle registration document now has two places for entering mileages on transfer, one in the red tear-off section for when the vehicle is transferred to a trader, and the other in the main blue section. The more of us enter mileages on these forms the less likely we all are to have our legs lifted with clocked cars.

Misdescribed

" As a member of the RAC for more than 30 years I sought their advice over the purchase of a 'grey' import being offered by a Kent dealer. This was described in the dealer's Internet advertisement as a 1995 Honda Prelude. On receipt of a favourable report from the RAC, for which I paid the premium price of £265 because it is an 'imported vehicle', I purchased it on 25 September last year for the sum of £12,000. I have now been informed by Kent police that the vehicle has been misrepresented to the DVLA and is actually a 1991 model, a fact which could easily have been determined by checking the engine number and VIN number with the manufacturer, or the date stamps on the vehicle's plastics. The vehicle is now unsaleable and I estimate my loss to be £6,000. The RAC Customer Relations department refuses to comment on the basis that it is too closely involved, but states that pressure of work precluded any check other than the standard HPI check and that the condition of the vehicle was such that it was not possible to distinguish between a 1995 and a 1991 model. "

In UK law, civil and criminal liability for the misdescription rests at the doors of the dealer who sold you the car. Do you have a print-out of the description from the website, tying it to the dealer? Was it described as a 1995 car on the invoice? If so, the TSO for the area where the dealer is located will help you take appropriate action against him. But shame on the RAC. What's the point of its clients paying extra for a special check on an imported vehicle if it does nothing to verify the date of manufacture? If the dealer hitches up his caravan and disappears, then I think you may have a strong case against the RAC for recovery of the difference in value between a 1991 Prelude and a 1995, which I estimate to be at least £3,500.

Changing the clock

" *I recently bought a used 1998 Ford Mondeo LX from a branch of a well known chain of garages. The mileage on the odometer said 1,297, and when I queried such a low figure the salesman assured me that they frequently had cars in with very low mileages. However, when the invoice and warranty arrived, they both showed a mileage of 11,479. In answer to my query about this, the sales manager said that the speedometer had been changed by the previous owner and that he would obtain and let me have a letter to that effect. So far, I have not received this.* "

It is a criminal offence to sell a car that has covered a higher mileage than indicated by the odometer unless the purchaser is specifically warned at the time that the mileage on the odometer is incorrect. Even then, a dealer is supposed to show 'due diligence' in checking the mileage with previous keepers, and odometers often carry a sticker informing prospective purchasers that these checks are in the process of being made. But, since your car must have been driven between the original speedometer failing and the new one being installed, it is impossible to determine accurately the true mileage the car has travelled. If you can prove what you have written, then there is a case to be made that the salesman committed a criminal offence and you should speak to the Trading Standards Office which covers the locality of the garage.

LIGHTS

Brakelight dazzle

" *I have read your comments over many months about inconsiderate drivers of automatics who sit in traffic queues with their foot on the footbrake dazzling the drivers behind them with their high-level brakelights. The glare in the eyes of the driver behind is unacceptable, especially at night. It is sloppy driving and should be actively discouraged. But what is the special feature of Vauxhall's new automatic gearbox, as fitted to the new Astra and the latest Vectra? It is a device that automatically selects neutral when the driver sits stationary in traffic in 'D' with his foot on the footbrake. (The transmission automatically re-engages 'Drive' when the foot is removed.) So, rather than discouraging drivers from sitting on the brakes and blinding the drivers behind (an offence under the RVLR 1989), Vauxhall is actually encouraging this sloppy and dangerous practice. Or had Vauxhall not realised the problem it was causing?* "

Probably they did not realise, just as Volvo failed to take account of slow-moving traffic queues when it first adopted high-intensity high-level brakelights on the 740/760 range. The good news is that the Astra automatic can easily be driven properly in traffic. Though you must put your foot on the brake to get it out of 'Park', it's easy to slip the lever into 'N' in traffic and, unlike VAG cars, you do not have to touch the brakes to get it back into 'D'. The best advice I can give if you find yourself behind a slob whose brakelights are detaching your retinas is to pull down the sun-visor, or hold your hand up between your eyes and the source of the glare. Do not sound your horn while stationary or flash the driver with your own lights, as these are both offences.

Light signals

" As a Canadian now resident in the UK, I find two British driving idiosyncrasies particularly confusing and annoying. One is the habit of 'flashing' other drivers. The other is when traffic on the motorway slows suddenly from high speed to a crawl, many drivers instinctively turn on their hazard warning lights. I'd be interested in both your opinion and the legal position. "

First, go out and buy yourself a copy of the *Highway Code*, available from any bookshop for £1.49. The current advice (Rules 90 and 91) is that you should flash your headlights only to let another road user know you are there. If another driver flashes his headlights, never assume it is a signal to go. Use your own judgement and proceed carefully. This clarifies the legal position because, if you act on the headlamp signal, or any other signal of another driver, the consequences are your responsibility, not those of the signalling driver. The trouble is, flashing your headlights is often the *only* way you can signal to another driver to proceed. Tinted windows, distance and ambient light all conspire against the other driver being able to see any hand signal you might try to make. Drivers use hazard warning lights to try to prevent themselves from being rear-ended when motorway traffic suddenly slows down. There is so much red light pollution on British roads that it is sometimes impossible to tell if brake lights ahead merely mean vehicles are travelling too close, are switching off their cruise controls or are stopping. If you are the last vehicle approaching a stoppage, you should brake, put your hazards on, keep your foot on the brake, leave plenty of room in front of you and watch your mirrors like a hawk so that if the vehicle behind appears not to be stopping you can give it more stopping distance by moving into the clear space in front of you. The same applies if yours is the last vehicle approaching a hazard after a blind bend.

Foggy thinking

" *Those of us who can remember London's 'pea-soupers' can recall that car foglamps were set deliberately low to enable the driver to see kerbs etc. beneath the level of the fog. Drivers nowadays seem to use them willy nilly in clear conditions, randomly blinding oncoming drivers, cyclists and pedestrians. Has the law changed?* "

No. It's all there in black and white in rules 94 and 95 of the new 'Highway Code'. These state, 'Use fog lights when visibility is seriously reduced, generally to less than 100 metres (328 feet). You MUST NOT use fog front or rear lights unless visibility is seriously reduced.' Under the Road Vehicle Lighting Regulations 1989 RVLR No. 27 (also in the 'Highway Code') it is an offence to use fog lights at front or rear unless visibility is seriously reduced. Fog lights must be fitted with their centres 24 inches from the ground or lower and may work independently of the headlights, in which case they must be fitted with a warning light. Fog lights must be a maximum distance of 16 inches from the sides of the car and a minimum distance of 14 inches apart. Driving lights (not fog lights) may be fitted with their centres less than 48 inches from the ground but must be wired through the headlights so that they extinguish on dipped main beam. No light on a car may be used in such a way that it causes undue dazzle or discomfort to other drivers and this, of course, includes high-level brake lights. The offence codes are CU 20, which carries three penalty points, and CU 60, which doesn't.

'Lighting-down' time

" I entirely agree with your and your readers' views on red light pollution caused by the excessive use of brakes on cars with high-level high-intensity brake lights. But what about headlamp pollution, especially from 'gas discharge' and Xenon bulbs? The brightness of these lights is a real menace, either from oncoming cars on motorways, or from those coming up behind you to overtake where the dipped beam shines straight into your mirrors. "

There is a solution to this, which I discovered when the lights of a Ford Cougar I was driving seemed to be bothering other drivers. Find the dashboard control which lowers the beams and turn them down. On busy motorways you have your night vision and the lights of other vehicles to see by, so turning down the beams does not reduce your vision. Using this control to set beams to their lowest level (level 4) can also be enough not to dazzle oncoming motorists while driving on the right-hand side of the road on the continent. Considerate Volvo drivers should also beam down their 'daytime running lights'.

MAINTENANCE

How often?

" *I recently purchased a Honda Civic Aerodeck 1.5LS VTEC-E. During the purchase, the local dealer advised servicing on a 6,000-mile or annual basis. In the service record, which I have now read, Honda quite clearly base the servicing requirements on a 9,000-mile or annual interval. Please, which is correct? I am sure you will understand that I don't want to spend more than is necessary, but nor do I want to undermine the warranty and I would appreciate your independent advice.* "

I must have issued this advice several thousand times. Now I'm going to issue it yet again. If you want your engine to last and also want to minimise problems (*particularly* if you are a very-low-mileage driver), then you should have the oil and filter changed at least every six months. Because this job is done on a ramp, it also gives the mechanic a chance to give the underside of the car a 'once over' and spot a problem, such as a near-severed brake pipe, that might be about to kill you.

Home-maintenance Merc

" *My son-in-law has thoughtfully bought my daughter a 1973 LHD automatic Mercedes 350SL for her 40th birthday. As the engineer of the family I shall be expected to learn everything about it and to advise and perhaps even work on it. Is there a Haynes manual available for it, and an owners club that we can join to get a quick boost of information?* **"**

Yes, there is a Haynes manual for American 350 and 450 SLs and SLCs from 1971–1980, price £11.96 + P&P, ref HO698, from Delta Press on 01442 877794 or Mill House Books on 01205 270377. The club is The Mercedes Benz Club, Brightstone, Over Old Road, Harbury, Glos GL19 3BJ, tel: 0707 1818868.

Taking a dip

" *What is the correct procedure for checking a car's engine oil level with the dipstick? With 40 years of motoring under my wheels I say: level surface, hot engine, switch off, leave for two to three minutes, then dip. My son, who knows more about cars than I ever will, says: level surface, cold engine, dip. He is supported by all the mechanics and engineers at my esteemed local garage. The handbook for my VW Vento implies that one can dip a hot engine.* **"**

To be absolutely accurate, your son and the mechanics are correct, because when the engine is cold, some of the circulating oil will have drained back to the sump. When dipping a cold engine you don't need to wipe the dipstick before taking a reading. If you want to dip a car when hot, you must leave it for at least a couple of minutes to allow surplus oil to drain back and you must wipe the dipstick before using it to take a reading. If the dipstick comes out way over the maximum level, oil has not drained back from the dipstick tube and is giving a false reading. You also need to be 100 per cent sure that the collar on the dipstick has not slipped, otherwise you will get a false reading.

100,000-mile servicing?

" I understand that cars are now being offered with longer intervals between oil services. However, I was taken aback to read that the Cadillac Seville STS can travel 100,000 miles without needing a service. Does that mean without even an oil change? If so, what sort of oil can protect an engine for that distance? "

The 100,000-mile interval is for a full service. By fitting a large and efficient filtration system, by sealing the transmission and by using advanced synthetic automatic transmission fluid which is not subject to the sort of contamination faced by engine oil, the ATF apparently lasts the life of the car. However, because engine oil is contaminated by heat and condensation, this does need to be changed when the car's diagnostic systems judges that it has deteriorated significantly, probably every 7,500 miles or so. It's impossible to give exact mileages for Cadillac oil changes because the deterioration of the oil will depend on how the car has been used rather than how far it has been driven.

First service

" I have just bought a new Renault Clio 1.4RT. The dealer enthused about how it needs a minor service only once a year and a major service every two years. I remarked that nevertheless I would be bringing the car in for its early 1,000-mile service involving a change of oil and a check-up, but the dealer told me this was no longer necessary. Can this be true? My use of the car will be a mixture of local trips and longer distances at higher speeds. "

The latest thinking is to run the engine on the factory running-in oil for the first year or 10,000 miles, in order to promote some wear and loosen the engine up. After that, whatever the manufacturer says, I still recommend at least two oil changes a year, before and after the winter, whether you do 2,000 miles or 20,000 miles a year.

Engine treatment ruins engine

" *I had been running a Fiesta with the 1.1 litre ohv Valencia engine for five years with no problems. But a 'friction-free' P.T.F.E. oil additive put an end to all this. Neat oil pumped to the exhaust, the plugs oiled up and the tappets needed adjusting almost weekly. I took the head off and found neat oil on top of the pistons, a build-up of solid P.T.F.E. on the exhaust valve seats, pushrods and all reciprocating parts built up with deposits of P.T.F.E. The piston ring oil scraper grooves and ring grooves were also heavily deposited. A set of new rings, valve stem oil seals and big end bolts has returned the car to its previous condition and it no longer uses any oil.* "

So much for 'miracle treatments'. But you don't say if the additive was added immediately after an oil and filter change, which may have made a significant difference.

Repair and servicing costs

" *I thought you might be interested in the repair and servicing costs of my modest Renault Clio 1,171 cc over 108,000 miles from September 1992 until September 1998. Repairs and replacements have totalled £1,851, including: 1 ECU at £586; 1 catalytic converter at £300; suspension arm bushes at £200; wheel bearings at £180; 5 tyres at £163; brake discs and pads at £125; 1 heater motor at £100; 2 exhausts at £78; 1 water pipe (and associated fittings) at £68; 1 clutch cable at £30 and 1 wheel trim at £21. Total servicing came to £1,592, including a cambelt change at 78,000 miles. Four MOT tests cost £108. So the total cost was £3,551. The engine has never used any oil between oil changes, but the clutch is now starting to slip. I estimate that depreciation over the six years has amounted to £5,000.* "

That's less than 8p a mile, excluding insurance, VED and petrol. But it's interesting that, without the ECU and cat failures, the figure would have worked out at just over 7p a mile. So in addition to the extra fuel used, these devices designed to help the environment have cost you 1p a mile.

British is best

" *You printed a letter in your column about the servicing and repair costs of a Renault Clio 1.1 over 108,000 miles (see above). I thought you might be interested in the costs for my rather larger 1990 Montego 1.6LX. It was bought second-hand in 1993 at 15,000 miles, has now covered 100,000 miles, and the cost of all servicing, MOTs, repairs and replacements has totalled £1,872. No oil is used between changes, engine and clutch are original and showing no signs of trouble, and the car has never failed to start. With total depreciation estimated at £3,000, the cost of 6.82 p a mile is what I would call cheap for reliable transport.* "

Not bad at all for a car that originally cost just £4,000.

Rubbed up the wrong way

" *My son's 1990 Cavalier 1.6 recently suffered a minor wiring short which resulted in some of the loom being burned. Fortunately, switching off the ignition stopped the short and extensive damage was avoided, but neither his insurers nor Vauxhall are prepared to foot the bill for the damage. Our local Vauxhall agent feels sure the problem was caused by the four-cable loom to the coil amplifier chafing against the battery tray. The black feed cable is not fused, and the loom of cables is not adequately protected by corrugated tubing as it is on the Vectra, so a short could result in a serious engine compartment fire. Please bring this to your readers attention.* "

This is a good general warning to bear in mind during any regular underbonnet inspection. As cars get older, and engine mountings softer, cables which may not have chafed earlier in the

car's life may begin to do so. Any sign of any such wear should set the alarm bells ringing because, as this reader points out, the cable which is losing its insulation through chafing may not itself be fused.

Spend and save

" *I am writing to thank you for your tips on engine maintenance that have enabled us to achieve an excellent improvement in fuel economy. In March I purchased a 2.0 litre 8v Cavalier automatic which, at the time, averaged 28 mpg. As a result of regular 3,000-mile oil changes, using semi or fully synthetic oil, running the car exclusively on Texaco CleanSystem 3, changing the spark plugs to NGK and fitting Continental Ecocontact tyres, the car now averages 38 mpg. Apart from the tyres, which needed replacing anyway, our outlay in implementing your tips has been approximately £70 and our saving to date has been £150, so we are already £80 in pocket.* "

38 mpg is very good for a Cavalier 2.0 automatic, despite its 'overdrive' 4th gear; 28 mpg is not good in trunk road and motorway use. Though an improvement of 2 mpg could be explained by higher ambient temperatures during the summer months, I have no doubt that the rest of the improvement is entirely down to the oil, fuel, spark plugs and tyres.

ASSYST-ance required

" *In June, I purchased a nearly-new Mercedes C250TD with the 'ASSYST' service interval display. Being a retired engineer brought up to change oils more frequently than manufacturer recommendations, even now I use a fully synthetic (Mobil 1 diesel), I have difficulty coming to terms with ASSYST currently telling me that the first service and oil change will be due at 13,300 miles. I have asked a number of different Mercedes sources how the ASSYST system calculates service intervals, ranging from photo cells across the sump to a system measuring the moisture content of the oil. Could you tell me what information is collected?* "

The ASSYST sensors measure oil level, oil temperature (including total time it remains below normal running parameters), coolant temperature (including total time below running temperature), engine speed, road speed, and load on the engine. From this information, the computer works out when the next service will be due. The more time the engine spends running cold, and the more time it spends under load, the shorter the service interval in terms of miles. So, in theory, a life of short runs from cold starts could bring service intervals down to 4,000 miles, while a life mostly running at normal temperature between 2,500 and 3,000 rpm could take service intervals up to 20,000 miles. If you don't want to take the ASSYST's word for it, intermediate oil changes can do nothing but good.

BMW service indicators

" *You answered a question as to what criteria are used by the Mercedes Benz 'ASSYST' service indicator. Could you tell me what system BMWs use? I have just bought a new BMW 735i and the answers I have been getting vary considerably.* "

The service indicators of BMWs prior to the 1997 model year calculated the need for services on the basis of engine time running, mileage and oil temperature. More time running at low oil temperature indicates more short runs from cold starts and hence the need for more frequent oil changes. From the 1997 model year the system computes the need for services on the basis of fuel consumption linked to a calendar. Since a car uses the most fuel on short runs from cold starts, when towing, and at extremely high speed, this simpler system does pretty much the same job, while the calendar calculates the need for time-based replacements such as coolant and brake fluid. Obviously the calendar chip is Millennium-bug-proof.

Soaring cost of service

" *I am the happy owner of a Toyota Soarer 4.0GT coupe which I have owned for two years. It is an excellent car and my second. Because the model is not imported into the UK by Toyota (GB) Ltd, both were personal imports, but, until recently, both were serviced by a Lexus agent. Now I am told that the Lexus agent can no longer service my car for insurance reasons. Is this a genuine problem, or is it part of a move to discourage individual imports direct from Japan? I am now looking for a convenient garage with the expertise to service my car.* "

There is a problem of liability insurance for an official Lexus agent, whose standard insurance covers it for its work on standard UK-supplied cars and is backed up by the UK company. But to cover itself to work on unofficial imports it would need to take out additional insurance, and if it doesn't service many of these cars this may not be cost-effective. Of course, this is also part of a move to discourage individual imports direct from Japan. But all is far from lost. Intech has set up a chain of garages throughout the country to service Japanese personal imports such as your Soarer. For details of the specialists nearest to you, tel: 01264 773888. An alternative supplier to Toyota (GB) for some parts is API, tel: 0500 830530.

'Hotstarter' for Saab

" I have recently purchased a Saab 9000 in excellent condition and am endeavouring to make sure that it stays that way. I am proposing to install a Kenlowe 'Hotstart' to eliminate much of the wear associated with cold starts, so I called Saab's technical helpline about this. I was amazed and disappointed to find myself speaking to a surly and totally unhelpful fellow. Apart from giving a curt comment that Saab have their own engine pre-heaters (not mentioned in any of the information I have seen) he was not the slightest bit interested. "

He is probably not allowed to be, because the manufacturer's liability insurance does not cover Saab for any advice given about non-Saab parts. Saab does offer its own engine preheaters in Scandinavia. I once attended a Saab lecture promoting them. I was told that if you are in a car park in Sweden in winter you can even plug your preheater to a power point in the parking bay to provide heat inside the car, or to keep the engine warm for when you wish to leave. Speak to the parts manager at your local Saab agent. (Non-Saab owners, contact Kenlowe on 01628 823303.)

'Man and machine in perfect harmony'

" *I have a 1990 Ford Sierra GLS which has now done 166,000 miles. Nothing remarkable in that, you may think. But it is still on its original exhaust system and there is no rust on the car anywhere. It uses no oil, but my one-man old-fashioned garage engineer has always fed it on synthetic oil. When we lifted the camshaft cover to replace the gasket, everything underneath looked new, with no signs of any black sludge nor gunge of any kind. Just goes to show what a bit of TLC can do.* "

Too right. There's also quite a healthy market for late, pre-cat 2.0 litre Sierras which are still in good shape.

Well oiled

" *The driver's handbook of my Ford Puma 1.7 specifies Ford Motorcraft 5W/30 engine oil, or an equivalent oil which meets the requirements of ACECA A1-96, B1-96 and Ford Specification WSS-M2C912. The handbook adds, 'If you are unable to meet these recommended oils, you must use SAE 10W/30, 10W/40 or 5W/40 API SH (Energy Conserving) oils... Use of these oils may result in reduced fuel economy and emissions.' Since the Puma 1.7 has a high-performance engine, the blocks of which are sent to Japan so that Yamaha can apply a special lining to the bores, I expected the servicing Ford agent to use the 5W/30 oil specified by Ford. Instead, I found that the garage had used the same 'top grade' oil it keeps in its bulk tanks and uses for servicing all Ford cars. I later discovered that this oil is SAE 10W/30, that 5W/30 is more expensive, and for that reason most owners are happy with 10W/30. Ford engineers tell me that 5W/30 is the recommended oil because it lubricates the engine faster during a cold start. How common a practice is it for franchised agents to standardise on a bulk oil? And am I entitled to expect the correct oil for my engine?* "

Most garages standardise on a bulk oil. Good ones specialising in modern cars of above-average performance tend to go for a semi-synthetic 5W/40 or 10W/40, or even a fully synthetic 0W/40. When I had our 98R Mondeo serviced by Dagenham Motors, Byfleet, they even itemised 5W/30 oil on the invoice. But garages which do a lot of fleet business have been known to use nothing more than a basic mineral oil because the fleets simply won't pay the extra cost of a good semi-synthetic or a fully-synthetic. Of course, you are entitled to have your engine filled with the correct oil, and you need to specify this at the time of booking the service and include it on the service order in writing.

Sludging Fiestas

Three readers have written of 'mayonnaise' in their 'Valencia' pushrod Fiesta engines which is not caused by cylinder head gasket problems nor by 'short-run syndrome'. It appears that the crankcase ventilation system of these engines is prone to trapping condensation which emulsifies the oil, further blocks the oil breather and simply gets worse. One reader's answer is to use a thinner Ford 10/40 oil and to change it twice as frequently as suggested (at least every six months or every 5,000 miles). He may do better still with Ford's excellent 5/30 semi synthetic oil. A reader from Bournemouth obtained an aftermarket 'emission filter' which enables the crankcase to vent separately rather than through the carburettor. And a reader from Nutlet pointed out that some Ford CVH engines have another cooling system problem in that the insert of the connector from the thermostat to the expansion tank is prone to internal corrosion, which restricts the flow and can cause the engine to overheat. Changing the coolant every two years, before the corrosion inhibitors in it degraded, should have prevented this.

Assault on battery

" *I have sometimes been told that, in winter especially, a battery is only just charging when everything electrical is switched on. The cure, it seems, is to wait until you no longer need the car for the day, switch everything off and then rev the engine for a few seconds. Is there any truth in this?* "

The first bit is true. The second isn't. Assuming there is no fault with the battery, it must be kept fully charged to 13.2–13.8 volts or its ability to hold enough charge to start the car will deteriorate. If you don't drive the car a significant distance every day, the best way to keep the battery in a fully charged state is to connect it to an Airflow Automatic Battery Conditioner (tel: 01635 569569) which very slowly tricklecharges the battery to the required voltage then maintains it there without affecting the car's electronics. (An ordinary charger could 'overcharge' the battery or spike the car's ECU.) These cost £40, and don't look like much for the money, but I've been using one for two years with great success and no ill effects.

Addicted to 'E's

" *I was browsing through your column when I came upon your response to the letter headed 'Assault on battery' (see above). I, too, have a Mercedes Benz 190E 2.6, but instead of being an 87E with 200,000 miles, mine is a 90G with 79,000. I love the car and look after it, using synthetic oil, servicing it every 10,000 miles, polishing it twice a year, etc. But can you tell me how many miles it has left in it, what its weaknesses are and what I should do to get the most out of it?* "

First, assuming you are doing around 10,000 miles a year, make sure you change the oil and filter every six months even if you stick to

10,000-mile servicing. Change the coolant and brake fluid every two years, and the ATF every two years. You are likely to need a new set of valve stem seals around the 100,000 mile mark (symptom: starts to use oil or begins to soot up its injectors), but this is a relatively simple 'head-on' job costing around £120. Exhausts tend to last five to six years. If any rust spots start to develop (on the sill in front of the rear wheelarch and on the arches themselves), have these attended to immediately. Also watch the steel coolant pipe across the front of the engine, as this, too, can rust. Some 190Es develop problems with their power steering, autobox or rear axle, but my father's 2.6 hasn't. It is still creamy-smooth and a real pleasure to drive.

Magnetic oil filter

" *Your readers might be interested in Camco 88's 'Magnom' magnetic engine protection modules. These comprise a magnetic element fitted either in an 'in-line' module or between a canister oil filter and its standard mount and gather metallic solids under 30 microns in size which would normally pass through the oil filter element. They can be cleaned every 6,000 miles, by which time most oil filters are replaced anyway.* "

From the description given, these devices do not restrict the flow of oil so would appear to be a good idea for anyone interested in ultimate engine protection, and especially anyone who races cars. More information from Peter Carter, Camco 88, Unit 5, Osnath Works, Lythgoes Lane, Warrington, Cheshire WA2 7XE, tel: 01925 445688.

Service with a stamp

" *I think that most readers would expect that a stamp by a national garage chain would indicate that their car had been serviced to the manufacturer's specification for a given mileage service. However, this is not the case with Halfords service stamps. I bought a 1995 Citroën Xantia LXTD on the strength of service stamps and invoices. I later found that the important 36,000-mile service, carried out at a cost of £114.85, had been little more than an inspection and a change of oil and filters. Citroën specifies that this service should also include a change of coolant and hydraulic fluid. Halfords tell me that when a service has been carried out to manufacturer's specification it uses a different stamp specifying exactly this.* "

A very sensible warning. Though no one is at fault here apart from the previous owner who commissioned the inadequate service, this same warning could apply to virtually any service carried out by an independent and not supported by a fully itemised invoice. Even a full service carried out by a franchised agent and stamped as such may only signify a service when the car actually needs major replacements such as brake discs, pads and exhaust. Stamps can, of course, also be no more than stamps, so never rely on them alone.

Preserve that Micra

In the past I have warned owners of Mk I Nissan Micras to change their timing belts regularly. But this may not be enough in itself. Failure of the water pump of a Mk I Nissan Micra will lead to timing belt failure and totally wreck the engine. David O'Brian, who runs API, the only second-hand Japanese engine supplier I recommend (0500 830530), has shown how honest he is by reminding us of this and also another Achilles heel of this engine. The engine has a mechanical fuel pump driven off the camshaft. After many years use, the fuel pump diaphragm fails, leaking neat petrol into the oil sump. This dilutes the oil to such an extent that severe engine wear results. In extreme cases, the petrol in the sump can explode and cause a nasty fire. So in summation, owners of Mk I Micras hoping to extend the lives of their cars well beyond their design life should change the timing belt and camshaft end seal regularly (preferably every three years); should keep a check on the water level and listen for the grating sound of a failing water pump – and if they hear it, stop using the car immediately. You should sniff the oil on the dipstick for petrol vapours at regular intervals. If you smell any petrol, stop driving the car and book it in for an oil, filter and fuel pump change. (Total parts and labour should not come to more than £100.) Mk I Micras were never designed to last beyond five years, but in the UK most have remained reliable well beyond this design life. This does not mean they will carry on indefinitely, and owners wishing to preserve their engines to the point where the car fails its MOT on corrosion should follow these tips.

Is 'history' worth having?

" *Just how much value is a full manufacturers service history when it comes to part-exchanging a motor? My BMW 316i automatic needed a major service inspection, 'Inspection 2'. My BMW agent quoted £500 for this service, including a timing belt change, carried out at its palatial premises. My local garage quoted £261 against a photocopy of the 'Inspection 2' schedule, including the timing belt change. It would not take many savings such as this to compensate for any reduction in p/x value. What is your opinion?* "

With a large, expensive car, it reduces the heavy depreciation to be able to offer a full manufacturer's agent service history – even though this does not necessarily mean that essential replacements such as brake discs, brake pads, timing belts, etc. have been carried out. With a comparatively cheap car such as a pre-September 1993-built BMW 316i (the point at which timing belts were replaced by chains), once the three-year so-called 'dealer warranty' is up you'll save more by cheaper specialist servicing than you'll lose on additional depreciation as long as you are prepared to sell the car privately. But, and it's a big but, you will miss out on 'in-service' modifications to the car carried out by franchised agents in accordance with 'technical service bulletins'. If the engine blows up as a result, you will then find any 'goodwill claim' against the manufacturer to fall on stony ground.

Handy handbooks

John Haynes (of Haynes Manual fame) has written to tell us that, after numerous requests from *Telegraph* readers, Haynes has now produced a manual for the Skoda Felicia. Other new Haynes manuals cover: Citroën Saxo; Citroën C15 and C15D van; Fiat Cinquecento; Fiat Punto; Nissan Micra 16v; Peugeot 406; Renault Laguna; Renault Megane; Renault Megane Scenic; Rover 100 Series; current Rover 200 Series from 1995; current Rover 400 series from 1995; Saab 900 from 1993–98; Vauxhall Vectra; Vauxhall Omega; VW Polo from 1994; and VW Passat from 1988–96 (updated).

'NEARLY-NEW'

HONEST JOHN'S LIST OF SPECIALISTS

Remember, most 'nearly-new' mass-market cars are ex-rental or from 'fast rotation' fleets. Availability and prices fluctuate wildly according to supply and demand, and big manufacturers such as Ford and Vauxhall have now cut back the number of cars they register through rental fleets and 'fast rotators'. You may save as much as £5,000 buying a nine-month-old 9,000-mile Mondeo or Vectra – but equally the saving may be as little as £3,000.

Beware of 'customer service returns' which can be faulty new cars rejected by customers, taken back by the manufacturers and auctioned off to the trade. And beware of Fiats lacking a 'red key' for the immobiliser system. Cars sold as 'new' may be unofficial imports.

Nearly-new specialists work on such low profit margins they cannot subsidise high offers for trade-ins.

- **LONDON:** The Great Trade Centre, Hythe Road (off Scrubs Lane – the original 'Car Supermarket') White City, London NW10. Tel: 0181 964 8080. (Advertises in the *Sun*, *Exchange & Mart*, *Thames Valley Trader*. Website: http://www.gtccar.co.uk.) Hertz Car Sales, Gillette Corner, Brentford. Tel: 0181 560 1202.

- **SOUTH:** Trade Sales of Slough, 353–357 Bath Road, Slough, Berks SL1 6JA. Tel: 01753 773763. (Advertises in 'Telegraph Motoring' – note that DEAL 2 prices are after £500 minimum part exchange, plus £99, and only for cars sold on finance.) CONCEPT, Lakeside, Weston Avenue, West Thurrock, Essex RM20 3FJ. Tel: 0800 783

3366. (Took over CARLAND after the 'car buying experience' failed.)

- **MIDLANDS:** Motorpoint, Chartwell Drive, West Meadows, Derby. Tel: 01332 347357. (Advertises in 'Telegraph Motoring'.) Rayns of Leicester, Thurcaston Road, Leicester. Tel: 0116 261 2200. Ian Shipton Cars, 24 Main Street, Stretton, Burton-on-Trent. Tel: 01283 542983. Concept at The Motor House, A5 Watling Street, Cannock, Staffs (1 mile from M6 J11). Tel: 01543 506060 or 0990 289227. Motor Nation, Mackadown Lane, Garrett's Green, Birmingham. Tel: 0121 786 1111. Bristol Street Motors, 156–182 Bristol Street, Birmingham B5 7AZ. Tel: 0121 666 6003.

- **WALES:** Carcraft at Empress Cars, Langland Way, Spitty Road, Newport, Gwent. Tel: 01633 284800. Ron Skinner & Sons, Roundabout Garage, A469 Rhymney, Gwent. Tel: 01685 842624, 01685 844370; sales hotline: 01685 844446.

- **NORTH WEST:** Fords of Winsford, Wharton Retail Park, Weaver Valley Road (off A5018), Winsford, Cheshire. Tel: 01606 861234; Faxback: 0891 715970. Reg Vardy Motor Zone, Albion Way, Salford, Lancs M5 4DG. Tel: 0161 737 7333. Carcraft, Molesworth Street, Rochdale OL16 1TS. Tel: 01706 752500. Reg Vardy Motor Zone, 608 Penistone Road, Sheffield S6 2SZ. Tel: 01142 834949. Reg Vardy Motor Zone, Chancellor Lane, Ardwick, Manchester M12 6JZ. Tel: 0161 273 2273.

- **NORTH EAST:** Reg Vardy Motor Zone, Stoddart Street, Shieldfield, Newcastle-upon-Tyne NE2 1AN. Tel: 0191 232 3838.

- **SCOTLAND:** Reg Vardy Motor Zone, 5 Seafield Way, Seafield Road (between Portobello and Leith), Edinburgh. Tel: 0131 669 3000.

NEW CAR PROBLEMS

Polo woe

" *Regarding your advice about something offering a bit more status than the Fiat Punto, you might be interested in my experience. I bought one of the first Polos in the UK and wrote to you in November 1996 about the high noise levels. You suggested a sound-proofing kit which I purchased, but I still found the car unpleasant on motorways. Then, at three years old and with 16,000 miles, it needed a new instrument cluster, the cost of which, to their great credit, VW offered to pay half. Other problems included moisture getting into the car causing condensation, the heater rear window element showing signs of failure, and a number of rattles from the doors, dashboard and radio. In February, I had the chance to buy a Fiat Punto Sporting at a very favourable price, so I did. I have to say that, after 1,600 miles, I am very impressed with the Punto. Apart from a very firm ride, it appears to be better built than the Polo – born out by the recent Lex reliability report. For me, aged 60 with a back problem, the driving position is better, the tyre, engine and wind noise are all very much less, and there are no rattles. Furthermore, it has an electric rather than a manual sunroof, electric window switches sensibly placed on the doors rather than on the dash, a conventional trip recorder, a six-speaker RDS radio, height adjustable headlamps, and a lot more.* "

But, the fact remains, in the words of a friend of mine, 'a bottle green two-door Polo with a sunroof carries more middle-class status than any other small car'. And, like Hyacinth Buckett, status was what my first correspondent was after. Your condensation problems were probably due to a blocked pollen filter.

Reputation rattled

" *We purchased a new Nissan Micra 1.0 16v in August 1995. The service from the car and the Nissan agent has been excellent apart from one aspect. When the car was a- year old the engine began to rattle, especially after a cold start. An apparently known fault in the timing chain tensioner was diagnosed and the tensioner was replaced under warranty (a nine-and-a-half-hour job). This spring, once again the engine became progressively noisier, so we took it back to the agent and once again they agreed to replace the tensioner under warranty. Now that the car is nearly out of warranty I am beginning to worry. How widespread is the problem, and how likely is it to happen again?* "

Tensioners have always been the weak point on engines with timing chains and, unlike a timing belt tensioner, they are buried in an oil-tight part of the engine block. In its check list, 'Parker's Guide' warns: 'Timing chains need careful servicing'. I think that six-monthly oil changes are essential on this model, especially when it does a very low mileage with a lot of cold starts, treatment that tends to emulsify the oil.

Sorting out a Skoda

" *I was interested to read reports on the new be-grilled Skoda Felicia and its performance in the 'Top Gear'/J. D. Power Customer Satisfaction Survey. I am one very dissatisfied customer. I bought my new Felicia 1.6 in January. The gears rattle at idle and the car will not drive straight. It veers to the left. Neither the dealer nor the company service centre will do anything about these ghastly faults except tell me that all 1.6 models are the same. How they came to earn the good publicity they did is a mystery to me.* "

If it pulls to the left on normal two-lane carriageways at town speeds, then the camber of the road is pulling it to the left. But if it pulls to the left from the right-hand overtaking lane of the motorway, then the suspension is incorrectly aligned and needs to be adjusted. A rattling gearbox idler shaft is an irritation, not a problem. Did the dealer make sure that the gearbox oil is up to the level? If he did, then have him completely drain the gearbox when hot and be there to witness what comes out. If there are any shards of metal in the oil, the cost of draining and refilling with clean oil should be down to the dealer. No shards of metal, the cost should be down to you.

Use your eyes

" *My wife and I are retired in our 70s and our hobby is fishing, so last year we decided to swap our two cars for a Honda CRV ES, with which we are extremely satisfied. On a recent fishing trip we went in convoy with a friend in his Discovery and, coming to a boggy meadow, we decided to park the CRV and use the Discovery. We then found out that there are no towing attachment points on the CRV – either front or rear, so, had we got bogged down, there was no easy way of pulling us out. I had to ask the agent three times before they told me there are indeed no towing points and that the vehicle 'should not be used in such conditions'. I was frankly astonished to hear this and furious that I had been encouraged to buy a car which they now say should not be used for the express purpose we told the agent we wanted it for. I would welcome your comments. How do you get a CRV out of a sticky situation?* "

There are two towing eyes built into the structure at either side of the front and one in the centre of the back, so I can only assume that the Honda agent must have misunderstood your question. He was right to point out that the CRV's off-road ability is limited, though. It's designed to handle

like a car, which it does very well, and drive to the rear wheels will only clutch in when sensors detect a lack of traction at the front. This, too, works very well indeed, as I discovered on a track through some woods which had degenerated into deep black, glutinous slime. So the CRV should be just the ticket for your fishing trips. But there is no way a CRV, RAV-4 or even a Freelander (without optional hill descent control) will come close to a vehicle such as a Discovery or Range Rover in serious off-roading ability.

M52 Factor

" *I am considering buying a nearly-new BMW 328i or 528i and understand there has been trouble with cylinder liners in aluminium engines up to March 1998 due to sulphur in UK petrol. Could you elaborate and indicate at what commission number the liners were changed?* "

The nickel-silicon cylinder bore liners could be attacked by sulphur in petrol, especially in engines subjected to short running periods from cold because this leaves a residue of neat petrol in the combustion chambers. If you are shown a service history which proves conclusively that the cylinder block has been replaced with an EU3 block under warranty or for 'goodwill' reasons, you should have no problem with any of these engines. The simplest rule of thumb is to avoid any six-cylinder BMW from 'M' to 'R'-reg. sold without a full BMW service history unless you are shown positive proof that it has steel rather than Nickel Silicon bore liners. Specific dates and engine codes to avoid are: 320i, 20 6S 3 from 12/94 on; 323i, 25 6S 3 from 5/95 to 9/98; 328i, 28 6S 1 from 4/95 to 4/98; 520i, 20 6S 3; 523i, 25 6S 3; and 528i, 28 6S 1, all from 5/96 to 9/98; 728i, 28 6S 1 from 1/96 to 9/98. 'EU3' engines with steel liners and no problems are designated: 20 6S 4; 25 6S 4; and 28 6S 2. All the 'new shape' E46 3-Series BMWs are OK.

Screechy steering

" On 17 August 1998 I took delivery of a new Vauxhall Astra Club. After 100 miles, an excessive whine developed in the power steering system. The Vauxhall agent admitted there was a noise and changed the offending part, but it made no difference. I was nevertheless assured that the noise did not portend a failure and took the car on holiday. The steering still whines, but Vauxhall Customer Care tells me that it could be the end of the year before a modification can be made to get rid of the noise. Is there any immediate danger from this fault in the power steering system? "

The fault is in the pump, not the rack, and affects some, but by no means all, of the new model Astras (it certainly was not present in the new Astras I drove). Vauxhall tells me it only occurs at low speed and, though it is annoying, it is not safety-related. Because of the volumes involved, it took until the end of 1998 to provide modifications for all cars affected and there was no point in recalling affected cars until the parts became available.

Too well oiled

" *I purchased a new Renault Clio in October 1997 and have become increasingly alarmed at its oil consumption. I measured it to be using one pint per 2,500 miles and complained to Renault, who replied that there would only be cause for alarm if oil consumption increased to one litre per 500 miles. Since then, my engine's oil consumption has increased to 1 pint per 1,200 miles. Do I have a problem?* "

Probably not. Modern engines are designed to use a little engine oil in order to lubricate their valve stems, a job previously carried out by lead in petrol. Excessive oil consumption is often caused by running a car in too gently. If the engine doesn't get revved early in its life, it can remain tight and use a lot more oil than an engine which has been loosened up. This should serve as a warning to all car owners to check their oil levels regularly – at least once a month and preferably once a week.

Surgeaway Jap

" *We finally succumbed to the lure of a Japanese car and bought a Honda Civic hatchback with the 1,500 cc VTEC engine. This year we have done 15,000 miles in it and all is well apart from the engine 'surging' between 60 and 70 mph in 5th gear. I think I can also detect equivalent sluggish areas. A friend who has the same model says that his is behaving in exactly the same way, though his previous Hondas did not. The dealer says it's nothing to worry about. Is it? We use Shell Premium Unleaded.* "

The 1.5 litre VTEC-E engine is designed to be 'lean burn' at light, constant throttle openings and because of this it can be remarkably economical for a petrol engine. What you are experiencing is the transition between 'lean burn' and the normal stoichiometric (Lambda 1) air:fuel ratio of 14.3:1. Nothing to worry about. There used to be a light in these cars to tell you when (or when not) the car was in 'lean burn' economy mode.

Honda hiccups

" *After months of agonising over what car to buy, I finally decided on a Honda Civic 1.4i 5-door last August, and that is when the nightmare began. To summarise, it was delivered with the wrong bumper, which I later found had been substituted because the original had been damaged. There was a problem with the accelerator cable, which had to be re-routed. A lock striker had to be re-sited. It crunches when I brake. There is a small hole behind the steering wheel. The weather seals on the doors are joined rather than continuous. The floor carpet is crooked. And one of the screen washers recently popped out of the bonnet. I feel that the car is not to a satisfactory standard and want to reject it.* "

Honda has suggested that if you feel that the car is faulty, you should pay for an independent inspection to confirm this (AA: 0345 500610; RAC: 0800 333660; ABS Vehicle Inspections: 0345 419926; AAA Motor Vehicle Inspections: 0705 0158123; Autocheck GB Ltd: 0181 678 7060). If the inspector finds that Honda or its agent has been deficient or negligent, Honda will abide by the inspector's decision. This is very good general advice to anyone who feels dissatisfied with a new car purchase. (For used cars, the inspection should be carried out *before*, rather than after, the purchase.) To your specific ongoing criticisms, the garage checked the brakes for more than two hours and could not replicate the 'rattle', and it will put the carpet right at the next service. But the split in the door seal is normal because the seal is not a continuous moulding, and the hole behind the steering wheel is a normal moulding mark.

Oil consuming Audis

" *I bought an Audi A4 2.4 V6 30v saloon exactly a year ago and wonder if you can offer any advice on how to reduce its oil consumption. Since new, despite driving it with care, the engine has only managed approximately 650 miles per litre of engine oil. When I first asked the agent about this at 3,000 miles he said it was merely due to the engine 'running in'. Now, at 20,000 miles, I have been given a photocopy of an official Audi document stating that it is acceptable for this engine to do only 600 miles (1,000 kilometres) per litre of oil. My previous car was an Audi 2.6 coupe which used 2 litres of oil in 10,000 miles. This high oil consumption is not mentioned in the sales literature of the A4 2.4, so I feel I ought to warn your readers.* "

One other possibility is that you have run in the car too gently. This can have the effect of preventing sufficient engine wear for it to loosen up, leaving the engine too 'tight' and leading to high oil consumption. But nine owners of the same engine responded. The A4 belonging to a reader from Emsworth used one litre of Esso Ultra in the first 3,000 miles, after which he had the oil changed. It has not used oil between changes since. A reader from Alderney, where there is not much room to use a car and consequently he has only done 4,256 miles, has already changed the oil so frequently it is impossible to calculate consumption. One from Inverness states that his A4 2.4 Tiptronic uses one litre of oil every 3,000 miles and that his son's A4 2.4 manual has no problems with oil consumption. Another Scot, this time from Glasgow, bought an 'ex-demonstrator', and from 8,000 to 23,000 miles has experienced oil consumption of around 750 miles per litre. A reader from Clanfield gets around 1,000 miles a litre, while one from Kelsall and another from Colchester both reckon to use around 3.5 litres of oil between 10,000-mile oil changes. Yet another suffered horrendous oil consumption during his first week of ownership, due to a faulty oil seal, after which it settled down to around 650–700 miles per litre. So, while five out of eight have suffered high oil consumption, two of those have not had unscheduled additional oil changes, making it difficult to draw any firm conclusions other than that 30 separate valve stem oil seals obviously increase the chances of a single stem seal failure.

All's well that ends well

" I personally imported a VW Passat TDI 110 bhp estate from France last November to use travelling regularly between the UK and Spain. In mid-December, I found rainwater was entering the car and, under the terms of the extra-cost pan-European three-year warranty, I took it to a UK VW agent for rectification. It went in on 4 January. The next day the agent phoned to tell me they had dismantled the interior and ordered new c-arpets, new main control unit and new wiring loom, which would take seven to ten days because they had to come from Germany. After the ten days elapsed and no parts arrived the agents told me they were too short of staff to chase up the parts. I then contacted VW Customer Services who told me the parts could take up to three weeks. So I bought an excellent ten-month-old 3,000-mile Fiesta 1.2iLX 16v with PAS from Motorpoint of Derby for £6,600 just to keep mobile, and then I contacted you. You checked with VW UK and found out that new ECUs are a problem because the unit has been superseded, and that wiring looms take three weeks from the order being received in Germany. The ECU has now arrived but the wiring loom hasn't, and on 8 March, after more than two *months with the agent, I took the car home on a trailer. It was filmed by Meridian TV on 9 March, who also conducted a telephone interview with What Car? magazine and interviews with me, my solicitor and The Consumers Association on 10 March.* **"**

I spoke again with VW on the evening of 9 March and I'm pleased to say that VW UK will be loaning you an equivalent car from its press fleet while it takes your car back to its HQ press garage and fixes it properly. The incompetent VW agents will get a sound rap on their ham-fisted knuckles for the way in which they have dealt with you.

Is it a whine, or a moan?

" *I bought a new Mercedes Benz from an MB UK agent at the end of 1998, and within 250 miles I noticed an abnormal whining noise at 50–55 mph. This has persisted and, despite the best efforts of my helpful MB agent, has defied all attempts at diagnosis. A wheel bearing was replaced without effect, and I suspect that either the back axle or the gearbox may be responsible. I do not wish to encourage further work on a car which is otherwise entirely satisfactory and which I had planned to keep for many years. However I fear some premature failure once the car is beyond its 12-month warranty. What do you suggest would be a sensible course of action?* **"**

Have the car checked out by an independent vehicle inspector. If he reports an unacceptable noise, then you can use this to invoke the Sale & Supply of Goods Act, 1994 on the agent who sold you the car, rejecting it as not being 'of satisfactory quality'. Quite how far this will get you is another matter, as case law on the act does not exactly help the private individual, particularly when a matter of months passes before the rejection. The four main used-car inspection organisations are AA: 0345 500610; ABS:

0345 419926; Green Flag/National Breakdown: 01254 355606; RAC: 0800 333660. Others are AAA Motor Vehicle Inspections (London area only): 0705 0158123; Autocheck GB Ltd: 0181 678 7060; D. S. Crawford (Central Scotland only): 0131 453 4393. ABS also offers a Helpline on 01625 576441.

No bearing on the matter

" *Last Wednesday I took my £22,000, three-year-old, 36,000-mile Honda Accord Aerodeck to the agent for a 36,000-mile service plus MOT and was astonished to find it had failed on a worn rear wheel bearing. This was not covered by the extended warranty I took out at an additional cost of £700 and I was faced with a bill of £200. Why did only one bearing wear? Can I expect the other to need replacing in the near future? How can I be sure that the worn bearing was not a faulty component or was not fitted incorrectly? I have written to the MD of Honda UK in protest asking for full reimbursement. Am I being unreasonable?* "

No. You should receive some form of goodwill payment, even if not the full cost. Wheel bearing life is not predictable. A faulty bearing, or one not 'thrust up' correctly, could be expected to fail sooner than yours did. But bangs from kerbs or potholes will also significantly shorten their lives. I have an old car which has had both rear wheel bearings and one front wheel bearing replaced in 14 years and 106,000 miles, but the other front one is still original.

Pug bugs

" *The positive battery terminal lead failed due to corrosion on my Peugeot 406 after 30 months and 24,000 miles. Peugeot 'Customer Relations' refused to consider an out-of-warranty goodwill claim submitted by their franchised agent. The total cost of the repair, including towing-in charges, was £208.53. I find it hard to accept that corrosion of a vital electrical connection such as this after 30 months is considered 'acceptable' by Peugeot. What do you think?* **"**

Though Peugeot replaced a car without quibble after six months of faults for a reader from Potters Bar, others have forwarded me the same particularly irritating letter which Peugeot 'Customer Relations' sends them in cases like this. It begins: 'I was sorry to learn of the difficulties you have encountered with your (106, 206, 306, 406). At Peugeot we pride ourselves on both the quality and reliability of our cars and it is always a cause for concern should any difficulty arise. Unfortunately, despite rigorous performance testing, it is not always possible to prevent...' blah, blah, blah. 'The 12-month New Car Warranty is provided to ensure...' blah, blah, blah. 'In the circumstances, we regret that as the New Vehicle Warranty has expired, we are unable to assist you financially.' In your case, if you have cleaned the white grease from the terminal and this has led to the corrosion, then the corrosion is down to you. If you have never touched the terminal, then, in my view, it's a case where 'Customer Relations' should have contributed at least part of the cost.

Poor performer

" *I own a Volvo V40 2-litre, purchased new in October 1997, and have been in dispute with Volvo ever since concerning its poor performance in terms of acceleration, fuel consumption and continuing lack of power. Volvo has checked the car out on a chassis dynamometer and suggested that its performance is OK. However, my previous 'J'-reg. 1.7 litre Volvo 460 was much nippier and my 'M'-reg. 2.0 litre Golf feels like a sports car in comparison. The agents and Volvo have suggested that my driving style is to blame. Can you suggest anything I can do? The AA, the RAC and MIRA do not wish to get involved by testing the car. The V40 has now covered 13,500 miles and the Golf 48,000 miles.* **"**

Peak power of 140 bhp in the 2.0 litre V40 engine is not developed until 6,000 rpm and peak torque of 135 lbs ft not until 4,500 rpm. The *Autocar* road test of this car, published 5 June 1996, criticised the engine for being extremely noisy at the high revs needed to achieve peak performance, and concluded, 'most drivers will forgo its performance advantage out of mechanical sympathy alone'. If you are not revving the engine, then the car will feel slow. But if, even when you do rev the engine, you feel that the performance does not come up to scratch, either have an independent dynamometer test done on the engine (check the 'Yellow Pages' for local car performance specialists), or try and persuade one of the magazines with proper testing gear such as *Autocar*, *What Car?* or *Auto Express* to figure it for you and compare it with their own road test data.

Out of line

" *I bought a new MGF VVC in Abingdon in April 1998 and, apart from odd bits of plastic trim dropping off, have been very happy with it. Then in March, after 9,500 miles, I had a flat tyre and was horrified to discover that all four tyres had been worn down to their wire carcasses on their inside edges. Rover said I had driven over too many pot holes and hit kerbs too often, but they still refunded me 50 per cent of the cost of the new tyres as a goodwill payment. They also re-did the wheel alignment under warranty, but the report did not look as if it had been too bad. I am now concerned that I will have to buy another new set of tyres in a few months time.* "

The fact that yours is a Fulham-resident car may explain the damage from high kerbs and other vicious 'traffic calming' measures. But there have been instances of misaligned subframes on MGFs which the type of alignment check you had would not necessarily pick up. Your best bet is to take the car to a body and chassis alignment specialist such as Autolign on 01604 859424, Popplewells on 01992 561571, or for a cheaper but 'state of the art' suspension alignment check take it to Micheldever Tyres on 01962 774437. The MGF internet bulletin board is a useful means by which owners can swap information about faults on: http://www.ipl.co.uk/cgi-bin/forum/MG/sub69/cmtlist.html.

ODDBALLS

Static

" *My daughter's new car is a Renault Scenic, and yes it does take the three children, two cellos, etc. The only drawback is the static electricity. Unfortunately, one granddaughter receives electric shocks when she steps out of the car. What is the cause, and what is the cure?* "

Though the DT's Motoring Editor, Peter Hall, covered triboelectrics in some detail in 1995, it is a question that keeps coming back. What happens is that static electricity is developed when two different materials come into contact and are then separated. They could, for example, be a shirt containing nylon and a wool jacket, or wool trousers and a nylon car seat. So it is you that becomes charged, not the car. Any static charge in the car itself constantly trickles to earth through the tyres which, because they contain carbon black, are conductive. If you get a shock touching part of the metal of the car with a finger it is caused by the static in your clothes discharging into the car body. But if you 'wipe' the car body with the fleshy side of your fist the discharge is spread and you probably won't notice it. Mazda fits a special button on the door through which you can discharge static, and a company called Statpad makes a key-fob that serves the same purpose, a sample of which I enclose. (Readers can order these at £4.95 each inc. p & p from Statpad Ltd, AMTRI House, Hurdsfield Industrial Estate, Hulley Road, Macclesfield, Cheshire SK10 2NE, tel: 01625 615524.)

A plea from a patriot

" *I am completely and utterly puzzled by the sale of Rolls Royce Motors to a foreign company. Why on earth is it not possible for the UK to retain even one totally British car manufacturer?* "

A reader from Pickmere sent us a quote from Thomas Edison of 100 years ago: 'The motor car ought to have been British. You first invented it in the 1830s [meaning steam-powered coaches]. You have roads second only to those in France. You have hundreds of thousands of skilled mechanics in your midst, but you have lost your trade by the same kind of stupid legislation and prejudice that has put you back in many departments in the electrical field.' Says it all!

Third world water

" *We believe we are the only charity to build water tankers for use in Africa and India. Trucks donated to the charity are brought down to our workshops in Cornwall where they are overhauled and where we build water tanks for those which arrive as chassis cabs. They provide better value for charitable contributions than new trucks. We also operate a water drilling rig in Africa. Our garage premises are the kingpin of our activities. The lease is due to run out on 1 August, but we have an option to purchase the garage for £70,000 by 1 September. We have raised £50,000 and were expecting the remaining £20,000 from a National Lottery Grant. This has been turned down and we are now suddenly faced with having to raise the £20,000 by 1 September or close down. Our charity provides a vital lifeline for hundreds of thousands of people. Please could I use your column to canvass for donations?* "

We ran the appeal, the charity, Action Water, got its money, bought its premises and kept going. But it still needs donations to carry on its work. Please call 01209 715385 or send your donations direct to: Action Water, Mount Hawke, Truro, Cornwall TR4 8BZ. My £25 is already on its way. (Action Water is a Registered Charity, No: 292673.)

Steering wheel allergy

" *I bought a new Fiat Brava 1.4S and took delivery on 25 March. That evening I made a journey of about 30 miles and next morning woke to find that my right hand was swollen. It was very painful and felt as if it had been stung by wasps. Over the next couple of days I tried to rest the right hand while driving but the left hand became similarly affected. Suspecting it was something to do with the car, my wife bandaged the steering wheel. On 29 March I spoke to my son, a medical doctor, because my neck and scalp were beginning to break out into a rash. By 1 April, as well as on both hands, I was starting to get rashes under the seat belt areas and on both hips. I consulted a GP who prescribed anti-histamines. For the next three days the condition became progressively worse, covering neck, buttocks and rear of legs. A fax was sent to the Fiat agent asking if they had experienced anything similar and asking if there was something in the plastic. The salesman phoned to say that a cleaner had been used on the steering wheel, seat belts and seats. I contacted the makers of this cleaner and spoke to the company chemist. He told me that the cleaner was not hazardous, but should be used in the correct concentration. He did not think it was a good idea to use it on steering wheels. By 9 April, after an uncomfortable weekend, I was in serious trouble, went to Exmouth Hospital Casualty department, and underwent a series of tests including blood, urine and X-rays. I was then given further medical treatment and told not to drive the car again. Since then I received further advice and discovered that my condition is what is known as 'Deep Seated Urticaria', caused by vibrations fed through the handlebars of my motor mower and through the steering wheel of my car.* "

This is interesting, because it is rare and not all GPs are aware of it. A couple of things worth trying with the car are first to swap the tyres front to back (one of the fronts might have a slight moulding fault) and second to have the front wheel alignment carefully checked by an alignment specialist. Alignment of a new car can easily be put out of whack during transportation from the factory to the dealer.

More of Ted's Wisdom

" *If your car fails its MOT and the cost of repairing it to pass the test will be more than the car is worth, why not consider donating it to a 'Motor Project'? These are schemes which get young tearaways off the street and enable them to get speed and aggression out of their systems by driving cars in banger destruction derbys. They also have to prepare the cars and learn mechanics on the way. So if the car you donate is repairable, the 'Motor Project' will repair it, put it through an MOT, then sell it and channel the money back into helping more young people stay on the straight and narrow.* "

Ted frequently writes in to my column. And he's usually right.

Publicity vehicles

" *Well in advance of the Mini's 40th birthday, I have been converting them into eye-catchers. First was the 'Mini Garden', which had flower beds on the bonnet and roof, garden gates for doors and was featured on breakfast TV. Next was the 'Mini-sippi', a fully waterproofed convertible Mini with a rear paddle wheel which made several successful river journeys. Next, fed up with petty theft, I constructed the 'Un-stealable Mini', a Mini which carried a fully enclosing folding garage on its roof rack, and which resided in its 'garage' on my driveway. This year's project has been the 'World's Only Double-Decker Mini-Bus', which carried my whole family aboard around my back garden. Though I am in the motor trade, I have yet to make any money from sponsorship of any of these projects, and was hoping that through your column I might find a sponsor wanting to use the Mini Bus for publicity purposes.* "

Tony Anchors (aka 'Waspy') has been giving us a laugh at the auctions for years with photos of his creations, so it's only fair that he should make some money out of them. Anyone with an offer, please call him on 01235 819745.

Beware of low hanging balls

" *Here's an old garage parking tip which has nevertheless kept at least one couple from divorce. If your garage is barely long enough to accommodate your car, suspend a tennis ball on a cord from the ceiling so that it just touches the top of the windscreen. Then, next time you drive the car into the garage, the car will be correctly positioned to within a fraction of an inch the moment the screen strikes the ball.* "

Thank you for a good tip, still valid. The ball is rarely disturbed by wind unless the garage is open at both ends.

PARTS AND ACCESSORIES

Sticky moments

" *I have been looking unsuccessfully for an adhesive tape capable of sticking to painted surfaces. It can be found behind the trim of my 1987 Montego. My local Rover dealer could not help. Neither could the local car parts shops. An article in 'Telegraph Motoring' by your colleague Andrew English mentioned 'tank tape'. Could this be what I am looking for?* "

This is very sticky cloth tape. The black type (of which I always carry a roll) is referred to as 'gaffer tape' and can be found in film industry equipment shops. The other type, described as either 'tank tape', 'duct tape' or 'repair tape' is usually silver and you can get it from any DIY shop or hardware shop. Also useful for sticking trim in place are double-sided mirror pads from the same sources.

Wind deflectors

" *We had a Wolseley which was fitted with side-window wind deflectors and they were a boon for providing fresh air ventilation without buffeting. They also allowed a flow of fresh air in the rain and stopped the car misting up.* "

You can still buy TUV-approved window deflectors from £49.95 a pair from Clim-Air UK, 1 Station Parade, Sidcup, Kent DA15 7DB, tel: 0181 309 7744. They also do TUV-approved sunroof wind deflectors at the same price.

Supercharger – super price

" *I have owned from new a 'J'-registered VW Corrado G60 which I have had serviced every six months and, on your advice, changed the timing belt. I have always enjoyed driving the car, but now, at 31,000 miles, a dark cloud has appeared in the form of a supercharger oil leak. This unit is not repairable and a replacement will be £1,905, including VAT. VW Customer Services is considering some goodwill help with the cost, which I much appreciate, but is there an alternative?* "

Few owners are happy about coughing up two grand for a new supercharger so, sooner or later, someone had to start rebuilding them. Happily, you have not yet blown yours and cracked the casing, so it's an ideal candidate for Jabbasport's £320 rebuild service (tel: 01733 571769). I can't vouch for this service, I merely found the name in *Rabbit*, the magazine of Club GTi. If readers want to join this club, write to Sean Grenyer, Club GTi Membership, PO Box 2747, Brighton BN2 4HT. Also, new G40 and G60 superchargers imported from Germany are available for £1,250 + VAT from GPC on 01582 596971 – a £500 saving.

Big bang

" *I have a Rover 623iS, the engine of which failed at 109,000 miles on the motorway after a three-mile journey. First the engine emissions warning light came on, then, when I stopped, the coolant warning light came on. An RAC patrol found oil in the radiator and it was later ascertained that the cylinder head had cracked. I have now been quoted £3,500 for a new engine, which I can't afford. Can you help?* "

No problem. Your Rover is actually a Honda Accord 2.3iSR in tweeds and shares the same 158 bhp 2,259 cc twin-cam four with the Prelude 2.3i 4WS, so any of these engines would suit. As it happens, Japanese engine suppliers API found a genuine 623i 2.3 engine for you at £1,295 plus VAT, and recommended an honest garage local to you to fit it (API, tel: 0500 830530). I think this is a better idea than trying to recondition your high-mileage and broken engine which would need an expensive new cylinder head anyway. But do make sure the expensive ignition igniter is still with your old engine. The reason why your head cracked is most likely to be failure on the part of the servicing garages to replace the coolant. MEG coolant only lasts three years at most before the corrosion inhibitors in it degrade and the engine becomes a corrosion battery. Either this ate away at a weak part of the head, or, more likely, created a sludge which blocked water passages creating localised overheating. If this occurred in a different part of the head from the temperature sensor, it would not register on the temperature gauge. This is why the first warning light to come on was the emissions light, the sensor of which registered water or oil in the exhaust emissions. Let's hope it did not damage the catalytic converter.

Speedo repair service

" *The speedometer of my 1989 'G'-reg. Renault has broken. The garage has told me it cannot be repaired and that a new one will cost £600–£700, which seems to me to be rather excessive. Can it be repaired for less?* "

Speak to Speedograph Richfield of Nottingham on 0115 926 4235. This company also offers a service whereby it converts a speedometer from mph to kph by fitting a small ratio corrector box into the drive cable. If the cost of a repair still seems to be excessive, check out the Renault breakers advertising in *Exchange & Mart* for a replacement speedo from a car they are dismantling for parts. If the speedo cable has lost its nylon drive cog into the gearbox, then you have a different problem altogether.

Triumphant

" *I friend of mine who is living overseas wants to obtain a spare parts catalogue for a Triumph Spitfire. Can you help?* "

There are two answers to this question. If he wants a Parts List, these cost £27.50 for Mks I & II combined; £15.95 for the Mk III; and £15.95 for the 1500 from 1975 on, prices plus p&p from Mill House Books on 01205 270377. If he wants a catalogue of available parts from a parts supplier, then Rimmer Bros do one for all Marks of Spitfire free of charge in the UK, £2 p&p for Europe, and £4 p&p for the rest of world. Rimmers also have catalogues for the Herald, the GT6, the Stag, the TR4 4A, 5 and 250, the TR6, the 2000/2500, the Dolomite Sprint, and the Rover SD1, available on the same basis; and for the TR7/8 at £3. You can also have a complete set of ten for £10 in the UK, £15 in Europe or £35 in the rest of the world. Tel: 01522 568000; email: sales@rimmer.netkonect.co.uk.

Well and truly shafted

" *My problem is with Ford Sierra spare parts. In mid-July the short driveshaft with two UJs from the transfer case to the front diff of my Sapphire 4x4 failed. I ordered a replacement through my Ford agents and have rung them constantly since but, at 17 September, I am still waiting for the part to arrive. It's a pity I can't charge hire of a replacement car to Fords because that would surely induce them to get their finger out.* "

This rang a bell about a warning we published some time ago from our old friend Dave Brodie of BBR (tel: 01280 702389). The drivetrain of cooking Sierra 4x4s, Sierra Cosworth 4x4s and Escort Cosworth 4x4s is virtually identical and relatively bulletproof. But if the drivetrain is subjected to 'shunt' (often due to nothing more than the water temperature sensor sending the wrong messages to the ECU), the first parts of the drive train to go are the UJs at either end of this shaft. Dave was unaware of any shortage of this particular part, but suggested that the best way to short-cut the system would be to buy a copy of *Motoring News* and start phoning around the Cosworth 4x4 specialists advertising in the back.

Good in parts

" *My wife has a 1993 'K'-reg. Micra 1.0 which started to cut out, and the local Nissan agent diagnosed distributor trouble. He warned that the cost of a new one was £250 + VAT and suggested that, since he could not get the parts to recondition the old unit, I might prefer to try an auto dismantlers. In fact, it turned out that a new distributor was £450 + VAT, but I found a number (0800 525 030) which I phoned and was told my request would be 'put on the net'. Within an hour I had received five calls from salvage specialists offering me the part at prices from £50 + VAT to £100 + VAT. This was on a Thursday. The distributor arrived at 10.30 am Monday and the car was back on the road again by 11.00 am. I thought your readers might like to know about this invaluable service.* "

Others offering a similar service are Find a Part One Call on 0891 662706, Premier Spares on 0800 092 6700, and 1st Choice Spares on 0906 910 8400.

The curate's *œuf*

" *In May I purchased a used Xantia TD, and when the dealer's MBI has expired I propose to carry out my own servicing. I bought the parts for this from an E. Leclerc hypermarket in France. All were made by the same parts manufacturers who make them for Citroën, and the Citroën part numbers applied. For an air filter element, oil filter, fuel filter element and front and rear disc pads I paid a total of £55.60 at the hypermarket against the £135.02 the same parts would have cost me from a UK Citroën agent. It's a pity I couldn't bring back a tanker load of diesel at the same time, as that is only 37p per litre in France.* "

Some of the price difference is accounted for by the continued overvaluing of Sterling as a result of the UK's high base rates, and its value as a hedge against the Euro. The rest is due to the fact that we have no direct equivalent of E. Leclerc in the UK. Who ever heard of a UK supermarket or hypermarket offering car parts at such rock bottom prices? Come to think of it, who ever heard of a UK supermarket offering anything at rock-bottom prices apart from steam-baked bread and baked beans ?

How many wheels?

" *I recently acquired an old Morgan in rather poor condition. If you know of anyone in the UK who could supply me with spare parts for this car I would be most grateful. Unfortunately I don't know the type and series of this car as it came without any paperwork.* "

The first, most obvious, question is how many wheels? If it's a four-wheeler, your first port of call should be the Morgan Sports Car Club, c/o Mrs Carol Kennett, Old Forge Lodge, Ogston, Highham, Derbyshire DE55 6EL, tel: 01773 830281, fax: 01773 521816. If it's a three-wheeler, go for The Morgan Three Wheeler Club Ltd, c/o

E. Eyes, 280 Commonwealth Way, Abbey Wood, London SE2 0LD, tel: 0181 311 7282. Somewhere, probably on the bulkhead, there will be a plate giving the chassis and engine number. From this, the appropriate club should be able to tell you which model you have. The biggest problem with an old Morgan is the body. If there's any woodworm or rot in the frame, restoring this car will be no picnic.

Burst bubble-top

" My brother-in-law accidentally broke the passenger-side tinted blue mirror 'T-top' of his 1980 Chevrolet Corvette. Could you suggest a possible supplier, please, and so lift his depression? I have not seen anything so gutted since I put some trout in the freezer. "

Talk to Tom Falconer at Claremont Corvette, Malling Road, Snodland, Kent ME6 5NA, tel: 01634 244444. If he can't fix you up with the part direct, he will be able to put you in touch with a supplier in the USA.

Noise nuisance

" I have a Maestro 2.0 litre diesel van of 1990 vintage which has done 70,000 miles. It is fine except that it is so noisy and agricultural, particularly when cold and accelerating, that it is embarrassing. Any suggestions, please? "

Noise is a characteristic of direct-injection diesels. Modern DI's combat it by cladding the engines with large sound-absorbing structures. There is a possibility that the sound absorber from current Rover 2.0 litre DI could be adapted to fit your engine. Ask your Rover agent. In a van, of course, the sound is exaggerated by the drumming of the unlined load area. A kit from

BJ Acoustics (tel: 0161 627 0873) may help to deaden this noise.

Right key, wrong keyhole

" *A fortnight ago I wrote to you complaining that, while my 1996 VW Polo saloon was at the VW agents for a check on the power steering, the driver's door lock failed. Apparently a piece of metal inside the lock barrel had sheared off, making it impossible to lock the car. My VW agent informed me that the entire mechanism would need to be replaced, but that no spare parts were currently available. Your answer to this was that the car is, in fact, a re-badged Seat Cordoba, built at Martorell in Spain, and that a Seat agent might have the parts. So I went to my local Seat agent and was delighted to have them fit a small replacement part (cost £1.21) in half an hour (total cost, £20). The manager told me that VAG was changing its part supply system so that all Audi, Seat, Skoda and VW parts would be sourced from the same UK parts centre, so problems such as the one I experienced would not occur in the future.* "

This says a lot about the Seat agent but not much about the VW franchise.

Unshockable?

" *My brother in Australia is in the process of restoring a 1938 Morris 8 Series 2 Tourer which he bought from the original owner. He is now desperately trying to get hold of a set of four reconditioned Armstrong hydraulic shock absorbers for the car. He will be visiting the UK soon and could take them back with him. Unfortunately, Harry Edwards and The Morris Club were unable to help.* "

Try Graham Brown at the Vintage & Classic Shock Absorber Co., 203 Sanderstead Road, South Croydon, Surrey CR2 0RN, tel: 0181 651 5347. However, Graham does point out that, despite the freight costs, and assuming the original items are repairable, it's always better to have the originals rebuilt than to try and find replacements.

Good service and bad

A reader from Bromley has written to tell us of how, faced with the alternative of fitting a new £400 starter motor to his 1995 Accord, Honda agents Gilberts Motors of Catford found a small firm which could make replacements for the faulty parts, leaving him with a total bill of just £68. Another reader, this time from Enfield, was not so lucky, either with his choice of dealer or choice of car. All the franchised Nissan agents he approached told him they could not supply him with a separate distributor rotor arm for a 1994 Nissan Sunny 1.4. Instead, he faces the cost of a new distributor at £409.24 + VAT. The Nissan Motor Co. itself confirmed that the rotor arm was not available separately. A phone call to Gilberts Motors (0181 698 7067) to put him in touch with the small specialist firm was recommended.

Milosovich Motors

" *One thing NATO planners neglected to take account of was the effect of a prolonged Balkans war on Yugo drivers. The spare parts situation is a nightmare. Any idea where I can get hold of some?* "

NATO has even bombed the Zastava factory which built Yugos. However, a Yugo parts specialist is GGB Engineering Ltd, 98 White Hart Lane, London N22 5SG (tel: 0181 888 2354. GGB, who also operate mail-order, carry parts for Alfa Romeo, Fiat, Lancia and Lada cars. Some Fiat parts will fit Yugos or can be adapted to do so. Your other possibility it to buy a running 'doner car' at a part-exchange auction where even one-owner examples fail to sell for more than £100.

POWER STEERING

Kas and PAS

" *Some nine months ago my wife bought a Ford Ka in the basic version. She now finds the steering too heavy. I have tried over-inflating the front tyres, which helps a little. Obviously we would lose a lot getting rid of it. As all Kas now have power steering, it might be possible to add PAS now. Any comments on the practicability and the price of this idea?* "

The parts are there, but it will mean a new steering rack rather than merely powering the existing rack. If the Ford agent is reluctant to undertake this job, try Power Steering Services on 0181 853 3343 or Steering Developments on 01442 212918 for alternative quotations. Reckon on £750 to £1,000, so also ask your Ford dealer about a part-exchange which, when everything is taken into account, could work out a better deal.

PAS saving

" *You often mention that power-assisted steering and air conditioning absorb a certain amount of engine power. Is it possible to give some idea of how much, in bhp?* "

The PAS pump takes roughly 3–5 bhp, and an aircon pump between 5 bhp and 10 bhp. How much this affects the performance and fuel consumption of the vehicle depends on a lot of other factors such as power and torque output in relation to the weight of the vehicle and contents, the speed at which it is being driven, the gradient it is being driven on and whether it is automatic or manual.

PAS retro-fit

" *My Golf Mk II 1.6CL automatic will be ten years old in February. It is in sparkling condition, is serviced every six months, and has done just 22,450 miles. I would like to keep it and have power steering fitted – but have been quoted £4,000 for the work and been told the car is only worth £1,000.* "

You're being taken for a ride. Your car is worth between £1,250 and £1,750 as a private sale and with power steering fitted could be worth as much as £2,500. The cost of power steering, using new parts, should not exceed £1,200 + VAT. Using used parts from a Golf 1.8GL or Golf 1.6 Driver automatic it should be about half this price. Try TSR on 01278 453036 (VW/Audi specialist – prices from £650 + VAT), A&C Vehicle Services of Leek, Staffs, tel: 01538 398227 (VW/Audi specialist – prices from £500 + VAT), Power Steering Services on 0181 853 3374 (prices from £2,000 + VAT using new parts) and Steering Developments Ltd on 01442 212918 (prices from £1,900 + VAT using new parts).

RECALLS
1994–1999*

1994 Recalls

- Citroën Xantia (May 1993 – Oct 1994): Parking brake modification.

- Citroën ZX range (Mostly Volcane May 1992 – Oct 1992 and 16v 1992–1994): Brake pipe chafing.

- Ford Escort/Orion 1.3 and 1.4CFi (92 VIN NE, NL, NY, NS, NT; 93 VIN PJ, PU, PM, PP, PB, PR, PA, PG, PC, PK): Electrical check.

- Ford Mondeo (92 VIN NY, NS, NT; 93 VIN PJ, PU, PM, PP, PB, PR, PA, PG, PC, PK, PD, PE; 94 VIN RL, RY, RS, RT, RJ, RU, RM): Headlamp failure.

- Honda Civic 3-door, 4-door, CRX automatics: auto gear indicator may show wrong transmission mode.

- Mazda Xedos 6 (VIN JMZ CA1***01100001 – 01119137): Engine may stop without warning.

---

* SMMT Recall Hotline: 0171 235 7000 – ask for Consumer Affairs Department. Or Department of Transport Vehicle Safety Branch: 0117 954 3300. Please note, these lists include known 'in-service modifictations' as well as official safety recalls.

- Mazda MX3 1.6 & 1.8 (VIN JMZ EC13**00100001 – 00113020): Front coil spring failure.

- Nissan Micra (Sep 92 – June 94 VIN 000001 – 237783): Floor may crack next to handbrake.

- Renault 19 Phase II (Apr 92 – Mar 94): Faulty seat belt pretensioners and bonnet catch.

- Renault Safrane (Dec 91 – Mar 94): Heat shield required to protect fuel tank from exhaust.

- Rover 800 (VIN RS 100001 – 117697 and RS 150000 to 187439): Front seat belt security.

- Saab 9000 (VIN N1041085–N1049024 and P1000001–P1015289): Fuel leak.

- Saab 9000/Turbo (VIN N1000001–N1049024, P1000001–P1042386, R1000001–R1027659): Oil leak and faulty brake light switch on some models.

- Saab 900 (VIN R2000001–R2028886): Delayed braking action.

- Saab 900 5-door (VIN R2000001–R2022754): Cracking of driver's seat rails.

- Seat Ibiza (1985–1991 VIN 09045074–D119002): Fuel leak.

- Skoda Favorit (VIN P0670305–R0916381 and P5019665–R5043486): Wheel bearing failure.

- Suzuki Vitara (Sep 1993 – Jul 1994): Wheel bearing failure.

- Vauxhall Cavalier TD (Mar 1992 – Mar 1994 VIN NV201488 – R7560941): Loss of braking efficiency.

- Volvo 440/460/480 2.0 litre (440 VIN 419000 – 602090; 460 VIN 419001 – 602089; 480 VIN 586300 – 590058): Airbag may deploy accidentally.

1995 Recalls

- Alfa 164: to VIN 6272929: Corrosion of front suspension spring support.

- Ford Fiesta: VIN prefix SK, SD: Tyres may be incorrectly fitted.

- Ford Fiesta/Escort: VIN prefix SE: Brake lights may not work.

- Ford Fiesta/Escort/Mondeo diesels: VIN prefix SY, SS, ST: Brake vacuum pump may not create enough vacuum for servo.

- Ford Escort: VIN prefix SE, SL: Loose rear brake cylinders.

- Ford Escort: VIN prefix SC, SK, SD: Possible damage to seat belt webbing.

- Ford Mondeo: Fuel pipe.

- Ford Mondeo: RP, RB, RR: Static sparks may occur when refuelling.

- Ford Fiesta, Escort and Mondeo diesel (from June 1995): Check brake vacuum pump.

- Ford Maverick with Michelin 215/80 R15 tyres: VIN prefix PM, PP, PB, PR, PA, PG, PK, PD, PE, RL, RY, RS, RT, RJ, RV, RM, RP, RB, RA: Tyres may lose pressure.

- Land Rover Discovery VIN LJ163104 to LJ172980 and LJ501920 to LJ504252: Check seat belts.

- Range Rover (new model): VIN LP311035 to LP312917: ABS braking hose may fail.

- Mercedes Benz E-Class: Passenger footrest.

- Nissan Primera: VIN 000001 to 472213: Front brake hoses may chafe.

- Nissan Terrano II with Michelin 215/80 R15 tyres: VIN 200000 to 242699: Tyres may lose pressure.

- Peugeot 306: Check accelerator cable.

- Peugeot 405: 1995 model year to VIN 71339513: Airbag may fail to inflate in an accident.

- Renault 5 Campus 1.4: VIN C4070510214892 to C4070511788781: Car may pull to left when braking.

- Renault Espace 2.1TD first reg. 3/93 – 6/94. Install fuse in preheater wiring circuit, and re-route wiring away from main loom and install clip to keep it away to prevent risk of insulation damage.

- Saab 900: VIN R2027373 to S2009903 and S7000001 to S7013081: Welds missing from seat frames.

- Saab 9000 (*manual with TCS): VIN N1000001 to N1049024, *P1000001to P1042386, *R1000001 to R1026535: Loss of brake pressure and/or ABS.

- Vauxhall Astra: Fuel pipe, airbag.

- Vauxhall Astra TD: VIN S5000001 to S5241939; S2500001 to S2707652 and S8000001 to S8216827: Chafing of wiring harness and possible fire risk.

- Vauxhall Combo van, Corsa, Astra, Cavalier and Omega: Static sparking during refuelling.

- Vauxhall Astra: Airbag may fail to inflate in an accident.

- Vauxhall Omega 16v: VIN R 1000001 to S1155206: Fuel feed pipe may chafe. Reposition and clamp into place.

- Vauxhall Frontera: VIN NV500400 to RV628644: Faulty bonnet safety catch.

- Volvo 760: VIN 37400 to 39877 and 16300 to 38007: Battery short circuit leading to possible fire risk.

- Volvo 850: VIN 078000 to 120420 and 175000 to 220678: Fault with jack which could allow the car to fall.

- VW Golf/Jetta 1.6 & 1.8 1983A to 1989G: Bypass valve to be inserted into heater pipe; heater matrix to be replaced if degraded.

- VW Golf GTi, 16v, VR6, Convertible: VIN 1HPW 439315 to 1HSW 418237 and 1ERK 000001 to 1ESK 025159: Headlamp failures. Headlight switch on RHD models can overheat, leading to headlight failure. 28,000 cars affected.

- VW Passat: VIN3ARE 0000001 to 3ASE 142536: Headlamp failures.

1996 Recalls

- Citroën ZX ('facelift' model from June 1994): Faulty seat belt pretensioners and, on cars so fitted, faulty airbag sensors.

- Daewoo Nexia (to May '95): Check engine bay wiring harness routing (helpline: 0800 060606).

- Ford Fiesta March 1989F – September 1990H: Check for possibility of front seatbelt inertia reel locking mechanism failure.

- Ford new Fiesta and Courier van 1996 model year (47,500 cars): Check for faulty piston seal in hydraulic clutch master cylinder. Check for contamination of brake fluid and incorrect front brake hose routing.

- Ford Mondeo (all): 'Free recall' (per What Car? 9/96 p. 132) to replace valve sticking valve stem seals – work will usually be carried out when car is in for a routine service.

- Ford Mondeo (1996 model year with hydraulic clutch – excluding V6): Check, replace if necessary clutch master cylinder/slave cylinder. Check front brake callipers.

- Ford Galaxy (April '96 – July '96): Check for overheating of brake system.

- Ford Galaxy 2-litre with airconditioning (Jan '95 – Feb '96): Air conditioning compressor may seize up.

- Ford Scorpio (Aug '94 – Jul '96): Check for sticking throttle due to corrosion by road salt.

- Ford Scorpio (Feb '96 – March '96): Rear axle mounting may loosen.

- Hyundai Lantra: (1991 – 1996): Check for fracture of rear suspension bolt.

- Mazda new 121 (Fiesta based) 1996 model year: Check for faulty piston seal in hydraulic clutch master cylinder. Check for contamination of brake fluid and incorrect front brake hose routing.

- Mercedes Benz C-Class: Check for sticking bonnet catch and safety catch which may lead bonnet to fly open.

- Mercedes Benz E-Class: Airbag may inflate on wrong side.

- Mitsubishi Colt, Shogun and Sigma (1991 – 1994): Check for loss of brake fluid.

- Peugeot 306 (July 1993 – February 1996 – 150,000 cars): Underbonnet wiring may chafe leading to short circuit and fire.

- Peugeot 405 (Sept '93 – May '95): Check for seepage of fuel from feed pipe.

- Peugeot 406 1.8i and 2.0i petrol: Free upgrade of engine management chip if owner complains of 'rough' running, flat spots and lack of power on hills.

- Peugeot 806 (Sept '95 – Oct '95): Check airbag trigger.

- Porsche 911 (1989 –1993): 54,000 cars worldwide recalled (2,966 in UK) to check universal joint in steering column which may fail. Early signs are noises or free play in the system.

- Proton Compact: from October 1995. Fuel pump call allow fuel to leak when tank is brimmed.

- Renault Espace – on original tyres (March '91 – Oct '92): Check for separation of tyre tread.

- Renault Laguna and Safrane (May '94 – Aug '94): Automatic transmission may lock up.

- Renault Laguna and Safrane (Jul '94 – Dec '94): Airbag warning light may be faulty.

- Renault Laguna (April '96 – Aug '96): Fuel injection system computer may be faulty.

- Rover 400 (new model): Driver's seat lock does not always click into place properly. May mean seat slides when car is being driven. Most likely on cars with several drivers where seat is moved to and fro.

- Rover 600s built between 12/94 and 12/95: Check to ensure steering rack mounting bolts are secure – sympton of problem: stiff steering.

- Saab 900 convertible (1993 – 1995 = old model): Check for loss of steering control.

- Seat Toledo (1993 – 1995): Cooling fan motor may seize.

- Toyota Carina E: Anti-roll bar linkages may fail (first sign is a rattling noise). Covered under 3-year warranty. Only affects 2 per cent of cars.

- Vauxhall Vectras built between 8/95 and 2/96 (40,000 cars): Check front seatbelt mounting bolts and tighten if necessary.

- Vauxhall Frontera Sport: Fit heat shield between exhaust system and petrol tank (fire risk). Replace catches for removable roof section.

- VW new Polo (to June 1996): Steel wheels may lead to loss of tyre pressure.

- VW Golf/Jetta 1.3 1983A to 1989G, 4-cylinder VW Passats and Corrados 1988F – 1989G: bypass valve to be inserted into heater pipe; heater matrix to be replaced if degraded.

- VW Golf, Passat and Corrado VR6 (1993 – 95): Cooling fan motor may seize.

- Volvo 440, 460, 480 (1991 – 1995): Fire risk from faulty electrical connections.

1997 Recalls

- Audi A3, A4, 1997 ('96 model year) A6s built Feb – March 1997: Check front seatbelt top mounting height adjusters.

- Audi A6 2.8 V6 (built 1997–98): Rumoured recall issued in April concerning driveline.

- Audi 80, A4, A6: 50,523 cars recalled due to possibility of 'inadvertent deployment of airbags'.

- Bentley Azure: 101 cars recalled due to danger of fire from a short circuit.

- BMW E36 3-Series (from January 1996): Tighten stub axle bolts.

- BMW E36 3-Series (77,000 cars). Possibility of corroded steering shafts.

- BMW 2.8 litre six cylinder engines: Possibility of premature bore wear, not mileage or age related, repaired under warranty. (Not an official recall.)

- BMW M3: Faulty bearings in Variable Valve Timing mechanism can deposit shards of metal in engine. Official recall. 400 cars affected.

- Citroën Saxo: Driver's seat.

- Ferrari F355: 120 cars recalled due to 'fire risk caused by possible fuel leak'.

- Fiat Bravo/Brava (17,000 cars): Petrol may contaminate brake vacuum diaphragm leading to loss of power assistance.

- Ford Mondeo 24v 1/8/94 – 14/6/96 (9,000 cars): Free official recall to replace catalytic converter closest to exhaust manifold.

- Jaguar XK8: Rear suspension.

- Jeep Cherokee (January 1993–1997 model year RHD): Check for stress fractures around steering box mounting (19,200 cars affected).

- Jeep Grand Cherokee. 2,536 cars recalled due to danger of fire from a short circuit.

- Chrysler Jeep: 567 cars recalled due to possibility of 'inadvertent deployment of airbags'.

- Land Rover Discovery (22,723 vehicles): Possibility of failure of RHS door latches.

- Mercedes Benz: all cars with 'Brake Assist' (170,000 cars Worldwide): The 'Brake Assist' system, which is designed to apply the brakes fully in an emergency, may give too much 'assistance' during light braking. 1997 recall to disconnect the system. Supplies of modified component available from early 1998.

- Mitsubishi Colt: 213 cars found to have potentially defective braking system.

- Peugeot 106 (15,821 cars): Ignition switch harness may foul on steering column.

- Peugeot 306: possible starter motor fault on 1996 model cars. Free replacement.

- Peugeot 306: 2,060 cars found to have potentially defective braking system.

- Peugeot 406 (13,412 cars): Ignition switch harness may foul on steering column.

- Peugeot 406: 333 cars found to have potentially defective braking system.

- Proton Persona: 1,797 cars found to have potentially defective braking system.

- Renault Megane and Scenic: 7,434 cars found to have potentially defective braking system.

- Renault Laguna (12,494 cars): Engine ECU may malfunction causing exhaust manifold to overheat and set fire to bulkhead insulation

- Rolls Royce and Bentley: 29 LHD cars found to have potentially defective braking system.

- Saab 900. (all current-shape models: 21,661 cars). Corrosion on the throttle housing can cause a sticking throttle. Relevant parts to be replaced with brass items which cannot corrode.

- Seat Alhambra: Brake problem.

- Suzuki Vitara: Steering fault.

- Vauxhall Corsa/Astra/Vectra 1993 – 1996 1.4 & 1.6 16v only (27,000 cars): Possibility of faulty cambelt idler pulley which can snap cambelt.

- Vauxhall Astra 1.4 litre models: Oil pump may fail. Vauxhall will replace faulty component free of charge on cars less than three years old. Will consider part-payment for older cars, but not for engine damage as a result of continuing to drive with the oil light on indicating no oil pressure.

- VW Golf Mk III. (single headlight models). January 1997 recall for headlight failure. Headlight switch on RHD models can overheat, leading to headlight failure. 9,700 cars affected.

- VW Golf Mk III and Vento 1994 – 97. September 1997 recall for headlamp modification for all cars. Total 150,000 cars affected.

- VW Golf Mk III and Vento with electric front windows (16,000 cars): Insulation on power cable may chafe and short circuit. Needs protective shield in cable opening of door.

- VW Sharan: brake problem.

- Volvo 850 (1996 and 1997 model years): Check for sticking throttle.

1998 Recalls

- Audi A3: 2,822 cars recalled due to possibility of rear seat belt fixing brackets cracking.

- Audi A4, A6, A8 with 2.8 litre V6 30 valve engine: 4,574 cars built between August 1997 and February 1998 recalled due to possibility of jammed throttle.

- BMW E30 3-Series (1983–90) 170,000 UK-market cars recalled because valve in radiator cap may seize up, over-pressurise cooling system and cause hot coolant to leak into cabin..

- Chrysler Voyager and Grand Voyager (old model not marketed in UK): Recall in USA after fatalities due to faulty rear door latches. Voluntary recall in Europe.

- Citroën Xsara: 14,000 owners of cars built September 1997 – February 1998 notified that may be a delay in airbag inflating in the event of an accident. Also possibility of faulty seatbelt pre-tensioner.

- Ferrari F355: Possible fault with steering column bolt.

- Fiat Punto (March '97 – Nov '97 build): Faulty seat belt pre-tensioner.

- Fiat Tempra 1.8, 2.0 and 1.9TDS (1993 – 96): Front coil springs could fracture.

- Fiat Bravo/Brava 1.4 and 1.6 with ABS built before Oct '97: Check for chafing of brake hoses.

- Fiat Marea 1.6 16v, non-ABS: Check for chafing of brake hoses.

- Ford Ka with ABS (Mar '98 – Sep '98): Brake master cylinder may fail.

- Ford Fiesta, Courier, Courier Combi (July 1995 – June 1996 – 67,000 cars): Possibility of brake failure due to front brake pipe chafing on bracket. Modified pipe and bracket to be fitted to both front brakes. (Announced radio 12/2/98)

- Ford Fiesta with ABS (Mar '98 – Sep '98): Brake master cylinder may fail.

- Ford Fiesta (with passenger airbag built August '96 – Feb '98): Passenger airbag may go off while car is stationary.

- Ford Puma with ABS (Mar '98 – Sep '98): Brake master cylinder may fail.

- Ford Escort (with passenger airbag built August '96 – Feb '98): Passenger airbag may go off while car is stationary.

- Ford Mondeo (with passenger airbag built August '96 – Feb '98): Passenger airbag may go off while car is stationary.

- Ford Mondeo V6 with ABS(Dec '97 – Jan '98): ABS System may fail.

- Ford Scorpio (with passenger airbag built August '96 – Feb '98): Passenger airbag may go off while car is stationary.

- Ford Explorer (1996 – 98): Oil pump recall notice issued January 1998. Explorer TSBs (Technical Service Bulletins) include curing transmission shudder. Accelerator may be jammed open by the driver's floormat.

- Hyundai Accent built 1994 – 1997: Possibility of road salt corrosion to front coil spring causing spring to damage tyre.

- Jaguar XK8 and XJ8 (July – October 1997 – 11,221 cars): May suffer sudden deceleration due to weak retention bracket on accelerator cable. Extra clip 'costing pennies' solves the problem. (Announced on radio 7/2/98)

- Land Rover Freelander: Clutch system for part-time four-wheel-drive system found to be failing. Replaced 'in service' by Land Rover agents. (Not an official recall.) Worldwide recall of all Freelanders built June '97 – June '98 (22,300) due to possibility of rear suspension collapse owing to faulty welding on suspension arms.

- Land Rover Discovery (Jan '94 – Mar '97): Airbag may go off involuntarily.

- Land Rover Range Rover Classic (Jan '94 – Mar '97): Airbag may go off involuntarily.

- Land Rover Range Rover V8: All current-shape models: official recall to check and replace underbonnet cooling system hoses.

- Lexus LS400 (built April '95 – June '96): Risk of underbonnet fire due to faulty wiring.

- Lotus Esprit: 200 V8 models recalled for new timing belt, idler pulley bearings, new clutch and 5th gear locknut, cost to Lotus at least £1,500 per car. Also check rear alloy wheels for hairline cracks.

- Mazda 121 (Fiesta shape, built Dec '95 – June '96): Possibility of brake failure due to front brake pipe chafing on bracket. Modified pipe and bracket to be fitted to both front brakes.

- Mazda 626 (Nov '96 – May '97): Possibility of timing belt failure leading to total loss of engine power and power assistance to steering and brakes.

- Mazda 626 diesel (to May '98 build): Faulty fuel injector may stall engine.

- Mercedes Benz V-Class and Vito van (1996 – 98): Tread may separate from tyres.

- MGF (Aug '95 – Jul '98): Faulty driver's seat belt.

- Nissan Almera (Dec '97 – May '98): Inertia reel seatbelts may not lock on impact.

- Peugeot 106 (Jan '98 – Mar '98): Engine wiring harness may chafe.

- Peugeot 306 (Sep '97 – Oct '97): Steering wheel hub may crack.

- Peugeot 306 (Nov '97 – Apr '98): Front suspension may collapse.

- Porsche 911 Carrera (1998 model: 540 UK cars): Wrong size pulley fitted driving ancillaries drive belt which may slip affecting PAS, brakes, water pump and alternator.

- Proton Persona and Compact with 13" wheels (Aug '97 – Aug '98): Front tyres may lose pressure.

- Renault Clio (June '97 – Nov '97): Possibility of 'inadvertent deployment of airbags'.

- Renault Megane Scenic (June '97 – Sep '97): Roof bars may fail under load. Replacements redesigned and sourced from a different manufacturer.

- Renault Laguna. 'Plip' key transmitters can go out of sequence due to static or fiddling with them in the pocket. Improved 'plip' key transmitters now available free of charge to Laguna owners. (Per BBC 'Watchdog' 12/2/98)

- Renault Laguna diesel: Cambelt tensioner may lead to premature failure of cambelt – to be checked as a TSB item at services.

- Renault Laguna (June '97 – Dec '97): 17,000 cars recalled due to possibility of 'inadvertent deployment of airbags'.

- Skoda Felicia (with airbag): Wiring for airbag may chafe.

- Suzuki Vitara 2-door (Oct '91 – Oct '93): Front seat belt stalk may fracture.

- Vauxhall Corsa diesel (K to N reg: 26,000 cars): Live cable may rub against bonnet hinge, lose insulation and cause a fire. (3/6/98; Helplines: 01189 458500, 0800 455466.)

- Vauxhall Corsa 1.0 12v (P to R reg: 8,000 cars): Cable may touch engine inlet manifold. (3/6/98; Helplines: 01189 458500, 0800 455466.)

- Vauxhall Vectra (all 200,000 built 1995 – 98): Handbrake cable subject to premature wear. Modified cable free replacement service.

- Vauxhall Vectra automatics: In-service modification to autobox ECU mapping.

- Vauxhall Sintra: Catches for removing the seats may sever fingers. Covers to be fitted to seat release lever mechanism.

- All 16-valve and 24-valve Vauxhalls from 'L'-reg. to 'P'-reg; also Vectras and Omegas 'P' to 'R'. General warning issued to refer vehicle to a Vauxhall agent to have timing belt and timing belt idler wheel replaced before car reaches 40,000 miles or 4 years old, whichever comes first. Otherwise idler wheel may disintegrate and timing belt snap, wrecking engine.

- VW Passat (Dec '95 – Mar '98): May be airbag activator fault.

- VW Passat Synchro (Dec '97 – Apr '98): Throttle and brake hose problems.

- VW Passat: 11,450 Passats built between May – November 1997 recalled due to potential fault affecting front seat belts. Involves replacing complete belt units.

- VW Sharan (Aug '96 – Feb '98): Loss of power due to wiring loom failure.

1999 Recalls (up to close of press)

- Alfa 156, June, 1999: Safety recall No 4054 to modify rear hinge mounting on all four side doors to prevent hinges splitting from doors.

- Bentley Arnage: Possibility of short-circuit in heated seats.

- New BMW E46 3-Series from April 1998: Safety recall over failure of brake pedal clip which can allow the pedal to become disconnected and over sensitive side airbag trigger switches. (Daily Telegraph 28/5/99.)

- Fiat Barchetta: Problem of sticking control valve for engine variable valve timing – makes engine sound like a diesel. Announced on BBC Watchdog 21/1/99.

- Ford Focus: 61,000 card built September '98 – March '99 recalled for better waterproffing of alternators to prevent short-circuits. Anounced Daily Telegraph 16/7/99.

- Lexus GS300: All GS300's built July '95 – July '97 recalled to replace potentially faulty suspension links. Announced June 1999.

- Rolls Royce Silver Seraph: Possibility of short-circuit in heated seats.

- Rover Mini: 5,000 Minis built from August 1996 recalled for rectification of a braking system fault. Announced on BBC radio news 14/5/99.

- Saab 9000 range 1993 and 1994 (5,300 cars): Possibility of moisture corrupting computer chips which control passenger airbag trigger mechanism.

- Seat Arosa: Cold weather fault with the 1.4 automatic, manifesting itself in a loud noise when changing up from 1st to 2nd gear. Replacement parts are fitted free. Announced Auto Express 24/2/99.

- Vauxhall Corsa 1.4 and 1.6 16v (Sept '93 – Sept '96): Timing belt and GF50 plastic idler pulley must be replaced before 40,000 miles or 4 years old whichever comes first or pulley may disintegrate and belt snap leading to engine failure and loss of power assistance to steering and brakes. (Helpline 01582 427200.)

- Vauxhall Astra: Noisy power steering pump on some 1998/1999 model year Astras. Will be replaced FOC. Announced Auto Express 24/2/99.

- Vauxhall Astra 1.4, 1.6, 1.8, 2.0 16v (Sept '93 – Sept '96): Timing belt and GF50 plastic idler pulley must be replaced before 40,000 miles or 4 years old (see Corsa).

- Vauxhall Cavalier 2.0 16v and 2.5 24v (Sept '93 – Sept '96): Timing belt and GF50 plastic idler pulley must be replaced before 40,000 miles or 4 years old (see Corsa).

- Vauxhall Vectra 1.6, 1.8, 2.0 16v and 2.5 24v (Sept '93 – Sept '98): Timing belt and GF50 plastic idler pulley must be replaced before 40,000 miles or 4 years old (see Corsa).

- Vauxhall Calibra 2.0 16v and 2.5 24v (Sept '93 – Sept '96): Timing belt and GF50 plastic idler pulley must be replaced before 40,000 miles or 4 years old (see Corsa).

- Vauxhall Omega 2.0 16v, 2.5 24v and 3.0 24v (April '94 – Sept '98): Timing belt and GF50 plastic idler pulley must be replaced before 40,000 miles or 4 years old (see Corsa).

- Vauxhall Frontera 2.2 16v petrol (April '95 – Sept '98): Timing belt and GF50 plastic idler pulley must be replaced before 40,000 miles or 4 years old (see Corsa).

RESTORATIONS

'Rubber bumper' resto

" I have a 1980 MGB Roadster which has been laid up for the past three years. It is in reasonable condition. I am now considering either having it restored or selling it to a restorer. Could you please indicate the approximate value if I decide to dispose of it to a restorer and the best way to proceed? "

How long is a litre of oil? The answer depends on the state of the car. If it has rust in the seams, floor and sills, the restorer could be looking at a re-shell and the restoration cost could well exceed £10,000 for a car which is then unlikely to be worth more than £8,000. If it's not too bad and can be made road legal reasonably cheaply it's probably worth about £2,000 as it is and is best sold through the photo ads in *Classic Car Weekly* (£20 a week, tel: 01733 465430). But it urgently needs to be MOT-tested and put onto a SORN certificate, because Euro moves are now afoot to seek out and dispose of all unregistered 'end of life' cars not in established collections.

Minimum rust

" I have a 1987 'E'-registered Mini 'Jet Black' which I bought when it was two years old for £3,000. I generally use it for pottering about, which has

kept the mileage down to 45,000. Although it passed its MOT in May and the engine is brilliant, it has started to rust badly under the headlamps and sills and my garage has indicated that it would be unlikely to pass another MOT. I looked at trading it in, but was shocked to find that the most I was offered was £600. I am very fond of the car and have three boys, the eldest of whom is eleven. I had visions of passing the car on to him when he reached seventeen. Is it worth getting the rust seen to, and how much would a respray set me back? I still see lots of older Minis knocking about, which is testament either to their endurance or to the determination of their owners. **"**

Your problem isn't just the body rot, to which Minis are prone. It's severe structural rust in the front and rear subframes. The engine will also need a modified cylinder head to run on cheap unleaded petrol from 2,000. The head will cost you about £200 (see 'Fuel & Emissions' for suppliers), but I can't even begin to estimate the cost of body and subframe repairs. I suspect you have an honest garage man who knows that the cost of getting the car up to scratch will simply not be worthwhile. Think about switching to a later 'H' or 'J'-reg. Mini that will run on unleaded without the baggage of a catalytic converter. Also think about upgrading to a Rover Metro with the 'K' Series engine; these are starting to look very good value these days.

If you can't beat it, have it re-built

" *I found that there simply was no modern substitute for my 89,000-mile 'F'-reg. Nissan Prairie. So, instead of replacing it, I had it completely revamped by Walden Motorsport of Sawston, Cambridge (01223 835848), a company you have featured before. They fitted new shock absorbers, reconditioned the gearbox, rebuilt the engine to a higher specification, replaced the brakes, repainted it in silver and replaced the underbody protection. I now have a Prairie which drives even better than when new, accelerates more quickly, is slightly faster and uses less fuel. No other* *vehicle has ever approached the Mk I Prairie for practicality. It's a pity they stopped making it.* "

I checked back with Walden Motorsport to confirm the condition of this Prairie in the first place. If a Prairie has started to rust and sag in the middle, its construction is such that it cannot be saved. Fortunately, this one was structurally sound and worth re-building, but this won't always be the case. Walden Motorsport offer the same service for many other makes of cars, especially Vauxhalls.

'Old Fords never die'

" *Twenty-one years ago my Mk I Granada Ghia was sold by Tandridge Motors (now Asta Motors) in Oxted, Surrey. It still has the original engine, rebuilt only once at 275,911 miles. It now shows 310,000 miles and the car has been restored to showroom condition in a combined operation by E.G. Green & Son (bodywork), tel: 01892 822992; Serck Marston (radiator), tel: 01622 756595; Spit & Polish (alloy wheels), tel: 01732 367771; Allen & Povey (interior trim), tel: 0181 304 0262; and Ambassador Car Mats (custom floor mats), tel: 01257 472315. It is now on display at Asta Motors, Oxted.* "

These were quite nice old cars and a giant leap forward from their predecessors – the disastrous Mk IV Zephyrs. It's nice to see one being preserved. This is also a useful list of telephone numbers for anyone contemplating having a similar job done on an old favourite.

Corvette re-cons

" *In Bob Murray's article about Corvettes, he quoted Tom Falconer as stating that 'a complete engine re-build would cost well under £1,000'. I have been quoted £3,500 locally. So who is Tom Falconer, and how does one get in touch with him?* "

Tom Falconer runs Claremont Corvette and, with six books to his credit, is the UK's top Corvette expert. He confirms that a 'tired engine', already out of the car, could be rebuilt with new rings, mains, ends, camshaft, lifters and timing gear for a total of around £1,000. More work, such as a rebore, balancing, chemical cleaning and painting or plating, would naturally cost more. Claremont Corvette is based at Malling Road, Snodland, Kent ME6 5NA, tel: 01634 244444. Another reader I put in touch with Claremont was referred on to Dart Corvette Sales & Service, Penhurst Road, Leigh, nr Hildenbridge, Kent, tel: 01732 838551. And there is, of course the Classic Corvette Club (UK) Ltd, c/o Andy Greenfield, 17 Sudeley Gardens, Hockley, Essex SS5 4XQ, tel: 01702 200881.

Of Minor concern

" *I have just acquired a 1968 Morris Minor 1000 which I intend to restore over the next three years and present to my daughter once she passes her driving test. However, I admit to being unsure where to start. Are there any publications which deal with the complete restoration of a Morris Minor? Or is there some organisation which can give me an idea where to start?* "

Providing you have bought a car which is structurally sound (many old Minors aren't), then you couldn't have picked a better car for a home restoration. First, join the Morris Minor Owners Club, PO Box 1098, Derby DE23 8ZX, tel: 01332 291675, website: http://www. MorrisMinorOC.co.uk. The club publishes its own manual of technical tips on restoration, backed up by a technical helpline. Providing the car is not too far gone, you should have a lot of fun working on it and joining in the club activities. But I would urge you to seriously consider updates such as Marina running gear and brakes, an unleaded cylinder head conversion and other modifications that make the car much better and safer to drive in 1990s traffic.

She sells MG shells

" My son-in-law in Cyprus has a 1963 MG Midget. He wishes to restore the car and requires a new body shell. Can you please offer any advice on a likely supplier? "

British Motor Heritage has a factory in Witney, Oxfordshire, which builds new shells for MG Midget Mk IIIs (1966 on), MGB roadsters, MGB GTs, Triumph TR6s and Mini Mk IVs (1976–89). They are supplied through specialists and the advice line on 01993 707200 will direct you to the right one. In your case, the biggest supplier is Moss International Ltd, International House, Hampton Farm Industrial Estate, Hampton Road West, Hanworth, Middlesex TW13 6DB, tel: 0181 867 2000. The price for a Midget Mk III primed shell is £2,500 including VAT (subtract VAT for export). But, unfortunately, a 1963 Mk I has different doors (no wind-up windows), different rear panel (no proper folding hood) and very different rear spring hangers (quarter rather than semi-elliptics).

Registering a rebuild

" I wonder if you would have the time to run through the attached file of correspondence on my Saab 96 V4 GLS. The car was built in 1979 and I have owned it for 14 years since it was originally imported in 1982. Before I rebuilt the car it bore the registration mark LGK 916Y, from the original date of importation (rather than build date, as is the current system). The rebuilt car retains its original body/chassis, apart from bolt-on replace-

ment wings, etc. It has its original engine, gearbox and springs. But the rear axle was replaced in 1986 and I have converted it from LHD to RHD so it has a replacement steering assembly. The Local VRO has inspected the car twice, but insists on re-registering it with a new chassis number and a 'Q' plate. How can I get a clear statement of their basis for doing this and challenge it? "

On the basis of its inspections, the DVLA has now allocated the car a new chassis number (contradicting the number stamped on the actual 'chassis'), and a 'Q' plate, and it has voided both the original registration, LGK 916Y, and the registration MOO 778J from which some 'donor' parts such as the steering rack and column came. But on the basis of the DVLA's leaflet INF26 detailing registration of rebuilt and radically altered vehicles, I agree with you – the car appears to qualify to keep its originally allocated number-plate. To qualify to keep an original registration the car must notch up 8 or more points from the following list:

- Original chassis or both sub-frames and bodyshell, or a new bodyshell supplied by the manufacturer   5 points

- Original suspension   2 points

- Original axles   2 points

- Original transmission   2 points

- Original steering assembly   2 points

- Original engine   1 point

SAFETY

Flyopen bonnets

" *Some time ago I purchased an 'H'-reg. VW Polo for my wife from a large dealership. It came with a fresh MOT. Days later she had the frightening experience of the front-opening bonnet flying open while she was driving. The safety catch had corroded and stuck open. More recently, I purchased an 'H'-registered Volvo 740SE Estate for myself, again from a garage and again with a fresh MOT. This car also had a stuck-open bonnet safety catch. I write to urge all your readers who have front-opening bonnets to check that the safety catches are functioning properly and, if not, to free them off with a penetrating oil and to then protect them with a liberal coating of grease. I also feel that a check on the function of the bonnet safety catch should be part of the MOT inspection.* "

Good point, and good advice – especially to readers who live in areas where the roads are heavily salted during winter.

Belting about in older cars

" *Can you tell us the law regarding carrying small children and infants in pre-war motor cars? My vehicles are a five-seat, four-door saloon in which I have devised my own child locks for the rear doors (I take the inside handles off) and an open two/four seater with a single door.* "

According to *Hughes Guide to Traffic Law For the Enforcement Officer*, a 'small child' (under

12 years, under 4ft 11in tall) must wear a front seatbelt, or otherwise must not be carried in the front at all. Larger children must wear front seatbelts where they are fitted but if not fitted they can still travel in the front. If rear belts are not fitted and front belts are, children must transfer to any unoccupied front seat and wear the belt. There is much more to this, so better to read the 'Highway Code' or to buy *Hughes Guide to Traffic Law For the Enforcement Officer* from Motorvation Consultants Ltd, price £15 (annual update service £8), PO Box 3250, Milton Keynes MK6 3ZT, tel: 01908 676008. The danger in a pre-war car is not the accident you might cause but the accident another driver might cause by overestimating the speed the old car is travelling. Today's roads are not safe places for small children in old cars to travel.

Rear seat safety

" *We have a 1989 Vauxhall Carlton Estate and three children, two aged six and one of three. The three-year-old is still in a car seat, but growing fast, and is already 3ft 5in tall. When he grows out of his car seat, I don't really want him in a lap belt. I have spoke to Vauxhall who say they do not make or know of anyone who does make a three point centre seat belt for my car, or indeed for any car not designed for it. Do you know of anyone who makes such a kit, or will I have to change my car?* "

The old strap-hanger harness bar for estate cars has not been manufactured for about five years because there is now a new EU standard and no one has been able to make a harness bar that complies with it. The In-Car Safety Centre (01908 220909) offers a device known as the 'Vario' which fits over the centre child's stomach and can be used by children up to six or seven years old. The Quickfit Safety Centre

(0181 206 0101) offers a range of three-point centre rear belt fittings tested to EU standards by the TNO in Holland or by the TRL. All the cars I am about to list come with a proper lap and diagonal centre rear seat belt, either as standard or as an option. They are: Alfa 156 (£97.53 option); new BMW 5-Series; Citroën Xantia Estate; Ford Mondeo from 1997 model-year; Honda Accord from 1999 model-year; Land Rover Freelander five-door; Land Rover Discovery from 1999 model-year; new Mazda 626 from July 1997; Mercedes C Class estate; Mercedes E Class estate from May 1996; Mercedes E Class saloon from June 1998; Mitsubishi Galant from 1998 model-year; Mitsubishi Space Star; new Nissan Primera SLX; Peugeot 306 Sedan; Peugeot 406; Renault Laguna from 95M; Renault Megane and Scenic; Renault Espace from 1997 model-year; 'new' Rover 200; Rover 600 from 1997 model-year; Rover 75; Rover 800 4-door from 94M; Saab 900 from 94L; Saab 9-3; Saab 9-5 (saloon and estate); New Seat Toledo (from 1999 model-year); Toyota Camry from 1997 model-year; Toyota Corolla from July 1997; Toyota Avensis; Vauxhall Astra from April 1998; Vauxhall Vectra from 1997 model-year; Vauxhall Omega; 1998 VW Golf IV (£100 optional extra); new VW Passat (£100 optional extra); Volvo S40; Volvo V40; Volvo S70; Volvo V70; Volvo 850; Volvo S80; Volvo 940; Volvo 960,; Volvo S90; Volvo V90.

Tightening your belts

" *The rear seat belts of my December 1996 Nissan Primera are causing me some concern. An intermittent fault seems to make the belts tighten so much that the wearers feel obliged to unbuckle them – even while travelling. This is without the belts being put into the ALR mode for fitting a*

child safety seat. Have you or any of your readers experienced this kind of problem? "

The idea of the ALR is to switch the belts from 'inertia' to 'locked' mode in order to keep a child seat secure. The method of engaging it is to slowly pull out all the seat belt webbing from the reel, then allow the belt to retract slowly and feed it into the reel to take out any remaining slack. As you do this, you will hear a clicking sound. To switch the belt out of ALR mode, the method is to open the buckle and allow it to retract fully to the stowed position. Next time you pull the seat belt out it will have reverted to inertia mode. If this reader is following these instructions to the letter and this is not happening, then there is a fault and his seatbelts are permanently in ALR mode. What might be causing this is that his passengers are very large and cannot get the seat belts around themselves without pulling them all the way out of the reels. Nissan GB confirmed this opinion. The rear belts are not designed to accommodate extremely large people or to hold rear-facing baby seats. The front belts are much longer, to cope with the range of front seat positions and to accommodate rear-facing baby seats or large people.

Bagged

" *Many current passenger cars are now fitted with driver's airbags. In the case of a head-on accident where the airbag does not inflate, would you say that the car manufacturer bears some responsibility for the non-functioning of this particular piece of equipment?* "

It isn't as simple as that. European airbags are set to trigger at an impact of around 15 mph into a solid object. American airbags were originally set to trigger in a 5 mph impact. The trouble is, the trigger that measures the weight of impact can never be 100 per cent reliable because impacts themselves are different. A car under braking hitting the back of another car which is itself under braking may undergo too soft an impact to trigger the airbag. The other factor to take into consideration is the high cost of an airbag going off. If this happens due to an over-sensitive trigger in a situation that causes no other damage to the car, replacing the airbag and repairing the damage they caused can cost as much as £5,000 in some cases. In any case we shouldn't rely on passive safety devices. We should always leave what Paul Ripley describes as a 'control space' between our car and the car in front, even if this means moving to a lane to our left.

Amazingly lucky escape

" *In August, my husband had a terrible accident in our Jeep Grand Cherokee. He was sitting in the vehicle with the engine running, his foot on the brake and the gear selector in reverse. He then got out of the car without shifting the selector from 'R' to 'P'. The car remained stationary while he walked behind it, but then began to reverse, pinning him against our gate. It then broke through the gate, ran my husband over and continued over the road until it crashed into a brick wall. As we ran to it, we heard the engine sound alter as it changed gear into 'D', at which point our two-year-old son ran out of the gateway straight into its path. The Jeep knocked him over, passed completely over the top of him and crashed back into our gate pillar where it eventually stopped. My husband pulled our son out from beneath the back of the Jeep unharmed apart from a bumped head and bruised foot. My husband suffered from severe grazing and bruising. I feel that two questions arise from this incident: How can it be possible to get out of an automatic car while it is still in gear? Surely there should be more safety precautions. And how can an off-road car, or any car for that matter, jump gear at all? Chrysler Jeep's response was that the vehicle is fitted with an interlock system that prevents the selection of forward or rearward drive without the foot brake first being depressed, and that 'it is strongly recommended that the gearshift lever be left firmly in 'P' (Park) before leaving the vehicle.' Jeep felt that the change of gear from 'R' to 'D' was 'a direct result of the sudden change of inertia when the vehicle came into contact with the brick wall'.* "*

I have heard of other cases when automatic vehicles 'changed themselves' from 'R' to 'D' or 'D' to 'R' as the result of an impact. It's also quite common for owners of automatics with American-style foot-operated parking brakes (which include current Mercedes models) to simply leave the vehicles in 'P' and not bother with the parking brake when they get out. To protect drivers from making the same severe error your husband made, it should be possible to for an auto electrician to install a warning buzzer that sounds if a door is opened when the vehicle is in gear with the engine running.

Being seen

" *Driving in the dark as we often must do now that winter's here, I am appalled at the dull clothing of most pedestrians and cyclists which makes them very hard to spot on the roads. Rule 3 of the current 'Highway Code' clearly states, 'Wear or carry something that will help you to be seen. Light coloured, bright or fluorescent items will help in poor visibility. At night use reflective materials (e.g. reflective armbands and sashes), which can be seen in headlights up to three times as far away as non-reflective materials.'* "

Useful advice well worth repeating, because a significant proportion of non-driving pedestrians are completely unaware that the first section of the 'Highway Code' is devoted to them. An investment of £1.49 could save your life. Road menders fluorescent safety waistcoats only cost £10–£15 from builders' merchants and industrial clothing suppliers. It's a good idea, too, to keep one in the spare wheel compartment, in case you have to change a wheel in the dark at the side of the road.

Safe in a crash

" *My wife and I were recently involved in a severe head-on crash. I was driving an 'H'-registered VW Polo. The other vehicle was an 'M'-reg. Transit. My wife and I were severely injured and the Polo is a write-off. The Transit driver, who now faces charges, was unhurt. The crash design of the Polo may well have saved our lives, but it is equally apparent that driver and passengers stand a better chance in a larger vehicle. Should I therefore buy a Transit van and hope I don't hit anything bigger?* "

Polos have always had front and rear 'crumple zones' surrounding a 'rigid safety cell'. The first models were advertised as being 'Crunchy on the outside, hard in the middle'. And the current Polo came out top of the class in the latest

NCAP crash safety survey. But a larger vehicle designed along the same principles should provide even better protection. I recently renewed acquaintance with VW's Caravelle 2.5 TDI and was reminded of another advantage of vehicles like this. The view over the tops of surrounding cars is excellent, giving the driver ample opportunity to spot approaching hazards and take action.

Shunt protection

" *I have followed the results of the recent NCAP tests, but none of them include a rear impact test. As about 90 per cent of drivers follow much too close, are there any comparative statistics for the ability to withstand a rear-end shunt?* "

Yes, but they are held by the manufacturers. Saab, Volvo and Mercedes Benz conduct extensive research into the ability of their vehicles to withstand all types of impacts and this greatly exceeds the limited independent comparative work done by NCAP. For example, a ceiling-high load in an estate car can shift forwards with such force it decapitates the rear seat occupants. However, Saab's 9-5 estate has a load tie hook system which is so strong it can take the entire weight of the car. The Saab 9-5 saloon came top in its class in the NCAP side and offset front impact tests, so the Saab 9-5 Estate would currently seem to represent the safest car to be in during most types of accident.

Accident kit

" *Your readers might be interested in our 'Stop Camera Action' car kit which provides all the essential ingredients for recording the evidential aftermath of an accident. This includes a disposable flash camera, pen, standard European accident report statement form and a high-visibility reflective waistcoat which can not only be used at the scene of an accident, but also worn for changing wheels and essential roadside repairs. The kit will retail at accessory shops and service stations for no more than £14.99. If your readers have any problems finding one, please phone Unique UK on 01754 763457.* **"**

I'll go along with this because, though a reader could assemble the kit himself, the price for the complete kit is fair and reasonable.

Airbag safety

" *I am 5 ft 2 in tall and am interested in the type of injury that can occur to those who are nearer than 25 cm to an airbag when it goes off. If injury is inevitable, then I would have to consider having the airbag either disarmed or removed. What I want to avoid is the sort of incident where a minor collision causes serious injury as a result of this supposed safety device going off.* **"**

On 14 April 1999, an inquest jury returned a verdict of accidental death on a woman allegedly killed by her car's airbag in a head-on collision. Inevitably there were calls for an inquiry. According to a *Daily Telegraph* report, 'the airbag knocked her back against the headrest with a force equivalent to someone falling off a building. Both the hospital doctor who tried to save her and the police expert who examined her Rover 414 car believed her death was cause by the airbag.' It is the first known death by this cause in Europe, but in the USA 130 deaths have been recorded when drivers sat within ten inches of the steering wheel. The report went on to talk about adopting 'intelligent airbags' and switching mechanisms to switch them off if a driver's seat is moved too closely forward. But, of course, the last things modern cars need is more high-tech equipment, because it merely means more to go wrong. The best advice for those short of stature is to sit in a variety of cars with height and reach adjustable steering and seats, for example the Ford Focus, Ford Mondeo, VW Golf, VW Bora or Seat Toledo. If, with the seat a long way forward, the steering wheel can be pushed to a minimum ten inches from the driver, even in the unlikely event of an airbag going off with the force described, the driver would be sufficiently far away for it not to matter. If you disconnect an airbag, you may find that your or the third party's insurer disclaims responsibility for any injury, and the car manufacturer almost certainly will.

SECURITY

Fobbed off

" *Complaints about the unreliability of keyfob transponder immobilisers brought forth an explanation from the Radio Society of Great Britain.* "

Before the EC Electromechanical Compatibility Directive of 1996, all very-short-wavelength transmitters operated in the UHF waveband at 418 MHz. Because this is a protected waveband in which only very low power transmissions exist, there is only a very small chance of mutual interference. But the Directive settled on an immobiliser frequency of 433.92 MHz with a maximum permitted unlicensed power of 0.25mW.

Unfortunately, in the UK, 433.92 MHz is in the middle of a band used by the MOD for its MOULD national radio network. The MOD is the primary user of this band. For Radio Amateurs there is an Internationally allocated band of 430 MHz to 440 MHz. In the UK, Radio Amateurs are classed as secondary users of the band, but powerful signals exist from UK and continental static and mobile radio stations. Trafficmaster also uses the 433 MHz band and is classified as a secondary user.

The Wireless Telegraphy Act of 1949 requires

that secondary users of any waveband *must* accept interference. And since keyfob transmitters are required by the EU directive to operate at the extremely weak power of 0.25 mW, they will almost always be overridden by a stronger signal.

The signal receivers in car systems can be of very poor quality and are sometimes unable to filter out radio signals on frequencies close to 433.92 MHz. These overload the front of the transmitter so it cannot 'hear' the signal from the keyfob. It's like two people trying to whisper to each other in a football crowd after a goal. To overcome this, a reader from Marlborough sends the following suggestions: first, hold the fob as close as possible to the receiver; second, wait in case the stronger signal decreases in strength or stops; third, get into the car with the key and push it to another location where the fob will disarm the immobiliser.

The other key-fob problem is synchronisation of the rolling codes of 'Thatcham'-approved immobilisers. The car's receiver knows that the next signal it should receive should be based on the on it received previously. But if one of more of these signals are blocked by a stronger signal, the code sequence goes out of step and the receiver ignores any further signals from the transmitter fob.

There are various routines to re-synchronise the fob transmitter, which usually mean opening it and pressing two buttons at the same time, but may be more complicated.

My Marlborough correspondent suggests that car buyers should insist on a system that operates on 418 MHz rather than 433.92 MHz. Owners with problem systems operating on 433.92 MHz might seek legal advice as to the 'satisfactory quality' of their systems under the 1994 Sale and Supply of Goods Act. (getting redress under the Act is easier said than done, but there may be a basis for a Small Claims Court action.) He feels that the AA and RAC should press the DTI to persuade Brussels to remove the 433.92 MHz immobiliser allocation.

Another correspondent, this one from Newbury, sent me a similar letter and an extract from *Radcom*, the Radio Society of Great Britain's magazine. This tells us that the Society has formed an EMC Committee which is campaigning for an improvement in the performance of 433.92 MHz radio-activated vehicle key entry systems. The 'RAKE' group has produced a document entitled 'Guidelines for Manufacturers of Vehicle Key Systems'. (Radio Society of Great Britain, Lambda House, Cranbourne Road, Potters Bar, Herts EN6 3JE, tel: 01707 659015; fax: 01707 645105; website: http://www.rsgb.org.uk.)

Unwanted immobilisations

" *I drive an Astra GTE 16v which I had fitted with a Vecta immobiliser when I purchased it in 1992. Recently, the car started cutting out while I was driving it and, after replacing the fuel pump relay, the cause was eventually narrowed down to the Vecta. Some circuits were isolated and I had to pay a bill of £35.25. Then, in May 1998, I had the same problem again. The Vecta people told me they were aware of the problem and removed the immobiliser. Now, if I want it replaced, I have to pay for a new one. What concerns me is I never wanted it, I was told to have it by the insurance company. So I was told to fit a device for security which, if it fails on a fast main road or motorway, could endanger my life.* "

You have a point. The other little problem that could always occur with aftermarket immobilisers is that they pack up while you're on your holidays in Southern Spain or Italy. For questions about alarms and immobilisers, the Association of British Insurers runs a helpline on 0990 502006.

'Red Key' remedy

" *I recently wrote to you about an ex-rental Fiat Cinquecento I bought which came without a 'Red Key' to reset the car's combined ECU and immobiliser. You expressed doubts about having a new key correctly programmed. However, branches of MINIT UK now offer precisely this service for '70 per cent of immobiliser keys on the spot'. Prices start at £12.95, rising to £19.95, and the key they cut and programmed for our Cinquecento works perfectly.* "

As long as you have successfully disconnected the battery, reconnected it, and used the replacement master key to re-set the immobiliser system to work with the other keys you hold, I believe you. However, without an original red key to copy, all your new key will be is a copy of the other standard immobiliser keys.

Locked out

" *Four months ago, we purchased a two-year-old Mercedes C200 Elegance. Since that date, the infra-red remote locking system has proved to be totally unreliable, in that one key or the other fails to open or close the system, and we are afraid of being locked out sooner or later. The Mercedes agent who supplied the car cannot rectify the system and suggests we pay £6,500 over and above the £20,000 we paid for our car in order to obtain a model with a manual locking system. We live in a remote area of Herefordshire and are both disabled. Can you please help us resolve this problem?* "

After a spate of this type of problem, the Motor Insurance Repair & Research Centre, Thatcham, has issued a press release on the subject. Its first, very simple, piece of advice is to *always use the fob, not the key*. MIRRC believes that confusion arises partly because too few buyers of new and used modern cars read their vehicle handbooks and partly because casual drivers such as parking attendants and valet staff use the key to get into the car instead of the fob. Using the key instead of the fob may well put the transmitter and receiver out of synchronisation. Second, change the batteries of all fobs at the recommended intervals stated in the handbook, or at least every 12 months (particularly important with infra-red systems). Third, keep the key and fob on the same keyring. Fourth, keep your spare key and fob fully operational and in a safe place. Fifth, understand the manufacturer's procedure for obtaining a new remote control and key which, for security reasons, may take up to a week.

The salesman at your Mercedes agent may have thought that you would never manage to understand your system, which is why he recommended you to switch to a car with manual locking. But follow MIRRC's advice and you should have no further problems.

Alarming story

" *I purchased a VW Golf Mk IV in August and the specification includes a factory-fitted intruder alarm. After the BBC 'Watchdog' report, Mk IV Golfs so fitted were re-called for the system to be modified to prevent it being set off by heavy rain hitting the car. The modifications consist of a pair of ugly sensors fitted to the tops of the 'A' pillars which I find detract from the appearance of the interior of the car. I contracted to purchase a Golf with a totally integrated system. Instead, I have two carbuncles fitted to the tops of the 'A' pillars and am told that my insurance is likely to increase if I remove them. Would you care to advise me, please?* "

Yes, with the same observations I gave to VW. I had one of these pre-modified Golfs on loan and the alarm went off during a storm in the middle of the night. So I sleepily crawled out to the car and did what I have always done to prevent precisely the same thing happening with the alarm of my 12-year-old VW. I turned the heater to maximum heat, which has the effect of closing the fresh air vents into the car, and I set the directional controls to send any air which did come through to the footwell. Result: no more false alarms from changes of air pressure inside the car. Pressing the air recirculation switch with the ignition on should have the same effect on a car so fitted.

Dis-car-nected

" I have need of another Dis-car-nect. This is a device, fitted between the negative terminal of the car battery and the earth cable, which enables the battery to be disconnected simply by turning a knob, thus allowing the car to be disabled by removing the knob completely. It was marketed by a company by the name of Richbrook International, which seems to have disappeared. Incidentally, here in France I have just purchased a Fiat Seicento with power steering and metallic paint for Ffr 51,000 on the road (£5,374). "

Richbrook International have moved, and are alive and well at 18 York Road, Wimbledon, London SW19 8TP, tel: 0181 543 7111. They still sell the Dis-car-nect, and other devices such as an electrical master switch which can be hidden anywhere in the car. But, due to lack of demand, they have stopped importing Store-Tech plugs, designed to absorb condensation moisture from inside the combustion chambers of a stored car.

STARTING AND RUNNING PROBLEMS

Intermittent faults

Some common causes of intermittent faults are as follows:

● **Carburettor icing** The air entering a carburettor needs to be heated because, at speed, condensation in the air can freeze in the air intake, restricting the orifice and cutting off the air. Once the car has stopped for a short time, the residual heat of the engine melts the ice and the car can be re-started. If water-heated, check water pipes; if electrically heated, check electrics. If the air filter trunk has a 'summer' and 'winter' setting, switch it to the winter setting so it picks up hot air from the exhaust manifold.

● **Faulty carburettor** The Pierburg carburettors of older VWs can suffer loosening of the brass needle valve seat when the engine is hot. This leads to flooding of the carburettor, giving an over-rich mixture which makes the engine difficult to start. Stripping the carb, pushing the needle valve seat firmly home, and peining the surrounding aluminium to keep it in place will solve the problem for a while.

● **Faulty fuel pump or relay** An electrical contact in the relay to the fuel pump or the fuel pump itself could break or 'dry out', causing intermittent mis-fires in a fuel-injected car. After correction, the condition of the catalytic converter (if fitted) should also be checked.

● **Air leaks** in the injection system or the diaphragm pressure switch.

● **Badly routed cable** An electrical engine management cable routed over a part of the engine subject to movement could rub the insulation from the cable leading to a short.

● **Faulty contact or internally broken cable** Any engine management system cable suffering such a fault can lead to intermittent breakdowns. For example, 'The earth contacts at the plenum chamber to rocker cover were producing a short circuit caused by two unsecured bolts on the rear rocker which had become stripped.' (Alfa 164 Cloverleaf).

● **Dried-out coil or ignition system contacts** The remedy for this is to check all contacts and clean where necessary.

● **Coil failure; Spark plug or spark plug cable failure** The insulation of the cables from the distributor to the spark plugs can eventually break

down, but first try cleaning any accumulated dirt from the outside of the cables as this can harbour moisture which diverts the high tension current.

● **Blocked exhaust system** In pre-cat days, rust caused by condensation inside one of the silencer boxes could eventually block passages in the exhaust, preventing the car from 'exhaling', and stopping the engine. The same can happen if the ceramic core of a catalytic converter breaks up and blocks the rest of the exhaust system.

● **Dirt in fuel** Swarf or rust in a steel fuel tank can block the fuel pipe or fuel filter causing an excess of back pressure (this cause of intermittent faults is less common now that many cars have plastic fuel tanks).

- **Fuel line air lock** Often due to a sticking gravity valve, this can stop a carburetted car where the fuel is sucked by an engine-driven pump rather then pumped from the tank by an electric pump.

- **Blocked fuel tank breather (pipe or filler cap)** By preventing air being drawn into the fuel tank to replace the fuel sucked out, this can stop a car.

- **Faulty inlet air temperature sensor** Part of the 'choke mechanism' on a fuel injected car which sends messages to the ECU, which then decides to enrich or lean-off the fuel/air mixture.

- **Faulty fuel flow meter or air flow meter** This can cause intermittent or total failure in a fuel injected car.

Thanks to Colin Marshall and Keith Rhoods at Wheelbase garage, Hersham (01932 252515), and to BBR, which now offers a motor fault-finding helpline (0897 161123, 9.00–5.30, and calls cost a maximum of £1.47 a minute).

A reader from Dorchester came up with a novel reason for intermittent failures I had not encountered before. His heavy house keys were on the same ring as his ignition key, and the motion of these caused the key to move slightly in the ignition switch, separating the contact. A new ignition switch solved the problem.

Erratic automatic

" *I purchased a 'G'-reg. Peugeot 205 automatic with power steering. The car has developed a stalling problem. I took it to a Peugeot agent, but he could not solve this. On my own, I had the distributor cap and coil replaced, and had the battery checked. When it stalls it feels like it's running out of petrol. I then let it sit for five minutes and it will start. Can you help me?* **"**

The carburettor may simply be clogged up with tarry deposits from the petrol and all it may need is a carb-cleaning fuel additive, so try this cheap solution first. But the problem you describe was common on early carburated 405s, 309s fitted with the same 1.6 litre XU petrol engine and the 205 automatic which was the only 205 with a carburated 1.6 litre XU engine. Stalling happens when the engine runs too hot and causes fuel evaporation in the carburettor. The standard cure, which should have been carried out on most cars 'in service', was to fit a different main jet to improve the fuel flow, and to fit a new fan thermostat that switches the fan on at a lower temperature, keeping the engine cooler. If the carburettor itself is worn out, it can be replaced by a new Weber 36 TLC, part number 15310.799, which costs £249 from Webcon on 01932 788805. One other, less likely possibility with this engine, but one which fits your symptoms, is carburettor icing (see 'Intermittent Faults' above).

Down to earth

" *Recently I went to the aid of a young lady neighbour in distress whose Mini would not start. I eventually traced the reason to the battery earthing strap in the boot. The self-tapping screw which held it to the boot floor had stripped its thread. A nut, bolt and non-slip washer solved the problem, but I wonder just how many starting problems are down to a simple earthing fault?* **"**

Lots. And not just in the obvious places either. The sensors (air flow, air temperature, fuel flow, etc.) in a fuel injected engine also need to be earthed to the car's body, and if they lose the earth the car won't go.

Bravo/Brava HT leads

" *I have suffered an HT lead failure on my 'P'-registered Fiat Brava. Prior to the 24,000-mile service at Reg Vardy, Springburn, Glasgow, I was told that occasionally the HT leads fuse to the spark plugs. Apparently this is a '1 in 25 possibility'. When I went to collect the car, one of the HT leads had been found to be suspect and the whole HT wiring loom needed to be replaced at a staggering £93.00 including VAT. The customer care manager said she would take this up with Fiat.* "

Another reader had HT lead problems on a Panda. But so far yours is only the second complaint about Bravo/Brava HT leads. If any reader ever experiences a misfire in a catalysed car, for whatever reason, stop immediately and do not continue to drive, otherwise you could destroy the matrix of your very expensive catalytic converter.

No choking

" *I have a 'P'-reg. Nissan Micra automatic. Twice I have had to call out Nissan Assist because it would not even attempt to start in the garage. The first chap said it was 'flooding', not my fault, and it happened once in a blue moon. The second chap was much more helpful. After some detective work, we narrowed it down to the fact that the previous time I had started up the car it was only to move it out of the garage, wash it and put it back. Apparently, with the fuel injection automatic enrichment system, after you first switch on the engine you should drive the car for about ten minutes before you switch it off. Seems wrong, but nobody warns you. Also, he showed me how to remove a fuse, turn the ignition once or twice, replace the fuse and Bingo!, it goes!* "

There's a much bigger issue here than you and a lot of other readers realise. Starting a car engine and then switching it off again almost immediately always was extremely bad practice. For a cold engine to fire, it needs a rich fuel–air mixture, the residue from which will tend to wash out the cylinder bores immediately after switching off. Starting from cold also creates a massive amount of condensation, both inside the engine and inside the exhaust system, which does not fully dry out if the car is not driven for 10–15 miles. And, to compound all this, modern catalysed fuel injection cars are set up to run through a two, three, and sometimes four stage cold-start cycle. If this is not completed, the car can massively over-fuel and the ECU shuts down the engine to prevent fuel damage to the cat. So, if you want to clean your car and if your garage and drive are on level ground, it's far better to push the car in and out of the garage. Avoid any really short trips. And, if forced to take one, try to balance it with frequent longer trips of ten miles or so. You should also change the oil and filter of a little used car at least every six months because, by the end of that six months, the oil will be contaminated by unburned petrol and condensation.

Same fault seven times

" I bought a new Citroën AX Neon in January 1994 and have had a number of problems with it, most of which were either fixed under warranty or free of charge as a matter of goodwill. However, the throttle potentiometer has been found to be faulty no less than seven times: in May, June and July of 1995; in May 1996; in February 1997; and in April and May of 1998. "

This letter is the much-edited tip of a rather large iceberg. Part of it is the result of my correspondent moving from Norfolk to Kent. I talked this over with Citroën UK and discovered that, over time, the Norfolk Citroën agent had isolated the problem, caused by electrolytic corrosion in a connecting block rather than a fault with the potentiometer itself. It took the same sort of time scale for the Kent agent to arrive at the same conclusion. Each time a new potentiometer was connected to the old connector block the electrolytic corrosion began again until contact was partially lost. The same can occur with Peugeot 106s because the same parts are used.

A raw deal?

" *A simple question, the answer to which never appears in 'road tests': how is one supposed to anticipate an engine's oil consumption? I have the misfortune to have purchased a new Seat Alhambra TDI. Between August last year and its first service at 10,000 miles it has consumed 3 litres of engine oil. When I say 'consumed', I mean 'burned', not leaked. To my astonishment, Seat tells me this is within normal tolerance and their engines can use up to 1 litre per 1,000 km or 625 miles. This engine, by the way, is the Audi 1.9 diesel used throughout the VW/Seat/Audi and now Skoda range. Am I being picky or am I getting a raw deal?* "

There are three possibilities here. The first is that the engine is simply 'bedding in'. This can take 15,000 miles with a TDI and VWs are filled with a special blend of recycled oil specifically for 'running in'. The second is that you're not booting it enough. If direct-injected diesels aren't given enough welly early in their lives they don't tend to bed in properly and can become oil burners. The third is that you have a dodgy turbo oil seal and engine oil is exiting via this and the exhaust pipe. Get someone to follow you and if they notice a puff of blue/black smoke whenever you accelerate (not just when pulling out to overtake after being stuck behind something) then ask your Seat agent for a new turbo under the car's three-year warranty. Once you've got this sorted out, if I was you I'd ignore the 10,000-mile oil change intervals and have the oil changed by your Seat agent every 5,000 miles until out of warranty. Then switch to Mobil-1 diesel and change it yourself every 5,000 miles.

Killer slime?

" *Some months ago you mentioned a VAG TDI 90 bhp engine that, in spite of oil changes at manufacturer-stipulated intervals, expired before it reached 150,000 miles. I have recently been made aware of what I regard to be a potential defect in these engines which, in my opinion, will seriously reduce their life expectancy. This is the massive build-up of black sludge in the inlet manifold in the area of the exhaust gas recirculation outlet and is caused by the virtually unrestricted flow of exhaust gas mixing with the copious oil vapour from the breather in the turbo-charged air from the intercooler. VW believes this is okay, but I envisage it leading to piston rings sticking, bore wear and the build-up of deposits on inlet valves by the muck that is actually drawn into the engine rather than being left deposited on the walls of the inlet manifold. Amounts of up to 3 mm have been seen in engines of under 40,000 miles. Presumably the build-up will continue to the point where airflow is restricted, causing black smoke, power loss, high fuel consumption and MOT test failures. To establish the amount of sludge in an engine, all that is needed is to remove the hose where the inlet tract joins the manifold and look in.* "

I phoned the expired engine's engineer owner, who confirmed that he had found so much black sludge in his inlet manifold he had to use cleansing agents and 'a teaspoon' to get most of it out. But this wasn't the cause of his disaster. The previous week, the engine's head gasket had failed and been replaced by his local VAG agent. At the time, with the head off, it was noted that there was some bore wear. With the head back on, during a 1,000-mile return journey the car began blowing out a lot of blue smoke and using oil. The owner thought that either the rings had worn, a piece of debris from replacing the head gasket had broken an oil ring on one piston and badly scored the bore, or that the replacement head gasket had given way and was letting oil into a combustion chamber. He simply bought a used replacement engine and won't know the true cause of the original failure until he has the engine rebuilt. But, in conversation, he also confirmed that he had changed the engine oil 'every 4,000–6,000 miles' using Morris Oil (once), VAG oil (once) and mostly Millers XFE semi-synthetic. The oil was changed earlier than the 6,000-mile change point because 'the engine would start to clatter after 4,000–4,500 miles'. I put the sludge question to VW UK and their answer was, just as they told him, that the sludge is benign. Based on engine life tests, VW now allows 10,000-mile oil changes and says that TDIs simply do not suffer from an increase in oil consumption unless something breaks or is ingested into the engine.

TDI engine life

" Further to the letter about sludge and its effect on VAG TDI engines (see 'Killer slime?' above), I have nothing but praise for mine. Contrary to the 150,000-mile engine life achieved in the letter, mine was still going strong when I sold it after four-and-a-half years and 200,000 miles. The engine had needed a new head gasket at 130,000 miles, but the car was still on its original clutch, still on its original exhaust system (including the catalytic converter) and was only on its second timing belt which had been changed at 98,800 miles. Oil changes were at 10,000-mile intervals, and the car was only using half a litre of oil in between changes when I sold it. "

The reasons why your engine did not sludge up are partly the high rate at which you clocked up the mileage, keeping the engine hot and driving out moisture, and partly your driving style. But it's good to know that a life of 150,000 miles is far from universal.

The M52 factor

" *I am contemplating purchasing an 'M'-registered BMW 525iSE Touring from a friend. It is a high-specification version and will have done around 70,000 miles, almost exclusively motorway travel, and has a full service history. Having been a company Mondeo man for many years I am looking for a little more refinement and comfort in retirement. I would like the car to last for about eight years and another 80,000 miles. Can I reasonably expect the engine to do 150,000 miles without major problems and expense? Should I be worried about the rumours that some UK petrol can have a detrimental effect on the bores of six-cylinder BMW engines? This car has been run exclusively on supermarket 'own brand' unleaded.* "

525s and 325s don't suffer M52 factor because they have M50 iron block engines. As long as you use semi or fully synthetic oil, change it and the coolant regularly (twice as often as scheduled), and use decent high-detergent petrol such as Texaco or Shell, the engine should have no problem clocking up 150,000 miles and should be game for at least 100,000 more.

Stammering Gentry

" *In March 1992, I bought a new Peugeot 205 Gentry, based on the catalysed 205GTi 1.9. I have been in semi-retirement since 1995 and the car has been used very lightly, covering just 59,000 miles in total. Over the last 12 months it has become very difficult to start when hot. Earlier this year, the agent fitted a new chip, but my own feeling is that this has little to do with the problem. I regularly check the coolant level because the thermostatic fan seems to cut in frequently – seemingly without regard to the ambient temperature.* "

The estimable John Simister has mentioned this to me before and subsequently covered the solution in detail in the January 1999 issue of *Practical Classics* magazine. It seems that the main reason why Peugeot 205 GTi 1.6s and 1.9s suffer problems of hesitancy in the fuel delivery is poor quality components in the ECU. These are affected by 'background electronic noise', but our old friends BBR have a cure which costs £121 in kit form or £176.25 fitted. Speak to Dammon Butler at BBR, tel: 01280 702389.

Running-on

" *I recently purchased a 1996 Alfa Romeo 155 2.0i Twin Spark with about 20,000 miles on the clock. On two separate occasions recently, having switched off the ignition and take out the key, the engine continued to run. As soon as I tried to put the car into gear, the engine stopped running. I have been driving for 20 years, mainly Fords, and this is the first car that has not responded to the ignition key.* "

Because the engine conks out when you try to put it into gear, I suspect that the problem is confined to just one cylinder. It could be an excess of carbon on one of the two spark plugs which continues to glow red hot when the ignition is switched off and then ignites any residual fuel/air sucked into the combustion chamber. So, first, check the plugs – all eight of them. If you find that several bear carbon deposits, change all eight plugs and start running the car on decent petrol such as Texaco CleanSystem 3 Super or Shell Super, both of which contain adequate detergents to keep the fuel system clean. Running a car like this on the cheapest 'premium unleaded' petrol available is likely to result in the sort of problems you describe. Other reasons for running-on are air leaks in the inlet manifold, over-advanced timing (unlikely in an ECU-controlled engine); incorrect valve clearances, and silt in the cooling galleries causing localised overheating.

Well, bowl me over

" I have a Passat estate with an ignition key immobiliser. I began to experience trouble starting the car. It would fire up, then peter out, and would do so between twice and seven times before the engine would run normally. The fault was intermittent and the car would sometimes run perfectly for three or four days before it recurred. The VW agent could find no fault, but suspected the immobiliser. Then it dawned on me. Just before the problem started, my bowling club issued us all with a circular disc containing a micro-chip with which to gain entry to the club. I kept mine on the car keyring. When I removed it I had no more trouble, so the chip must have been interfering with the car's immobiliser system. I hope my experience is of help to readers who encounter a similar problem. "

I'm sure it will be. There has been a problem with the signal receivers in the steering columns of the very similar Audi A4 (see 'Fobbed off' in the Security section above) and the bowling club micro-chip signal must have interfered with this.

Stuttering Skoda

" After reading favourable comments in your column I decided to buy a Skoda Felicia diesel. I have found it to be an excellent car and superb value for money, but one drawback niggles. The car starts as soon as the glow-plug light goes out and for the first 100 yards it runs perfectly. I then suffer a bout of kangaroo jumps as the car stutters. Sometimes this is slight. But on occasion it can be quite alarming. Thereafter the car runs superbly. Two Skoda agents have had a look, but could find nothing wrong. "

Two suggestions. You may be setting off from cold before the engine has reached operating temperature and then changing into too high a gear too soon. Or there may be condensation water in the fuel. This collects in the base of the fuel filter and there should be instructions in the owner's handbook telling you how to drain it periodically. There is now a Haynes manual for this car.

Rogue Rover

" *I have a 90,000-mile 1989 Rover 820iSE automatic. After about two miles of driving, the engine starts to vibrate excessively and lose power. This continues for about a mile, then disappears. The agents tell me they won't be able to diagnose what is wrong unless it occurs when they are testing the car. My service engineer thinks it might be an electrical fault. Another engineer thinks the valves may be sticking. Do you think I should have a top-end overhaul, or renew the fuel injection ignition controller?* "

The M16 engine is prone to a number of faults at the mileage yours has reached. But because the hesitation in yours seems to clear itself after a mile, it can't be the usual burnt-out valves. The simplest and cheapest first-stage remedy is to empty a bottle of fuel injector cleaner into the petrol tank, then fill up with Texaco Clean-System 3 petrol (or Shell, Esso or Elf if you can't find Texaco). That may clear up the problem, but if it doesn't I would suspect either a serious build up of filth in the throttle body or a dickey air flow or air temperature sensor in the fuel injection system sending the wrong message to the ECU. If the engine has not had a recent timing belt, belt tensioner and camshaft end-seal replacement, it needs one, and because it's quite easy to put the belt on one or two notches out, I'd have this work done by a Rover agent or Rover specialist.

STORING A CAR

Car cryogenics

" *My father has now given up driving and we were wondering what to do with his 'F'-registered Fiat 126 Bis, which has covered just 28,000 miles and is in very nice condition. We have no need for a second car and we know its current value is very little. But we do have the space to keep it in dry storage and wonder if it might become collectible and start to appreciate in a few years time.* "

Unfortunately, the water-cooled 652 cc Bis was a model which tended to develop severe engine problems at around 30,000 miles as well as severe rust. But suggestions which should benefit all readers wishing to put a car into storage are as follows.

First, put the car on a SORN (Staturory Off Road Notification), which keeps it registered but necessitates an annual MOT. It's best to time the MOT halfway through the SORN year in case you have to do some work to get it through. Fail to keep an old car registered on a SORN and under new EU environmental laws it could be taken away and disposed of. During the summer it will be better for the car to be driven a reasonable distance occasionally (do you know anyone with trade insurance and trade plates who could do this without the necessity to tax and insure the car?). During the winter it will be better to lay the car up. Briefly, prior to laying up, completely drain and thoroughly flush the cooling system using a product such as Holts Radflush Parts 1 and 2. Refill the cooling system with a pre-mixed MPG Trigard coolant such as Comma Coldstream, which lasts four years rather then the two years of conventional MEG coolants and the year or less of Methanol coolants. Renew the engine oil and filter, grease the battery terminals with petroleum jelly, don't garage the car until it is thoroughly dry (best to take it for a long run immediately prior to laying up to evaporate any condensation in the exhaust system). To prevent rust in the tank and fuel system, drain the tank and replace the petrol with paraffin. When you leave the car, either disconnect both terminals of the battery or buy an 'Airflow' battery conditioner, follow the instructions, and leave it connected. Unlike a conventional battery charger, the 'Airflow' keeps the battery fully charged but not over-charged, with a very low amp current which does not interfere with the car's ECU, immo-biliser, or any other electronics. It's £40 well spent, and is available from Airflow UK, tel: 01635 569569. Store the car in a dry, well-aired garage, shed, barn or warehouse (the more air around the car the better). Consider investing in a dehumidifier or a 'Carcoon' (tel: 0161 737 9630). Leave the windows slightly open. Cover the car with a cotton sheet. Pump the tyres about 5 psi over pressure and move the car backwards and forwards occasionally to prevent the tyres flat-spotting. Give the battery a top-up charge once a month, press the clutch and brake pedals a few times every fortnight. There's not much you can do about the brake discs rusting except to store the car when dry in a dry place. Leave the handbrake off to prevent the cable stretching and the rear brakes seizing on. Before re-starting, drain the paraffin and either fit an in-line fuel filter if the car does not have one, or replace the fuel filter if the car does have one to be sure of picking up any debris or gums from the tank. When you want to re-start the car, either turn the engine over with a wrench or turn it over using the starter motor with the ignition disconnected to circulate some oil before starting it.

TAX

What's an historic vehicle?

" *I have two cars which I consider to be 'classics'. One is a 1974 'M'-registered MG Midget Mk III which has done 18,281 miles from new and is a concours winner. The other is a 1973 'M'-registered MGB GT V8 which has covered 42,527 miles and is one of only 2,591 ever made in right-hand drive. Under the new 'Historic Vehicles' rules, these are condemned forever to be considered as taxable old bangers, yet a 1972 Citroën Dyane is regarded as a VED-exempt 'classic'. I know the case is being argued by the Federation of Classic Car Clubs, but surely a fairer system would be to offer vehicles more than 25 years old a reduced rate of VED, or VED exemption if the car is only taken onto the roads at weekends or bank holidays, with VED payable if it is used during the week. If a punitive rate of VED based on engine size is introduced for cars such as my MGB GT V8 I am afraid that the car will have to be laid up. If this happens to all such cars then it will have a devastating effect on the UK's huge 'classic car' industry, on which many thousands of people depend for their employment.* "

Some sensible points raised here, despite the fact that there are many who would consider the Citroën 2CV and Dyane to be more 'classic' designs than an MGB V8.

Car or cash?

" *I currently travel 10,000 business miles a year, have a lease car provided by my employers, and contribute £84 a month towards it for private use. I purchase all the fuel and charge it back to my employers at 4.5 pence a business mile. My employers are now offering a scheme whereby I provide my own vehicle. In exchange, they will provide an £801pa lump sum (taxable), plus 34.4 pence a mile up to 8,500 miles and 12.5 pence per mile thereafter. I would be grateful for your advice as to which you consider to be the most advantageous.* **"**

I can't answer this because it depends on too many variables. There are two levels of tax-free mileage rates – up to 4,000 miles and over 4,000 miles – but the levels themselves depend on the engine size of the car. The other factor is the amount of your private mileage. Work this out, then contact Crown Leasing on 01487 773322 who will tell you which is the best way to go taking account of all costs and tax implications. Their full address is: The Green, Abbots Ripton, Huntingdon PE17 2PF. Crown Leasing uses Price Bailey Chartered Accountants at Walsingham Chambers, Butcher's Row, Ely, Cambs CB7 4NA, tel: 01353 662516 for Inland Revenue negotiations.

Benefit-in-unkind

" *If list prices of cars in the UK are considerably higher than equivalent cars in Europe, then, because benefit-in-kind tax is based on UK list prices, all company car drivers must be paying more in car benefit tax than we should be. Maybe it's time for company car drivers to at least complain and pressurise their fleet operators to source their cars from Europe, thus both reducing the list prices and P11D values and saving themselves paying some income tax. In the meantime, my £20,500 company car is shortly due for replacement and I intend to ask for a 'top of the range' van instead, saving myself £120 a month in income tax.* **"**

You're right. Company drivers are unfairly discriminated against in this way. But the fact is, fleets of 25 cars or more buy more than 60 per cent of all new cars sold in the UK, and smaller fleets absorb another 10–20 per cent. Big fleets buy cars at huge discounts on their list prices – sometimes combined discounts, rebates and volume bonuses amounting to as much as 40 per cent of list. Yet company drivers are taxed on the UK 'list prices' which are only ever paid by private buyers who have more money than sense.

Fuel price profiteering

" I am a regular reader of your column as well as the motoring magazines. I am deeply concerned about the pricing of motor fuel in the UK. I have just returned from New Zealand, where diesel fuel is a third of the price it is here. The oil companies always escape a proper answer to this question with the excuse that the high cost is due to national taxes. What is the truth? "

Different countries have different tax regimes. In the UK it is the current government's policy to subsidise low direct taxes with high indirect taxes on alcoholic drinks and on petrol and diesel fuel. The current rate of tax on unleaded petrol retailing at 71.9p a litre is 417 per cent. You pay 13.98 pence for the petrol, plus 57.92 pence in tax. Tax on ordinary diesel retailing at 74.9 pence per litre is 454 per cent. You pay 13.53 pence for the fuel and 61.37 pence in tax. The one fuel for which oil companies do over-charge is Superunleaded. When you pay 83.9 pence a litre for this, 64.83 pence goes in tax but you pay an unacceptable 19.07 pence for the fuel. You should only be paying about 15 pence, plus tax, as in all other EU countries. From 1 October 1999 the fuel tax on Super will be reduced to 49.21 pence, plus VAT on the fuel duty and VAT on the fuel itself, so if the price of Superunleaded

is not reduced to between 77 and 79 pence a litre, then the oil companies will be ripping us off and the matter should be referred to the MMC.

Fuelling discontent

" *I write in connection with an absurd situation, which needs your urgent intervention. The price of diesel in France is now so much lower than the price in the UK that, on a single fill, a lorry can save itself between £300 and £400 after the crossing charges have been taken into account. This means that lorries registered in France and Belgium can come into the UK, undercut British firms while working all week, and return to the mainland on Friday to repeat the exercise the following Monday. The effect of this will very rapidly be that hauliers in my constituency and over a wide swathe of the UK will be put out of business. It goes without saying that the UK Government receives not a penny in either tax or duty from these incoming lorries. I have sympathy for the desire to reduce the number of lorries on the roads, but I have absolutely no sympathy with a policy which simply substitutes French and Belgian lorries for the British lorries which provide jobs for British people. Could you please do something about this immediately? I am releasing this letter to the media because it is of such tremendous local concern.* "

This is a letter from the MP Andrew Rowe to Deputy Prime Minister John Prescott, which was copied to me. It was sent before the March 1999 budget, which raised tax on diesel yet again and put British lorry drivers' livelihoods under even greater threat.

'Cash for Car' PCPs

" *Because of the considerable tax benefits to our employees, we are thinking of offering them cash instead of company cars. However, some of them are worried about the financial liability of a personal contract purchase scheme in the current economic climate. Their main fear seems to be, 'What happens if I leave the company or lose my job for one reason or another?' Are you aware of any company offering PCPs that provide protection in these sort of cases?* "

The other problem currently experienced with PCPs (personal contract purchases) is that, because used car values have fallen heavily over the past six months, many schemes are not providing the expected equity to finance the deposit on the next PCP contract. Crown Leasing gets round this by working on minimal deposits and never making any such promise. Crown also provides the answer to your question in the form of employee protection cover against early termination of the PCP for reasons of redundancy, unemployment, resignation, death, long-term sickness, vehicle write-off or theft of the vehicle. The average cost is £350 per three-year contract and, even taking this into account, many employees will be financially better off on a 'Cash for Car' PCP than they are with a company car. More information from Nick Moger of Crown Leasing on 01487 773322.

Tax refund

" *Further to your article about which cars qualify for reduced-rate VED, I have a question. My wife taxed her Micra 1.0L for 12 months from 1 March 1999. As a result of the Budget, will she be entitled to a partial refund, and if so how should she apply?* "

Around 2 million 'keepers' of cars of 1,100 cc or less and first registered on or after 1 January 1973 are entitled to a partial refund of VED already paid for periods from 1 June 1999 onwards. The DVLA wrote to them about this in May 1999. From 1 October 2000 the rates will change again, as from that date VED will be based on CO_2 output which does not necessarily favour the smallest engines. (See 'VED reform' below.)

VED reform

" *I recently acquired a copy of the Treasury's paper entitled 'Consultation on reform of Vehicle Excise Duty to ensure a cleaner environment'. I found it rather difficult to understand and am little wiser as regards how one can 'ensure a cleaner environment' by reforming VED other than to increase it to such a level that motorists are forced off the road. Do you have any comments to make about the future of VED in the UK?* "

What they're going to do, as from 1 October 2000, is tax cars on the amount of CO_2 emitted per km. All manufacturers are required to provide this information, and the figure ranges from 119 g of CO_2 per km for a Seat Arosa or VW Lupo SDI to 438 g/km for a Rolls Royce limousine. In-between figures are 150 g/km for a Mitsubishi 1.8GDi petrol or a Citroën Xantia

HDI diesel; 190 g/km for a Rover 200Vi; 221 g/km for a VW Golf 1.8GTi Turbo; 275 g/km for a new Mercedes S320; and 398 g/km for a Range Rover 4.6HSE. The Treasury has stated that the new tax system will not be 'banded', and will be simply administered according to individual CO_2 output. My guess is it will be a straight £1 for every gram of CO_2 per km for cars for which CO_2 figures are available, and a straight £10 per 100 cc engine capacity tax for older and non-cat cars. (See 'They must be choking' in the Fuel & Emissions section for comment on the true value of taxing CO_2.)

Spanish tax avoidance

" *I took note of fuel prices when I was in Fuengirola, Spain. Apply an exchange rate of Ptas 250 to £1 and they translate to 'Leaded Super' 45.96 pence a litre; 'Super Plus unleaded' 47.56 pence a litre; 'Premium Unleaded' 43.56 pence a litre; and 'Diesel plus' 35.16 pence a litre. Our Government rigidly applies an annual escalator in fuel duty which has made UK fuel by far the most expensive in Europe.* "

It's no coincidence that the report, 'Source Apportionment of Airborne Particulate Matter in the United Kingdom', was launched in January 1999, just before the budget increases in fuel tax which increased the duty and VAT on the price of petrol and diesel to well over 400 per cent and to over 80 per cent of the price we pay at the pumps. The UK price of diesel, on top of Europe's highest weight-based annual vehicle tax, is killing off the UK haulage industry, and a number of big operators are now moving their bases to France so they can remain competitive. Soon we won't merely have sold off our car industry to foreigners, we won't have a road transport industry either. A reader from

Keyworth wrote to suggest that if readers are not happy about the punitive levels of UK fuel tax, they should lobby their MPs and motoring organisations. The AA and RAC make gestures but don't do enough these days to fight on behalf of their beleaguered ordinary members.

Tax cows

" The Chancellor has again used the fuel duty escalator to force road users to pay an unfair share of Government revenue. To add insult to injury, spending on roads is decreasing – especially on essential maintenance. In my area alone, at least 70 per cent of roads require rebuilding or re-surfacing, and many are in a dangerous 'third world' condition. What other group of 32 million electors would tolerate such contemptible treatment? What it needs is an organisation that will promote vigorous opposition to further increases. If there is no change by the next election, road users should remember that they have sufficient pencil power to overturn even this Government's majority. "

There is The Association of British Drivers, c/o The Secretary, ABD, PO Box 19608, London SE19 2ZW, tel: 07000 781544, Website: http://www.abd.org.uk. There is also Mike Rutherford's 'The Motorists Association', PO Box 325, Longfield DA3 7JU, email: mike.rutherford@news-of-the-world.co.uk. When I asked Mike why he was running an alternative motorists group to the ABD, he came up with the very sensible reason that the only way to combat the large number of loud but tiny anti-car groups was to come up with a large number of loud but big pro-car groups. The fact is, for many people, there is no viable alternative to the car. For example, one reader lives 36 miles from his office. His alternative to commuting by car would be to catch a bus at 5.20 am which would get him to work at 8.48 am, providing it ran on time, with a similar three-hour journey home. Decades of underinvestment in public transport have left it in such a parlous state that, for it to provide any sort of alternative to the car, at least £100 billion would need to be spent. The Government gets enough income from motorists to pay for this, but it only channels £9 billion in total into all forms of transport from the £35 billion it takes in motoring taxes every year.

If it moves, tax it

" *The state of England's roads is going to deteriorate at an even faster rate over the next few years. The Government is shortly to 'de-trunk' more than 75 of Britain's roads, handing over the responsibility of their maintenance, and the funding of that maintenance, to county councils. The Government has stated that it will provide additional funding to councils to cover this additional burden for a maximum of two years, after which the entire cost of maintenance will have to be borne from local sources. The Government states that the transfer will give more power to local democracy. It will do nothing of the sort. It is merely a means of the Government passing the buck to county councils in order to drastically cut spending on road maintenance without seeming to do so itself. Memories are short. In the early 1970s, the state of Britain's roads was very poor. At that time, most of the road network was under the responsibility of the county councils. In 1974, the Government took over direct responsibility for many of the main routes, following which the state of the roads was substantially improved. These are the roads the government now wants to 'de-trunk'.* "

There may actually be a more sinister motive to this than most of us ever imagined. When plans were mooted to plant more trees to absorb more CO_2 at the Kyoto conference in December 1997, a delegate actually stated, 'The trouble with this idea is that planting trees will not lead to the societal changes we want to achieve.' What they want to do is curtail our movement.

It's difficult to imagine a 21st century in which people are restricted by lack of adequate transport to the sort of areas they moved around in during the 18th century. And when the Government has stopped us moving about, where is it going to get the £30 billion a year in clear revenue it used to get from motorists? By hitting every single person in the country for an extra £500 a year in other forms of taxation, that's how.

TIMING BELTS AND CHAINS

Timing trouble

" On 14 May, watching BBC 'Watchdog', I was concerned to learn that on some Vauxhall models, including Cavaliers, a problem has arisen causing loss of power and considerable engine damage. Apparently this is caused by the failure of an idler pulley, part number GF50, and can affect models registered between September 1993 and September 1996. I own a Cavalier 2.0i automatic registered December 1993 which has done just 24,000 miles (I am retired and now 80 years of age). The RAC is said to be concerned about the safety aspect of such a failure at speed and would like there to be a safety recall. What advice can you give on this matter, please? "

Phone your nearest Vauxhall franchise and book the car in for a timing belt replacement, specifying that you also want the tensioner and any idler wheels replaced. Your car is well over-due for a timing belt replacement anyway, and when cars are in for this job at Vauxhall agents, the suspect idler pulleys are routinely replaced as an 'in-service modification'. The problem is mainly with GF50 plastic idler pulleys on the 16v and 24v engines fitted to Corsas, Astras, Tigras, Cavaliers, Vectras and Calibras between September 1993 and September 1996 ('L' to 'P') and, as announced on 'Watchdog' on 21 May, all petrol engined 'P' and 'R'-reg. Vectras, Omegas and Fronteras. The Vauxhall Customer Service Helpline is on 01582 427200. Anyone worried about imminent failure and in possession of a few tools should remove the engine timing belt cover and inspect the plastic idler pulleys for signs of cracks. If you find any, don't start the engine.

Brace yourself for a belting

" *I have an 'L'-registered Metro which is now five years old but has covered just 10,000 miles. When I took it in for its service and MOT I was told it was due for a new timing belt and that the cost would be £300. Do you think this is exorbitant?* "

Yes, if all you're getting is a belt. The new Garage Fix-it Prices service on the Internet (http://www.Driversclub.com) gives prices of £120 for a petrol engine and £160 for a diesel engine using original-equipment parts. But if your car needs more than this, such as a new camshaft end-seal and a new timing belt tensioner, and you're also having the car serviced at the same time, this could bump the cost up to £300. It is certainly time the belt was replaced.

Snap

" *I have a 1992 Peugeot 405 estate which failed on the road with a broken cam belt at 90,000 miles. The car had been serviced from new by a Peugeot agent but in the service specification for this model there was no requirement to change the belt at any stage. A replacement engine would have cost £2,000, but this would not have been reflected in the value of the car so I was forced to trade it in at half its pre-breakdown price. Who is responsible for advising a change of cambelt – the manufacturer, the agent or the customer?* "

In the absence of specific guidance from manufacturers, I have spent the last five years advising readers to change their timing belts every three to four years and every 35,000–40,000 miles. This advice has been printed in my column and my books over and over again.

Chain reaction

" *I agree wholeheartedly with your reply to the reader whose Peugeot cambelt had snapped (see 'Snap' above). In the past, mainly due to advice from a garage-owning cousin of mine, I have replaced the cambelts of all my cars so fitted every 30,000 miles. But you did not mention the mileage or age at which a timing chain should be changed. I have a Nissan Primera 1.6 which is four years old and has just had a 36,000-mile service. I asked about changing the timing chain and was told it was not necessary until the car was five years old or had done 54,000 miles, whichever came first. Do you think it would be wise to mention that chains have a longer life?* "

I have before and, because new information on belt and chain life keeps coming in, I will again. The two problem areas of timing chains are the tensioner and the oil feed. The timing chain on the old 2,599 cc six-cylinder 12v Mercedes engine lasts virtually forever, as long as the oil is kept reasonably clean. (As far as I'm concerned, this means six-monthly rather than annual oil changes, even for cars which do low mileages.) The 2.0 litre twin-cam Primera 16v also has a fairly bulletproof chain, as do all current BMWs and all Mercs from 1989 when the last 'Simplex' chains were switched over to 'Duplex'. But the Primera, Sunny and Almera 1.6 litre 16v engine has not one, but two timing chains – a primary chain low down in the engine and a secondary chain driving the cams. There's more to go wrong, so more reason to follow the manufacturer's advice. 16v Micras in which the oil has not been changed regularly enough can also develop tensioner problems, and it's an expensive job to replace chain and tensioner in these engines. Saab's 2.0 litre and 2.3 litre engines are developed from that of the old Triumph Dolomite and TR7. The Triumph engine did have a tensioner problem which Saab solved, but the evidence suggests that, depending on their oil change regime, Saabs can require a new timing chain at around 100,000 miles. Older four-cylinder Mercedes with 'Simplex' (single link) chains tend to need their chains and tensioners replacing at around the 60,000-mile mark. Tellingly, GM Vauxhall, which started the trend to timing belts with the Victor FB, has reverted to chains for its new family of direct-injected 16v diesel engines and I have yet to hear of chain failure on any of these.

Premature failure

" *I own a 1993 BMW 316i, which has been serviced according to the dashboard service indicator at BMW agents throughout its life. The owner's manual states that the timing belt should be changed every three years or 36,000 miles, whichever comes first. It was changed on 1 May 1996 at 59,000 miles, so, in theory would have been due to be changed again by 1 May 1999 or by 95,000 miles, whichever came first. It snapped on 28 September 1998 at 86,000 miles, resulting in such extensive engine damage that a replacement engine has been advised. A new engine is £2,800, plus fitting, and the service manager of my local BMW franchise believes that BMW will contribute 50 per cent of the cost of this. However, I have now discovered that BMW advises a change of timing belt at every 'Inspection 2' service and that later models have timing chains instead of belts. Does this amount to an admission that BMW timing belts were of 'unsatisfactory quality'? And should I press for the later timing chain engine to be fitted instead of a replacement with a timing belt?* "

This is a huge expense for a failure which certainly isn't your fault. But it's not unreasonable for you to be charged half the price of the replacement engine because you will effectively be getting a new engine rather than one which has done 86,000 miles. I can't say whether BMW will be willing to fit the later 1994 model-year chain-cam engine, but regard this an example of continuous product improvement rather than an admission that the old engine was not 'of merchantable quality' under the old 1979 Sale of Goods Act under which this car was purchased. After all, BMWs had been fitted with timing belts rather than chains for many years. Your other possibility is to seek out a second-hand chain-cam engine and ancillaries from a crashed car, which may work out at less than the £1,400, but you will need to have it fitted by an independent BMW specialist. The *Exchange & Mart* BMW breaking section is your best source of a fresh engine, not the replacement engine specialists in the front of the magazine.

Land Rover timing belts

" *I am a motor mechanic by trade and have just replaced the timing belt of my 1996N Land Rover Defender 90 TDI at 14,000 miles. The reason was premature wear due to misalignment of the timing gears and tensioners during production. I know of several other Land Rover TDIs with similar problems. One snapped at 11,000 miles and another had three belts fail before 54,000 miles. I assumed that replacement would be under warranty, but my claim was turned down. A modification kit is now available to extend belt life, consisting of a main timing casing, gear and pulleys, seals, gaskets, engine oil separator and injection pump bracket. To Land Rover's credit, this is very cheap at £91.57. I would like to advise all your readers with low-mileage TDI Land Rovers to take a peep with a torch through the wading plug hole in the bottom of the timing belt cover. If they see any rubber debris, they should get their belts changed pronto before they snap and cause severe engine damage.* **"**

A timely warning for which late Land Rover TDI owners will be very thankful.

Belting story

" *My wife has a 1994 'M'-reg. VW Golf 1.6CL which has now done just 29,503 miles. In April this year it had a 30,000-mile service, which included a new alternator drive belt. Then in September a new alternator was fitted. In November, this belt snapped and part of it got behind the timing belt cover, disturbing the valve timing and resulting in engine damage. Both the AA and the VW agent think that a stone must have flown up, got between the belt and the pulleys and caused the belt to snap. The garage has been helpful and kept the cost to me down to £604. But I also had to pay £247 for a hire car to keep my wife on the road. Is the AA and garage explanation plausible?* **"**

Yes. I checked with independent VW specialists Wheelbase of Hersham (01932 252515). If the alternator belt snaps and gets trapped between the pulleys and timing belt cover, the timing belt could itself be damaged. The alternator belt is self-tensioning by means of a sprung bracket, so it could not have been over or under-tensioned by a mechanic. A stone or other foreign body flung up from the road surface is the most likely explanation.

Water pump wrecks engine

" *I was driving my wife's 40,000-mile 1986C Nissan Micra 1.0 litre recently when the engine developed a noise, so I pulled over and switched off. I got a tow to a local garage, where the diagnosis was that the water pump had seized, tearing some teeth from the recently fitted timing belt and leading to valves hitting pistons. 'Parker's Guide' lists a seized water pump and corrosion in the cooling system as problem areas on pre-1993*

9-valve Micras. Yet I had changed the coolant regularly. Would you therefore recommend changing the water pump at the same time as the cambelt on these cars, especially on older models which cover low annual mileages? "

On Mk I Micras, yes. And, though the water pumps on older 1.0 and 1.3 litre Polos and Golfs are more robust, they are also driven by the timing belt rather than by an external auxiliary belt, so water pump failure will have the same result as on your car. Mk I Micras were well loved for their abstemious fuel consumption and legendary reliability, which far exceeded their design life of three to five years, and you've done well to get 13 years out of yours. Mk II Micras with 16v engines have timing chains rather than belts, but require frequent oil changes if problems are to be avoided. API (0500 830530) can supply a standard complete second-hand MK I Micra engine, imported from Japan and delivered to a local garage, for £280 + VAT, warranted for six months. (Note that the Japanese carburettor might not be compatible with UK petrol.) API can also supply a 'Premier' reconditioned second-hand engine with new timing belt but with no ancillaries such as carburettor for £455 + VAT delivered and with a 12 months warranty. All Japanese Micra engines run on unleaded petrol.

Well and truly Porked

" *I am the very proud owner of a 91J Porsche 944 S2, which I bought four years ago at 35,000 miles and which has now expired at 85,000 miles. It has been regularly serviced by the same Porsche agent and the last service was a 24,000-miler at a Porsche agent 500 miles before the engine failure. I was initially told that the timing belt had broken and, because it was still under warranty, Porsche would pay for the replacement. Two days later, I was told that the failure was caused by the movement and loss of the nylon tensioner guide and this had resulted in extensive damage which would cost £5,000 to repair. The Porsche Users Club of Great Britain tells me that these tensioner guides should be replaced every two years at a cost of £17 + VAT. Is there any article by any motoring correspondent relating to the replacement of this component?* "

The best way to get to the truth in a matter like this is to talk to independent Porsche specialists who don't have a position to defend. Paragon Porsche told me that a 944 S2 has both a timing belt and a balancer shaft belt, each of which have their own tensioners. Porsche recommends that they are all replaced every 48,000 miles or every four years, whichever comes first, and your service book should contain a reminder card about this. However, fitting both belts is not easy and it is absolutely vital that they are fitted and tensioned correctly. When both belts have been fitted, the car must be taken back to the agent for the belts to be re-tensioned at between 1,000 and 2,000 miles. New belts and new tensioners should have been fitted to your car at the 84,500-mile service and you should have been due to bring the car back to have them re-tensioned. But if any part of this job was missed out to save money, it's down to who made the decision – you or the Porsche agent.

TOWING

Commodious towcar required

" *Seven years ago I bought at auction a 1989 'F'-reg. Rover 820 fastback and it has served me well. Now I hope to replace it with a large estate in which to haul around musical instruments and sailing gear and to tow racing dinghies. The Citroën XM estate appeals in this respect. I have between £6,000 and £7,000 to spend at auction, so what can I get for this kind of money?* "

Right now, the UK used car market is on its back with its legs in the air – no sector more so than large models with 'a bit of a reputation'. Enormous improvements were made to the XM in Summer 1994, so don't consider buying earlier than 'M'-reg. (unless it's one of the first Mk IIs registered in June or July 1994). Your budget might even buy you a 2.5TD VSX estate. The thing is, there aren't many of these cars around, so you could spend months visiting ex-fleet auctions without ever finding one. If you're on the Internet, try running a search on these websites: http://www.auto-hunter.co.uk/car and http://www.autotrader.co.uk.

Towing hitch

" *A recent amendment to the law requires some privately owned vehicles to be fitted with tachographs when towing trailers. For example, a van towing either a goods trailer or a caravan may be required to be fitted with a tachograph because the towing vehicle has the capacity to carry goods. Similarly, a car towing a trailer capable of carrying goods may also be required to be fitted with a tachograph. To enable your readers to get to grips with the implications of this change in the law, The Trailer and Towing Advisory Service has produced a 15-page booklet which details the amendments, incorporates relevant extracts from the legislation, and gives a guide to drivers' hours. The cost is £20 plus £1 post and packaging, or alternatively we charge £40 to answer a legislative enquiry. The person to contact is Steve Hanley, TTAS, 16 Moor Drive, Helensburgh, Argyll & Bute G84 7LE, tel: 07079 017244; email: stevehanley@btconnect.com; fax: 0143 667 8686.* ”

£21 is a lot of money for 15 pages. And Brian Bate of the National Trailer and Towing Association Limited strongly disputes this interpretation of the way the relevant EU directive has been incorporated into UK law, suggesting that towers arm themselves with DETR booklet GV262 (revised 8/98) instead. For more information, phone or fax Brian Bate directly on 01926 335445.

Off the hook

“ *I change my Rovers every 18 months and my garage always removes the tow bar and fits it to the new vehicle every time. However, this time they refused, on the basis that there is now an EEC law which states that this practice is now illegal. Can you confirm this is correct, please?* ”

Yes. EC Directive 94/20/EC, effective from 1 August 1998, decrees that all tow balls fitted to new cars must conform to EU Whole Vehicle Type Approval Standards. A tow bar transferred from an older car might or might not meet these standards. Originally, it had been proposed to ban cars from being fitted with protruding tow bars when not actually towing – particularly because of the anonymous damage they can do in car parks. And many European manufacturers developed 'quick release' removable tow bar systems, though companies such as Witter in the UK did not. In the end only Italy was sensible enough to incorporate this into national law. A very strange situation exists in the UK in that some EU Approved removable towbars do not conform to UK regulations. If a towbar is not 'quick release' or folding, it should at least be possible to unbolt the ball, leaving nothing protruding beyond the bumper to damage other cars.

Towing the line

" *My 2.0 litre Vectra has developed a fault in its automatic gearbox at two years old and 26,000 miles. An automatic gearbox specialist has diagnosed it as hardened seals, allowing leakage of the ATF past the control pistons, probably caused by the gearbox overheating. I am now faced with the prospect of either changing the car or paying £600 to have all the seals replaced. Should I forget about towing with an automatic? Should I have the car repaired and fit a transmission oil cooler? Or should I switch to a different make of automatic car? Vauxhall has agreed to pay 50 per cent of the cost of the repair.* "

What has happened is that you have overheated the ATF while towing your caravan, most probably up long motorway inclines. The reason is that the Vectra's gearing in 4th is comparatively high to help the car deliver its excellent 'solo' fuel economy. This is masked when driving solo by a small amount of torque converter slippage. But when towing a caravan the slippage increases considerably and overheats the ATF, 'cooking' the transmission seals. You should have fitted a transmission oil cooler. You should also consider manually holding the car in 3rd when towing up motorway inclines to prevent any 'hunting' between gears and slippage. Vauxhall's offer of 50 per cent is fair. But next time you are choosing a tow-car, seriously consider a Subaru Legacy. Their flat-four engines develop comparatively high torque. Top gear is relatively low, which is good for towing. And four wheel drive provides excellent grip both on the road and on the often wet grass of a caravan site.

Keeping your cool with a caravan

" *I have a Mercedes E200 estate which I use for caravan towing and which has a four-speed automatic gearbox. I now want to change it for an ex-demonstration E300TD automatic estate, which has a five-speed automatic gearbox, but have run into two problems. One is the astronomically expensive price of the official MB tow bar. The other is that I have been told that if I want to use the car for towing I must have the cooling system upgraded. I will be fitting a Witter or equivalent, instead of the MB tow bar, but what should I do about the cooling system?* "

The automatic gearbox of another reader's Vectra estate burned itself out (see 'Towing the line' above), and I explained why a few weeks ago. The problem arises when an automatic car is fitted with a 'tall' top gear for economy. Depending on the weight of the caravan, the overall gearing and the incline being ascended, the autobox torque converter will either slip and get very hot, or the box will 'hunt' between the two highest gears. It would obviously help the box if you were to shift it manually from 5th to 4th on inclines when towing, and sometimes even to 3rd. But an additional gearbox ATF oil cooler is the solution proposed by MB. I think the agent may also have quoted you for a socially responsible removable tow bar, such as those made by Brink, to prevent parking damage to other evhicles when not actually towing.

But, so far, these are only required by law if leaving the tow bar in place when not towing would obscure the towing car's number plate. New Witter equipment conforms to the way Directive 94/20/EC has been interpreted by the Vehicle Inspectorate in the UK. Having avoided a dangerously snaking caravan on the M18 recently, I don't recommend anyone to tow a caravan without fitting a stabiliser bar. Also, make sure the nose weight of the caravan is correct, and never tow a caravan on tyres more than six years old because, though they may look fine externally, the inside of the carcass could have dangerously deteriorated.

Fit to burst

I received a worried letter from a reader from Bedford concerning pre-puncture and post-puncture liquid tyre sealants. Post-puncture sealants are only intended to effect a temporary repair, after which, under BS AU 159, the tyre must be removed from the rim, the carcass thoroughly inspected and a proper vulcanised repair made. Sealants sold as preventing punctures can not only leave the driver unaware of tyre damage, but can make a such a serious mess of the inside of the carcass it cannot be properly repaired. Despite this, it appears that a lot of motorists are treating liquid tyre sealants as a permanent cure. This is particularly dangerous among caravan owners, to whom 'puncture preventing' sealants have been actively marketed. There can't be many of us who have not witnessed the result of an unstabilised caravan tyre blowout. Now that summer is here and readers are planning long car or car and caravan journeys which subject tyres to extreme conditions, we should all remember to have any aerosol liquid sealed tyre properly repaired. We should, in any case, inspect all our tyres thoroughly for tread depth, cuts, nails and sidewall deterioration (caravan tyres particularly) and ensure that they are inflated to the correct pressures for the weight carried and the speeds we will be driving.

Overheated about caravans

" There can be another, simpler, reason for overheating when towing a caravan. It is under-inflation of the tyres on the caravan. Using the correct tyre pressures on caravans is critical when towing. "

Not just correct pressures; the condition of the tyres is critical too. All too often a caravan spends most of its life suspended on its jacks and the tyres begin to perish. It isn't until the owner takes it on its annual big trip that a tyre bursts, the caravan jack-knifes, the owner's holiday is ruined and, more to the point, thousands of motorists are delayed on the motorway. If I see this happen half a dozen times every summer the total rate of incidence must be huge.

So you think you can tow?

On the otherwise excellent BBC programme 'So You Think You Can Drive?', Nick Ross made an over-simplification that could get towers into trouble. A question asked, 'If your towed caravan begins to snake, should you slow down or speed up?' The answer given on the programme was 'Speed up'. But this takes no account of what caused the snaking in the first place. If, for example, it is a rapidly-deflating caravan tyre, speeding up will only increase the speed at which the inevitable accident occurs.

TYRES

False economy?

" *I have a Vauxhall Cavalier 1.7 LSTD which I bought from my son at 30,000 miles. The front tyres were new Michelin Energy and the rears were also Michelin. I have been amazed at the economy of this car. It regularly returns 55 mpg on motorway trips and 52 mpg on shorter runs. All the tyres, front and back, were down to less than 3 mm of tread by 72,000 miles, so I changed them all. I was quoted £60 a wheel for Michelin Energy or £39 for Vredesteins, so I plumped for the Vredesteins. I now find that my mpg has dropped by about 5 mpg, but I have also noticed that the trip meter seems to be recording slightly shorter distances. Could this be because the new tyres are slightly bigger. Can the type of tyre really affect fuel consumption?* "

A number of readers have praised Michelin Energy tyres, both for their longevity and for the fact that they do seem to save energy. The average improvement in fuel consumption is in the order of 5–10 per cent. But your new wheel and tyre combinations also have a greater circumference than your old worn tyres, so the odometer will record a slightly shorter distance which means that the true drop in mpg is not as bad as first seemed. Because the Vredesteins are unlikely to last as long as the Michelins, the extra investment in Energy Tyres would have paid off handsomely if you kept the car another 40,000 miles.

Pulling to the left

" *The reader who complained of his Skoda pulling to the left (see 'Sorting out a Skoda' in the New Car Problems section) ought to try swapping his front tyres left to right. I once had a Morris 1300 which exhibited the same tendency. The agent checked the tracking, which was spot on. It was only when I switched the tyres that the fault was cured.* "

Good point. This is a solution that quite often works – even for Formula 1 cars.

Giving it the boot

" *I am interested in buying a Mazda MX5, but have identified a problem with it to which no dealer has been able to provide a solution. The MX5 has a space-saver emergency wheel. If you have the misfortune to have to use it, where do you put the wheel you have taken off? It will be too big to go into the boot even if it is empty and there is no room inside the car.* "

Unless the boot is full of luggage, this is a non-problem, because the punctured road wheel and tyre will fit into the boot. There is even more room inside the boot of the new MX5, which is much more capacious than the old model. Goodyear has now come up with a new type of tyre which fits standard rims and which can be 'run flat' for up to 50 miles, removing the need to carry an emergency tyre.

Unidirectional tyres

" *I recently required a replacement tyre for my VW Passat because I had used the spare to replace the punctured tyre. I was surprised to be asked, 'which side of the car will you be using it?' I replied it was for a spare and was told, 'You can't do that. The tyre is supposed to rotate one way only.' Please could you advise if your readers should have two spare wheels? I needed a tyre for the spare wheel and bought one by a different manufacturer which was cheaper.* "

You've answered your own question. Buy a multi-directional tyre for the 'emergency' wheel and stop calling it a 'spare'.

Punctured pocket

" *It's not just in France that tyre rip-offs can occur. The same thing happened to me on the Isle of Wight. Somebody stuck a long nail into the tyre of my Mitsubishi Carisma. There was a garage further down the road, so I had them fit a new Dunlop SP200 185/65 HR14. The bill was a jaw-dropping £90.80. A few days later, back home in Oxfordshire, I checked what the price would have been at my local Mitsubishi agent. £52.80, including valve, balancing and VAT. So I wrote to the garage suggesting they had made a genuine mistake and asking for an appropriate refund. I wrote again, recorded delivery, on 11 June, but by 22 June had still not received a reply. So, readers beware. You don't have to go to France to get ripped off.* "

Micheldever Tyres (01962 774437) quoted £43.12 for the latest 200E 'Energy' version of this tyre, fitted, balanced, re-valved and inclusive of VAT. They also came up with an explanation as to why the Isle of Wight tyre was £90.80. If the fitter sourced the tyre via 'official' UK channels it would cost him considerably more than benefiting from the relative strength of sterling and sourcing the tyre in Continental Europe. There are tyre people like Micheldever who buy at the lowest possible rates on world markets then pass on the savings to their customers. And there are tyre people who don't.

Check your spare

" *I have a Vauxhall Vectra fitted with four-stud wheels. It wasn't until I had a puncture that I discovered the spare was a five-stud wheel from a high-performance version. You might want to warn Vectra owners to check their spare wheels.* "

Said and done.

Tyre changing nonsense

" *I drive 30,000 miles a year and change my tyres frequently. Because my cars are front-wheel-drive (Audi 80 and then Saab 900) I have always had the new tyres fitted to the front wheels. But on a recent visit to a tyrefitters I was told that this is wrong. New tyres should go on the rear wheels to give better control when braking and also better control in the event of a front tyre failure. I wonder if this is to ensure a quick return visit to the fitters, because if the worn rear tyres were transferred to the front they would wear off more quickly than if left at the rear. I have never had my request for new tyres on the front queried before. What is the correct advice?* "

Put the new tyres on the wheels that need them. On a front-wheel-drive car, the front tyres can wear at two to three times the rate of the rears.

But, like the rear brakes, the rear tyres of a front wheel drive car don't do much work, and you need the most grip on the front. Do remember, though, that new tyres provide comparatively poor grip until they are 'scrubbed in', which can take up to 500 miles. It's also a fact that, *in dry conditions only*, a tyre on which most of the tread has been worn off has more surface area, which is why a car can seem to grip and handle best just before the tyres have to be changed.

Front tyre wear

" *After two years and 11,866 very happy miles in my 1996 VW Polo 1.4CL, I was shocked to be informed by the VW agent that the front tyres needed replacing. Other members of the CSMA have complained about comparatively short front-tyre life on front-wheel-drive power-steered cars (14,000 miles on a Mondeo; 17,165 miles on a VW Polo diesel). VW Customer Care wrote to tell me that, because of the forces front tyres have to cope with on a front-wheel-drive car, the front tyres will wear at a far greater rate than the rears. What are your feelings on this matter?* "

Front tyre life of between 4,000 miles and 20,000 miles is normal on a front-wheel-drive road car. The wear rate depends on how the suspension is set up, the performance level of the car, the rate at which the car is accelerated, the speeds at which the car is driven round corners and, crucially, whether the driver uses power-assisted steering to turn the wheels while the car is stationary.

The 108,000-mile tyre

" *I have owned a Vauxhall Nova since 1988 and recently had to replace the two rear Michelin MXL tyres prior to the car's MOT because the side-walls had become cracked. The mileage on these tyres was 108,000. Is this a record?* "

Probably. But readers should please remember that cracked or otherwise decomposed tyre sidewalls are actually more dangerous than low tread depth because a cracked sidewall can lead to a blown tyre at any time.

Going round in circles

" *There is a recommendation in the driver's handbook of my new Nissan Micra 1.3GX to rotate the tyres after 6,000 miles. In my understanding, tyre rotation went out of favour over 30 years ago. The reason is that each tyre develops a wear pattern within the first thousand miles of use and this wear pattern helps to maximise its footprint on the road, after which the rate of wear slows down. If tyres are rotated, increased wear results while each tyre in its new location re-develops its footprint. The Micra handbook also suggests bringing in the spare tyre. This gives the combination of a new tyre and a part worn one on the same 'axle'. I believe that, for a front-wheel-drive car, the best course of action is to leave the tyres where they are, checking occasionally for uneven wear pattern due to suspension misalignment. When the front tyres are worn to around 2.0 mm, a new tyre of the same pattern should be purchased for one side and the unused spare utilised for the other side.* "

On a front wheel drive car, I do what you do. If the car has a 'space-saver' emergency wheel, I replace both front tyres together. BBC 'Watchdog' provided all 4x4 owners with another useful lesson about tyre replacement. If four wheel drive is permanently available automatically (as is the case with all Land Rovers and Range Rovers, Audis, Subarus, Toyota RAV 4s, Honda CRVs, etc. and when 'part-time 4wd' is selected in a Jeep Cherokee) all four tyres must be replaced at the same time or it will confuse the system and possibly lead to failure. Happily, these cars tend to wear all four tyres at an even rate, but a problem occurs in the event of one part-worn tyre suffering an irreparable puncture. This needs to be replaced with a similarly part-worn tyre rather than a new one.

Reply re-aligned

" *You recommend Micheldever Tyres (01962 774437) for its state-of-the-art suspension alignment bays. I thought your North Western readers might like to know that at First Stop Tyreworld in Croft Street, Widnes (0151 424 5961), we have the same sophisticated equipment.* "

Fair do's. If you've got it, shout about it.

'Bumpy Ride' – the sequel

" *Other readers have written about the 'bumpy ride' of the Mk II Mondeo. We changed from a 1996 2.0 litre GLX, which had a very compliant ride with superb handling, to a 1998 2.0 litre Ghia which has a noticeably 'livelier' ride. As you suggested, I experimented with tyre pressures and the ride is now better. The car is fitted with Firestone Firehawk 'fuel saver' tyres, which I think may be the cause of the poor ride, but I note that you recommend Pirelli P6000 or Continental Eco Contacts, and I will try these when the current tyres wear out.* "

I received a lot of letters along the same lines and will try and answer them all in one go. Standard four-cylinder 'facelift' Mondeos come with three different tyre sizes. LXs have 14" wheels shod with 185/65 tyres. Ghias have 15" steel or alloy wheels with 195/60 tyres, Verona, Si, Ghia X models and others fitted with optional alloy wheels have either 15" wheels with 205/55 tyres or 16" wheels with 205/50 tyres. The lower the profile of the tyre (the number following the '/'), the less it is able to cushion road shocks, and if the car is fitted with slightly stiffened suspension (as is the case with the Si and the Ghia) these road shocks will be amplified. The Mondeo is also extremely sensitive to variations in front tyre pressures. A couple of pounds above the standard 31 psi greatly amplifies road shocks. A couple of pounds below absorbs shocks at the expense of some tyre squeal and increased tyre wear. In my opinion, the best all-round factory-fitted compromise is the LX suspension with 185/65 x 14 Continental Eco Contacts. Not only do these provide impressive grip, good 'feel', low wear rates and low road noise, their low rolling resistance also helps with fuel consumption – witness my 2.0iLX which is averaging 36 mpg.

Under too much pressure

" My wife recently bought a Mazda Demio with which she is very pleased except that the ride is rather hard. When the car was delivered by the local Mazda agent the tyre pressure had been set at 35 psi, whereas the handbook and the door frame sticker both give the recommended tyre pressure for normal use as 29 psi all round and 32 psi (front) plus 41 psi (rear) when fully loaded. The car has 60 profile tyres. When my wife discussed the difference with the agent he replied without any explanation that it was their practice to set the pressures at 35 psi. Who is right? The car certainly rides better with a lower pressure but we are reluctant not to accept the agent's advice. "

The agent is arrogant and stupid. Agents routinely over-pressure tyres of cars which sit in stock to help prevent the tyres 'flat spotting', and if he had any courtesy or common sense he would have told you this. You should set the pressures to the levels recommended by Mazda for the sort of use you wish to put the car to, and if you have any doubts about the information supplied with the car call Mazda Customer Care on 0845 6013147.

Solid wheels

" *I recently bought a Rover 618iS direct from Rover through a trading agent. I tested the car on local roads limited to 40 mph and 50 mph and was very satisfied. The agent mentioned that the car was fitted with 'alloys'. However, first time on a motorway, my wife and I could not hold a conversation. The road noise was incredible. The local Rover agent confirmed that the wheels and tyres were standard equipment for the model. These are 205/55 x 16. Am I stuck with this, or is there a way of solving the problem without it costing a great deal of money?* "

Avoid motorways with high noise surfaces. Or put an ad in you local paper offering to swap your 16" wheels and tyres for either the 15" alloy wheels with deeper profile tyres from a 618iL or the 14" steel wheels with even deeper profile, narrower tyres from a base model 618 or 620. Remember, low-profile tyres greatly improve the steering, handling and roadholding of a Rover 600. The car will feel lighter and understeer more on narrower, deeper profile tyres.

USED CAR PROBLEMS

Malevolent Maestro

" *I have a 1983 MG Maestro 1.6 with 33,000 miles on the clock. At over 63 mph the engine surges and loses power. The rev counter jumps all over the show. Any advice on this would be appreciated.* "

This is a real timewarp question because the MG Maestro 1.6 was a completely hopeless car from launch. All Maestros built between 1983 and 1985 suffered appalling build quality, 1.6s have engine oil leaks, badly-breathing crank-cases, duff gearboxes, and the twin-carburettor set up on 1.6 MGs is notorious for a litany of problems. You could try and sell it to someone who doesn't know any of this, but the 'honest' solution is to park it in the corner of the garden, take the seats out, and use it as a greenhouse. (Later Maestros were vastly improved, particularly the 2.0 litre fuel-injected MG version.)

Drum Concerto

" *I have a 1994 'M'-registered Honda Concerto 1.5 auto which is fitted with a sliding sunroof. I have always been very satisfied with the courteous and efficient service provided by my local Honda franchise, but now a problem has arisen. For some time I had been aware of a drumming noise which has built up over the years. I have checked and dismissed causes such as a loose hardboard boot floor over the spare wheel and a mis-hung rear silencer, and eventually isolated the cause to the roof panel astern of the sun-roof. A strengthening bar is fitted across it to which the roof panel should be bonded, but on mine the bonding has separated leaving the bar to drum against the roof. Old-shape Rover 200s have an identical body and I have identified the same problem in some of them. Now I am faced with a bill of £123 to put matters right, as must countless other owners of Honda Concertos and old-shape Rover 200s. Honda will not meet the cost under its anti-perforation warranty.* "

Other readers have complained of noises from their Rover 200s and you seem to have put your finger on the cause. What must have happened is that the bonding agent has melted in the extreme heat to which a car roof can be subjected, even in an English summer. This is part of the gradual deterioration every car suffers from the moment it rolls off the production line. Though it's irritating, I don't think it can be put down to a manufacturing defect unless you can prove that the bonding between the bar and the roof was never applied. If this turns out to be the case, then Honda should put its hand up and bear the cost of the repair.

Problem areas

" *I bought your last* Book of Motoring Answers *and found it most helpful and interesting – particularly the references to cars with built-in major expenses down the line such as Mondeo and Vectra clutch replacement and the combined alternator and brake vacuum pump on Vauxhall/Isuzu 1.5 litre and 1.7 litre turbodiesels. What other cars have this sort of trap in store for the unknowing motorist? Or, if the list is shorter, what cars don't have them?* "

You will find a comprehensive list in *The Daily Telegraph Book of How to Buy and Sell Cars*, price £6.99, ISBN 1-84119-035-7. Since this section takes up most of the book, and includes most recalls over the past four years, it would be impossible to reproduce it here.

Reliably informed

" *It is some time since I saw a reliability table published. The last one I have on file is 12 April 1996 for 'L'-registered cars, when the top seven places were filled by Japanese vehicles. Has a later table been published?* "

Yes, for 'M', 'N' and 'P'-registered cars. Quentin Willson appealed to owners of 'P'-registered cars to complete J D Power questionnaires during the winter 1998 series of BBC 'Top Gear'. The results were broadcast in Spring 1999 and published in the May 1999 issue of *Top Gear* magazine. The Consumers Association also published the results of its annual survey with the June 1999 issue of *Which?* using information supplied by *Which?* subscribers. The Data Protection Act prevents proper random surveys of car ownership satisfaction in the UK.

INDEX